THE
IRAQ
WAR
and its
CONSEQUENCES

Thoughts of
Nobel Peace Laureates
and Eminent Scholars

THE IRAQ *and its* WAR CONSEQUENCES

Thoughts of
Nobel Peace Laureates
and Eminent Scholars

Editors

IRWIN ABRAMS

WANG GUNGWU

World Scientific

NEW JERSEY · LONDON · SINGAPORE · SHANGHAI · HONG KONG · TAIPEI · BANGALORE

Published by

World Scientific Publishing Co. Pte. Ltd.
5 Toh Tuck Link, Singapore 596224
USA office: Suite 202, 1060 Main Street, River Edge, NJ 07661
UK office: 57 Shelton Street, Covent Garden, London WC2H 9HE

British Library Cataloguing-in-Publication Data
A catalogue record for this book is available from the British Library.

THE IRAQ WAR AND ITS CONSEQUENCES
Thoughts of Nobel Peace Laureates and Eminent Scholars

ISBN 981-238-588-6
ISBN 981-238-590-8 (pbk)

Inhouse Editor: Juliet L C Lee

Printed in Singapore by World Scientific Printers (S) Pte Ltd

We must be the change we wish to see.

Mahatma Gandhi

Foreword

September 11, 2001 was a turning point for the United States in the way it saw the world. In that context, some would say that the Iraq War sixteen months later, in March–April 2003, was something of a turning point for most other countries in the manner they saw the United States, especially with regard to its ambition to create a new world order. Although the latter may be a bit overstated, it indicates how strongly the Iraq War has impacted all of us.

The essays collected in this volume come from many sources. They are by distinguished people who have long been concerned with the need for a stable world in which wars would become more easily avoidable and the desire for world peace is universally shared. For such people, it is understandable that the debates over the invasion of Iraq have stirred fears that there will now be many new sources of conflict. Not least is the danger that more countries will take confrontational approaches on the grounds that the known measures for resolving conflict have failed us. Although we will need to examine why the Iraq War became inevitable, it is not enough to dwell only on the rights and wrongs of the war. What exercises most of the contributors to this volume is what can be learnt from it. Thinking ahead about the consequences may not be easy, but it is not too early to consider how such wars might be avoided in the future.

The consequences for Iraq and its people are indeed tragic. The problems they have created for the Middle East are likely to stay deadlocked and intractable. As for the United States' relations with most countries in the world, they have become increasingly challenging and may remain uncertain for quite a while. Therefore, the two issues that should now take precedence over others are (a) the credibility of the United States, the world's strongest power, as the leader in a world that still strives for peace, and (b) the viability of the United Nations, especially its Security Council, as the organization that could implement the measures essential to that peace.

The two are closely related. The United States went to war in Iraq ultimately because it concluded that the UN Security Council is no longer able to enforce its own resolutions and is but a toothless body whose will could be easily flouted. The United Nations sought hard to avoid war and demand compliance from the Iraqi regime. When that failed, it wanted a degree of legitimacy for the violent retribution to follow, but its outdated machinery was unable to provide that.

For the United States, efforts are being made to reshape its alliances with its past and present partners and find new terms for trust and future cooperation. The results are not encouraging. The image that it is committed to do it alone whenever conditions are not to U.S. liking may not be an entirely accurate one, but that is now a commonly held perception. The several efforts so far to dispel this view are widely seen as unconvincing. This volume of essays includes some ideas of what the U.S. and its partners might be able to do to have that image softened if not dismissed.

As for the United Nations, the feeling that peace is too important to be left to a self-interested Security Council is too widespread to ignore. But without a restoration of faith in having an organisation that could effectively monitor and supervise peace measures, all moves to reform the UN would be seen as too little too late. Above all, its future without a broad reconciliation with the United States that regains room for its future action leaves it as helpless as a landed whale. This would be to no one's interest. For all who care for peace in the world, every effort must be made to resolve these two issues as soon as possible. Perhaps some of the essays in this volume could contribute to the dialogue that such a process will need.

Wang Gungwu
Director, East Asian Institute
National University of Singapore
August 2003

Introduction

Historians fashion their centuries not by the calendar but by events, thus the nineteenth century in many history classes begins in 1815 with the Congress of Vienna, and ends in 1914, with the First World War. It may be different with the twenty-first century. It was in 2001, often considered the first year of the new century, that the United States found that it was no longer shielded from foreign attack by its two oceans, but vulnerable to the criminal designs of terrorists in airplanes. The United States, now the most powerful country in the world, responded to the attack by announcing a war against Terror, attacking first far-off Afghanistan, the terrorist base, and then Iraq.

It must really be left to historians in the far future to decide whether these events represent a watershed between two centuries. To an American like myself who lived through them the world seemed a very different place than when as a student it took me more than a week by ship to reach Europe from our shores, when the United States was only one of the powers called Great, when the geographic area known as the Near East was not very near at all, and when there was an association of states called the League of Nations, of which the United States was not even a member.

The events I have lived through in the last few years have had what seemed like world-shaking consequences. The terrorist attack on September 11, 2001 brought expressions of sympathy to the American people sent from all over the world, which demonstrated a sense of common humanity that was most unusual in its extent and depth. I remembered fifty years ago when there was talk of One World, but this world-wide unifying phenomenon was something different. Of course technology has brought the world closer together, as I realize every day when I sit down at my computer to communicate with the editorial executives in Singapore. When the United States attacked the Talibans and the Al-Qaeda in Afghanistan, there was still support and understanding for the United States, but the world wide feeling of unity was dissipated when the United States led a war against the state of Iraq, after attempting, but failing to convince major states on the UN Security Council that Iraq under Saddam Hussein, who was said to have weapons of mass destruction at the ready, actually represented an imminent threat to the United States, no longer invulnerable behind its oceans, and to other countries.

The U.S. war, supported by Great Britain and a number of minor states, led to another mass movement of opinion, this time in opposition to the United States. There was an unprecedented world-wide demonstration for peace; millions of people in many countries marched to protest what they felt was an unjustified war, holding up anti-American signs (but often making clear that they were opposing the government, not the American people). In the United States, however, the majority, with memory still fresh of the attacks that had been made against their country on its own soil, supported the war. After 9/11, public opinion around the world had been pro-American, sharing its grief. Now, however, world public opinion was divided as it had been during the Vietnam War.

It was in this situation that the publishers of World Scientific Publishing Company of Singapore decided to have a book done that would discuss some of the questions arising from the Iraq War. What had been the most important objectives of the United States in going to war? Was the war justified according to the UN and other international agreements? Was the war being conducted with respect to international obligations? What about the opposition to the war? How were human rights affected? What would be the future of the United Nation? Of multilateralism? Was the U.S. on a continuing unilateral course? How would Iraq be reconstructed? What would it cost?

To answer such questions and others they might raise themselves, WSPC appointed two co-editors — Prof. Wang and myself — who recruited two groups of authors, Nobel peace laureates and eminent scholars in various fields, mainly American and British. We were given the title of "The Iraq War and Its Consequences". The result was a collection of essays on the origins of the war, its conduct, its aftermath, and the future of the UN and human rights. The essays were written at different stages concerning the war, and while some of the pieces are original and written for this volume, others are reprinted from earlier publications.

The international developments up to the present has been left to the authors. At the present writing the United States is considering turning back to the UN for assistance, both for financial aid and to provide adequate security for the Iraqis. This could mean political cooperation once more between the major powers, but to lay the foundations for an enduring peace in the Middle East by developing positive relationships between western and Islamic civilizations, based on respect for human dignity and individual rights, would still be a significant challenge.

Of the peace laureates, those who have held political office, former President F. W. de Klerk of South Africa, José Ramos-Horta, now Foreign Minister of East Timor and David Trimble, leader of the Ulster Unionist Party of Northern Ireland, tend to support U.S. policy. All three are concerned about the Middle East as a whole and see the need to disarm Saddam as a necessary move in stabilizing the region and even in changing its undemocratic ways. Both de Klerk and Ramos-Horta write knowingly about American leadership, its potential and its responsibilities. Ramos-Horta, as befits a new foreign minister, gives us a *tour de monde* of recent international history.

Those active in the organized peace movement, such as Mairead Corrigan Maguire, co-founder of the Community of the Peace People of Northern Ireland, Jody Williams, International Ambassador of the International Campaign to Ban Landmines, and Cora Weiss, writing for the International Peace Bureau, are very critical of the United States. Maguire also tells of her personal witness protesting the sanctions against Iraq and demonstrating for peace in the United States. Williams writes a well documented article against the United States policy. She and Maguire recently took part in a peace vigil in front of the White House and were led away in handcuffs by the police. Weiss, also president of the Hague Appeal, speaks for a large part of the organized peace movement.

Joseph Rotblat, nuclear physicist and former president of Pugwash Conferences, and Bernard Lown, writing for International Physicians for the Prevention of Nuclear War as its co-founder, have for many years sought to explain the danger to human life on the planet of nuclear weapons, which they point out is increasing. The Dalai Lama writes clearly and simply about the bases of peace, and Mary Ellen McNish, Executive Secretary of the American Friends Service Committee, and Brian Phillips, representing the two Quaker bodies which shared the 1947 prize, also write from their pacifist religious convictions. We also include the Open Letter by Irene Khan, Secretary-General of Amnesty International, sent to the Heads of State on the eve of the war, reminding them of their obligations under the Geneva Conventions, while Christian Dominicé, Secretary-General of the Institute of International Law, discusses the impact of the war on international law. Peter Hansen, Commissioner-General of the UN Relief and Works Agency for Palestine Refugees, writing in his own name, tells of the unfortunate situation of human rights in a related conflict.

Among the scholars is the Iraqi exile, Faleh A. Jabar, who presents a personal account of how he and others in London welcomed the news of the fall of Saddam Hussein. Other scholars have reservations. In a speech in March, 2003, Frank von Hippel of Princeton says that President Bush who wants to establish democracy in Iraq should reestablish "a democratic process of foreign-policy making in the U.S.". Joseph Stiglitz of Columbia University, Nobel laureate in economics, predicts how a war would have severe effects on the American economy. However, William Hartung (with Ceara Donnelley) of the World Policy Institute, in a hard-hitting factual account, shows how the privatization of Iraq reconstruction means high profits for American corporations.

As might be expected, Noam Chomsky of MIT, the prominent social critic, writes compellingly in disapproval of the United States war policy, while Mahmood Mamdani of Columbia University, critical from a different angle, describes the American move from alliance with Iraq against Iran to punishment of Iraq for the invasion of Kuwait and to the subsequent punishment "by proxy" through the UN "genocidal" sanctions regime.

Professor Richard Falk of Princeton gives a closely reasoned answer to the question, "Is the UN now irrelevant?" This can be compared with the account of the U.S. and international law by Christian Dominicé in Section I. Professor Robin Lakoff of the University of California, Berkeley, gives a fascinating linguistic analysis of President Bush's rhetoric.

Two archeologists, Lord Renfrew of Cambridge University and Professor Benjamin Foster of Yale tell the sorry tale of the efforts in vain from the beginning to persuade the invading forces to protect the Iraqi museums from the expected looting of precious artifacts. Sir John Daniel of UNESCO, in writing of the reconstruction of education in Iraq, reminds us of the spectacular Arab achievements in scientific and intellectual history long before western Europe even entered its medieval age. Also writing about nation-building, Professor John E. Dower of MIT, a Pulitzer Prize winner, shows how the postwar reconstruction of Iraq would be very different from that in Japan.

Professor Roland Paris of the University of Colorado looks ahead toward the problems of nation-building and also touches upon the Bush administration's preference for unilateral policies to multilateral engagements, while Professor Lisa Martin of Harvard presents a solid discussion of the background of multilateralism in American policy. Eric Stover, Director of Human Rights Center at the University of California, Berkeley, reports on incidents of the violation which he observed on assignment in Iraq; Professor Rosemary Foot of Oxford University discusses human rights as it evolved in American foreign policy and its prospects in three areas in the Pacific; and Helena Cobban, specialist in international relations at the University of Virginia, proposes a way to improve human rights in a state abusing individuals without going to war against that state.

Dr. Svetlana Broz of Sarajevo, from her hopeful research in the Balkan conflicts, reports on evidence of altruistic acts in war time.

Professor Akira Iriye of Harvard sees the conflict between the U.S. and Europe in cultural, rather than political terms, with Europe historically closer to the Middle East and the U.S. motivated more by power. He strongly agrees with the resolution of the UN General Assembly in 2001, calling for "dialogue between civilizations", thinking of the Islamic civilization and the West.

In that hope we end the volume with a special feature, the universalist sermons delivered by Bishop Gunnar Stålsett of Oslo, former deputy chairman of the Norwegian Nobel Committee, one in Oslo on the eve of the Iraq War, the other at the memorial service in Oslo for the victims of the bombing of the UN headquarters in Baghdad in August 2003.

Stålsett spoke of the dying words of Sergio Vieria de Mello, head of that UN unit, then trapped beneath tons of concrete after the bomb blast, "Don't let them pull the mission out!" That message, referring to the mission to bring peace to Iraq after the war, serves to tell all of us not to let war makers like the bombers who wrecked the UN building and murdered many of its staff succeed. Not to let them end the efforts of peacemakers anywhere, those who are working to build an enduring foundation of world peace, based upon human dignity and individual rights for all.

May the essays by our authors play some part in helping us to think through the questions raised by the Iraq War and Its Consequences and to play our own part in the quest for world peace. Perhaps some day that unifying moment of sensing our common humanity after 9/11 can be recaptured and will endure.

Irwin Abrams
Distinguished University Professor Emeritus
Antioch University, Ohio
September 2003

Contents

Part I

Contributions from Nobel Peace Prize Winners

Individuals

Part II

Contributions from Eminent Scholars

Part III

Sermons in Closing ...

PART I

CONTRIBUTIONS FROM NOBEL PEACE PRIZE WINNERS

NOBEL PEACE PRIZE WINNERS: INDIVIDUALS

Tenzin Gyatso, 14th Dalai Lama of Tibet
NOBEL PEACE LAUREATE 1989

Tibetans believe that, in the person of Tenzin Gyatso, the Dalai Lama has come to them for the fourteenth time. To devout Tibetans, he is the reincarnation so enlightened that he could ascend to the highest spiritual state but instead, to serve his people, he has returned again and again to take rebirth. The following is the English translation of His Holiness the Dalai Lama's statement to the Buddhist devotees on the first day of the Great Prayer Festival, March 11, 2003, in Dharamsala. The prayer session was held in view of the threat of war in Iraq. The statement is translated and issued by the Department of Information and International Relations, Central Tibetan Administration (Dharamsala, India).

War is Anachronistic, An Outmoded Approach

War, or the kind of organized fighting, is something that came with the development of human civilization. It seems to have become part and parcel of human history or human temperament. At the same time, the world is changing dramatically. We have seen that we cannot solve human problems by fighting. Problems resulting from differences in opinion must be resolved through the gradual process of dialogue. Undoubtedly, wars produce victors and losers, but only temporarily. Victory or defeat resulting from wars cannot be long-lasting.

Secondly, our world has become so interdependent that the defeat of one country must impact the rest of the word, or cause all of us to suffer losses either directly or indirectly.

Today, the world is so small and so interdependent that the concept of war has become anachronistic, an outmoded approach. As a rule, we always talk about reforms and changes. Among the

5

old traditions, there are many aspects that are either ill-suited to our present reality or are counterproductive due to their short-sightedness. These, we have consigned to the dustbin of history. War too should be relegated to the dustbin of history.

Unfortunately, although we are in the 21st century, we still have not been able to get rid of the habit of our older generations. I am talking about the belief or confidence that we can solve our problems with arms. It is because of this notion that the world continues to be dogged by all kinds of problems.

But what can we do? What can we do when big powers have already made up their minds? All we can do is to pray for a gradual end to the tradition of wars. Of course, the militaristic tradition may not end easily. But, let us think of this. If there were bloodshed, people in positions of power, or those who are responsible, will find safe places; they will escape the consequent hardship. They will find safety for themselves, one way or the other. But what about the poor people, the defenseless people, the children, the old and infirm. They are the ones who will have to bear the brunt of devastation. When weapons are fired, the result will be death and destruction. Weapons will not discriminate between the innocent and guilty. A missile, once fired, will show no respect to the innocent, poor, defenseless, or those worthy of compassion. Therefore, the real losers will be the poor and defenseless, the ones who are completely innocent, and those who lead a hand-to-mouth existence.

On the positive side, we now have people volunteer medical care, aid, and other humanitarian assistance in war-torn regions. This is a heart-winning development of the modern age.

Let us pray that there be no war at all, if possible. However, if a war does break out, let us pray that there be minimum bloodshed and hardship.

Tenzin Gyatso, 14th Dalai Lama of Tibet

Importance of Nonviolence and Harmony

These days, when television and other media tend to focus on conflicts between people and nations we may sometimes forget that we human beings are part of one great human family. All human beings are basically the same, wherever we come from, whether we are rich or poor, educated or uneducated, following this religion or that, believers or nonbelievers. As human beings, we are all fundamentally the same emotionally, mentally and physically. There may be a few small differences in the shape of our noses, the colour of our hair and so on, but these are insignificant; basically, we are the same. We all have the same potential to undergo both positive and negative experiences. We all have a most remarkable quality, the ability to develop infinite altruism and compassion and a brain capable of unlimited knowledge and understanding. This intelligence needs to be used in the right way, for it is also capable of unlimited destruction. Most important, we have the same potential to transform our attitudes. And this is what I think is essential: to recognise that we can each transform ourselves into a better, happier person.

I believe that life is meant to bring us happiness. Negative actions always bring pain and sorrow, but constructive action brings us pleasure and joy. The most important thing is transforming our minds. In our daily lives compassion is most effective. We all want to be happy and one of the most important foundations for happiness is mental peace. From my own limited experience I have found that the greatest inner tranquility comes from the development of love and compassion. The more we care for the happiness of others, the greater our own sense of well being. Cultivating a close, warm-hearted feeling for others automatically puts the mind at ease. This helps remove whatever fears or insecurities we may have and gives us the strength to cope with any obstacle we encounter. It is the ultimate source of success in life.

As individuals what is particularly important is that we develop a kind heart, a sense of love, compassion and respect for others. I believe it is important that issues like working for peace in the world do not merely remain the business of politicians and diplomats; we should all be involved. The shape of the future is of great interest to all of us. I am convinced that even if only a few individuals try to create mental peace and happiness within themselves and act responsibly and kindheartedly towards others, they will have a positive influence in their community.

The twentieth century was marred by conflict and war. There-fore, it is especially important that we take steps to ensure that this new century will be characterized instead by nonviolence and dialogue, the preconditions of peaceful coexistence. I do not imagine that we will ever create a human society in which differences and conflicts do not occur, but we have to develop confidence that dialogue and the support of friends are a valid alternative to violence in all our relations.

I am not an expert in these affairs, but I am quite sure that if problems can be discussed according to nonviolent principles with a calm mind, keeping in view the longterm safety of the world, then various solutions can be found. Of course, in particular instances a more aggressive approach may also be necessary.

Terrorism cannot be defeated by the use of force alone. Force is not the answer to this complicated problem. In fact the use of force does not solve any problems. The use of force often leaves destruction and suffering in its wake, hurting more people and deepening wounds. Human conflicts should be resolved with compassion. The key should be the use of nonviolence.

Human conflicts do not arise out of the blue. They occur as a result of causes and conditions, many of which are within the protagonists' control. This is where leadership is important. It is our leaders' responsibility to decide when to act and when to be restrained. In the case of violent conflict it is important to restrain the situation before it gets out of hand. Once the causes and conditions for violent clashes have ripened, it is very difficult to calm them down again. Violence undoubtedly breeds more violence. If we instinctively retaliate against violence done to us, what can we expect other than that from our opponent who will also feel justified to retaliate in turn? Preventive measures and restraint have to be adopted at an early stage. Clearly leaders need to be alert, farsighted and decisive.

Everyone wishes to live in peace, but we are often confused about how it can be achieved. Mahatma Gandhi pointed out that because violence inevitably leads to more violence; therefore if we are seriously interested in peace, it must be achieved through peaceful and nonviolent means.

We must continue to develop a wider perspective, to think rationally and work to avert future disasters in a nonviolent way. These issues concern the whole of humanity, not just one country. We should explore the use of nonviolence as a longterm measure to control terrorism of any kind. But we need a well thought out, coordinated longterm strategy. The proper way of resolving differences is through dialogue, compromise and negotiations, through human understanding and humility. We need to appreciate that genuine peace comes about through mutual understanding, respect and trust. As I have already said, human problems should be solved in a humanitarian way, and nonviolence is the humane approach.

Rt. Hon. David Trimble
NOBEL PEACE LAUREATE 1998

Born in Bangor on October 15, 1944, Trimble co-won the Nobel Peace prize with John Hume for their work in securing the Belfast Agreement. He was First Minister of the North Ireland Assembly 1998–2000. He is also a Member of Parliament of the Ulster Unionist Party (since 1995).

The United Nations Left Us No Option But to Act

We had no doubt about the nature of the regime in Iraq. We had no doubt about the threat, about the wars that have been started, or about the weapons of mass destruction that have been accumulated and used. There was also no doubt about what the United Nations required. There were United Nations resolutions that required Saddam Hussein to disarm. There was certainly a failure to comply. There was a material breach before Resolution 1441, and there was a material breach when Allied troops went into Iraq.

It was only the credible threat of force that has achieved the little progress that had been there up until that point, and that made Saddam Hussein permit the admission of inspectors. That came after the failure of earlier UN resolutions. All the resolutions in the 1990s failed. The UN and the world community allowed themselves to be bluffed and manoeuvred out of Iraq. Against that background, 1441 had to be clear, and backed up by a credible threat of force. That credible threat had to be maintained.

The paradox is that, in order to obtain compliance with UN resolutions, there had to be the threat of force. Because Saddam Hussein failed to comply, it was inevitable that that force would have to be used. Those who supported the UN and its resolutions, including 1441, must be aware that, as a consequence, they had to support the credible use of force, right down to the point of its use. Those who failed to do so weakened the UN gravely.

The UN had been weakened badly enough by the failures of the 1990s. It again set its hand to trying to carry through its will in this matter, and it had to succeed. If it did not, enormous damage would have been done to the possibility that the UN can be credible in the future, and that will have implications for world peace. The paradox is that those who want peace and a UN that succeeds in the world had, therefore, to support the use of force when that became necessary.

I appreciate that some people find that difficult to live with. Some of those who were reluctant to go down the route that I have described were well meaning, and others were engaged in wishful thinking.

Other people were influenced by less noble motives. I have been distressed by the degree of anti-Americanism that has been expressed in recent months, and the personal hostility to the President. I consider that wholly misplaced. I have been appalled at some of the comments about President Bush, and at the false caricature of him that has been presented. I base that opinion not only on the fleeting personal acquaintance that I have had with him, but on what he has said and done over the past couple of years, which I looked at closely.

The record has been clear, especially in the period since September 11. The U.S. moved slowly, deliberately and proportionately. That was the evidence.

People were right to be concerned about what would happen in Iraq and the region if force had to be used. However, we must realise that the region is highly unstable. That was another of the lessons of September 11: it brought home to us just how unstable the region is. We need to think about the causes of that instability, and about how we can resolve or do something to improve the situation there.

This is a complex issue. If there were no oil in the region, there would be a series of failed states there. The region has failed to deal with the challenge of modernisation.

I am talking about the Middle East region as a whole and the Arab states there, not about Islam. A distinction must be drawn between Islam and what is happening in the Middle East in respect of a particular and virulent strand of that religion. That strand is a distortion of Islam.

We need to ask why modernisation has failed. Saddam grew out of the Ba'ath socialist party, although he was, in fact, a crude anti-Semitic nationalist. Why have such people obtained and retained power? How do we change that?

How can we change the culture in the Middle East and the orientation of those states because, until we do that, we will not achieve stability? Just talking about the problem in Israel and the Palestinian areas is not terribly helpful. That problem cannot be dealt with in isolation. It is part of the instability generally, and dealing with that instability generally will make it easier to deal with Israel and Palestine; but we cannot deal with that in isolation.

Some spoke of containment and deterrence as a way of dealing with the problem in Iraq. Those concepts worked well during the Cold War, but the world has changed since the Cold War ended. We had to recognise that containment and deterrence would not work in the situation that confronted us.

In the modern world, we face danger from what are called rogue states, terrorist groups with a global reach and weapons of mass destruction. As a consequence of the Cold War, there is a lot of expertise and matériel floating around the world that is not as well guarded as it should be.

Perhaps we did not fully appreciate the problem before September 11, but the events of that day should have concentrated minds on the matter. The significance of September 11 is that it made people realise that a different approach was needed if we were to deal with the problems caused by WMD, terrorist movements and rogue states.

That different approach was symbolised in 2002 by the passing of resolution 1441. The international community decided to proceed by a route different from that offered by containment and deterrence, and to go back to the weapons inspections that had taken place immediately after the 1991 Gulf War. In that way, a serious effort was made to disarm Saddam Hussein.

However, that approach was no longer tenable when the French said that they would veto a resolution whatever the circumstances. The French were not saying, "Give it another month or couple of months." If the French position had been to give the approach a little more time, it would have been possible to maintain the credible threat of force. However, as soon as the French said that they would exercise their veto whatever the circumstances, they destroyed the credible threat of force used through the UN channel.

The UN route was therefore blocked. The British and U.S. Governments spent a week seeing whether they could unblock it, or find some way around the blockage. I was surprised that they spent so long coming to terms with the French position, which effectively closed down the UN route.

Why did the French do this? Their actions are different from the normal French way of operating, with which we are all familiar. In the past, yes, the French had been awkward and difficult. They hung on until people have met the requirements of what the French regard as their national interest, or until people recognised the French position. They did not like being taken for granted, but in the past they usually came into line.

There were indications that the Russians were going to do the same. Whatever their public position, the Russians had a shopping list. I am very glad that the Americans were not tempted to accede to the list, as the reports that I heard suggested that it contained some pretty gruesome items. Be that as it may, the Russians were operating in their normal way, and one expected the French to do likewise. The question was, why did the French adopt the position of saying that they would exercise the veto, whatever the circumstances?

I suggest it went back to the French view of themselves in Europe. The French believe that they should lead Europe, and that Europe should be another pole of power in the world — a challenge or a rival to the U.S.

What were we to do when it was obvious that the UN route ended? We were not where we wanted to be and the situation was not ideal, but we had to operate in the circumstances that then prevailed. Were we just to strike camp and go away? Was the United States going to allow itself to be humiliated by the French? No, it would not, and nor could anyone reasonably expect that. Nor would it have been reasonable to think along those lines. If resolution 1441 was right, ensuring compliance with it was also right. The French action, therefore, was an unreasonable threatened exercise of the veto.

We had to make a choice in the circumstances we found ourselves in. We had to consider the consequences of that choice, some of which were unknowable and unpredictable. There was an element of risk in the choice that we made, but we had to make it. The situation was imperfect — this is an imperfect world — and the issue could be easily compartmentalised. In that situation, however, we did not have much of a choice and that is why I supported the actions of the British and American Governments.

Jody Williams
NOBEL PEACE LAUREATE 1997

Born in 1950 in Vermont, U.S., Williams was the founding coordinator of the International Campaign to Ban Landmines (ICBL), the coalition which spearheaded the global movement to outlaw anti-personnel mines (APLs) and deal with their long term impact. Williams currently serves as Campaign Ambassador for the ICBL.

Iraq and Preemptive Self-Defense

Overview

In December 2001, Nobel Peace Laureates convened in Oslo to help mark the 100th anniversary of the Nobel Prizes. Coming not long after the terrorist attacks on the Twin Towers in New York City and the Pentagon, that issue was much on the minds of those of us there. I argued then that despite the constant refrain that "everything had changed" as a result of the spectacular attacks, I believed that, in fact, many things were very much the same as they had ever been — only worse. The events leading up to the U.S. invasion of Iraq about 15 months later and the unfolding aftermath of that invasion have done little to change my opinion.

What may have changed as a result of September 11 is the American psyche and its new-found sense of vulnerability in the world. In my view, what has not changed is that for the Bush administration it has been very much "business as usual" in the sense of those in power taking advantage of uncertainties and fear to advance their own political and ideological agendas.

17

I believe that the Bush administration took advantage of the fear and uncertainty engendered by the horrific attacks of September 11 in two ways. First, the administration used the attacks to put forth a national security policy of preemptive self-defense as if it were a direct response to September 11. Instead, it is but one element of a longer-standing, post-Cold War political vision of unrivaled U.S. power developed by members of the administration, first floated during the first Bush administration, then released in September 2002 as the "National Security Strategy of the United States of America".[1]

Second, they sought to finish the work many felt had been left undone in the first Gulf War and used the new security policy as a justification to invade Iraq to remove Saddam Hussein from power and, in their view, pave the way for a "reverse domino theory" of radical transformation of the Middle East — another element of their over-arching political strategy.

Domestically, they were helped in promoting the push to war by major media outlets that acted more like public relations firms for the administration's war agenda than objective news sources that supposedly are the underpinnings of the much-lauded American free press. Meaningful public debate was stifled and opposition to the war was largely ignored by the press. The U.S. Congress, cowed by the high-flying rhetoric of "patriotism" and "security for the homeland", rushed to a vote to support Bush's war of "preemptive self defense" against Iraq. In so doing, they further eroded their Constitutional responsibilities regarding the declaration of war and endorsed the Bush administration's radical departure in U.S. national security policy essentially without meaningful debate.

Internationally, the administration tried to use similar manipulations, coupled with intense political and economic pressure, to achieve international support for the invasion. They had hoped to build upon the surge of global sympathy toward the U.S. in the

---

[1] "The National Security Strategy of the United States of America," White House Office of Homeland Security, September 2002, available at: http://www.whitehouse.gov/nsc/.

aftermath of September 11 and the international cooperation that developed in the administration's war on terrorism resulting from those attacks.

In the process of taking the U.S. to war, the Bush administration alienated some of its closest allies and much of the Arab world, particularly through its actions in the United Nations and its dealings with UN weapons inspections during the lead up to the invasion. The majority of the international community did not accept the assertions that Saddam possessed weapons of mass destruction (WMD) that posed such imminent threat to international security that newly initiated UN weapons inspections — which were making some progress — could not be given more time before resorting to the use of force to disarm the regime.

I do not believe that a national security doctrine based on preemptive self-defense serves the best interests of the people of the United States. I believe that preemptive self defense threatens to dramatically destabilize international security and international law and that the Bush administration has set a dangerous precedent the ramifications of which will be felt for years if not decades.[2] At the same time, I do not believe that the invasion of Iraq had much to do with an "honest" application of such doctrine, but rather was carried out to advance U.S. interests as defined by the archconservatives of the Bush administration.

As the invasion and the post-invasion occupation of Iraq are playing out, those around the world who have always held the motive for the Bush administration's drive for regime change suspect are finding their beliefs confirmed. By their unilateralist actions toward Iraq, the Bush administration has further alienated an international community already deeply concerned by the administration's policies — policies that seem determined to undermine international law and multilateral cooperation, such as it is.

---

[2] In an op-ed in September 2002, General Wesley Clark commented on the preemptive doctrine, writing, "It is a doctrine that could be used by others to overturn much of the practice of international law, which we ourselves have helped engineer since World War II." See Wesley K. Clark, "USA-Iraq II: Necessity and efficacy," *Chicago Tribune*, September 15, 2002, p. 11.

Iraq: The Spin and the Lead-Up to War

The Bush administration — and its primary ally British Prime Minister Tony Blair — tried to spin the case that the Iraqi regime posed such an overwhelming and immediate threat to national and global security that "preemptive self-defense" gave cause for a just war against Saddam Hussein. This doctrine, spelled out in the administration's September 2002 national security strategy document states:

> "We will disrupt and destroy terrorist organizations by: direct and continuous action using all the elements of national and international power. Our immediate focus will be those terrorist organizations of global reach and any terrorist or state sponsor of terrorism which attempts to gain or use weapons of mass destruction (WMD) or their precursors; defending the United States, the American people, and our interests at home and abroad by identifying and destroying the threat before it reaches our borders. While the United States will constantly strive to enlist the support of the international community, we will not hesitate to act alone, if necessary, to exercise our right of self-defense by acting preemptively against such terrorists, to prevent them from doing harm against our people and our country; and denying further sponsorship, support, and sanctuary to terrorists by convincing or compelling states to accept their sovereign responsibilities."[3]

The primary justifications for a war of preemptive self-defense against Iraq were that Saddam's regime supported terrorists in general, had links to Al-Qaeda in particular, and was continuing to develop weapons of mass destruction (WMD). As that argument spun out, the Bush administration consistently stated that there was

---

[3] "The National Security Strategy of the United States of America," The White House, Washington, DC, September 17, 2002, available at: www.whitehouse.gov/nsc/nss.html; see also "National Strategy to Combat Weapons of Mass Destruction," U.S. Department of Defense, December 2002, available at: www.defenselink.mil/pubs/.

a direct link between Saddam and Al-Qaeda, implying that, through that link, he was responsible either directly or indirectly for the attacks of September 11. The administration also argued that because of his support for various terrorists and their networks, at some point Saddam would likely provide WMD to those terrorists to attack the U.S. and its assets, if he did not use them himself against the U.S. or its allies in the region.

While always asserting those fundamental arguments to justify a preemptive war, the administration sought to soften the image of the invasion by also arguing that it was seeking regime change because it sought to free the Iraqi people from decades of despotic rule. Administration officials argued that the long-suffering Iraqi people deserved freedom from the dictator and the right to form their own government and use the riches of Iraqi oil to benefit all the people of the country. In particular, the administration used this argument to play to the best side of the American psyche — the belief that most Americans share that this country really does stand for freedom and justice and democracy and self-determination for all under all circumstances.

These were the essential elements that the administration also took to the United Nations as they attempted to rally the support of both the U.S. Congress and the international community for action against the Hussein regime. On September 12, 2002, Bush addressed the UN in the push for a new UN resolution requiring the regime to give up WMD and stop support for terrorism in order to avoid war.[4] On October 11, 2002, both Houses of the U.S. Congress voted to authorize an attack on Iraq if the regime refused to give up WMD as required by UN resolutions. In commenting on the passage of the resolutions, Bush declared, "America speaks with one voice." Further, he said, "The Congress has spoken clearly to the international community and the United Nations Security

---

[4] "Remarks by the President in Address to the United Nations General Assembly New York, New York," The White House, Office of the Press Secretary, September 12, 2002, available at: www.whitehouse.gov/news/releases/2002/09/20020912-1.html.

Council. Saddam Hussein and his outlaw regime pose a grave threat to the region, the world and the United States. Inaction is not an option, disarmament is a must."[5] On November 8, the Security Council unanimously passed Resolution 1441, which established an enhanced inspection regime to disarm Iraq, to be carried out by the UN Monitoring, Verification, and Inspection Commission (UNMOVIC) and the International Atomic Energy Agency (IAEA).[6]

Even as the weapons inspectors were resuming their activities, the Bush administration increased rhetorical and real pressure on the Iraqi regime, and began to move troops into the region. Even as Hussein grudgingly began to cooperate with the inspectors, the Bush administration, under pressure from its primary ally British Prime Minister Tony Blair, agreed to press for another UN resolution that would grant it international legitimacy to go to war.

On January 27, 2003, Mohamed ElBaradei, Director General of the IAEA, reported to the Security Council the results of the first 60 days of activity of the weapons inspections resumed under Resolution 1441. In opening he recalled the accomplishments of the inspections carried out between 1991–1998: "In September 1991, the IAEA seized documents in Iraq that demonstrated the extent of its nuclear weapons programme. By the end of 1992, we had largely destroyed, removed or rendered harmless all Iraqi facilities and equipment relevant to nuclear weapons production. We confiscated Iraq's nuclear-weapons-usable material — high enriched uranium and plutonium — and by early 1994 we had removed it from the country. By December 1998 — when the inspections were brought

---

[5] "Senate Approves Iraq War Resolution," *CNN.com*, October 11, 2002. One of the few consistently vocal dissenters to U.S. policy toward Iraq has been Senator Robert Byrd (D-WVa); at the time of the October 11, vote, he equated the Iraq resolution to the Gulf of Tonkin Resolution of the Vietnam War. That resolution was the result of false claims by the Johnson administration of attacks against U.S. ships on the Gulf of Tonkin and was used to justify further buildup in the Vietnam War.

[6] United Nations Security Council Resolution 1441, S/Res/1441/2002, November 8, 2002, available at: www.un.org/documents/scres.htm.

to a halt with a military strike imminent — we were confident that we had not missed any significant component of Iraq's nuclear programme."[7]

After then describing the progress and challenges remaining under the resumed inspections, ElBaradei concluded, "We have to date found no evidence that Iraq has revived its nuclear weapons programme since the elimination of the programme in the 1990s. However, our work is steadily progressing and should be allowed to run its natural course. With our verification system now in place, barring exceptional circumstances, and provided there is sustained proactive cooperation by Iraq, we should be able within the next few months to provide credible assurance that Iraq has no nuclear weapons programme."

Almost as if the IAEA had never reported on the progress of the inspections, on February 5, 2003, in a dramatic bid to convince a skeptical world of the imminent need for war, U.S. Secretary of State Colin Powell presented the administration's case to the United Nations as prelude to its push for a second UN resolution for war.[8] In his address, Powell presented evidence of the administration's allegations that the Iraqi regime was in "material breach" of Resolution 1441 — continuing its WMD development and its ties to terrorists — which justified going to war. Much of the evidence he presented was based upon undisclosed sources, and documents and intercepts subject to various interpretations.[9] Many of the claims

---

[7] Mohamed ElBaradei, "The Status of Nuclear Inspections in Iraq," Statement to the United Nations Security Council on behalf of the International Atomic Energy Agency, New York, January 27, 2003, available at: www.un.org/News/dh/iraq/elbaradei27jan03.htm.

[8] Secretary Colin L. Powell, "Remarks to the United Nations Security Council," The U.S. State Department, February 5, 2003, available at: www.state.gov/secretary/rm/2003/17300.htm.

[9] The White House, "U.S. Secretary of State Colin Powell Addresses the UN Security Council, February 5, 2003, available at: www.whitehouse.gov/news/releases/2003/02/20030205-1.html. For a point-by-point discussion of the elements of the speech, see "Powell's February 5th Presentation to the UN," Center for Cooperative Research, available at: www.cooperativeresearch.org/wot/iraq/colin_powell_february_5_presentation_to_the_un.html.

Powell made have subsequently been demonstrated to be false as the Bush administration's evidence in its case for war has unraveled over the past months, as described below. While Powell made an eloquent presentation, the evidence he presented did not convince a skeptical world of the need for immediate action.

By mid-February 2003, of the 15 members of the Security Council, only Britain, Spain and Bulgaria supported the resolution. Speaking from his ranch in Crawford, Texas, on February 22, Bush stated that this was the last opportunity for the UN to "show its relevance."[10] The U.S. exerted tremendous pressure on members of the Security Council to support the resolution, for which it needed nine votes and no vetoes in order to prevail. But when it became apparent that a war resolution would not pass, with France and Russia in particular continuing to vow to veto such a resolution, the administration decided to not press for a vote and go to war unilaterally with what it would call "a coalition of the willing".

On March 17, 2003, in an address to the nation, President Bush gave Saddam Hussein an ultimatum: leave Iraq within 48 hours or face war. In his address, Bush gave his view of the global strains caused by the press for war, stating,

> "Today, no nation can possibly claim that Iraq has disarmed. And it will not disarm so long as Saddam Hussein holds power. For the last four-and-a-half months, the United States and our allies have worked within the Security Council to enforce that Council's long-standing demands. Yet, some permanent members of the Security Council have publicly announced they will veto any resolution that compels the disarmament of Iraq. These governments share our assessment of the danger, but not our resolve to meet it. Many nations, however, do have the resolve and fortitude to act against this threat to peace, and a broad coalition is now gathering to enforce the just demands of

---

[10] "Bush: Clear UN Resolution on Tap," *CBSNEWS.com*, February 22, 2003, available at: www.cbsnews.com/stories/2003/02/23/iraq/main541608.shtml.

the world. The United Nations Security Council has not lived up to its responsibilities, so we will rise to ours."[11]

Two days later the U.S. launched its invasion of Iraq with a "decapitation attack" aimed at Saddam Hussein and his two sons.

The Spin — Myth or Reality

On May 1, 2003, after a dramatic photo-op fighter jet landing on the aircraft carrier the USS Abraham Lincoln, standing before a huge banner hung on the ship which read "Mission Accomplished," Bush declared major combat operations of the war to be over.[12] However, on July 16, a little less than three months later, as organized attacks on occupation forces were on the rise, the new commander of U.S. Central Command General John Azibaid acknowledged that U.S. occupying forces in Iraq were facing a "classical guerrilla-type campaign".[13] No weapons of mass destruction have as yet been found in the occupied country and the administration's arguments for war have been rapidly losing currency — a currency that many believe they never should have had in the first place.

The Bush administration was helped tremendously in advancing its war agenda domestically by the U.S. media. Embracing the administration's arguments for its post-September 11 policies, both at home and abroad, media outlets gave virtually no room for dissent or even objective discussion — particularly in the lead up

---

[11] "President Says Saddam Hussein Must Leave Iraq Within 48 Hours," Remarks by the President in Address to the Nation, The Cross Hall, The White House, Office of the Press Secretary, March 17, 2003.

[12] "Bush to Declare Major Combat Over in Iraq," *Associated Press*, April 30, 2003.

[13] Jonathan Marcus, "U.S. faces up to guerrilla war: It has taken a change in command for senior U.S. officers to utter the 'G' word about Iraq," *BBC News*, July 17, 2003, available at: news.bbc.co.uk/1/hi/world/middle_east/3074465.stm; Vernon Loeb, "'Guerrilla' War Acknowledged: New Commander Cites Problems," *Washington Post*, July 17, 2003, p. A1.

to the Iraq invasion and during the war itself, when U.S. reporters were "embedded" with advancing U.S. troops. The "embedding" of media was only the most overt aspect of the administration's policy of misinformation and propaganda to achieve its goals vis-à-vis Iraq.

Almost as soon as Bush began his rhetorical assault on the imminent threat of Saddam's WMD, time after time it would be revealed that "evidence" he cited was false, non-existent or distorted. One of the first examples I remember was his October 2002 statement that an IAEA report on Hussein's nuclear capacity alleged that the regime was "six months away" from developing a nuclear weapon. Almost immediately the IAEA refuted the allegation, pointedly noting that no such report existed at all. While Bush's claims were put out loud and clear, the subsequent disclaimer by his spokesperson Ari Fleisher was barely noted by the media. It still remains a piece of misinformation barely touched upon by the media.[14]

Other WMD evidence used both by Bush and high-ranking members of his administration has also proven to be either completely false or to have been made "more forward leaning" in order to bolster the position that the administration wanted to prove.[15] The most notorious example of the use of false information is Bush's statement in his January 28, 2002 State of the Union Address that Hussein sought uranium for nuclear weapons in Africa. The statement was based, in part, on documents that supposedly demonstrated the regime's attempts to buy uranium from Niger, which had been discredited many months earlier by U.S. intelligence

---

[14] Dana Milbank, "For Bush, Facts Are Malleable," *Washington Post*, October 22, 2003; "MEDIA advisory: Bush Uranium Lie is Tip of the Iceberg: Press should expand focus beyond '16 words'," *Fairness & Accuracy In Reporting*, July 18, 2003. For an analysis of 16 major distortions by the administration to justify the invasion, see *Council for a Livable World*, "Iraq: 16 Distortions, not 16 Words," July 31, 2003, available at: www.clw.org/16distortions.html.

[15] John W. Dean, "Missing Weapons Of Mass Destruction: Is Lying About The Reason For War An Impeachable Offense?" *FindLaw*, June 6, 2003; James Risen and Douglas Jehl, "Expert Said to Tell Legislators He Was Pressed to Distort Some Evidence," *New York Times*, June 25, 2003.

agencies and proved to be complete forgeries.[16] The CIA had successfully argued for removal of a similar statement from an earlier speech given in October by Bush because it knew the "evidence" to be not credible. It also has argued that it pressed the White House to drop the Niger allegations from Bush's address.[17]

An example of making information "more forward leaning" is the case of aluminum tubes bought by the Iraqi regime that the U.S. administration declared Iraq was planning to use for producing nuclear bombs. Although many experts stated that the tubes were not for nuclear production and the whole debate about the issue was highly controversial and highly charged, Bush administration officials advanced it as yet more proof of its case for war. One article outlining the evidence for war wrote of the dismay among some intelligence analysts who had participated in the aluminum-tubes debate at how administration officials were presenting the issue. One said, "You had senior American officials like Condoleezza Rice saying the only use of the aluminum really is uranium centrifuges. She said that on television. And that's just a lie."[18]

---

[16] Articles and analyses of the evidence presented by the Bush administration to justify attacking Iraq abound. See, for example, William M. Arkin, "A Hazy Target; Before going to war over weapons of mass destruction, shouldn't we be sure Iraq has them?" *Los Angeles Times*, March 9, 2003; Seymour M. Hersh, "Offense And Defense," *The New Yorker*, April 7, 2003; Robin Cook, "Shoulder to Shoulder and Stabbed in the Back," *Los Angeles Times*, June 6, 2003; John W. Dean, "Missing Weapons Of Mass Destruction: Is Lying About The Reason For War An Impeachable Offense?" *FindLaw*, June 6, 2003; John B. Judis & Spencer Ackerman, "The Selling of the Iraq War: The First Casualty," *The New Republic*, June 30, 2003; Dana Milbank, "White House Didn't Gain CIA Nod for Claim on Iraqi Strikes: Gist Was Hussein Could Launch in 45 Minutes," *Washington Post*, July 20, 2003; Dana Priest, "Uranium Claim Was Known for Months to be Weak: Intelligence Officials Say 'Everyone Knew' Then What the White House Knows Now About Niger Reference," *Washington Post*, July 20, 2003.

[17] Edward T. Pound and Bruce B. Auster, "The Plot Thickens: New Evidence fails to resolve mystery of Bush's State of the Union misstep on Iraq," *U.S. News & World Report*, July 28–August 4, 2003.

[18] John B. Judis and Spencer Ackerman, "The Selling of the Iraq War: The First Casualty," *The New Republic*, June 30, 2003.

It has been widely reported that Vice-President Cheney, and other administration allies such as Newt Gingrich, went repeatedly to CIA headquarters to press for interpretations of information to support the push for war.[19] According to one report, both Cheney and his chief of staff, Lewis "Scooter" Libby, visited the CIA for briefings. One senior administration official said, "Nearly every day, Cheney and Scooter hammered the agency on Iraq or terrorism. Over time, the agency got tired of fighting."[20] But apparently, even this pressure did not satisfy the needs of the administration. Defense Secretary Donald Rumsfeld set up a shadow agency, the Office of Special Plans (OSP), to compete with the CIA and its military counterpart, the Defense Intelligence Agency in interpretation of data.[21]

The other primary argument for the invasion was the "bulletproof" evidence, as declared in September 2002 by Donald Rumsfeld, that Saddam Hussein had ties with Al-Qaeda.[22] President Bush and his advisors repeatedly talked of these ties, with the barely veiled implication that because of the links Saddam was in some way responsible for the attacks of September 11. Yet, these claims proved even weaker, if possible, than the evidence provided regarding the WMD in Saddam's possession.

---

[19] John B. Judis & Spencer Ackerman, "The Selling of the Iraq War: The First Casualty," *The New Republic*, June 30, 2003; Julian Berger, "The Spies Who Pushed for War," *The Guardian* (London), July 17, 2003; Jim Lobe, "The Other Bush Lie," *TomPaine.com*, July 15, 2003; Ray McGovern, "Not Business as Usual: Cheney and the CIA," *Alternet*, June 30, 2003, in this piece McGovern writes, "As though this were normal! I mean the repeated visits Vice President Dick Cheney made to the CIA before the war in Iraq. The visits were, in fact, unprecedented. During my 27-year career at the Central Intelligence Agency, no vice president ever came to us for a working visit."

[20] Edward T. Pound and Bruce B. Auster, "The Plot Thickens: New Evidence fails to resolve mystery of Bush's State of the Union misstep on Iraq," *U.S. News & World Report*, July 28–August 4, 2003.

[21] Julian Berger, "The Spies Who Pushed for War," *The Guardian* (London), July 17, 2003.

[22] John B. Judis and Spencer Ackerman, "The Selling of the Iraq War: The First Casualty," *The New Republic*, June 30, 2003.

On June 15, 2003, retired General Wesley Clark was inter-viewed on NBC television's "Meet the Press" where he stated that the Bush administration began trying to implicate Hussein imme-diately after the September attacks. Clark said, "Well, it came from the White House, it came from people around the White House. It came from all over. I got a call on 9/11. I was on CNN, and I got a call at my home saying, 'You got to say this is connected. This is state-sponsored terrorism. This has to be connected to Saddam Hussein.' I said, 'But — I'm willing to say it, but what's your evidence?' And I never got any evidence."[23]

According to the non-profit media watchdog Fairness & Accuracy In Reporting, "Clark's assertion corroborates a little-noted CBS Evening News story that aired on September 4, 2002. As correspondent David Martin reported: 'Barely five hours after Amer-ican Airlines Flight 77 plowed into the Pentagon, the secretary of defense was telling his aides to start thinking about striking Iraq, even though there was no evidence linking Saddam Hussein to the attacks.' According to CBS, a Pentagon aide's notes from that day quote Rumsfeld asking for the 'best info fast' to 'judge whether good enough to hit SH at the same time, not only UBL.' (The initials SH and UBL stand for Saddam Hussein and Osama bin Laden.) The notes then quote Rumsfeld as demanding, ominously, that the administration's response 'go massive...sweep it all up, things related and not'."[24]

Others in and around the Bush administration began publicly trying to connect Saddam to Al-Qaeda and thus to the September 11 attacks. On behalf of the administration, James Woolsey, a former director of the CIA and a current member of the Defense Policy Board, went to Europe to seek evidence to back the claim. His

---

[23] *Fairness & Accuracy In Reporting*, "MEDIA ADVISORY: Media Silent on Clark's 9/11 Comments: Gen. says White House pushed Saddam link without evidence," June 20, 2003.
[24] *Ibid.*

evidence — that Mohamed Atta, the leader of the 9/11 attacks, had met with an Iraqi intelligence official in Prague — was not supported by U.S. intelligence or by Czech officials.[25] In February 2003, the *New York Times* reported that an FBI official said, "We've been looking at this hard for more than a year and you know what, we just don't think it's there."[26] Additionally, a classified British intelligence report seen by BBC news stated, "There are no current links between the Iraqi regime and the Al-Qaeda network."[27]

Despite the lack of support for such a connection, administration officials have continued to make the claim. On May 1, 2003, when President Bush declared the major operations in the invasion of Iraq to be over, he said, "We have removed an ally of Al-Qaeda. No terrorist network will gain weapons of mass destruction from the Iraqi regime."[28] Again, during a July 30 press conference, Bush stated his confidence that evidence would be found to prove a connection between Saddam Hussein and Al-Qaeda.[29]

The U.S. Media Bias and Government "Information Warfare"

It can be difficult to understand why much of the American public still wants to believe the nearly mythological justifications for the invasion. I can understand why people outside the United States cannot understand the "gullibility" of the American public and are confused by the claims of seemingly uniform support for the Bush

---

[25] John B. Judis and Spencer Ackerman, "The Selling of the Iraq War: The First Casualty," *The New Republic*, June 30, 2003.

[26] James Risen and David Johnston, "Split at C.I.A. and F.B.I. On Iraqi Ties to Al-Qaeda," *New York Times*, February 2, 2003.

[27] "Leaked Report Rejects Iraqi Al-Qaeda Link," *BBC News*, February 5, 2003.

[28] Walter Pincus, "Oct. Report Said Defeated Hussein Would be Threat," *Washington Post*, July 21, 2003, p. A1.

[29] Mike Allen and Dana Milbank, "Bush Takes Responsibility for Iraq Claim," *Washington Post*, July 31, 2003, p. A1.

administration's policies. But from inside the country, it is easier to understand.

Particularly since September 11, the mainstream American media has been mostly uniformly in support of an aggressive war on terrorism and a "muscular" U.S. foreign policy. In the immediate aftermath of the September attacks, it was considered "unpatriotic" at best and "treasonous" at worst to publicly ask any questions about the root causes of terrorism. Additionally, the mainstream media consistently presented positions that reinforced the administration's point of view and left little room for debate and discussion, particularly in the lead-up to the war and during the invasion itself. For example, one survey of 414 Iraq-related stories on the three major U.S. networks between September 2001 and February 2002 found that all but 34 of the stories were sourced out of the White House, Defense Department or the State Department.[30]

The situation did not improve once the invasion started. Fairness & Accuracy In Reporting (FAIR) began a three-week study on 19 March 2003, the day after the war began. They canvassed 1,617 on-camera sources appearing in stories about Iraq on the evening newscasts of six U.S. television networks and news channels.[31] The major findings include the following: "Nearly two thirds of all sources, 64 percent, were pro-war, while 71 percent of U.S. guests favored the war. Antiwar voices were 10 percent of all sources, but just 6 percent of non-Iraqi sources and 3 percent of U.S. sources. Thus viewers were more than six times as likely to see a pro-war source as one who was antiwar; with U.S. guests alone, the ratio

---

[30] In 2001, a total of 14,632 sources were interviewed by the three major network's evening news broadcasts. Of these, the percentage who were white: 92, the percentage who were male: 85, the percentage who were Republican, when party noted: 75, and the percentage who were the President: 9; see "The Usual Suspects," *Utne*, November–December 2002; see also the website of *Fairness & Accuracy In Reporting* website, available at: www.fair.org.

[31] The news programs studied were ABC World News Tonight, CBS Evening News, NBC Nightly News, CNN's Wolf Blitzer Reports, Fox's Special Report with Brit Hume, and PBS's NewsHour With Jim Lehrer.

increases to 25 to 1... Looking at U.S. sources, which made up 76 percent of total sources, more than two out of three (68 percent) were either current or former officials...In the category of U.S. officials, military voices overwhelmed civilians by a two-to-one margin, providing 68 percent of U.S. official sources and nearly half (47 percent) of all U.S. sources. This predominance reflected the networks' focus on information from journalists embedded with troops, or provided at military briefings, and the analysis of such by paid former military officials."[32]

At the same time, despite the largest public protests in the streets of American cities since the height of the Vietnam War, coverage of the massive displays of opposition to official policy was barely acknowledged, let alone covered. The *FAIR* study cited above found, for example, that "just 3 percent of U.S. sources represented or expressed opposition to the war. With more than one in four U.S. citizens opposing the war and much higher rates of opposition in most countries where opinion was polled, none of the networks offered anything resembling proportionate coverage of antiwar voices".[33] In the face of such a barrage of biased reporting, it is very difficult for individual citizens to believe that their opposition opinions, or even basic questioning of events, are anything but rare, isolated, and perhaps, even "unpatriotic".

As Chris Hedges, a non-pacifist war correspondent for about 20 years, writes in his recent book *War is a Force That Gives Us Meaning*, "The effectiveness of the myths peddled in war is powerful. We often come to doubt our own perceptions. We hide these doubts, like troubled believers, sure that no one else feels

---

[32] Steve Rendall and Tara Broughel, "Amplifying Officials, Squelching Dissent: FAIR study finds democracy poorly served by war coverage," *FAIR*, May/June 2003, available at: www.fair.org/extra/0305/warstudy.html.

[33] Steve Rendall and Tara Broughel, "Amplifying Officials, Squelching Dissent: FAIR study finds democracy poorly served by war coverage," *FAIR*, May/June 2003, available at: http://www.fair.org/extra/0305/warstudy.html. The antiwar percentages ranged from 4 percent at NBC, 3 percent at CNN, ABC, PBS and FOX, and less than 1 percent — one out of 205 U.S. sources — at CBS.

them. We feel guilty. The myths have determined not only how we should speak but how we should think. The doubts we carry, the scenes we see that do not conform to the myth are hazy, difficult to express, unsettling. And as the atrocities mount, as civil liberties are stripped away (something, with the "War on Terror", already happening to hundreds of thousands of immigrants in the United States), we struggle uncomfortably with the jargon and clichés. But we have trouble expressing our discomfort because *the collective shout* [emphasis added] has made it hard for us to give words to our thoughts. This self-doubt is aided by the monstrosity of war...".

And this is just the domestic public face of the administration's attempts at molding U.S. public opinion — and information abroad, for that matter. In a presentation in April 2003 in Washington, DC, one university professor analyzing the situation noted the administration's "attempts to assert 'full spectrum dominance' over all levels of wartime communication...effacing the traditional boundary between battlefield deception and public sphere propaganda".[34] Further, he stated, "According to defense analyst William Arkin, the Bush strategy lays out goals for information warfare that pursue D5E: 'destruction, degradation, denial, disruption, deceit, and exploitation.' Arkin notes that the wide array of sites and practices of information control brought into the range of this policy 'blurs or even erases the boundaries between factual information and news, on the one hand, and public relations, propaganda and psychological warfare on the other.'"[35]

The administration sought to carry out this strategy through an office in the Pentagon called the Office of Strategic Influence (OSI), created shortly after September 11 to generate support for the war

---

[34] Gordon R. Mitchell, "Legitimation Dilemmas in the Bush National Security Strategy," Paper presented at the Eastern Communication Association Conference, Washington, DC, April 23–26, 2003.

[35] William M. Arkin, "Defense Strategy: The Military's New War of Words," *Los Angeles Times*, November 24, 2002, cited in Gordon R. Mitchell, "Legitimation Dilemmas in the Bush National Security Strategy," Paper presented at the Eastern Communication Association Conference, Washington, DC, April 23–26, 2003.

on terror.[36] The OSI considered a range of options from standard public relations to the covert planting of disinformation in foreign media — an operation known as "black propaganda".[37] Yet when plans for OSI were leaked to the *New York Times*, it reported "even many senior Pentagon officials and congressional military aides say they know almost nothing about its purpose and plans".[38] With the leak of its creation to the press, the controversy generated resulted in Rumsfeld's shutting OSI down within one week[39] — the day after Bush proclaimed zero tolerance for lies by American officials and vowing to "tell the American people the truth".[40]

While OSI might have been publicly closed, it is likely the policy itself continued. As a *Newsday* columnist wrote at the time of the closing, "But don't worry, Rumsfeld's people were whispering yesterday around the Pentagon. They'll keep on spreading whatever stories they think they have to — to foreigners especially. Call it the free flow of misinformation. Who needs a formal office for that?"[41]

---

[36] "New Pentagon Office to Spearhead Information War," *CNN.com*, February 20, 2002, available at: www.cnn.com/2002/US/02/19/gen.strategic.influence/.

[37] Tom Carver, "Pentagon Plans Propaganda War," *BBC World News*, February 20, 2002, available at: news.bbc.co.uk/1/hi/world/americas/1830500.stm. In this article Carver wrote, "Some generals are worried that even a suggestion of disinformation would undermine the Pentagon's credibility and America's attempts to portray herself as the beacon of liberty and democratic values."

[38] James Dao and Eric Schmitt, "Pentagon Readies Efforts to Sway Sentiment Abroad," *New York Times*, February 19, 2002, available at: www. commondreams. org/headlines02/0219-01.htm.

[39] For a full transcript of Rumsfeld's remarks to the press at the announcement of the closing of OSI, see "U.S. Closes Office of Strategic Information: Says effectiveness damaged by media," U.S. Department of State, International Information Programs, February 27, 2002, available at: usinfo.state.gov/regional/ nea/sasia/text/0227rmfd.htm.

[40] Norman Soloman, "Pentagon's Silver Lining May be Bigger Than Cloud," Media Beat, *Fairness & Accuracy In Reporting*, February 28, 2002, available at: www.fair.org/media-beat/020228.html.

[41] Norman Soloman, "Pentagon's Silver Lining May be Bigger Than Cloud," Media Beat, *Fairness & Accuracy In Reporting*, February 28, 2002, reporting on *Newsday* column by Ellis Henican, available at: http://www.fair.org/media-beat/ 020228.html.

On November 18, 2002, en route to a meeting of defense ministers in Chile, Rumsfeld himself told reporters on his plane, "And then there was the Office of Strategic Influence. You may recall that. And 'oh my goodness gracious isn't that terrible, Henny Penny the sky is going to fall.' I went down that next day and said fine, if you want to savage this thing fine I'll give you the corpse. There's the name. You have the name, but I'm gonna keep doing every single thing that needs to be done and I have."[42] Despite the controversy generated when the creation of OSI was revealed, these comments about the continuation of the policy went essentially unreported. As reported by FAIR, "A search of the Nexis database indicates that no major U.S. media outlets — no national broadcast television news shows, no major U.S. newspapers, no wire services or major magazines — have reported Rumsfeld's remarks."[43]

In the period leading up to a possible second UN resolution to endorse the war in early 2003, when it was revealed that the administration's National Security Agency was "conducting a secret 'dirty tricks' campaign against UN Security Council delegations in New York as part of its battle to win votes in favor of war against Iraq", much more concern was generated in the international media than in the U.S. press.[44] The activities included intercepting the home and office phone calls as well as email of country

---

[42] Media Advisory, "The Office of Strategic Influence is Gone, But Are Its Programs in Place?" *Fairness & Accuracy In Reporting*, November 27, 2002. The full transcript of Rumsfeld's remarks are available at the U.S. Department of Defense website at: www.dod.gov/news/Nov2002/t11212002_t1118sd2.html. For discussion of the continued programs, despite closing of OSI, see *NPR's On the Media*, "Global Information War in the Works?" an interview with William Arkin on WNYC on December 13, 2002, available at: www.wnyc.org/onthemedia/transcripts/transcripts_121302_information.html.

[43] Media Advisory, "The Office of Strategic Influence is Gone, But Are Its Programs in Place?" *Fairness & Accuracy In Reporting*, November 27, 2002.

[44] Martin Bright, Ed Vulliamy, and Peter Beaumont, "U.S. National Security Agency Memo Reveals Spying on UN Delegates," *The Observer* (UK), March 3, 2003, available at: reclaimdemocracy.org/weekly_2003/spying_on_un.html.

representatives to the United Nations in order to gather information as to how they might vote on the resolution.[45]

If the Invasion of Iraq Wasn't About WMD and Al-Qaeda, What Was It About?

While the Bush administration, with the support of much of the mainstream American media, had — at least until mid-2003 — been able to control or at least contain the domestic perception of why it went to war against Iraq, much of the rest of the world did not buy into that perception. As the evidence used by the Bush administration regarding Hussein's WMD continues to publicly unravel and no evidence of an immediate threat to international security by such weapons is found, the preemptive rationale for the invasion is even less credible than before the invasion. The widely shared beliefs outside the United States that real reasons for the invasion were to gain control of Iraqi oil and to set in place a firm precedent for a U.S. policy of preemptive self-defense as part of a larger strategy of global political and economic dominance gain even more strength.

Some members of the Bush administration have also long sought a radical transformation of the Middle East, which would have at its core the removal of the Hussein regime and insertion of U.S.-style governance. In this scenario, a "reverse domino theory", set in motion by the toppling of Saddam Hussein, would result in the blossoming of democracy throughout the region. For these policy theorists, preemptive self-defense and regime change in Iraq are not post-September 11 constructs. They are elements of a larger

---

[45] Martin Bright, Ed Vulliamy, and Peter Beaumont, "U.S. National Security Agency Memo Reveals Spying on UN Delegates," *The Observer* (UK), March 3, 2003, available at: reclaimdemocracy.org/weekly_2003/spying_on_un.html.

post-Cold War strategy for the U.S. developed over more than a decade.[46]

Deputy Defense Secretary Paul Wolfowitz, one of the primary intellectual architects of a radically transformed post-Cold war strategic policy for the U.S., first floated the vision during the first Bush administration.[47] In 1992, Wolfowitz, then serving as under secretary of defense for policy, was charged by then Defense Secretary Dick Cheney to draft a "Defense Planning Guidance" (DPG), which would outline policy in a second term for then-President Bush. Wolfowitz's draft argues for a new military and political strategy in a post-Cold War world in which containment has no place. The draft calls for a muscular American foreign policy in which the country should "should be postured to act independently when collective action cannot be orchestrated".[48]

The primary objective of this U.S. policy, according to that DPG, should be to prevent the emergence of a rival superpower. To achieve this objective, "First the U.S. must show the leadership necessary to establish and protect a new order that holds the promise of convincing potential competitors that they need not aspire to a greater role or pursue a more aggressive posture to protect their legitimate interests. Second, in the non-defense areas, we must account sufficiently for the interests of the advanced

---

[46] Todd S. Purdum, "The Brains Behind Bush's War," *New York Times*, February 1, 2003; Thomas Donnelly *et al.*, "Rebuilding America's Defenses: Strategy, Forces and Resources for a New Century," Project for the New American Century Report, September 2000, available at: www.new americancentury.org/ RebuildingAmericasDefenses.pdf.

[47] For an interesting discussion of the development of the policy, see Nicholas Lemann, "The New World Order: The Bush Administration may have a brand-new doctrine of power," *The New Yorker*, April 1, 2002. The article talks about Cheney's tasking both Wolfowitz and Powell to come up with strategies for American foreign policy after the Cold War, but Cheney being more taken with Wolfowitz' bolder and broader thinking on the subject than with Powell's more moderate vision.

[48] Todd S. Purdum, "The Brains Behind Bush's War," *New York Times*, February 1, 2003; "Chronology: The Evolution of the Bush Doctrine," *Frontline: The War Behind Closed Doors*, available at: www.pbs.org/wgbh/pages/frontline/shows/ iraq/etc/cron.html.

industrial nations to discourage them from challenging our leadership or seeking to overturn the established political and economic
order. Finally, we must maintain the mechanisms for deterring
potential competitors from even aspiring to a larger regional or
global role".[49]

The draft also outlined several scenarios in which U.S. interests
could be threatened by regional conflict, including blocked access
to vital raw materials, primarily Persian Gulf oil, and the proliferation
of weapons of mass destruction and ballistic missiles. Of seven
regional scenarios laid out to make the case, the two primary
examples were Iraq and North Korea. When the 46-page classified
draft was leaked to the press, the controversy generated resulted in
orders for Defense Secretary Cheney to rewrite the draft and in the
new version there is no mention of preemption or U.S. willingness
to act alone.[50]

But in the post-September 11 world of the new Bush administration, preemptive self-defense as a basis for U.S. national security
re-emerged. On September 17, 2002, Bush issued his administration's vision of national security in its document "The National
Security Strategy of the United States".[51] On September 22, 2002,
in an address at West Point, Bush stated that in the post-Cold
War world containment does not work and his national security
policies would be predicated on preemption. Recognizing American
hegemony, he stated "America has, and intends to keep, military

---

[49] "Chronology: The Evolution of the Bush Doctrine," *Frontline: The War Behind
Closed Doors*, available at: www.pbs.org/wgbh/pages/frontline/shows/iraq/etc/
cron.html.

[50] "Chronology: The Evolution of the Bush Doctrine," *Frontline: The War Behind
Closed Doors*, available at: www.pbs.org/wgbh/pages/frontline/shows/iraq/etc/
cron.html; "Excerpts From Pentagon's Plan: 'Prevent the Re-Emergence of a New
Rival,'" *New York Times*, March 8, 1992; Patrick E. Tyler, "U.S. Strategy Plan Calls
for Insuring No Rivals Develop," *New York Times*, March 8, 1992.

[51] "The National Security Strategy of the United States," September 2002, available
at: www.whitehouse.gov/nsc.

strengths beyond challenge."[52] Both strategic aims — preemption and hegemony — echo the pivotal objectives of U.S. military strategy Wolfowitz had outlined in 1992. However, this time public response to the policy was muted at best in an American psyche traumatized by September 11.

When Bush pressed for war with Iraq to remove the imminent threat of WMD, he also talked about the need for regime change — that the Iraqi people deserved to live without the fear of the dictator. It is highly unlikely that the American public or U.S. Congress would have supported regime change for its sake alone — thus the "evidence" of WMD and links to Al-Qaeda — to make war more palatable. But regime change is one component of the administration's larger political strategy of a "reverse domino theory" for the Middle East, and in their view, reason enough to go to war.

When Bush addressed the UN in September 2002 to press for what became Resolution 1441, he hinted at this vision. He said, "The people of Iraq can shake off their captivity. They can one day join a democratic Afghanistan and a democratic Palestine, inspiring reforms throughout the Muslim world."[53] A reporter for the *Los Angeles Times* commenting on the UN speech noted that while the headlines focused on the call to disarm Iraq, Bush was actually endorsing the conservative vision of the reverse domino theory. The article said, "This theory has become a central — perhaps *the* central — justification for war in conservative circles, especially among the neoconservative foreign policy intellectuals."[54] Under this scenario,

---

[52] "Complete Text of Bush's West Point Address," *NewsMax Wires and NewsMax*, June 3, 2002, available at: www.newsmax.com/archives/articles/2002/6/2/81354.shtml.

[53] Stephan Richter, "Reverse Domino Theory," *The Globalist*, February 20, 2003, available at: www.theglobalist.com/DBWeb/StoryId.aspx?StoryId=2957. For full text of Bush's remarks at the United Nations, see "Remarks by the President in Address to the United Nations General Assembly New York, New York," The White House, Office of the Press Secretary, September 12, 2002, available at: www.whitehouse.gov/news/releases/2002/09/20020912-1.html.

[54] Ronald Brownstein, "Still a Few Dots to Connect in Iraq Domino Theory," *LATimes.com*, September 23, 2002, available at: www.latimes.com/la-na-outlook23sep23(0,2724543).story.

regime change in Iraq would have multiple benefits: it would reduce reliance on Saudi oil; would allow the U.S. to withdraw its forces from Saudi Arabia, which has been a source of significant agitation in the Arab world; and would send a sobering message to hostile regimes in the region.[55]

Another common perception around the world is that the invasion had much more to do with control of Iraq's oil than its possible WMD. While not much of the U.S. public is aware of it, an April 2001 blue-ribbon study by the Council for Foreign Relations and the James A. Baker III Institute for Public Policy at Rice University, entitled "Strategic Energy Policy Challenges for the 21st Century", was covered by both the British and Australian press in October 2002 and has been called a hidden blueprint for the Bush administration's policy toward Iraq.[56] The report, commissioned by former Secretary of State James Baker and submitted to Vice President Dick Cheney, warns of potentially serious energy shortages within five years unless corrective action is taken. With chilling disregard for international law, it suggests that the United States consider military intervention in Iraq to maintain the stability of Persian Gulf oil supplies.

Coincidentally, perhaps, around that same period the controversial and highly secretive energy task force convened by Vice President Cheney to help develop the Bush administration's energy policy was also investigating Iraq's oil industry. Task-force related U.S. Commerce Department papers, dated March 2001, included a document entitled, "Foreign Suitors of Iraqi Oilfield Contracts", which listed foreign companies that were pursuing business with the

---

[55] Ronald Brownstein, "Still a Few Dots to Connect in Iraq Domino Theory," *LATimes.com*, September 23, 2002, available at: www.latimes.com/la-na-outlook23sep23(0,2724543).story. For discussion of the removal of U.S. troops from Saudi Arabia, see Sam Tanenhaus interview with Paul Wolfowitz, *Vanity Fair*, July 2003; see also: "Wolfowitz says Saudi troop withdrawal was 'huge' reason for war with Iraq," *AP*, in *The Atlanta Journal-Constitution*, May 30, 2003, available at: www.ajc.com/news/content/news/0503/30wolfowitz.html.

[56] "Strategic Energy Policy Challenges for the 21st Century," available at: www.rice.edu/projects/baker/Pubs/work.

regime. In its report, released in May 2001, the task force recognized the Middle East as being "central to world oil security".[57]

An international perception that much of the reason for war had to do with control of the oil was further bolstered by the fact that Halliburton, the oil company once headed by Vice-President Cheney, was handed a lucrative contract in Iraq just after the war was launched. The contract was given directly to the company without any public competitive bidding.[58] In April, the U.S. Army stated that Halliburton had already been paid over $50 million of a contract that could be worth up to $7 billion over a two-year period.[59] Reportedly, classified Halliburton documents indicated that the plans for the contact began to be developed at least as early as October 2002.[60] Bechtel, another company with close connection to the Bush administration, was also awarded a contract in April worth up to $680 million for rebuilding "vital elements" of Iraq's infrastructure. According to some estimates, the cost of rebuilding Iraq could reach $200 billion.[61]

---

[57] H. Josef Hebert, "Cheney Task Force Eyed on Iraq Oil," *Associated Press*, July 2003.

[58] "Halliburton Handed No-Bid Iraq Oil-Fighting Contract," *Agence France-Presse*, March 25, 2003, available at *Common Dreams News Center:* www.commondreams.org/headlines03/0325-11.htm.

[59] "Halliburton's Iraq role expands: Halliburton's role in post-war Iraq includes operating Iraqi oil fields, new documents reveal," *BBC News*, May 7, 2003, available at: news.bbc.co.uk/1/hi/business/3006149.stm.

[60] "Halliburton signed pre-war deal to operate Iraq's oil industry," *Alexander's Gas and Oil Connections, Company News: Middle East*, Volume 8, Issue 12, June 13, 2003, available at: www.gasandoil.com/goc/company/cnm32400.htm.

[61] Mark Gongloff, "Bechtel wins Iraq Contract: Private contractor wins State Dept. contract, worth up to $680 million, to rebuild Iraq's infrastructure," *CNNMoney*, April 17, 2003, available at: money.cnn.com/2003/04/17/news/companies/bechtel/. In discussing the close ties to the Bush administration, the writer notes that former Secretary of State George Schultz is on the board of Bechtel and that its CEO, Riley P. Bechtel, was recently named to Bush's Export Council, an advisory committee on international trade. Another commentator noted that Schultz also chaired the advisory board of "The Committee for the Liberation of Iraq," which, according to its website (http://www.liberationiraq.org/) ceased

Skepticism was also fueled by the fact that one of the few Iraqi ministries that the U.S. invasion forces managed to guard and protect was the Oil Ministry — at the same time that U.S. troops seemed unable or unwilling to secure the Iraqi facility housing its uranium supplies.[62] The U.S. Central Command acknowledged that the Tuwaitha Nuclear Research Center, which was the headquarters of Saddam's former nuclear program and a storage site for uranium, was looted.[63]

On May 22, 2003, the UN adopted Security Council Resolution 1483 which lifted sanctions against Iraq, provided for the termination of the Oil-for-Food Program within six months and transferred responsibility for the administration of any remaining activity to the occupying authority.[64] Not only did the resolution grant legal immunity through 2007 to the revenue generated by newly authorized oil exports, a development that will effectively protect Iraq's petrodollars from creditors, but it also gave authority to the U.S.-led coalition forces over the formation of Iraq's new government and the disposition of oil revenue.[65]

---

operations "Following the successful Liberation of Iraq….." Some of the other members of the Committee's advisory board include Newt Gingrich, James Woolsey, Richard Perle, William Kristol.

[62] "Thanks for ousting Hussein, 'Now please go home,'" *Washington Post*, April 22, 2003; "Conflict in Iraq: Concerns and Consequences," Bulletin #14, available at: www.basicint.org/iraqconflict/index.htm.

[63] Jalal Ghazi, "A Radioactive Mess," *Pacific News Service*, May 6, 2003.

[64] United Nations, "Implementation of Oil-for-Food: A Chronology," Office of the Iraq Programme, Oil-for-Food, August 4, 2003, available at: www.un.org/Depts/oip/background/chron.html.

[65] Suzanne Goldenberg, "UN mandate oils wheels for reconstruction of Iraq," *The Guardian*, May 23, 2003, available at: www.guardian.co.uk/Print/0,3858,4675308,00.html. For an interesting discussion of issues related to oil and the occupying authority, see "Iraqi Oil, Today and Tomorrow," a report by Robert E. Ebel, Director, Energy Program, Center for Strategic and International Studies, submitted to the Subcommittee on Energy and Air Quality, Committee on Energy and Commerce, U.S. House of Representatives, Washington, DC, May 14, 2003, available at: www.csis.org/hill/ts030514ebel.pdf.

The resolution also called for a Development Fund for Iraq to be set up under Iraq's central bank, with an international advisory board — including representatives of the UN, the International Monetary Fund, the World Bank and the Arab Fund for Social and Economic Development — which will appoint independent auditors for the fund. Money in the fund is to be "disbursed at the direction of The Authority in consultation with the Iraqi interim authority" and used to meet humanitarian needs, economic reconstruction and the repair of Iraq's infrastructure, the continued disarmament of Iraq, the costs of indigenous civilian administration and for "other purposes benefiting the people of Iraq".[66] A U.S. State Department release about the fund stated, "The president said the Department of the Treasury in consultation with the departments of State and Defense will be responsible for the fund."[67]

The same day as the UN vote, Bush issued an executive order that declared "null and void" any claims against either the Development Fund for Iraq or revenues from the sale of Iraq's oil and natural gas. The executive order found that "the threat of attachment or other judicial process" against these economic resources "obstructs the orderly reconstruction of Iraq, the restoration and maintenance of peace and security in the country, and the development of political, administrative, and economic institutions in Iraq. This situation constitutes an unusual and extraordinary threat to the national security and foreign policy of the United States and I hereby declare a national emergency to deal with that threat".[68] The Hussein regime had foreign debts totaling about

---

[66] United Nations, Security Council Resolution 1483, S/1483/2003, May 22, 2003.

[67] U.S. Department of State, "U.S. to Create Development Fund at Iraq Central Bank," International Information Programs, Washington File, May 23, 2003, available at: usinfo.state.gov/regional/nea/iraq/text2003/0523bank.htm.

[68] The White House, "Executive Order Protecting the Development Fund for Iraq and Other Certain Property in Which Iraq as An Interest," Office of the Press Secretary, May 22, 2003, available at: www.whitehouse.gov/news/releases/2003/05/20030522-15.html.

$383 billion, according to analysis by the Center for Strategic and International Studies and the U.S. Government Accounting Office.

With some concern that U.S. reconstruction funds might run out by the end of the year, some U.S. contractors rebuilding Iraq are reportedly pushing a funding proposal that could indebt the country even more. Halliburton and Bechtel, the government's two main contractors in the reconstruction of the country, and other firms are lobbying to have the U.S. Export-Import bank to finance projects now in Iraq in exchange for a share of future Iraqi oil revenues. That would make the bank, a U.S. government agency, another in the long line of creditors any future government would have to face. While there are some questions about the legality of the U.S. government accepting loans on behalf of an Iraqi government that does not yet exist, some argue that such loan monies could be placed in a fund controlled partially by Iraqis appointed by the U.S.[69]

The day before the Security Council vote on Resolution 1483, in a news conference at the United Nations, George Soros announced that his Open Society Institute would be setting up a watchdog group to guard against abuses in how the U.S. manages Iraqi oil resources while it occupies the country. Noting concerns around the world at how the U.S. would manage the oil reserves because a small number of U.S. corporations had already received huge reconstruction contracts without competitive bidding, Soros said, "It is very much in the interest of the United States to allay these fears, and we want to help."[70] Soros had also called upon Security Council members to amend the draft resolution before its passage to strengthen safeguards against abuse.

---

[69] Shane Harris, "The future of Iraq: A mixture of debt and oil," *GovExec.com*, July 9, 2003, available at: www.governmentexecutive.com/dailyfed/0703/070903h1.htm.

[70] Irwin Arieff, "Soros Watchdog to Monitor U.S. Use of Iraqi Oil," *Reuters*, May 21, 2003, available at: www.commondreams.org/headlines03/0521-04.htm.

Conclusion: Rewriting History and the Impact on U.S. Credibility Around the World

As the Bush administration has increasingly struggled to contain the unraveling of the evidence used to justify its unilateral invasion of Iraq, Bush and other members of his administration have charged that critics of the Iraq policy and those seeking full disclosure of the process leading to the invasion are attempting to "re-write history". The administration continues to cling to its increasingly discredited arguments for war and attempts to dismiss the calls for investigation of the steps leading to war as mere "historical review" no longer worthy of comment in the face of the enormous task of the here and now: stabilizing and rebuilding Iraq.

On July 14, 2003, Bush himself made this most startling revisionist statement about the lead-up to the invasion. In remarks from the Oval Office of the White House after a meeting with UN Secretary General Kofi Annan, he said, "The large point is, and the fundamental question is, did Saddam Hussein have a weapons program? And the answer is, absolutely. And we gave him a chance to allow the inspectors in, and he wouldn't let them in. And therefore, after a reasonable request, we decided to remove him from power..."[71] It was, in fact, the Bush administration that pushed the passage of UN Security Council Resolution 1441 demanding that the regime allow the resumption of weapons inspections — and weapons inspections resumed and were making progress. It was the Bush administration that opposed extending the timeframe of those inspections and, without UN support, invaded Iraq.[72]

---

[71] U.S. Department of State, "Remarks with UN Secretary General Kofi Annan," President George W. Bush, Remarks in Photo Opportunity, The Oval Office, The White House, Washington, DC, July 14, 2003, available at: www.state.gov/p/io/rls/rm/2003/22389.htm.

[72] Dana Priest and Dana Milbank, "President Defends Allegation on Iraq: Bush Says CIA's Doubts Followed Jan. 28 Address," *Washington Post*, July 15, 2003.

In the weeks, and now months, after Bush declared the end of the major combat operations in Iraq, and as the search for WMD has continued to turn up nothing, the administration has struggled to deal with the issue. The challenge for them has been heightened with the continued revelations outlined above about the misinformation and manipulated "evidence" used to try to convince the U.S. public, its Congress, and the international community of the need for war.

The senior architects of the Iraq policy have been re-writing the history of their certainty that Saddam was on the brink of reconstituting his WMD program. On May 5, Rumsfeld said that there were teams investigating suspected sites and "of course the reality is that, if we have knowledge of a site — and a suspect site is probably the way we should phrase it — it's very likely things are not there."[73] By the end of May, he stated, "It is also possible that they decided that they would destroy them prior to a conflict."[74] Then, on June 6, speaking to members of the U.S. House of Representatives, Rumsfeld said he was sure WMD would be found, but U.S. teams needed more time — the same time the Bush administration denied the UN weapons inspections, renewed under UN Resolution 1441 and unilaterally cutoff by the administration after its failed attempt for a second war resolution and the subsequent invasion of Iraq.[75]

After a July visit to Iraq, Deputy Defense Secretary Wolfowitz even stated that finding WMD was not a primary concern. Speaking to reporters on his trip back to the U.S., Wolfowitz said, "If you

---

[73] "Rumsfeld: WMD Unlikely to be Found at Suspected Sites," *CNN.com*, May 5, 2003, available at: http://www.cnn.com/2003/WORLD/meast/05/04/sprj.irq.main/.

[74] "Rumsfeld: Saddam may have destroyed WMD before attack," *Pravda*, May 29, 2003, available at: http://english.pravda.ru/mailbox/22/98/387/10133_rumsfelllllld.html.

[75] "Rumsfeld Sure WMD Intelligence Will Prove Correct," United States Marine Corps, Headquarters, Washington, DC, Press Release # 0609-03-0608, June 6, 2003, available at: http://www.usmc.mil/marinelink/mcn2000.nsf/template releaseview1/3F88CA91ADD833D485256D400037ADD9?opendocument.

could get in a relaxed conversation with Iraqis on that subject they'd say why on earth are you Americans fussing so much about this historical issue when we have real problems here, when Baathists are killing us and Baathists are threatening us and we don't have electricity and we don't have jobs. Those are the real issues."[76]

While occupied Iraq is facing real issues of insecurity, guerrilla war and an uncertain future, few in the international community will accept the premise that addressing the misinformation and manipulations used by the Bush administration to justify its invasion of Iraq is "fussing about" a "historical issue". As evidenced by the inability of the U.S. government to gain support for a second UN resolution backing its desire for war, there was not widespread acceptance of the evidence put forth by the U.S. for the urgent need for war. The Bush administration, prior to its invasion of Iraq, was already seen as dramatically isolationist, bent on undermining international treaties and multilateral forums for addressing issues of global impact.

The Bush administration used the newfound vulnerability of the American public after the terrorist attacks of September 11 to advance a post-Cold War political and military agenda long under development by members of the administration. As a senior administration official reportedly observed, inside the government, the terrorist attacks were "a transformative moment" not because they revealed a threat previously unknown to the government, but because of the drastically reduced resistance of the American public to military action abroad. With the attacks on the U.S., "the options are much broader".[77]

While the Bush administration's post-September 11 national security strategy based on preemption did not stir much debate inside the U.S., it did abroad. Many argued that it would create precedents that would make the world much less secure rather

[76] "Wolfowitz Not Worried About WMDs," *CBSNEWS.com*, July 22, 2003, available at: www.cbsnews.com/stories/2003/06/25/iraq/.

[77] Nicholas Lemann, "The Next World Order: The Bush Administration may have a brand-new doctrine of power," *The New Yorker*, April 1, 2002.

than more. To now find that the evidence used to justify its first preemptive action — the invasion of Iraq — was based not just on uncertain intelligence, but on "forward leaning" interpretation of intelligence as well as outright lies to justify policies already in motion puts U.S. credibility further at risk. The strategies and tactics used by the Bush administration to achieve its ends left, in the words of one commentator, "diplomacy in ruins". The impact of its increasingly tattered credibility on both U.S. and global security remains to be seen.

José Ramos-Horta
NOBEL PEACE LAUREATE 1996

Currently the Minister for Foreign Affairs and Cooperation, Timor-Leste, the Hon. Ramos-Horta co-won the Nobel Peace Prize with Bishop Carlos Filipe Ximenes Belo, the former apostolic administrator of the Dili Diocese, Timor-Leste.

The Post-Cold War and the Unipolar World: Can the U.S. Lead?

The post-World War II world witnessed some major conflicts that have cost the lives of tens of millions of peoples and displaced tens of millions more. And we thought we had been shocked into a permanent state of mind, emotionally, intellectually and morally in opposing wars, any war.

The Iraqi invasion of Iran in the 1980s resulted in the death of over a million people. Chemical and biological weapons were unleashed on civilians and combatants. The West turned a blind eye when Kurdish and Iranians were gassed to death by the thousands by the butcher of Baghdad. After all, the choice was a simple one between two evils. One greater evil was the Ayatollahs who had established a Middle Ages theocracy in Iran, bent on exporting their own stupidity around the world and respected no boundaries and other beliefs.

The other evil was Saddam Hussein and his Sunni minority loyalists in Iraq who had consolidated power over a tribal country, slaughtering into submission the Shia majority and Kurdish minorities, and thus presented Iraq as a model of a secular Arab regime friendly to the West and former Soviet Union. He was courted by all — the U.S., UK, France, Russia and other smaller players, each trying to outdo the other in securing weapons exports and oil contracts. The Soviets came on top in weapons sales, followed by the French. The British and the Americans were side-lined into embarrassing third and fourth places respectively. The dictator's ego was catapulted to illusions of grandeur and conquest.

As the Middle Ages Ayatollahs mismanaged their revolution with Stalinist-style purges that deprived the country of many of its professional military officers, Saddam Hussein moved in. The two sides fought relentlessly in a savage and fanatic manner, the Grand Ayatollah Khomeini launching human waves of his youth into World War I style frontal assault against a bigger and better equipped army. And just like in some of the most barbaric scenes of World War I trench warfare, chemical and biological weapons were unleashed, gassing to death tens of thousands of Iranian soldiers and civilians.

The Northern Iraq Kurdish town of Hallajbah was gassed into an agonising death for its women and children. An estimated five thousand died. Where were the peace marchers? After all, if anyone deserves a few hours of our slogans and a few miles of power walk, they are the most underdog of all, the wretched of the Earth — the Kurdish. They number some 30 million and are unwanted in Turkey, Iraq, Iran, Syria — the four nations making common cause when it comes to suppressing their own Kurdish. The Kurdish, in their spare time, slaughter each other.

The Iran-Iraq War lasted eight years ending in 1988. Back then we did not have the benefit of minute-by-minute TV coverage by embedded journalists, but there was enough graphic media coverage that would galvanize peace-mongers into action.

But there were no peace marchers. I remember wondering where were the thousands who took to the streets in the West in protest against the Vietnam War and later against the deployment of cruise missiles in Europe? They seemed to have evaporated, or if they were still lurking around, their self-righteous souls were not perturbed by the images of dark-skinned medievals killing each other. This was perhaps because the favourite target of the peace marchers was, for once, not involved in the war. The U.S. and Europe watched the Iraq-Iran War in tranquility and with glee.

Some aided the lesser evil with weapons. Arabs and Muslims were not able to help end the war.

Soon after the end of the Iraq-Iran War, the same regime in Baghdad unleashed yet another invasion, this time against the State of Kuwait, its small, rich Arab neighbour. An impressive coalition of countries, led by the U.S., intervened and Kuwait was freed but not without wanton destruction by the retreating forces that set on fire hundreds of oil wells. This was the first time ever that a regime launched an environmental war. Some Arab countries joined in the coalition for the liberation of Kuwait. Egypt and Syria and Saudi Arabia were with the coalition. Yemen stayed out and its sympathies were with Iraq. The Palestinians made the costly mistake of siding with Iraq.

A great Arab statesman, the late King Hussein of Jordan, also decided to oppose the coalition intervention to liberate Kuwait. King Hussein was an extraordinary leader, a survivor, a man of courage who made peace with Israel even though his kingdom could be said to be essentially a Palestinian entity, as some 60 percent of his citizens are Palestinians. Jordan is even more unfortunate as it shares borders with some of the most implacable Israelite foes — Syria and Iraq.

Saddam Hussein dragged his nation into two tragic and sense-less wars, ruining his once prosperous country and condemning his people to a life of fear and servitude. Other leaders lose their job or even their head when they lose a war. Former Argentinean dictator General Galtieri was deposed after he led the botched invasion of Malvinas in 1982. Richard Nixon was forced out of office for cheating. Joseph Estrada of the Philippines is languishing in jail for being too much of a crook. Imelda Marcos was disgraced for allegedly collecting too many thousand pairs of shoes while many of her female compatriots walk barefoot and can hardly afford a meal a day.

But Saddam Hussein was to be different. He invaded his Muslim neighbours, slaughtered millions of his own people — Kurdish, Iranians and Kuwaitis — blew up oil fields, unleashed chemical and biological weapons, sponsored with cash Palestinian extremists and suicide bombers, and yet seemed unmovable and untouchable. Well, now he is gone somewhere.

In the 1990s the European continent that believed it had shaken off the demons of war of a recent past woke up to the tragic ethnic wars in the Balkan region. The last chapter of the Balkan wars was the war in Kosovo in 1998. We witnessed close-up U.S. air supremacy as it bombed the defiant Serbia into submission and how it saved a small Muslim community that was being driven off their homes by Serbian ultra-nationalists. I supported this NATO intervention. But, I ask, every time we want to save someone do we also have to bomb some other people? Serbia was carpet-bombed, destroyed, and proud Serbians who fought bravely on the side of the Allies during World War II are still licking the wounds of their collective humiliation and are still paying for their sins and crimes.

Following the September 11 terrorist attacks in New York and Washington, we woke up to the Taliban rule in Afghanistan that took us back to the savagery of the Middle Ages. Our memory has to be fresh still to the 1994 genocide in Rwanda, and the countless wars being waged in Africa, parts of Asia and Latin America.

With only few notable exceptions, for the most part the international community failed to preempt the occurrence of violence and to intervene when violence began. More often than not the UN was paralysed and hostage to the narrow interests of some of its members. We had illusions that the (mis-)use of the veto was a fact of the Cold War and it would be less and less exercised in the new world order. However, with notable exceptions, national interests endured beyond the Cold War, and the Security Council has remained hostage to them.

I will put forward a question — was the bipolar world that prevailed during much of the 50 years after the end of World War II up to the implosion of the USSR a safer and more just world? During much of the life of the bipolar world, we witnessed numerous intra-state and inter-state conflicts, involving directly or indirectly the two rival superpowers that dominated the bipolar power system.

The U.S. and the USSR fought or sponsored wars in Latin America, Africa and Asia in their attempt to exercise influence and control over strategic areas of the world such as Central America, the Horn of Africa, Southern Africa and Southeast Asia, most of which with no real value as providers of raw materials. Somalia was both a tragedy created by the stupidity and miscalculation of its dictator Siad Barre and by the Cold War rivalry between the U.S. and USSR. The U.S. fought a senseless ugly war in Indochina, and the USSR had its own Vietnam in Afghanistan.

The nuclear threat was much more real then than today although we are very far from getting rid of these abominable weapons. The sudden collapse of the USSR and the end of the Cold War ushered in a new era, a more promising New World Order free from the nuclear threat and proxy wars sponsored by the two superpowers. Human Rights and the struggles for democracy that were hostage and fell victim to the Cold War gained new life and momentum. Soon after the end of the Cold War we saw the beginning of the end in rapid sequence of the class of military regimes in Latin America, Africa and Asia. Much to the consternation of the enemies and critics of the U.S., the American Empire emerged triumphant, as there was no doubt that the collapse of the totalitarian communist system and beliefs was a vindication of Western liberal thought and values. Marxism was thoroughly discredited.

Much has been written and said, always in the language of frustration and regret, that the world we are living in today is a unipolar one based on the unchallenged American economic and military power. But I dare to say, "Is it so bad?" The alternative, the past bipolarity — built on two rival ideological systems and military adversaries — gave us a fragmented world with many wars that resulted in tens of millions of the dead and the ever present nuclear nightmare.

The counter-force to the U.S. was the USSR with its Stalinist brutality and expansionist doctrine; it was not a rival benign superpower democracy. Can we forget the incredible scenes of jubilation when the Berlin Wall came down in 1990 following

Soviet capitulation? There were celebrations by tens of millions when the rotten Soviets' totalitarian system imploded.

The U.S. was the winner but so was Europe and so was all humanity. However, while Europe remained divided along their own individual national interests without a real political unity and a strong economy and defence, the U.S. harvested the fruits of the collapse of the Soviet Empire. But Europe should not have to be a rival or a balance, but rather the transatlantic alliance plus Canada and Japan should forge a strategic partnership in the fight for world peace and prosperity. Differences and occasional conflicts will continue to occur but this trilateral partnership of open societies with solid democratic foundations will be able to resolve them.

There is no equal or rival to the U.S. today and, whether we like it or not, the U.S. is the world's unchallenged sole superpower and will remain so for many more years, perhaps as many as 30 years or more until the emergence of or two new superpowers, China and India. However, there are too many question marks about the future stability of the two Asian giants. Will China continue its impressive economic growth of the past 10 years? Will it remain politically stable and united? Or will it implode and fragment? The same questions can be asked of the future of India. So it seems that we are all going to live under the shadow of the Star and Stripes for many generations to come.

Those who regret the current unipolar world seem to blame the U.S. for its status. The facts are that the U.S. is the sole surviving superpower because of its highly educated people, its ingenuity, creativity, the ability of its industries and commerce to a continuing process of reform and adaptation, its diversity, intellectual and political dynamism, and its investment in research sciences and technology. Its universities produce far more Nobel Laureates in sciences, medicine and economics than Europe, Japan and Russia combined. It is a superpower partly by default, by the failures of others, and by design, because it wants and plans to be a superpower.

Many resent the Americans and accuse them of arrogance and insensitivity. But hundreds of thousands of Americans gave their lives for others. They fought with unique bravery in Europe, North Africa, and the Pacific and in the malaria infested jungles of Asia and saved the world from Hitlerian domination.

One wonders, if the U.S. had not entered World War II, and had not stayed on in Europe after the war, what languages the Europeans would be speaking today, and what language Asians would be forced to learn and use. There would be no European Union and no peaceful and democratic Japan.

For 50 years, the U.S. provided the only credible deterrence in Europe against Soviet expansion, and it continues to be the only credible security balance and has thus averted catastrophic wars in the Indian subcontinent, Middle East, Korean Peninsula, China Straits, etc. It checked Soviet attempts at encroaching on the vast African continent. The Soviets did succeed in gaining some strong footholds in the Horn of Africa and Southern Africa, but by and large the Continent was largely a U.S. preserve. In the face of the frequent street protests and criticisms from certain Asian circles about U.S. military presence in the region, I would advise my fellow Asians to pause and think about the consequences of a U.S. disengagement from Asia.

An American retreat from Asia would precipitate an uncontrollable arms race between or among rival neighbours that would almost inevitably result in warfare including nuclear war and set back the impressive economic and human development of the past 20 years. This does not suggest that Asians would not be capable of resolving their differences through patient diplomacy. However, the facts are that U.S. power has avoided warfare between India and Pakistan, a second invasion of South Korea by the North and a serious clash in the South China Sea involving China and Taiwan.

The American Revolution, its Constitution and liberal ideas, its dynamic culture and arts have had a profound influence on the rest of the world for most of the past century. From some good quality to many trashy Hollywood materials, from the famed jeans to the obviously unhealthy Coca Cola and Pepsi, KFC and MacDonalds, from Elvis Presley and Liz Taylor to Madonna and Jennifer Lopez, the rest of us buy, read and consume "made in USA". We all know about the Kennedy dynasty and its aura and drama, and the Kennedys continue to have a pop star status around the world. We watch countless American TV series and were glued to the TV over Bill and Monica's indiscretions. We do not pay much attention to other juicy stories originating from elsewhere in the world.

Third World dissidents from the left and right have found a safe haven in the U.S. campuses, from where they lecture on the evils of American imperialism. Other dissidents went to Moscow to live out their dreams of a utopian socialist classless society and were confronted instead with the ugly and tragic reality of the communist system.

While the much talked about melting pot is still very much a partial truth, the U.S. has progressed in racial relations. It absorbs like no other country an extraordinary diversity of peoples from all over the world, offers them opportunities that exist nowhere else, and at the same time benefiting from this vast diversity of cultures and talents. Afro-Americans, Asian-Americans, Jews and Latinos can be seen everywhere exercising political and intellectual influence, holding leadership positions in every sphere. This is the secret of U.S. endurance and supremacy. It imposes itself on the rest of the world through its cultural and intellectual vitality, mastery of sciences and technology, ethnic and cultural diversity, and its intelligence in absorbing the best brains and talents the rest of the world can offer. While Europe, Japan and Russia remain provincial and frozen in their prejudices about foreigners, particularly those of darker skin, the U.S. head-hunts for brains of all colours and persuasion, offering scientists from countries as diverse as India, China, Africa, Russia and Poland a chance to fulfill their life-long dream to excel in their profession and earn fabulous rewards.

This does not in anyway suggest that the U.S. is a benign power, a sort of a giant Mother Theresa. Its history is one of conquest and suppression, of greed and violence verging on barbarism. The Americas are a testimony of U.S. imperial arrogance. Vietnam and Cambodia were carpet-bombed back to the Stone Age. It cultivated and propped up despotic regimes all over the world. It still does. But we commit an error when we make sweeping judgments about this great country. It has many virtues, some ugly and sinister motives, depending upon who is in Washington, who gets elected to the White House, who gets elected to the mighty Congress, etc. It was John Kennedy who captured the imagination of his people and of millions around the world with his vision and promise.

Being the wealthiest nation in the world, a nation of immigrants and refugees, a country that possesses the most advanced science and technology, it should lead and lead means setting examples of behaviour and compassion, with greatness of heart and humility. True leaders do not impose, threaten or bully others into submission. True leadership lies in one's ability to develop consensus, work out compromises, and then forge a common and effective strategy.

The U.S. can be a force for change and good; it can be a benign power, upon which rests the world's security and well-being. It can turn the world into a much safer, better living common home for all of us, as long as it has the humility of the truly great and walks half-way to meet its fellow human beings, to acknowledge its own limits and errors, and to share with the rest of us a more compassionate vision and agenda.

The U.S. can use its enormous power in leading the fight against poverty, the debt trap that stunts progress in many parts of the world, and against malaria, HIV, and other preventable diseases that afflict tens of millions of the poorest in the world. This is after all the only surviving superpower, whose wealth and security depend upon the state of the rest of the world. The gigantic and hungry U.S. economy feeds on the wealth of others but at the same time, the economies of much of the world are dependent on the U.S. market for their growth and for the well-being of their people. We are in a mutually interdependent world, locked in an economic embrace, feeding on each other, destined to find ways of how we can all survive and prosper.

The rest of the world was in shock and mourned in the aftermath of September 11. But some did not fully grasp the American determination to fight back an enemy that dared to attack them on their very own soil. The first country to experience American anger was the stone-age rulers of Afghanistan who had been foolish and irresponsible enough to allow their country to be a training ground for extremist foreign mercenaries from the Arab world and Pakistan. The next terrorist domino to fall was Iraq. I will not need to dwell on the details of the nature of that despotic regime.

Were there other options other than military intervention in Afghanistan and Iraq? In the case of Afghanistan, I did not believe then and do not believe now that diplomacy had any chance of success. The nature of the regime was known to all. It harboured the Al-Qaeda terrorists, offered them sanctuary, training ground and freedom of movement to stage their terrorist attacks around the world. By choice and because of its own belief, the Taliban regime fell hostage to the Al-Qaeda network and was no longer capable on its own to clear the terrorists from its soil, even if it wanted.

Were there diplomatic options that would have averted a war in Iraq? I believed so then. In an article published in the *New York Times*[1] and one following article published in the *Chicago Tribune*,[2] I appealed to the U.S. to show patience and give more time to the weapons inspectors, while at the same time to allow the UN Secretary-General to try to persuade Saddam Hussein to leave office. I believed then that given time and as long as the Europeans stopped undermining the U.S. threat of use of force, Saddam Hussein could have accepted exile in Syria. For me there was no doubt that the real and only culprit in the Iraq crisis was Saddam Hussein and no one else. He was a master of brinkmanship, of deceit and a gambler. He believed he could pull it off once again, that President George W. Bush would back off. Saddam Hussein was banking on the growing peace movement and the divisions within NATO and Europe.

---

[1] See my op-ed "War for Peace: It worked in My Country" in the *New York Times*, February 25, 2003.

[2] See my op-ed "The Peaceful Exit of a Madman" in the *Chicago Tribune*, March 18, 2003.

The U.S. was confronted with a real dilemma. If it backed down under the pressure of the street demonstrations and the increasingly stronger appeals from some of its own friends and allies, the most despotic regime on earth would score another win once again, thus fuelling its arrogance. The peace movement would have scored a major victory but it would have been a hollow victory, as the real winner would be the dictator and the losers its many hundreds of thousands of victims.

I am opposed to violence and wars, any war. But sometimes, we must ask ourselves some troubling questions. Should we continue to oppose the use of force even in situations of genocide and ethnic cleansing? There have been strong and valid arguments against a unilateral U.S./UK intervention in Iraq on the technical grounds that the Security Council is the only source of international legitimacy for armed intervention. That may be so, but as someone who has had direct experience in my country, my family being victims, I dare to pose some naive questions.

How does one fight Osama bin Laden and his legions of fanatics? One option is prayer. Another is appeasement. Another is the use of intelligence, serious intelligence, and prudent force. Let us have no illusions that there can be a reasonable exchange of views, rational dialogue and a modus vivendi, co-existing between the rest of the world and the fanatics.

Extremists existed in many cultures, religions and regions. Christians cannot be too proud of their dark history of fanaticism and intolerance. After all, slavery, colonialism, genocide and the holocaust were made in Europe and exported to the rest of the world. The Europe of enlightenment engineered two world wars and many smaller wars.

It is a fact that the terrorist network that spans the globe mostly originates from the Middle East and some Muslim countries. While some hold high the banner of the Palestinian suffering and humiliation as their rallying cry against Israel and the West, others have a more ambitious agenda, and that is the overthrow of the secular regimes in all lands inhabited by Muslims with the imposition of conservative theocratic rule inspired by the experiences of the Ayatollahs in Iran and the Taliban in Afghanistan. These are their models.

Poverty has little to do with the spread of terrorism but it does provide a fertile ground for the recruitment of foot soldiers. However, the brains behind Islamic fundamentalism and their main followers are educated, middle-class and upper-class fanatics who care little about the poorest of the poor in Asia and Africa. They want power and want to impose their own vision of the world on everyone.

I return to the question of when and how should the use of force be acceptable.

If one accepts as valid the proposition that the Security Council is the only source of legitimacy for armed intervention, does it follow that any unilateral intervention is illegitimate, even when that intervention ends a genocide?

Let me offer an example for reflection — the case of Cambodia under the Khmer Rouge regime in the 1970s. The Cambodia tragedy of the 1970s unleashed by the Khmer Rouge regime with almost universal indifference and the complicity of many is now almost three decades old and has faded in our memory. The world knew, or at least, the U.S. and much of the West as well as Cambodia's neighbours knew, that an evil regime was deliberately cleansing the nation and causing the death of hundreds of thousands of innocent human beings. Vietnam finally intervened unilaterally in 1979, putting an end to the Khmer Rouge rule. Were Hanoi's motives purely humanitarian to save a people? I would say, I really do not care. They were the ones who ended the genocide in Cambodia.

This was the Cold War era. The USSR and Vietnam were seen as more dangerous than the rival Chinese communists, who were supporting the Khmer Rouge regime. So we witnessed the unthinkable, the most distasteful Cold War twisted rationale — the U.S. and the rest of the world aligned itself with the most wretched regime on Earth, simply because they wanted to punish and stop Vietnam. The new pro-Vietnam regime installed in Phnom Penh was ostracized by much of the world, while the Khmer Rouge regime retained its seat in the UN General Assembly.

As far as I remember, there was only one individual in the U.S., a prominent liberal Senator, George McGovern, who called for armed intervention. The Security Council did not even discuss the Khmer Rouge genocide. In any case, if anyone had any inclination to bring this matter to the Security Council it would have been vetoed by China.

There was no chance the Security Council would act, even assuming there was a general political will to intervene. When we visit the genocide museum in Phnom Penh, we cannot help but be angry and ashamed that humanity did nothing to save the three million that perished before Vietnam's intervention. I talked with some Cambodian survivors of the Khmer Rouge, and they remember with gratitude Vietnam's intervention. And yet Vietnam was condemned and sanctioned by certain powers for having intervened and ending the genocide in Cambodia.

The Tanzania intervention, also in 1979 in Uganda, put an end to the Idi Amin grotesque rule. The Organization of African Unity and the Security Council didn't do anything for reasons of state sovereignty and the principle of non-interference. Was the Tanzanian intervention so immoral, wrong and illegitimate? And that intervention was ordered by one of the greatest African statesmen, Julius Nyerere.

Was it wrong that Bill Clinton and Tony Blair mobilized NATO to intervene in Kosovo in 1999, bypassing the Security Council? Well, they saved hundreds of thousands of Kosovars. This was the first time in NATO's 50 year history that it intervened to save an ethnic minority, a Muslim community that was being slaughtered in the heart of Christianity.

Maybe one thing one can say is that Bill Clinton was smarter than George W. Bush. He didn't go through the Security Council because he knew the Russians would have vetoed any attempt at having a resolution authorizing armed intervention in Kosovo. Or we could try to be generous and give credit to the Bush Administration for attempting to secure the endorsement of the Security Council for an intervention in Iraq.

One can argue still further. Was it right and moral that the world did nothing to preempt the unfolding of the Rwanda genocide? If we continue our line of argument that the Security Council must always be the only source of legitimacy for armed intervention, it could follow that the inaction on Rwanda was right, since no action can be taken outside the Security Council authority. Should we put our faith in a highly political body? Should the Security Council be always at all times the only valid source of legitimacy for an armed intervention? If not, then we should deal with the next question — which party carries the legitimacy to intervene? The only existing superpower with enough fire power to shoot its way through?

Allow me then to explore some ideas, not very new, that could lead to an improved United Nations security arrangement that would in turn avoid the temptation or need for interventions outside the UN mandate. The existing UN collective security mechanism is out-dated and undemocratic, a product and relic of the Cold War that no longer meets the challenges of today's world and does not reflect today's economic, demographic and strategic realities. There is an obvious need for reform and I list some ideas.

First, there is a need for an expansion of the membership in the SC to include new Permanent Members that would reflect 21st century realities and challenges with a demographic, economic and strategic balance. The new expanded SC should include countries like India, Indonesia and Japan; Brazil and Mexico; Egypt and South Africa; Germany and Poland.

Second, the veto power should be eliminated and replaced by a 2/3 majority vote for waging wars under Chapter VII. The veto power was used and abused and was responsible for the inaction of the SC.

The two-year rotation for non-permanent members should be shortened to one year so as to give a better chance for more members to serve in the SC.

I submit that in post-September 11 and post-Saddam, the U.S. must lead the fight against poverty as it does the fight against terrorism. The U.S. should also lead in gradually eliminating agriculture subsidies to farmers in the U.S. and Europe that kill competition and market access by poor countries. The U.S. and Europe gave away US$300 billion/year in subsidies to their farmers and only $50 billion in developing assistance to poor countries. France is the country that most heavily subsidizes its agriculture and most strongly opposes the scrapping the agricultural export subsidies.

The EU has a better approach in its relationship with the poor countries through multilateral treaties such as the Cotonou Agreement and the initiative called Everything But Arms that open up the European markets for goods from Africa, the Caribbean and the Pacific Islands. The U.S. should follow this European example.

The U.S. and some Western democracies, Russia, most Central and Eastern European countries, developing countries like China, Brazil and South Africa, are weapons-producing countries that flood the world and fuel conflicts. There has to be a strict code of conduct on weapons exports aiming at reducing the flow of conventional weapons to poor countries and regions in conflict. Certainly the control of the spread of weapons is not an easy task, but we could start by having a strict binding code of conduct along the lines of the Anti-Land Mine Convention.

The U.S., the EU and Japan should heed the calls for a debt pardon for the poorest and most indebted countries. I certainly would not endorse a debt pardon without some stringent condition. First on the list to have their debts cancelled are the LDCs, followed by all others with an annual per capita income of less than $1,000. However, some conditions should be attached, namely, significant reduction in defence expenditure; pro-poor sustainable development strategy; more resources put into education and public health; adoption and clear evidence of anti-corruption laws, transparency and accountability; evidence of functioning democracy, based on the rule of law, with free media, and independent judiciary; accession to Human Rights Treaties; and accession to the International Criminal Court (ICC).

For other heavily indebted countries with per capita income of over $1,000 or which are oil-producing countries, there could be other creative compromises such as a moratorium on debt payment for a period of up to five years. However, the same conditions listed above for the LDCs apply to them.

The U.S. should accede to the International Criminal Court, to Kyoto, as well as to UN Human Rights Conventions. It must set the example if it wants to lead. There are enough guarantees and safeguards in the Rome Statute against politically motivated prosecutions. We hope that the UN and the Europeans would find a compromise with Washington so that the U.S. would agree to accede to the Treaty. It makes no sense that the U.S. supports *ad hoc* tribunals for former Yugoslavia and Rwanda, but does not support the ICC.

After September 11 and the Afghan campaign, after the Iraq intervention and the ouster of a brutal and arrogant dictator, the U.S. must also show humility and leadership. It has the resources, the power and ingenuity that no other nation in human history has to effect positive changes in the world. However, leadership must be by inspiration and reason, by building bridges and consensus, and not by bullying.

It can lead through a reformed and strengthened UN, with a more patient and constructive approach, but also by working with and supporting regional organizations and vital institutions in dealing with challenges and cooperation in disparate regions of the world.

As a superpower the U.S. will not enjoy universal acclamation. It will be admired and respected, and sometimes feared and resented. There will be always enemies, arrogant leftists and religious fanatics. But it can win over the majority, the common people. Right now it has few friends.

Bernard Lown, MD
NOBEL PEACE LAUREATE 1985

Like all physicians of the International Physicians for the Prevention of Nuclear War (IPPNW)[1] — faithful to their Hippocratic oath — Dr. Lown, co-founder of IPPNW (since 1980), works to prevent what IPPNW regards as "the final epidemic". Although the prevention of nuclear war is still IPPNW's highest priority, the organization's mission was broadened in 1991 to include the prevention of conventional war. To this end, IPPNW seeks to prevent all wars, to promote nonviolent conflict resolution, and to minimize the effects of war and preparations for war on health, development, and the environment. Now organized in 58 national affiliates, IPPNW is the only international medical organization dedicated to the abolition of nuclear weapons. IPPNW's affiliates also work to end the threats posed by small arms and light weapons, landmines, chemical and biological weapons, and environmental degradation.

Seismic Change in Nuclear Policy[2]

A seismic change in American nuclear policy has been largely ignored by the media. The Pentagon's most recent Nuclear Posture Review (NPR) provides a chilling insight into new policies aimed to breach the nuclear firewall. This Strangelovian document lays out contingency plans for the use of nuclear weapons against at least seven countries, including Russia, China, Libya, Syria and, of course, the so-called "axis of evil" — Iraq, Iran, and North Korea. The NPR defines military objectives as those targets that are able to withstand

---

[1] IPPNW can be contacted at 727 Massachusetts Avenue, Cambridge, MA 02139, USA; email: ippnwbos@ippnw.org; website: www.ippnw.org.

[2] This article appeared in the May 2003 issue of IPPNW's news magazine *Vital Signs*.

65

non-nuclear attack, or countries using or threatening to use nuclear, biological, or chemical weapons, or "in the event of surprising military developments", whatever that maladroit locution denotes.

Since Hiroshima and Nagasaki, nuclear weapons were considered options of last resort, to be used only when a nation's very survival hung in the balance. With the NPR, nuclear weapons will be available to theater military commanders as conventional battlefield hardware. A British commentator reflected, "the possibility that the U.S. will resort to the use of nuclear weapons in a future conflict is greater now than at any time since the darkest days of the Cold War." The Bush Administration has indeed lowered the nuclear threshold. In the scary gobbledygook of the Pentagon's NPR, "We must be prepared to stop rogue states and their terrorist clients before they are able to threaten or use WMD [weapons of mass destruction] ... To forestall or prevent such hostile acts the U.S. will, if necessary, act preemptively." It continues, "The U.S. reserves the right to respond with overwhelming force, including through resort to all our options, to the use of WMD against the U.S., our forces abroad, our friends, and allies."

This means that any attack on U.S. interests, real or imagined, however limited, from whatever source, wherever in the world, involving any form of chemical, biological, or radiological weaponry, could trigger nuclear retaliation. The NPR shreds the Non-Proliferation Treaty (NPT). The U.S. thereby breaks a pledge issued in 1970 never to use nuclear weapons against a non-nuclear weapon state or against a signatory of the Non-Proliferation Treaty such as Iraq. In a deeper sense, the NPR abrogates a doctrine hallowed since the earliest days of the Cold War, namely, that the sole justification for stockpiling genocidal nuclear weapons is to deter their use — not to employ them in fighting wars. This horrendous precedent will set in motion uncontrollable forces with treacherous, far-reaching, and unpredictable consequences.

The NPR also discloses plans to expand greatly the nuclear war infrastructure. To develop a new generation of warheads, the Bush Administration is preparing to end its *de facto* compliance with the Comprehensive Test Ban Treaty. To enhance the planned "nuclear options capability", already in the development pipeline, is the "robust nuclear earth penetrator" for destroying underground targets and the "enhanced radiation weapon" intended to incinerate toxic agents. The U.S. is now spending 45 percent more on nuclear weapons activities than during the Cold War.

Why has there been no outcry about this barbaric policy shift? The projection of a U.S. military strategy based on the use of nukes, with unprecedented potential for first use against non-nuclear states, the prodigious investment of scarce funds for development of new nuclear weapons, and even the planned resumption of nuclear testing has been greeted by a muted acquiescence. Neither the media, the ethicists, the clergy, nor the intellectual classes — all those who pride themselves as guardians of our moral values — have raised a howl or even hiccuped a whisper of revulsion. After all, what is being prepared is the initiation of a type of industrialized genocide associated with Auschwitz, but on a far more colossal scale.

The silence must be carefully analyzed if effective opposition to the present nuclear posturing is to be roused. Public detachment relates to a concept that has been subtly espoused by the establishment and accepted by the entire political spectrum of opinion. It involves the concept of weapons of mass destruction or WMD. Included under this rubric are nuclear, chemical, and biological weapons. One three-lettered acronym equates the destructive consequences of these disparate instruments of mass murder. It has long been clear to the PR engineers who shape the mass mind that a particular meaning imparted by oft-bandied words helps mobilize public consent. Indeed, Saddam's alleged possession of chemical and biological weapons (CBW) and willingness to use them was a major selling point of the need to attack Iraq.

An examination of the development and historical uses of CBW indubitably demonstrates, that though these are able to inflict horrendous human suffering, they are orders of magnitude less dangerous and far less destructive than thermo-nuclear devices. A B52 loaded with tons of conventional explosives is potentially more devastating than any chemical or biological devices when deployed against developed rich societies. By contrast, a sizeable nuclear attack can make a huge continental country like the U.S. uninhabitable. Nothing remotely as destructive is possible with CBW.

Engendering equivalence in the public mind of these incomparably destructive weapons lowers public resistance against a nuclear response. It numbs people's moral restraint against resorting to genocidal weapons. It is time once again for anti-nuclear activists to break this psychic numbing.

Sir Joseph Rotblat
NOBEL PEACE LAUREATE 1995

Born in Warsaw in 1908, Professor Sir Joseph Rotblat is a Fellow of the Royal Society, Emeritus Professor of Physics at the University of London and Emeritus President of the Pugwash Conferences on Science and World Affairs. During World War II he initiated work on the atom bomb at Liverpool University, and later transferred to Los Alamos. When it became clear that Germany was not working on the bomb, he resigned from the project — the only scientist to do so before the bomb was tested. He has devoted the subsequent 50 years of his life to averting the danger posed by nuclear weapons, and was awarded the Nobel Peace Prize in 1995 jointly with Pugwash Conferences, the organization he helped to found. He is the author of about 400 publications. His latest books include A Nuclear-Weapon-Free World: Desirable? Feasible? *(1993),* World Citizenship: Allegiance to Humanity *(1997),* Nuclear Weapons: The Road to Zero *(1998), and* War No More *(2003).*

The Nuclear Issue: Pugwash and the Policies of the Bush Administration[1]

This paper is mainly concerned with the nuclear issue, specifically with the dangers to the world that may arise from the nuclear policies of the George W. Bush Administration. But in order to put these policies into a proper perspective, I have to start with observations on the general doctrines and strategies of this Administration.

---

[1] This is the abridged text of a speech given by Sir Joseph Rotblat, President Emeritus of the Pugwash Conferences, on the occasion of the 53rd Pugwash Conference on Science and World Affairs at Halifax, Nova Scotia, Canada on July 18, 2003.

I should declare, from the start, that I am strongly critical of the present U.S. Administration in its conduct of world affairs. In the highly charged political climate of the recent months — largely related to the Iraq debacle — anyone criticizing the Bush Administration has immediately been branded as anti-American, and placed in the defensive position of having to begin with a statement that one is not anti-American.

So let me say this clearly: I am not anti-American. On the contrary, I submit that it is the policies of the current Administration that should be called anti-American, because — in my opinion — they do not represent the views of the majority of the American people. I am convinced that these policies would not have been pursued if Al Gore had won the election in 2000. You will remember that — even with the distraction of Ralph Nader — Al Gore had a majority in the national vote, and it was only through some questionable manoevres that he was deprived of the Presidency. It seems to me very unlikely that, had he been elected, Al Gore would have alienated so many to such an extent.

It is important to note that the current polarization of the world is largely the consequence of the Bush slogan: "*You are either with us or against us*". This was initially applied to the campaign against Al-Qaeda, but it puts all those who do not fully agree with the Bush policies into the category of villains. There are many, perhaps a majority in the world, who are strongly against terrorists, and ready to join in actions against them, but are not happy with the Bush policies. These policies are seen by many outside the U.S. as aiming at establishing a U.S. hegemony in the world, and treating international undertakings with contempt, to be adhered to only if they suit the interest of the U.S.

What I find so repugnant about these policies is their blatant hypocrisy. The U.S. proclaims itself as the champion of democracy in the world, while actually imposing its will in a dictatorial manner. It is supposed to uphold the rules of law, yet violates legal commitments under international treaties. It castigates members of the United Nations for exercising their rights under existing rules but takes military action against a member state without the authority of the United Nations.

A central criticism of the United Nations made by the Bush team is that it is ineffective, a useless and enfeebled organ, incapable of taking decisive action. This sort of criticism has traditionally been leveled at democracies by totalitarian regimes. Long discussions and protracted negotiations are an inherent feature of a democratic system, in which the needs and aspirations of many groups or nations have to be reconciled in a peaceful manner. The Bush Administration has no truck with such approaches, even though it professes to champion democracy.

In my view, such policies are unacceptable in a civilized society because in the long run, they would spell the ruin of civilization.

The pursuit of these policies was evident in the campaign against Iraq. The stated justification was to disarm Iraq of weapons of mass destruction, but others see it primarily as an attempt to increase the U.S. influence in the Middle East. There is plenty of documentary evidence to support the thesis that the main reason for bringing down the Saddam Hussein regime in Iraq — and making similar threats against Syria and Iran — was to change the political configuration in the Middle East so as to give the U.S. political, economic and military control of that region. The history of these endeavours is now general knowledge.

The Al-Qaeda attack of September 11 provided the opportunity for these policies to be put into practice. The case for a *Pax Americana* had been set out, and its first stage was implemented in the war against Iraq.

The prolonged squabbles over UN Resolutions and inspections, aiming at giving legitimacy to the war, seem to have been just a charade, intended to create the impression that it was not the U.S. alone but a coalition that was involved in the anti-Iraq campaign. The decision to overthrow the Saddam Hussein regime having been taken much earlier, it was only the time for its implementation that had to be chosen. This was probably dictated not by the outcome of the Hans Blix inspections, but by the need to assemble the necessary military strength.

The military strength of the U.S. is truly awesome. Since the end of the Cold War, the Americans have built up an enormous military potential. Making use of the latest advances in science and the achievements in technology — and supported by budgets of astronomical dimensions — the U.S. has become the greatest military power that ever existed; nearly exceeding in sophistication all other nations combined. Against this might, the Iraqi army, with antiquated tanks and no air-power to provide cover, did not stand a chance.

Of course, the fact that Saddam Hussein's regime was rotten, and was kept from falling apart entirely by the terror imposed by a small number of thugs, contributed to its rapid demise. The claim by Rumsfeld *et al.* that Iraq posed a threat to other nations, including the U.S., was just laughable.

Indeed, the official reason for the military attack on Iraq — the removal of weapons of mass destruction — has proven to be completely indefensible, since no such weapons have so far been found, despite the intense search carried out by large groups of experts appointed by the U.S. As time goes on, and the WMDs are not found, there will be an attempt to play down the importance of finding them, but this will not alter the fact that the war was started on false premises.

All the same, it would be hypocritical for those of us who were against the war not to rejoice over the downfall of a tyrannical regime, and not to admit that this would not have come about so quickly without military intervention. But the price we paid for this is far too high: it has reinstated in world affairs the old maxim that *the ends justify the means.*

The events of the recent months are a severe setback to those who believe that morality and adherence to the rules of law should be our guiding principles. For the time being, the rule seems to be: *might is right*, and in submitting to this rule, the governments of many countries may be driven to adopt a pragmatic policy; they may be forced to acknowledge that there is now a single superpower; they may feel obliged to accept the role of the U.S. as the world's policeman.

But this cannot be a permanent solution. Even if the Americans were less arrogant in pursuing that role than they are now, a system with a built-in inequality is bound to be unstable. It is bound to create resentment, a resentment that will find expression in various ways, including an increase in international terrorism. This in turn will force the "policemen" to take countermeasures, which will make the inequality even more acute. Democracy in the world, as we know it today, would be ended.

This is a possible scenario, but it need not happen. My main hope is that the opposition to it will come from within the U.S. itself. At present, Bush is very popular and carries a majority of public opinion: this is the usual wave of patriotism which comes with a military victory, but it is already decreasing significantly. I believe that the strong antiwar demonstrations that we saw earlier are a true reflection of the views of the majority of the American people. Somehow, I do not see the American people accepting the role assigned to them by the clique that has hijacked the Administration. Public opinion is bound to turn when the dangers associated with the current policies become apparent. My main worry is that in the meantime these dangers may lead to catastrophic results. The greatest dangers derive from the nuclear doctrines pursued by the Bush Administration.

The elimination of nuclear weapons has always been the goal of Pugwash, following the call in the Russell-Einstein Manifesto. We have pursued this goal for moral reasons, because ethical issues have always played a major role in Pugwash: any use of nuclear weapons has been seen as immoral. But we have also seen in our goals a basic purpose: survival. Any use of nuclear weapons would carry the danger of escalation and a threat to our continued existence.

But the use of nuclear weapons is explicitly contemplated in the policies of the Bush Administration.

These policies seem to have two aims: one, a defensive strategy to make the U.S. invulnerable to an attack from outside; the second, an offensive strategy, to threaten an unfriendly regime with military action, including the use of nuclear weapons, if it attempts to acquire WMDs for itself.

For the first purpose, the decision was made to give a high priority to missile defence. As a first step, the U.S. abrogated the Anti-Ballistic Missile Treaty, which had been previously considered the bedrock of the arms control system. A hugely increased budget has been provided for a missile defence project, which is said to be essential in a world of potential threats from weapons of mass destruction.

But it is in the offensive aspect that the biggest changes have occurred. The new Nuclear Posture Review spells out a strategy which incorporates nuclear capability into conventional war planning. The previous doctrine of deterrence, by which the actual use of nuclear weapons was seen as a last resort, when everything else had failed, has been thrown overboard. In the new doctrine, nuclear weapons have become a standard part of military strategy; they would be used in a conflict just like any other explosives. This represents a major shift in the whole rationale for nuclear weapons.

The implementation of this policy has already begun. The U.S. is designing a new nuclear warhead of low yield, but with a shape that would give it a very high penetrating power into concrete, the *"robust nuclear earth penetrator"*. It is intended to destroy bunkers with thick concrete walls in which weapons of mass destruction may be stored, or enemy leaders may seek shelter.

To enable this project to go ahead the U.S. Senate has already decided to rescind the long-standing prohibition on the development of low yield nuclear weapons. Other types of warheads are also contemplated.

The new weapons will have to be tested. At present there is a treaty prohibiting the testing of nuclear weapons (except in subcritical assemblies), the Comprehensive Test Ban Treaty, which the U.S. has signed but not ratified. Given the contempt of the Bush Administration for international treaties, little excuse would be needed to authorize the testing of the new weapon. Indeed, the need to resume testing is now openly advocated.

If the U.S. resumed testing, this would be a signal to other nuclear weapon states to do the same. China would be almost certain to resume testing. After the U.S. decision to develop ballistic missile defences, China feels vulnerable, and is likely to attempt to reduce its vulnerability by modernizing and enlarging its nuclear arsenal. An opinion is building up that: "*China should realize that the present minimum nuclear arsenal is inadequate to meet the new challenges, and therefore should greatly expand its nuclear force to the extent that it can be actually used in different scenarios.*" At present this is a minority view, but it may become significant should the U.S. resume testing. Other states with nuclear weapons, such as India or Pakistan, might use the window of opportunity opened by the U.S. to update their arsenals. The danger of a new nuclear arms race is real.

If the militarily mightiest country declares its readiness to carry out a preemptive use of nuclear weapons, others may soon follow. The Kashmir crisis, in May last year, is a stark warning of the reality of the nuclear peril.

India's declared policy is not to be the first to use nuclear weapons. But if the U.S. — whose nuclear policies are largely followed by India — makes a preemptive nuclear use part of its doctrine, this would give India the legitimacy to similarly threaten preemptive action against Pakistan. George Fernandes, India's Minister for Defence, said recently: India had "*a much better case to go for preemptive action against Pakistan than the United States has in Iraq.*"

Taiwan presents another potential scenario for a preemptive nuclear strike by the U.S. Should the Taiwan authorities decide to declare independence, this would inevitably result in an attempted military invasion by mainland China. The U.S., which is committed to the defence of Taiwan, may then opt for a preemptive strike.

And we still have the problem of North Korea, described by Bush as one of the "axis of evil". Under the Bush dictum not to allow the possession of weapons of mass destruction by any state considered to be hostile, North Korea will be called upon to close down all work on nuclear weapons. It is by no means certain that Kim Jong Il will submit to these demands, and a critical situation may arise in that part of the world.

A major worry in this respect are developments in Japan. So far Japan has been kept out of the nuclear weapons club by Article 9 of its constitution:

"...the Japanese people forever renounce...the threat or use of force as means of settling international disputes."

However, partly at the urging of the U.S., strong tendencies are now appearing — with the backing of the Prime Minister, Junichiro Koizumi — to revise the constitution so as to make it legal for Japan to become a nuclear-weapon state.

Altogether, the aggressive policy of the U.S., under the Bush Administration, has created a precarious situation in world affairs, with a greatly increased danger of nuclear weapons being used in combat.

Moreover, if the use of nuclear weapons is made legal, it would preclude passing of laws to prevent the development of new types of weapons, with even greater destructive potential than current WMDs — a truly horrifying prospect. Sir Martin Rees, the British Astronomer Royal, gives civilization a 50/50 chance of surviving this century. Others believe that this is optimistic.

What should be the Pugwash stand on this matter? Does the new situation call for a corresponding change in our activities?

Any attempt to achieve our goals by persuading the Bush Administration to change its policies through logical persuasion, or by appealing to moral instincts, would be hopeless and a complete waste of time. But it may not be a waste of time if such an appeal is made to the general public. As I said earlier, hope lies in a change of public opinion, particularly in the U.S., to rise in opposition to the current policies, and throw them out in the process usually employed in democratic countries, namely, in free elections. Therefore, my suggestion is that the Pugwash effort should be towards an acceleration of that process in a campaign to influence public opinion, a campaign based on principles of morality and equity.

The immorality in the use of nuclear weapons is taken for granted, but this aspect is very seldom raised when calling for nuclear disarmament. We are told that a campaign based on moral principles is a non-starter, and we are afraid of appearing naïve, and divorced from reality. I see in the use of this argument evidence that we have allowed ethical considerations to be ignored for far too long. We are accused of not being realistic, when what we are trying to do is to prevent real dangers, the dangers that would result from the current policies of the Bush Administration.

The public at large is ignorant about these dangers and we urgently need a campaign of public education.

The other basic principle is adherence to international law. It is a *sine qua non* of a civilized society that nations fulfil their legal obligations and respect international law. World peace cannot be achieved without adherence to international treaties.

There is much deliberate obfuscation and brainwashing in this respect. Let me illustrate this with the example which happens to be at the heart of the problem, the problem of the Non-Proliferation Treaty (NPT).

Let me recall the salient facts about the NPT, to which 98 percent of nations have subscribed. In accordance with the treaty, all non-nuclear states that signed it undertook not to acquire nuclear weapons in any way. At the same time, the five states which officially possessed those weapons — by virtue of the fact that they had tested them by a certain date — undertook to get rid of theirs. The relevant Article VI reads:

> *"Each of the Parties to the Treaty undertakes to pursue negotiations in good faith on effective measures relating to cessation of the nuclear arms race at an early date and to nuclear disarmament, and on a treaty on general and complete disarmament under strict and effective international control."*

By signing and ratifying the NPT, the nuclear member states are legally committed to nuclear disarmament. The hawks in those states, in an attempt to retain nuclear weapons, utilized an ambiguity in Article VI, which makes it appear that nuclear disarmament is linked with the achievement of general and complete disarmament. But the NPT Review Conference — an official part of the implementation of the NPT — at its session in 2000, removed this ambiguity in a statement issued by all five nuclear weapons states. It contains the following:

> "...*an unequivocal undertaking by the nuclear-weapon states to accomplish the total elimination of their nuclear arsenals leading to nuclear disarmament to which all States Parties are committed under Article VI.*"

This makes the situation perfectly clear. The Bush policy, which is based on the continued existence (and use) of nuclear weapons, is in direct contradiction to the legally binding NPT.

But the Bush Administration seems to have managed to convince the public that only a part of the NPT, the part that applies to the non-nuclear states, is valid, and that therefore states which violate it — as Iran now stands accused of doing — must be punished for the transgression. The part concerning the obligation of the nuclear states is deliberately being obliterated.

What we are *not* being told is that these weapons are just as dangerous in the possession of friendly nations. We are *not* being reminded that — with the realization of these dangers — even the U.S. has undertaken to get rid of its own nuclear arsenal. We are facing here a basic issue in which the ethical and legal aspects are intertwined. The use of nuclear weapons is seen by the great majority of people in the world as immoral, due to their indiscriminate nature and unprecedented destructive power. Their possession — and therefore likely use — is thus equally unacceptable, whether by "rogue" or benevolent regimes.

The elimination of nuclear weapons has been the declared aim of the United Nations from the beginning, and resolutions to this effect are passed, year after year, by large majorities of the General Assembly. These resolutions are ignored by the nuclear weapon states, as are all attempts to discuss the issue by the organ set up for this purpose, the Conference on Disarmament in Geneva.

There is a need to keep hammering home the point that America's stand on the NPT issue is iniquitous. It has signed and ratified an international treaty which commits it to get rid of nuclear weapons, yet it is pursuing a policy which demands the indefinite retention of these weapons.

We have to keep on highlighting the fundamental inconsistency in the U.S. policies. The U.S. must make a choice: if it wants to keep nuclear weapons, then it should withdraw from the NPT (which would probably result in a massive increase in the number of nuclear weapon states). Otherwise, it must abide by the terms of the NPT and get rid of its nuclear arsenals. There is no third way.

I believe that a campaign to educate and influence public opinion, centered on the issue of the NPT, would stand a good chance of being successful.

Frederik Willem de Klerk
NOBEL PEACE LAUREATE 1993

Born in 1936 of a family long prominent in South African politics, de Klerk, the former president of South Africa, co-won the Nobel prize with the then President Nelson Mandela of the African National Congress for their efforts to end apartheid and for the first time to resolve peacefully a civil conflict by a head of government and the leader of the opposition forces.

American Leadership in a Globalised World: 9/11, Iraq and Beyond

If the world has become a globalised village, there can be little doubt that the United States is its Mayor and — its Chief of Police. America holds these positions — not because it has been elected to them — but because of its unchallenged military, economic and IT preeminence.

America's role as *de facto* global leadership bears with it heavy burdens and responsibilities:

- The United States has to spend a disproportionate share of its national wealth on the upkeep of its global military capability;
- its preeminence makes it a target for disaffected groups all over the world. Osama bin Laden would not have targeted the World Trade Centre and the Pentagon if they were not military and commercial symbols of the richest and most powerful country in the world;
- The price of global preeminence is, and always has been, unpopularity. America must endure the jealousy of some of its oldest allies, many of whom delight in taking pot-shots at her policies, while sheltering beneath her strategic umbrella;

81

- the United States is likely to be criticised, whatever it does. If it acts to enforce United Nations resolutions on Iraq, it is accused of imperialism. If it fails to intervene in other crises — such as the civil war in Liberia it is slated for being insensitive to the plight of Africans.

Unfortunately, this is the price that must be paid for being the only remaining super-power. It is a price that was well understood by other preeminent powers — from the Romans two thousand years ago to the British during the nineteenth century.

How then should America react to this burden? What challenges confront it as global Mayor and chief of police?

When the United States first ascended the stage of world power at the beginning of the last century, President Teddy Roosevelt's approach was to "speak softly and carry a big stick". He said that by so doing America would go far. He was right.

The big stick is undoubtedly necessary.

After the terrorist outrage of September 11, 2001 it was essential for the United States to use its big stick against international terrorism.

- It was right and proper to overthrow the Taliban regime which had provided the main operational base for the terrorist attacks against America.
- It was essential to put extreme pressure on any country providing a safe haven for Al-Qaeda;
- It was equally important to launch a global campaign to track down terrorists wherever they might be hiding.

The United States also decided to use the "big stick" by invading Iraq and overthrowing the despotic regime of Saddam Hussein.

We should have no illusions regarding the central issues involved in the in the United States decision to invade Iraq:

- The world, the Middle East and Iraq are all better and safer places without Saddam's regime which was one of the most brutal and evil of modern times.

- It was also clear that none of Saddam Hussein's undertakings could be taken seriously. He responded only to force or the credible threat of force.
- The United States and Britain were evidently convinced that Saddam's regime was in possession of — or about to acquire — weapons of mass destruction. Conclusive proof for the existence of such weapons has yet to be produced — but the search continues.
- Regardless of all these circumstances, the United States' action — steadfastly supported by Prime Minister Blair of the UK — does not enjoy universal support. It has caused strains in the United States relations with some of its oldest allies and has led to strong anti-American sentiment throughout the world. Much of this criticism can be ascribed to rejection of the United States' pre-eminent global postion and to allegations that America's action was prompted by its own national geo-political and economic interests. However, a great deal of the criticism has its roots in the view that the United States attack on Iraq lacked an unambiguous mandate from the United Nations — or at least broad-based international support. As such it is viewed as a retrogressive step away from the establishment of a gobal order based on international law.

The United States should also remember Teddy Roosevelt's advice "to speak softly". Military force has an essential place in international affairs — but at the end of the day it cannot create lasting solutions.

Military force also carries with it immense risks. It is much easier to start wars than to end them. Also, the outcome of war is always uncertain. Wars seldom turn out the way they were planned. The Austrians, the Russians and the Germans did not think at the beginning of the First World War that the result would be the destruction of their ruling dynasties. When Napoleon marched his Grand Army into Russia in 1812 he did not foresee the disaster that would soon befall him.

One should consider the necessity of "speaking softly".

"Speaking softly" requires a multilateral approach to international crises. It does not mean that the international community must forgo the option of using the big stick; but it does mean that if it is finally used there will less criticism and a greater chance of success.

The "speaking softly" option also recognises that long term solutions can be achieved only by addressing the root causes of conflict — which are often poverty, repression; ignorance and fanaticism.

It is not by accident that the country that Osama bin Laden chose as his refuge was also one of the poorest, most tyrannical, repressive and conflict-ridden societies in the world.

The long term way to combat terrorism must then include tackling the roots of poverty, repression and conflict.

In the new millennium it will be less and less possible to ignore the reality that a large part of the human population still lives in unacceptable poverty, misery and repression. Although the portion of the world's population living in absolute poverty has declined from two thirds to one third in the past forty years, the total number of people living below the poverty line has stayed about the same — at about 2 billion (because the world's population has doubled since 1960). At the same time, although the poor might not be getting poorer, the rich are certainly getting richer: the disparity per capita between the poorest and richest fifths of the world's nations has widened from 30 to 1 in 1960 to 78 to 1 in 1994.

In a shrinking world, the problems of one region will inevitably become the problems of other regions and ultimately of the whole world:

- Diseases like AIDS — which first appeared in Africa — do not observe international boundaries;
- As we saw a few years ago, economic crises in emerging markets can have serious negative consequences for the whole of the global economy;
- Conflicts and instability in distant societies can reverberate throughout the whole international community. The attacks on New York and Washington on September 11, 2001 brought this

fact home with chilling clarity. Who would have thought that religious fanatics hiding in caves in distant Afghanistan could possibly pose a threat to the hi-tech nerve centre of the world's most powerful economy in down-town New York?

• Whether we live in the first world or the third world, we all share the same fragile global environment. Global warming, the decimation of tropical forests and the extinction of animal and plant species will have long-term consequences for the whole planet.

In our globalised society such problems and conflicts will sooner or later breach international borders and affect the interests of us all. It is equally true that the problems confronting a globalised world can no longer be dealt with unilaterally by any single country — regardless of how powerful or rich that country might be. Problems of global development, global security and protection of the global environment can be dealt with only if the international community works in concert. The United States can play a pivotal leadership role in this process — but it cannot achieve success alone.

Under its leadership and the leadership of other prominent countries the international community should develop the policies, the resources and the will to tackle the root causes of global problems.

We need to recognise the symbiosis between stability, prosperity and freedom: Economic prosperity creates the environment in which democracy and free institutions can grow — and they, in turn, help to promote the stability that is essential for economic growth.

There is an undeniable link between peace, development, growth and democracy. Only a handful of the countries in the world with per capita incomes of less than US$500 are full democracies, while nearly all of the twenty richest countries — those with per capita incomes above US$13,000 — are democracies (the exceptions being a number of oil-rich states).

There is also a link between levels of development and peace. Eleven of the thirty poorest countries — including Afghanistan — have in recent years been wracked by devastating civil wars. On the other hand, none of the twenty richest countries have experienced serious internal conflict — with the exception of Northern Ireland.

How then can we achieve this symbiosis between economic development, stability and democracy?

In the sphere of the economy, the developed countries should do more to promote economic growth in the least developed societies.

- More attention needs to be given to the debt burden of the world's 41 most highly indebted poor countries — 34 of which are in Africa. Some steps are now being taken by the IMF to address this problem, but more needs to be done.
- Steps should also be taken to increase the third world's share in global trade. For example, Africa, with almost one-sixth the world's population accounts for only one fiftieth of global trade. Third World exports need more favourable access to first world markets. The unacceptable reality is that the world's most developed nations spend eight times as much in subsidies to their own farmers as they do on foreign aid.
- The poor countries also require higher levels of foreign and domestic investment. They have to achieve at least 5% per annum growth levels if they are to break out of the grip of poverty. And they are simply not getting the investment required to achieve this.

The international community also needs to continue its efforts to promote democracy and the rule of law in third world countries.

Twenty of the 45 countries of sub-Saharan Africa are presently — or have recently — been involved in wars. Much of this instability can be ascribed to the lack of democratic mechanisms and the rule of the law.

- The international community should do more to encourage third world countries to proceed with democratic reforms and to protect the basic rights of their citizens.
- It should also not hesitate to act against regimes that grossly violate human rights and that subvert democracy. The Government of Robert Mugabe of Zimbabwe is a recent prime example.

- It needs to adopt a much more proactive stance in defusing potential conflicts and in promoting the peaceful resolution of disputes.

One of the fundamental causes of conflict throughout the world lies in the inability of different ethnic and cultural groups to coexist peacefully within the same societies. In 2000, the first year of the new millennium, only two of the 27 significant conflicts that afflicted the world were between countries: the rest were within countries — primarily between ethnic, cultural and religious communities. The present or recent conflicts in the Middle East, former Yugoslavia, southern Asia, Rwanda, Burundi, Sri Lanka, East Timor and Kashmir all bear bloody testimony to this fact.

The current conflict in the Middle East is, unfortunately, a good example of both the challenge that the international community faces in this regard and of the risks that such conflict can hold for the entire world.

- The still unresolved problems between Israel and the Palestinians continue to destabilise the entire Middle Eastern region;
- The Israeli/Palestinian conflict has caused enormous strains in relations between Moslems throughout the world and the West — and in particular, the United States.
- The passions that it has unleashed have created the environment in which fanaticism and terrorism can flourish.

For all of these reasons the United States, as the preeminent world power, cannot afford to allow the conflict to spiral further out of control. Just as war is too important to be left to the generals, peace in the Middle East is too important to the key interests of whole international community to be left solely to the Israelis and the Palestinians.

It is accordingly most welcome that — hand in hand with its actions in Iraq — the United States has clearly spelled out its support for the peace process between the Israelis and the Palsetinians. In accordance with the goals set out in the "road map", the Israelis and the Palestinians are simply going to have to find some way of learning to live together. This means that both sides will have to take risks; both sides will have to make painful compromises; both sides will have to accept that military force, and suicide terrorist bombings will only accelerate their downward spiral into deepening conflict. At the end of that conflict, after immense and unnecessary suffering, they will still have to negotiate.

Although the situation is extremely complex and difficult, it is not hopeless. I recall the dreadful period that South Africa went through between 1984 and 1987. We also, were confronted by our own version of the *intefada*; we also resorted to draconian security measures to restore order; we also experienced growing international isolation and condemnation.

But we pulled back from the brink. We discovered that there was another way: that it was possible to solve our long-standing and bitter dispute through peaceful means. In the process, we learned the following lessons:

- We could not dictate with whom we would negotiate. Whether we liked it or not we had to sit eye-ball to eye-ball with people and parties that had been our bitter enemies;
- We found that the negotiations should be as inclusive as possible. For that reason we invited all parties with significant support to join the process.
- All sides had to take enormous risks;
- All sides had to make very painful compromises;
- All sides had to accommodate the reasonable concerns and interests of others.

Finally we emerged with a new constitution which guarantees the individual and collective rights of all our people and which is enabling us to live together with one another in peace and co-operation.

If we could do it, the Israelis and the Palestinians should also be able to do it. The United States and the rest of the international community can play a major role in this process

- by continuing to remain actively and impartially involved in the peace process;

- by urging the parties to cease all violent acts and to implement faithfully all the provisions of the "road map";
- by insisting that both sides should make the painful concessions that will be essential to reach a just and lasting peace; and
- by giving cast-iron guarantees that the agreements that the parties reach will be honoured by all.

The most eloquent response to the terror attacks of bin Laden would be to achieve a settlement that would ensure the security of Israel, living in harmony with a viable Palestinian state.

These, I believe, are the priorities that confront the United States in its global leadership role. The United States should take the lead in

- tackling the problem of under-development and continuing third world poverty;
- in promoting conditions in which democracy and basic human rights will be enjoyed by all mankind; and
- in finding peaceful solutions to the conflicts that continue to afflict the world — and particularly inter-community conflicts and the impasse between Israel and Palestine.

If the United States can do all these things there will ultimately be no place for the terrorists to hide. Then it will have faithfully carried out its historic global leadership role.

Mairead Corrigan Maguire
NOBEL PEACE LAUREATE 1976

Maguire founded the Peace People in 1976, with Betty Williams and Ciaran McKeown. Maguire was the aunt of the three Maguire children who died as a result of being hit by an Irish Republican Army (IRA) getaway car after its driver was shot by a British soldier. The deaths prompted a series of marches throughout Northern Ireland and further afield, all demanding an end to violence, and resulted in a 70% decrease in violence in the first six months of the Movement. Maguire and Williams went on to win the Nobel Peace Prize in 1976.

Iraq After First (1991) Gulf War

In March 1999, I took part in a seven-person Fellowship of Reconciliation (U.S.) peace Delegation to Iraq. Nobel Peace Laureate, Adolfo Perez Esquivel, was part of the Delegation. On previous occasions, some of the U.S. delegates (from Voices in the Wilderness, U.S.) had brought in medicines, medical journals and toys, to Iraq, and because of these actions they were facing fines of up to $163,000 — about 144,000 Euro dollars or £100,000.

All members of the Delegation were saddened and deeply shocked by what we saw in Iraq. Tragically, we discovered that not only were the children dying or being traumatised emotionally as a result of the First Iraqi War, but also by the continuing on-going U.S./UK bombing raids over Southern and Northern "no-fly" zones and the UN/U.S./UK Economic Trade sanctions, as a result of which the entire society of Iraq was slowly being destroyed.

On arrival in Baghdad, our first visit was to the Ameriyah Shelter. Here on February 12, 1991 (the end of Ramadan and Ash Wednesday), over 500 (some people say it was around 1,200) women, children and elderly men gathered in this underground shelter to celebrate a birthday and the ending of Ramadan. In the early hours of the morning, two U.S. bombs were accidentally dropped into the shelter. Only 17 people survived. The rest were incinerated in this huge modern day gas chamber.

We met a woman called Umm Reyda at the shelter. A mother whose two children and eleven relatives died during the bombing, she herself had survived as she had gone out to wash some clothes. This courageous woman had dedicated her life to acting as a guide to visitors and telling the story of the bombing raid, thus reminding us all of how terrifying these weapons of mass destruction that we have in almost every country in the world are.

The walls of the Ameriyah Shelter are charred black. On the ceilings of the shelter are charred hand and body prints of the dead women and children. On one wall was the outline of a woman who had been instantly incinerated. The whole concrete wall was charcoal black except for a white area, which bore the outline of a human figure with an arm outstretched. The hundreds of photographs of women and children reminded us that in modern warfare it is mostly civilians who are injured or killed, and there are no such things as "smart" weapons.

Later we visited the Al Mansour Paediatric Hospital. We saw children ill and dying from malnutrition, water-borne diseases such as cholera, dysentery, acute leukaemia and cancers. It was all the more harder to witness this knowing that the children are dying not as a result of natural disasters, but from preventable diseases, and many could be saved if only the UN economic sanctions were lifted.

Up to seven children died each day in this one hospital, due to the absence of medicine, technical equipment, electricity, and clean water. The Director explained that for even the few whom they saved, there was little hope of survival. This is because when these patients were sent home, there was no clean water, there was a shortage of food and a complete lack of vital aftercare services. He told us that women who have Caesarean sections performed must have them without anaesthesia, as do children who needed to have their teeth removed.

In the children's cancer ward we met four-year-old Ahkmed Tapir and his mother, Najia. The doctor in charge of this ward, Dr. Salma, explained that due to shortage of staff, the mothers stay with the children constantly and also help out with the hospital work. During our visit doctors repeatedly spoke of the increase in cancer rates and debilitating birth defects throughout Iraq, especially in the southern zones due to contamination from U.S./UK bombs. The doctors said they needed medical journals to help them understand similar radiation defects, but because of the sanctions they were not allowed to receive such journals. Indeed Voices in the Wilderness, U.S., has been threatened with prison and even now face enormous fines for having carried in medical journals. One of the saddest things for Iraqi parents was that they had no photographs of their dead children — this again due to sanctions and the economic situation in their country. Some Iraqi mothers asked the visitors to send them back copies of the photos they were taking of their children.

Later we visited Umm Amarik Research Centre, which studies the effects of the Gulf War violence and its aftermath. The Director told us that depleted-uranium coating on U.S. bombs had led to a dramatic increase in cancer and physiological abnormalities throughout the country. She explained that due to the sanctions, they are completely cut off from the outside world. The economy of this oil-rich country had been completely devastated by hyperinflation and debt and the people were reduced to selling their possessions in order to buy food or obtain medicine for their families. She asked us if, when we returned to Iraq, we could carry in newspapers, books, even airplane magazines, as they have no information from the outside world. She asked us to help break the silence in the Western media and governments and tell the truth about what was happening to the Iraqi people. That was in 1999.

At the UN Office of the Humanitarian Co-ordinator for Iraq, we were told that they supplied the North of the country with food and monitored the supply in the South, which was dealt with by the Iraqi authorities. They were satisfied that this was being done in as good a manner as could be expected. However, the real problem regarding food and medicines in stores was that they had not the cash to pay people for distribution. There were problems with transport and communication, and a shortage of cold storage for medicines due to the destruction of the electricity grids. During the Gulf War when almost 200,000 Iraqi people (soldiers and civilians) were killed, allied forces destroyed grain silos, schools, sewerage systems, hospitals, electrical grids, water purification plants — indeed all of the infrastructure of Iraq. As a result of the effects of the First Iraqi War and continued Economic Trade sanctions, the people of Iraq never had enough money to rebuild their infrastructure and their country. Everyone we met in Iraq called for the lifting of the Economic Trade sanctions. Without a doubt these sanctions comprised a new kind of bomb and they were even more cruel than weapons. Weapons kill quickly. Economic sanctions condemned the Iraqi people to a slow, painful death.

In 1999, the Iraqi people were also suffering under a cruel military dictatorship, led by Saddam Hussein. The effects of war and sanctions added to their suffering. We enquired then about the Iraqi regime's alleged weapons of mass destruction, and were told that UNSCOM had done its job so well, after the First Iraqi War, that Iraq was no military threat to anyone outside its own borders.

After our visit to Iraq in 1999, all members of the Delegation continued to call for the lifting of the economic trade sanctions and a nonviolent solution to the problems. Sadly the U.S. and British Administrations refused to talk to the Iraqi regime, choosing instead to keep on the economic sanctions and relentless bombing, even though it was patently obvious that these cruel actions were obviously failing to solve the problems but rather causing more immense human suffering.

Turning Point for World Events — September 11, 2001

Tragically World events took a turn for the worst, with the horror of the attacks of September 11. The horrific attacks in New York and Washington shocked the World.

Sometimes in history events take place that leave a lasting impression on people's minds, when, it would seem, the whole world becomes frozen in shock with the awfulness of a calamity. The destruction of the Twin Towers and the loss of over 3,000 lives, was such an event. The sympathy of the world lay with the victims and their families, coming as they did from not only the U.S. but also many other countries around the world. For a brief moment the entire human family was united in grief and brought sharply into the realisation of how vulnerable all of us are in today's world.

It was a wonderful opportunity to call for the human family to come together in order to begin tackling the roots of violence in our world. A wonderful opportunity to call for a partnership of energies and goodwill of all men and women to continue and increase their efforts to build a fair and just and equal world for all. A wonderful opportunity to call for respect for all human rights and international laws. A wonderful opportunity to support the work of the United Nations mandate to build peace amongst the nations. A wonderful opportunity to help people overcome their natural fear and insecurity, and assure them they are not alone, so together we can replace a growing culture of violence with one of peace and non-violence. A wonderful opportunity for the American Administration to show compassion and forgiveness and call for no retaliation, as many Americans and other people did, even when they had lost families in the tragedy.

Illegal Invasion and Occupation of Iraq — March 19, 2003

Sadly, those in political power in the U.S. Administration and British Government chose the alternative route of war and retaliation. First it was Afghanistan, then the withdrawal of weapons inspectors to facilitate a U.S. led invasion of Iraq. This preemptive strike against Iraq was not only immoral, but also illegal and against the wishes of the vast majority of the World's community. Before the second Gulf War, we saw the largest ever World peace movement — millions upon millions around the world saying "No to War against Iraq" and "War Not in our Name". I myself never experienced such an outpouring of antiwar feelings. In India before the Afghan War, I marched with hundreds of thousands of Indian people walking for peace. Indian peace activists expressed concern at the dangerous Bush Doctrine of Preemptive strike. The human and diplomatic costs of the doctrine could be enormous, and Indians knew that a heavy price would be paid in human suffering, if preemptive war by India against Pakistan were to happen. Washington would lack all credibility if it objected to such a course. Both India and Pakistan are nuclear states.

Afghanistan War (2001)

I flew from India to New York. On October 11, I walked with over 10,000 U.S. peace activists, with many amongst them whose family had died or been injured in the New York attack. They carried banners "Not in Our Names" calling for no retaliation after September 11 attacks. Along the route to Times Square, we heard the sad news that American planes had just left to bomb Afghanistan. In Boston, Belfast, Beirut, Baghdad, Berlin, and in almost every city of the globe, men, women and children in their millions walked to call for an alternative to war. The U.S. Administration, in spite of all of its diplomatic muscle, could not persuade a majority of the Security Council that war against Iraq was justified. History will record that this was a war the world voted against.

Attack and Invasion of Iraq — March 19, 2003

But sadly the U.S./UK led war against Iraq started on March 19, 2003. U.S. Peace activists (Voices in the Wilderness, U.S.) who were in Iraq during this attack witnessed the cruelty and depravity of "shock and awe". They reported that throughout the war, embedded journalists' reports were touted as fact while independent reports were often omitted or underplayed by mainstream U.S. media. In Washington at this time, I myself found it depressing to listen to evasions and distortions in the U.S. media, as the U.S. continued to pursue its economic and military interests through the invasion of Iraq. We were told that this war was necessary because Iraq had weapons of mass destruction and was a military threat — particularly to the U.S. The U.S. public was informed that Iraq could launch its alleged weapons of mass destruction within 45 minutes. This led to great fear amongst the American people — particularly those who remember the September 11 attack, and a real confusion in their minds and hearts about war, with many opting to support their President or otherwise be accused of being unpatriotic.

I witnessed the sad confusion amongst many American citizens, during my 30 days' daily vigil outside the Whitehouse. This was when part of my 40-day liquid fast and prayer started on March 19, 2003, the day after the attack against Iraq took place. I also was inspired during my 30 days' vigil at the Whitehouse, by the hundreds of thousands of people throughout America, who — although the war had started — continued to march, with leaflets to protest, lobby and refuse to pay war taxes, committing actions of civil resistance. I myself had the privilege of carrying out nonviolent civil disobedience on two occasions — one in New York and one in Washington — together with 60 other protestors. In the last year over 2,000 U.S. citizens have carried out nonviolent civil resistance and many are currently serving long prison sentences for nonviolent civil disobedience against the war and militarism.

We were also told this second war against Iraq was to obtain a "regime change". There are many brutal regimes around the World, but it is not the role of the U.S., or any other country, to invade these countries and kill off dictators or their families. Killing Saddam Hussein's two sons instead of capturing them by other means is wrong. One of their grandsons and bodyguards also died in this military action. Governments have to uphold the law and arrest suspects, produce evidence, and bring people to properly constituted courts for a fair trial.

Guantanamo Detainees

After September 11, 2001, the American Government began detaining people suspected of terrorist activities — mostly young Muslim men. Since then it has held hundreds of detainess in Guantanamo Bay in Cuba. In January 2002 it transferred prisoners from Afghanistan to the U.S. Naval Base in Guantanamo. There are currently (July 2003) more than 600 detainees of around 40 nationalities held in Guantanamo. This action is a continuing violation of human rights standards — hooding and shackling the prisoners who have no access to the courts, lawyers or relatives, facing the prospect of indefinite detention in small cells for up to 24 hours a day and the possibility of trials by executive military commission with the power to hand down death sentences and no right of appeal.

With such policies we are seeing the growth of the American Global Empire, which has never been seen before. This invasion of Iraq helped secure American oil interests and gave it a power base in Iraq. The U.S. has now military bases in 80 countries (no foreign country has a base in U.S.) with over one million service personnel in these bases, and in the following year the U.S. military budget will equal the military budget of all the other 191 countries in the world.

Other Anomalies

Current U.S. foreign policies such as the above do not begin to tackle the root causes of violence: on the one hand, poverty, injustice, lack of freedom, rights and dignity, while on the other hand, uncontrolled ambition, domination, subjugation, denial of rights, the use of torture. Such current U.S. policies are at best reactions to the symptoms. Not only do they fail to deal with the real problems, they become part of the problem. Tragically, they increase fear, anger, marginalization, and often cause people in their frustration to take up arms themselves and use violence in their misguided belief that violence makes a better world. A foreign power is on their doorstep, promising to rid them not just of a tyrant but of tyranny itself. If the foreign power shows that it believes in many of the very same methods used by the tyrant, it is almost inevitable that the oppressed people will themselves use violence to try to balance the scales, as they imagine, in their own favour. And we must recall that the "liberators" of Iraq were an essential and vital control element in the unjust and inhuman sanctions that had already contributed to the death of over a million Iraqi children.

So, as most of the millions who marched for peace foresaw and forewarned, the violent response to the violence of September 11 has itself produced yet more violence. The invasion of Iraq that resulted in thousands of deaths, both of Iraqis and invading soldiers has now produced the retaliatory violence that everyone but the invaders had expected. The killing and counter-killing continues daily. It is the age-old and wholly predictable reactionary cycle of violence and counter-violence.

The problems faced in most countries today are multi-layered and as such need multi-modal approaches in order to solve them. Only the people of Iraq, Iran and other Middle East countries can solve the problems with which they are faced, and the West, rather than fearing, isolating or marginalizing these forces of reform, should support them in their attempts to fuse democratic aspirations with their own culture and religious identities in these regions. Empowerment of the people, politically, financially and socially, in order that they themselves may solve their own problems in the way best suited to their own needs.

What's To Be Done?

I believe that the following steps would be a basis for a constructive though radical process of peace and nation building:

1) The United Nations Security Council should immediately re-claim for itself the moral right to be the sole authority, with the disputants, for resolving disputes throughout the World. It should therefore convene to decide on the rightness or wrong-

ness of the invasion of the United States and British forces of Iraq, without its own sanction. It should censure those nations who took part in, or collaborated with, the invasion if they deem it unjust. They should place the burden on those same nations of restoring the infrastructure that they destroyed or helped to destroy in Iraq, demand that they pour massive aid into the country as compensation for their misdeeds and insist that they withdraw from the country without benefiting from their illegal actions, having first supervised independent and free elections without their own interference. All of these acts of reparation by the occupying forces should be supervised by the Security Council of the United Nations. That part of the recent legislation pushed through the UN Security Council which guaranteed U.S./UK occupation for at least a year, should therefore be rescinded as a matter of urgency to be replaced by a more robust declaration that would, in line with the above, wrestle the authority of that body from the few that control it and put power back into the hands of all its members.

2) The occupying forces should be directed forthwith to supervise the entry of humanitarian aid and the distribution of such aid — whatever the sources — by qualified non-government agencies working with the local people. The occupying countries should be responsible for making such aid available.

3) The UN should insist on the cancellation of debt and compensation demands from the 1991 Gulf War. The Iraqi civilian population should not be forced to pay for the debts accrued by the Ba'ath regime.

4) The United Nations Security Council should insist that the U.S. and UK occupiers clean up all cluster bombs, mines and depleted uranium used in Iraq and proclaim an end to the development, production, distribution or use of these weapons by any country. It should hold weapons companies and their countries of origin accountable to Iraqis and insist they make compensation for damages done.

5) The United Nations Security Council should insist that none of the belligerents or their allies should profit in any way from the

wealth of the invaded country. In much the same way as Iraq was not allowed to profit from its invasion of Kuwait, neither should the U.S., the UK, or other invading countries profit from the invasion of Iraq. The International Community should demand that appropriation of Iraqi assets be concentrated within Iraq and supervised by a transparent, non-governmentally-aligned body until the people of Iraq can select a new government of their own.

6) The United Nations Security Council should insist on payment of reparations from the U.S. and UK to families of Iraqi civilians killed over the last 13 years of military actions and economic sanctions.

7) The United Nations Council should supervise and be responsible for the continuing search of weapons of mass destruction of Iraq. The standards applied to Iraq in this regard must be applied to all nations. Never again should weapons inspections be linked to economic penalties imposed on a civilian population, as was done in Iraq.

8) The United Nations Security Council must reject the Bush Administration Policy of Preemption as totally unacceptable, illegal and damaging to the UN and world order. Otherwise, we face the horrific prospect of living in a state of perpetual war.

9) The United Nations Security Council should insist that those detained as combatants in Camp Delta in Guantanamo Bay should be either repatriated or charged but not held in indefinite confinement and not returned to countries where they might face torture or death. These prisoners, while held, should be treated humanely, allowed sufficient air and exercise, not be subjected to long hours of investigation during normal sleeping hours, and not be subjected to physical abuse or torture. To ensure this, Camp Delta should be open to immediate inspection by independent human rights organisations such as Amnesty International.

The Status of the United Nations

In all of these recommendations I have put the onus of action on the United Nations Security Council. That body, sadly, appears to me to have abrogated its rights and ceded its moral authority in the face of severe pressures from the United States since the coming into power of the Bush Administration. It was pressure from Mr. Bush himself that forced Resolution 1441 from a reluctant Council. That resolution, whatever its intention, was sufficiently ambiguous to allow the hawks in the U.S. and UK to assert that it allowed them to invade Iraq. You may think that a United Nations of the calibre required is an impossibility in the present climate. If so, we should know that this is the case. Maybe we should be looking for its reform. And if reform is not possible maybe we should be working towards its disbandment and its replacement by a new, more moral, more thorough and more self-believing United Nations, under whatever name. This new body would outlaw, among other things, the buying of votes by bribes or threats, would expel any nation, however powerful, that transgressed its rules, and even exclude any nation, however powerful, that insisted on being excempted from the sanctions or rules of international law that apply to all its other member states.

If the raison d'être of a body is being challenged at will by its most powerful members, then, if those members continue to belong to that body, it will lose its efficacy.

The Power of the Individual

And what, you might ask, if this is not possible or if the new United Nations turns out like the old.

I am a believer more in the power of the individual than of large corporate bodies or institutions. I believe too in the essential goodness of people, which is not always reflected in the decisions of their governments. Individual people around the world, brought together more than ever in the past year by the unfolding events in

Iraq, have, in their hundreds of millions, told their governments that they were against the war. 90% of Spaniards and 90% of Greeks were against it, but their wishes were ignored. We must try to keep the spirit of the antiwar movement alive.

With regard to Iraq, individuals — whether they are leaders of Government, members of Parliament, religious leaders, non-government leaders, or just ordinary citizens — who believe in peace and humanity, can play their own individual part in helping to bring peace and humanity to the people there. We can visit Iraq to find out the facts, to see for ourselves the consequences of war. We can meet Iraqi people, write to them, build friendships with them, and show them that we cared and that we still care. The human contact and the human approach can destroy the propaganda of domination or hate.

I appeal to the people of goodwill from all countries to take part in this offensive of love. I appeal also to those peace-loving people in the United States, whose courage in the face of immense State power, I personally witnessed, to redouble their efforts in making their Government conform with international law in its foreign policy, to continue to stand up for the constitutional and human rights of all people and continue to build a nonviolent, truly humane society. I urge them in particular to continue to reject with all their nonviolent power the Bush Doctrine of Preemption.

Lessons From Northern Ireland

In Northern Ireland, we have learned that one cannot solve deep ethnic/political problems through military or paramilitary or any form of violent or unjust means. These means only result in a vicious cycle of violence. Also the means must be in accord with the ends, so if you want to build a peaceful democratic society, you can only do this through nonviolent means of dialogue and negotiations. This demands even greater courage. It may be slow and laborious but no one gets killed in the process of peace building and reconciliation. This applies no matter where you have violent conflicts. All wars and violent conflicts come to an end and the sooner the better. Today there is a New World consciousness amongst the human family, that we are interconnected, and that there is an alternative to Fight or Flight, that is, nonviolence. We are in a new era.

I believe WAR is dying, There are many reasons for this: our weapons are too dangerous; it's mostly civilians who die; we know of alternative ways to solve these problems; and most of all, deep down in their hearts all peoples know that it is wrong to kill each other. Increasingly people are uniting to say "no more war". More and more people are realising that War is not a good, glorious, noble or patriotic endeavour. It is seen in all its horror and cruelty and viciousness and barbarity. It is, thank God, like Slavery and Racism, passing into the history book.

Conclusion

Although, after the war, people expressed a sense of hopelessness, I myself am very hopeful for the future. I believe we live in an age of tremendous change, when ordinary people are beginning to take up their own responsibility and claim rights not only for themselves, but also for others around the world. There is a deepening awareness of the value of every human being and all of creation, and our need to take care of each other and the earth. This is a time of hope, and each one of us can make a difference by taking a stand for truth and living out our own lives as nonviolently and truthfully as possible. The words of a great American peace activist, Fr. Dan Berrigan, are a challenge to us all: "KNOW WHERE YOU STAND AND STAND THERE".

NOBEL PEACE PRIZE WINNERS: ORGANIZATIONS[1]

Peter Hansen
UNITED NATIONS RELIEF AND WORKS AGENCY, UN 1945

Borned in Aalborg, Denmark, Hansen is the Commissioner-General of United Nations Relief and Works Agency (UNRWA) — a subsidiary organ of the United Nations which co-shared the Nobel Prize with its Secretary-General Kofi Annan in 1945. Hansen is appointed by the UN Secretary-General after consultation with the Advisory Commission and is the only head of a United Nations body to report directly to the General Assembly. With headquarters in Gaza and Amman, UNRWA provides education, health, and relief and social services to some 3.6 million registered Palestine refugees living in Jordan, Lebanon, the Syrian Arab Republic, the West Bank and the Gaza Strip. With some 22,000 employees, mainly locally recruited teachers and health workers, UNRWA is the largest United Nations Agency in terms of staff.

Picking up the Pieces in Gaza[1]

Israel's Demolition Policy

There is a daily grind in Gaza — a grinding of bulldozer gears. The churning of heavy machinery and the crash of concrete on concrete accompany it. Together this is a soundtrack of misery and despair. It is the sound of another family home being demolished.

It is the unfortunate lot of many Palestinians that the loss of their homes to the maws of Israeli military bulldozers or powerful explosive charges is now so commonplace that it fails to make the grade as news. After all, something that happens every day, usually

---

[1] This article, written in the author's personal capacity, appeared in the *International Herald Tribune* on June 23, 2003.

more than once a day, eventually stops being news. But it doesn't stop being terrifying.

At the end of May 2003 a total of 1,134 homes had been demolished by the Israeli military in the Gaza Strip, making almost 10,000 individuals homeless. Unfortunately this is not a policy on the wane. During the first two years of the intifada the average number of homes demolished in Gaza — a statistical category both depressing and surreal — was 32 per month. Since the start of 2003 that average has risen to 72. Disturbingly, the publication of the "road map" to peace has so far had no impact.

Very few of the demolitions target the families of suicide bombers or of those wanted by Israel. Instead the victims are simply people living in the wrong place at the wrong time. Those living near the Egyptian border in Rafah in the south of Gaza have the misfortune of being in a place where Israel feels the need to widen its security zone at the border. Hundreds of homes, dozens of small shops, mosques and communities that once huddled there against the border have been churned into rubble.

In Khan Younis, the residents of a refugee camp who have the bad luck to overlook the Gush Qatif settlement block have similarly had their homes razed. Tanks and bulldozers come in the night. Instructions to evacuate are shouted through loudspeakers and families grab what meager possessions they can before their world comes crashing down. This is repeated over and over again, night after night, with an appalling regularity.

The United Nations, in the form of the UN Relief and Works Agency for Palestine Refugees (UNRWA), tries to pick up the pieces after these demolitions. As the agency responsible for the humanitarian needs of more than 75 percent of Gazans, it immediately supplies tents, blankets, food and drinking water to the newly homeless. If it has the funds, it helps out with rental costs for those refugees — the majority — without the income to cover their new accommodation costs.

And UNRWA picks up the pieces in other ways too. Its schools in Gaza are facing a tidal wave of traumatised children, many of whom have been roused from their beds by the bulldozers or lie awake, fearful that their home will be next. UNRWA now provides trauma counselling in each of its 169 schools for these innocent victims of the intifada.

In the longer term the agency has pledged to provide a new shelter for all of those whose homes have been lost. The costs of such a pledge are staggering — upwards of $21 million is needed just to assist those who have already been affected and more come every day. Furthermore Gaza is already one of the world's most crowded spots. There is precious little available building space — and finding plots that will be safe from any future demolition is proving difficult. So far the agency has been able to erect just 120 new homes — with another 185 under construction.

UNRWA this month issued an appeal to the international community for funds to support its emergency operations in Gaza and the West Bank. Included in that appeal is a request for $21 million to allow for the repair and reconstruction of damaged and destroyed refugee shelters in the Gaza camps. Another $1.1 million is needed in the West Bank.

As necessary as funding for new shelters is, money is not the answer. Israel has legitimate security concerns, and much suffering of its own, but its security is poorly served by a policy that creates fresh anger and despair every day. What is needed is a just and durable peace that will allow the children of Gaza to again sleep soundly at night.

Irene Khan
AMNESTY INTERNATIONAL 1977

Started more than four decades ago, Amnesty International (AI) is a world-wide voluntary activist movement whose members work to prevent violations of human rights.

Open Letter to Belligerents[1]

Amnesty International is fearful that one of the first casualties of any war in Iraq will be human rights. Iraqi civilians, refugees and combatants, all have rights, and as we have seen in recent wars in Kosovo and Afghanistan each of these groups can be abused.

Amnesty International demands a public commitment from your Government that it will abide by the basic and specific measures outlined below:

- Protect civilians by strictly adhering to the rules of international humanitarian law
- Refrain from using indiscriminate weapons
- Treat civilian detainees fairly and humanely
- Protect the rights of combatants
- Ensure the security and humanitarian needs of the Iraqi population are fully met

---

[1] This is an open letter from Irene Khan, Secretary-General of AI, to President George Bush, Prime Minister Tony Blair, Prime Minister José Maria Aznar and President Saddam Hussein, March 19, 2003. For more information please refer to AI's document "People come first: Amnesty International's 10-point appeal to all parties involved in possible military action in Iraq" (AI Index MDE 14/022/2003, March 18, 2003).

- Protect and assist refugees and internally displaced persons
- Make sure that perpetrators of crime are brought to justice under international law
- Commit to using the International Humanitarian Fact-Finding Commission to investigate violations of the Geneva Conventions
- Support and facilitate the deployment of human rights monitors in Iraq as soon as the security situation permits
- Support the UN in their humanitarian and human rights work

Amnesty International is writing to the Governments of the U.S., UK and Spain, who have declared their intention to launch military action against Iraq. AI demands adherence to obligations under international human rights and humanitarian laws in the event of war. Those intending to launch military action against Iraq have a particular responsibility to ensure that international human rights and humanitarian law are fully upheld.

Amnesty International is making the same demand of the government of Iraq which must equally abide by its obligations.

Mary Ellen McNish
AMERICAN FRIENDS SERVICE COMMITTEE
1947

A Quaker organization, the American Friends Service Committee (AFSC) co-won the Nobel Peace prize with Friends Service Council of Great Britain (also a Quaker organization) for their relief efforts after World War I and their assistance to refugees from World War II. McNish is currently the General Secretary.

A Second Moment of Hope

A strangely hopeful moment followed the dreadful attacks of September 11, 2001. The U.S. fractured since the Presidential election of the previous fall united in mourning. An international community alarmed by an increasingly aggressive American foreign policy sent countless messages of support. Nations that have suffered generations of conflict sent their goodwill. It seemed that following the terror of that day there was a moment of grace when divided Americans and a divided world might heal old wounds and move together to work for real security and lasting peace.

Instead, abroad we have seen two wars initiated by the U.S., while at home we have seen our democracy corroded by fear and incendiary rhetoric. The same American public who united to aid survivors of attacks and families of victims has returned to bitter division. A world community that had shown profound sympathy now views Washington as the capital of a rogue state. It is the noon of American arrogance.

Many in Washington have a clear vision of the future that they are working toward. Policies like "preemptive strike" and phrases

113

such as "projecting American power" camouflage a belief that might makes right and that America's greatness is in direct proportion to the amount that the people of the world fear American power.

In the last days of the first Bush Administration, a group of ideologues began to dream of the world as they thought it should be. Their plan, called Project for the New American Century, imagined America as a colossus astride the world. They favored unilateralism over cooperation. They eschewed international law. They believed that no other nation must ever be allowed to approach the United States as a global power. The brazenness of their vision alarmed George Bush, Sr., and during the Clinton Administration, they bided their time. But many found places for themselves in the current administration. And when a bewildered nation asked for answers after the attacks of September 11, their easy answers were readily at hand.

Now after the invasions of Afghanistan and Iraq, many Americans fear that these are only battles in a much larger "war on terrorism". They fear that other countries — some named in President Bush's 2001 "Axis of Evil" speech, and some not — may soon be the next targets of America's new global war. Iran, North Korea, Libya, Colombia and Cuba are seen by the U.S. Government as hostile or problematic. Plans are already underway to deal with them, sometimes openly, sometimes covertly.

The foreign policy implications of the war with Iraq are especially problematic. As bad as the invasion of Afghanistan was, the invasion of Iraq bore only the tiniest element of international legitimacy. While the UN Security Council put up a valiant effort to stop the invasion, after the initial war was over the same Security Council approved a resolution giving the United States and the United Kingdom "blank check" control over an occupied Iraq. The broad and ill-defined powers granted to the U.S. and UK as occupiers set a dire precedent for the way in which occupying powers will regard international conventions in the future.

The resolution passed by the Security Council is breathtaking in its grasp. It gives complete authority to the principal victors for all dimensions of post conflict Iraq, including humanitarian assistance, infrastructure repair, reconstruction, management of Iraq's oil resources, and oversight of both interim and future governmental structures. Finally, the resolution limits the role of the United Nations to symbolic advising and consulting.

All of this is done in the name of security.

But even among these compounded sorrows and outrages, as television has shown us the rubble of a Baghdad eerily reminiscent of lower Manhattan on September 11, there is a second moment of hope. While we have lost the unity of parties and nations that followed America's moment of shock and awe, there is a new unity afoot, perhaps stronger than the first, which was lost to expediency and acquiescence. Millions in the U.S. and tens of millions around the world reached across political and cultural divides to reject this second moment of aggression.

I believe that this was not a passing "antiwar movement" but the beginning of a truly global peace movement. Domestic and global revulsion at the use of naked aggression against a weaker state has created a backlash that may well make the noon of America's arrogance its nadir. Never have there been such strong cries for diplomacy and peacemaking as solutions to conflict.

In the eyes of the children of Iraq we have seen the terrible price paid when a state values power over well-being. In the U.S. people have begun to ask what our own seemingly endless crusade will cost in lives lost and in opportunities denied as resources flow toward the security state. It is no longer only religious leaders and secular visionaries who say that there can be no real peace until the basic economic and social needs of all people are met.

The American Friends Service Committee has been actively engaged in promoting peace and justice since its founding in 1917. At no time in the ensuing nine decades has AFSC's work been more vital than it is right now. With an open invitation to all people who share the Quaker beliefs in the inherent worth of every person, and in the power of love to overcome violence and injustice, AFSC continues to advocate for bold, creative programs that promote peace, justice, and human dignity.

AFSC lifts up a vision counter to the current vision of U.S. foreign policy, a vision that shows that these wars were not necessary. That vision includes:

- Ratification of the International Criminal Court so that wars are increasingly replaced with trials under the rule of law;
- Ratifying international agreements to stop the financing of terrorist groups;
- Limiting the trade in weapons, especially the small arms that fuel regional conflicts around the world;
- Strengthening verification procedures for chemical and biological weapons;
- Abiding by nuclear non-proliferation agreements and working toward nuclear abolition;
- Working to bring a just peace to Israel/Palestine to show that no conflict is intractable.

This is the message of peace as we answer the immediate reality of war. But even these are interim steps. Our vision is larger still.

We need to ask and answer "what are the alternatives to war?" As we know all too well, there are few alternatives once we are already at the brink of conflict. Lasting peace depends on the hard and proactive work of prevention. Our work at the American Friends Service Committee is to take away the occasion for war and to examine our own behavior for the seeds of war. But if we are to finally take away the occasion for war, we must lift up an articulate vision of the world we want.

Pie in the sky wishful thinking? It doesn't have to be. It is that hope, optimism and pragmatic thinking that has fueled AFSC's programs and actions since our inception.

Violent conflict seeks to change a physical reality. As people of love, we commit ourselves to fundamentally change the human heart. The path is arduous, requiring courage equal to that of any warrior. It is a journey of decades and centuries. We remember the words of William Penn, the founder of Pennsylvania, who tells us that, "force may subdue, but Love gains".

We do not face our path with grimness. We do not speak of how harsh necessity dictates our course. Instead, the path itself gives us strength. We draw strength from each person who joins us along the way. We feel ourselves growing into that which has been laid upon us.

We categorically reject a world in which policy is guided by fear of what might be. Instead, we believe that the final victory belongs to Love and that the day of victory will come only when we commit ourselves to living in its Spirit. Love sees possibilities; Love knows that the way will open; Love awaits us at the journey's end.

Brian Phillips, Ph.D.
QUAKER PEACE AND SOCIAL WITNESS 1947

Dr. Phillips is Course Chair and Senior Lecturer in Human Rights Practice for the Centre for Development and Emergency Practice at Oxford Brookes University. He is also a member of the Quaker Peace and Social Witness Central Committee of Britain Yearly Meeting, and was a Joseph Rowntree Quaker Fellow for 2001–2002.

At a Time of Our Own Choosing: A Quaker Reflection on the War in Iraq

It was in early April that one heard the phrase repeated with such frequency that it began to sound like a kind of mantra — *"At a time of our own choosing."* As U.S. troops rolled into Baghdad and British forces gained control of Basra, the words tripped off the tongue of yet another officer, politician or reporter with each and every news bulletin: *"At a time of our own choosing"*. On April 3, Frank Thorp, spokesman for the U.S. Central Command, announced that "coalition forces at this point are outside of the Baghdad airport and are positioning themselves to engage that fight *at a time of our own choice"*.[1] That same day, British Secretary of Defence Geoff Hoon proclaimed that "key suburbs of Basra have now been taken. We will go further into the city *at a time of our own choosing"*.[2]

---

[1] Kathleen Knox, "Iraq: New Push Brings U.S. Troops to Edge of Baghdad," *Radio Free Europe/Radio Liberty*, April 3, 2003.

[2] *Ibid.*

Commenting on the 3rd Infantry Division's entry into the centre of the Iraqi capital on April 5, U.S. Air Force Major General Gene Reuart was clear about the significance of this movement: "I think that the message...is to put a bit of an exclamation point on the fact that coalition troops...do in fact have the ability to come into the city *at places of their choosing*".[3] And by way of explaining the deaths of an estimated 2000 Iraqi combatants in Baghdad that day, U.S. Army Brigadier General Vince Brooks suggested that "it certainly demonstrated our ability to operate within Baghdad *at a time and place of our choosing*".[4] General Brooks's comment appeared in an American Forces Press Service release tellingly headed, "U.S. Forces Drub Baghdad Defenders".

This incantation of superior power, of awesome control, of an unequalled capacity for domination had apparently become near-obligatory as the military campaign reached its climax. There was to be no crude triumphalism in victory, or so we were repeatedly told by our leaders. Yet any sense of genuine humility about the undertaking in Iraq — let alone anything like a deep repentance about the human cost of the venture — was all but overshadowed by these innumerable proclamations of mastery.

The fashion for asserting ultimate, quasi-godlike capability has been a notable rhetorical feature of President Bush's "war on terror". And the particular tag line which became so disturbingly familiar in early April may have its origins in an address made by the President just days after the appalling violence of September 11, 2001. Standing in the pulpit of the National Cathedral in Washington, DC, at a service of prayer and remembrance, President Bush stated that his was a peaceful nation — "but fierce when stirred to anger". He then promised that although "this conflict was begun

---

[3] Jim Garamore, "Infantry Division Takes Drive Through Baghdad," *American Forces Press Service*, April 5, 2003.

[4] Gerry J. Gilmore, "U.S. Forces Drub Baghdad Defenders, WMD Search Continues," *American Forces Press Service*, April 6, 2003.

on the timing and terms of others", it would *"end in a way, and at an hour of our choosing"*.[5]

An Anglican theologian later told me that the real shock of George W. Bush's statement for him wasn't so much that a present-day political leader had uttered these words in a holy space. After all, official blessings upon military campaigns of all sorts were far from uncommon in church history. But what perplexed him most about this particular bellicose sermon had been the relative absence of any serious reflection on the appropriateness of the President's remarks among communities of faith in the days and weeks that followed.[6]

In the wake of the President's cathedral address (and all subsequent assertions of our unrivalled military power), Christians and *all* men and women of faith ought to be asking themselves some very challenging questions indeed. What does it mean that a President of the United States — a committed Christian himself — feels licensed to make such an absolute claim in a house of God? What do such declarations of invincible might mean for God's *sovereignty* in the world — and what do they say about our relationship to Him? Whose power *do* we worship? Who is *really* in control of our lives? How can one reconcile faithful living with an insistence on the ability to act *"at a time of our own choosing"*? In responding to acts of unspeakable violence with further violence calculated to induce "shock and awe", are we not at risk of seeking for ourselves an omnipotence that is the exclusive province of God Himself?

Such questions take us back to the terrible irony at the core of the attacks of September 11 — the fact that those responsible believed wholeheartedly that their actions displayed complete obedience to God. For millions of believers of the Christian, Jewish, Muslim and other faiths, the most monstrous crime perpetrated on

---

[5] George W. Bush, "President's Remarks at National Day of Prayer and Remembrance," September 14, 2001.

[6] Conversation with Simon Barrow, London Mennonite Centre, UK, September 21, 2002.

that day was undoubtedly the usurping of God's power to give and to take life away. This was radical disobedience — by any measure. Such acts of violence can never be service to God, but rather a case of human beings seeking to act as gods themselves. On that day, the hijackers and their accomplices had sought to appropriate for themselves and for their cause the very *sovereignty* of God. This was a kind of idolatry — idolatry of human power, of human agency — cautioned against in all the Abrahamic faiths. And within the Christian tradition, there is no more demanding teacher on this matter than Jesus of Nazareth himself.

Consider the second temptation of Christ during his forty days in the desert. Jesus was led to a towering height — as high as a plane might fly. And what did the Devil offer him? Nothing less than *sovereignty* over all the Kingdoms of the world. Think what a good man like Jesus might have achieved with this gift — with this total control of people, of communities and events? The good that could have been done — the wrongs that might have been righted! And all *"at a time of his own choosing"*. How effective he might have been! And what was Jesus' reply to the offer? "Worship the Lord your God, and serve Him only" (Luke 4:8). Radical obedience. His will — not ours. *Sovereignty* is God's. Usurping that role was not an option — no matter what spectacular benefits might have been there for the taking. What Jesus recognised and acted upon in that moment is what the hijackers failed to comprehend on the 11th of September — what Rowan Williams, the Archbishop of Canterbury, has rightly called "the great lie of religion: the god who fits our agenda".[7]

These questions of God's sovereignty versus a "god of our agenda" — questions of obedience, of power and powerlessness, of servanthood and idolatry — surface again and again at the heart of Jesus' ministry. And they are not just questions for the hijackers of September 11 or for those who would defend them or their actions on the basis of their faith. They are also questions for American and

---

[7] Rowan Williams, *Writing in the Dust: Reflections on 11th September and its Aftermath.* London: Hodder and Stoughton (2001), p. 9.

British Christians — and for the societies we seek to defend. As President Bush's fellow Texan, theologian Stanley Hauerwas, has written:

> Christians believe that the true history of the world, that history that determines our destiny, isn't carried by the nation state. In spite of its powerful moral appeal, this history is the history of godlessness...For what is war but the desire to be rid of God, to claim for ourselves the power to determine our meaning and destiny?[8]

In choosing to deploy overwhelming military might in Afghanistan and in Iraq, our Christian leaders seem to have opted for a vengeful God. This is a vision of God as a kind of miraculous magician — one which the great German theologian, Dietrich Bonhoeffer, had hoped we'd come to reject in the wake of the experience of the Second World War. In its place, Bonhoeffer calls us back to the paradox of the Gospels. He reminds us that Jesus' life and teachings reveal something rather different — that "God lets himself be pushed out of the world on to the cross. He is weak and powerless in the world, and that is precisely the way, the only way, in which he is with us and helps us".[9] Definitely **not** the god of our agenda. Definitely not about fulfilling our need, however wronged we may have been, to react *"at a time of our own choosing"*.

Since the seventeenth century, Quakers have sought to place their faith in the ultimate sovereignty of God, and have maintained a belief in the full equality and value of all human beings created in His image. In Quaker faith and practice, it is always the will of God rather than human will — that perennial temptation to claim our right to act *"at a time of our own choosing"* — which must take precedence. As the British Quaker, Isaac Pennington, wrote in 1661:

---

[8] Stanley Hauerwas , "Should War Be Eliminated?" in *The Hauerwas Reader*, edited by John Berkman and Michael Cartwright. Durham: Duke University Press (2001), p. 421.

[9] Dietrich Bonhoeffer, Letters and Papers from Prison. New York: Touchstone (1953), p. 360.

Give over thy own willing, give over thy own running, give over thine own desiring to know or be anything and sink down to the seed which God sows in the heart, and let that grow in thee and be in thee and breathe in thee and act in thee; and thou shalt find by sweet experience that the Lord knows that and loves and owns that, and will lead it to the inheritance of Life...[10]

Quakers as individual men and women have never been less fallible or less prone to the attractions of power than other human beings. As a community, we make no claim to spiritual perfection or moral spotlessness. But for over 300 years, the Quaker Peace Testimony — our corporate witness against "all outward wars, and strife, and fightings with outward weapons, for any end, or under any pretence whatsoever"[11] — has reminded us of the rigorous demands of Christ's way of nonviolence. This is the Truth by which we aspire to live — the Truth that enables us to know that the "spirit of Christ by which we are guided is not changeable, so as once to command us from a thing as evil, and again to move unto it...".[12]

Devout Christians who see things rather differently, George W. Bush and Tony Blair included, would probably begin to cite the arguments of the just war tradition here — and they would be fully entitled to do so. But regardless of one's understanding of precisely what the Gospel requires of us in this post-September 11 world, there can be no question that even the most reasoned argument for the necessity of military action made by Christian leaders ought to be accompanied by declarations of the most profound regret and a plea for God's forgiveness. The language we use creates our reality — shaping the way in which we think and act in the public space. And the danger is that in making or tolerating shameful boasts about our ability and our right to vanquish our enemy "*at a time of*

---

[10] Isaac Pennington, in *Quaker Faith and Practice*. London: Britain Yearly Meeting (1994), 26.70.

[11] Declaration to Charles II (1660), in *Quaker Faith and Practice*, 24.04.

[12] *Ibid.*

our own choosing" we will come to convince ourselves that our salvation lies in the deployment of our overwhelming strength alone.

In his image-rich appearance on the deck of the USS Abraham Lincoln on May 1, 2003, President Bush closed his speech and the Iraqi campaign with a quotation from the prophet Isaiah. The Commander in Chief told those assembled that in fulfilling the errand on which he had sent them, they had released a captive people from the dark and set them free. President Bush would do well to continue his study of Isaiah's words — recalling also the prophet's caution against the intoxications of military might and the seductions of the easy victory: "Alas for those...who rely on horses, who trust in chariots because they are many and in horsemen because they are very strong, but do not look to the Holy One of Israel or consult the Lord!" (Isaiah 31:7).

At a time when leaders of faith communities around the globe need to be stating ever more boldly that there can be no divine imperative or justification for violence, let us pray that our Christian political and military chiefs will have the grace to turn from the arrogant rhetoric that insists on the primacy of our own will and the indisputable rightness of our actions. Let us turn from the idolatry that worships our own capacity for brute force (however sanitised by high-tech weaponry) and which confuses righteousness with superior means. And let us never fail to remember, as the Quaker William Penn wrote in 1693, that "it is as great presumption to send our passions upon God's errands, as it is to palliate them with God's name...".[13]

---

[13] William Penn, in *Quaker Faith and Practice*, 24.03.

Cora Weiss
INTERNATIONAL PEACE BUREAU 1910

The IPB is recognized as the world's oldest and most comprehensive international peace federation. It brings together people working for peace in many different sectors, not only pacifists but also women's, youth, labour, religious and professional bodies. Weiss is currently the President of both the International Peace Bureau (IPB) and the Hague Appeal for Peace[1], organizations devoted to human rights issues and movements, to sow the seeds for the abolition of war and to make peace a human right.

The International Peace Bureau Seeks a World Without War

The murder of United Nations dedicated international civil servants in Iraq in August and the wounding of dozens more has devastated us. The International Peace Bureau calls for everyone to rededicate ourselves to the force of law, to multilateralism as a method of conducting international relations, to the United Nations as an irreplaceable institution, and to increased participation of organized civil society in the affairs of state. Perhaps this will help to raise the status of nonviolent, legal solutions to conflict over the beat of the drums of war.

---

[1] For those interested to know more, the following are the contact details: the Hague Appeal for Peace, 777 UN Plaza, NYC NY 10017, email: hap@haguepeace.org and website at www.haguepeace.org; the International Peace Bureau, 41, Rue de Zurich, CH-1201 Geneva, Switzerland, email: mailbox@ipb.org and website at http://www.ipb.org.

With humble pride we remind ourselves of the grand award bestowed upon the International Peace Bureau in 1910 and of the responsibility which it bears. The IPB, since 1892, the most comprehensive international peace network, is committed to disarmament[2] and a culture of peace. It was named a laureate, "in the spirit of Alfred Nobel's plan to support, accelerate and promote the peace movement." Thirteen of our officers have been named Nobel peace laureates, including Elie Ducommun, the first Secretary General of the IPB, and to our vice president, Bertha von Suttner (1905) who helped influence Alfred Nobel to include peace among the five prizes his will was to establish.

For over 100 years we have helped to strengthen local and national peace and disarmament organizations by exchanging their information, promoting their needs and demands through a vast international network and coordinating joint campaigns. What they all have in common, and what we are dedicated to achieving is an end to war. For centuries humanity had been engaged in slavery, colonialism and apartheid. They were virtually abolished after great cost to human life. The nature and lethality of weaponry today is such that neither humanity nor the precious planet we live on can survive much more of a beating brought about by war. So, if we could eliminate those once acceptable institutions, why not war?

The devastating consequences of the invasion of Iraq has made it clearer than ever before that the world must never abandon its commitment to international law, the Charter of the United Nations, and to multilateral decision-making.

The most significant achievement of civil society in the buildup to the war in February and March 2003 were the vast demonstrations from millions on the streets of major capitals to a few individuals on street corners holding candles of hope all saying "No War" in Iraq. Those demonstrations served as the conscience for at least six members of the United Nations Security Council

---

[2] The IPB's first Honorary President is Jayantha Dhanapala (Sri Lanka), who is the former UN Undersecretary-General for Disarmament.

who rapidly became known as the "U6", the undecided six, for their refusal to vote to take the world to war.

The International Peace Bureau participated in the mobilization of those demonstrations, encouraging members to take to the streets, to call their elected officials, to flood newspapers with letters, to let everyone know that war would not be legal, nor moral, nor right, nor a solution.

There was never any question in the minds of IPB officials as to the outrageous abuses of human rights perpetrated by Saddam Hussein and his regime. Many countries are guilty of official human rights abuses. With a few exceptions, no matter how egregious, they do not constitute a reason for war. Much as we opposed the possible presence of weapons of mass destruction, we could not support an invasion based on possibility and thus we called for adequate time for the international weapons inspectors to investigate and report. Without an international response consistent with international law, such a presence of prohibited weapons would also not constitute a rationale for war.[3]

IPB encouraged its members to help educate the public on issues of international law. We reminded them of the many years scholars and activists have spent developing alternatives to violence, educating on prevention of violent conflict and on conflict resolution. The methods are available in the same way the weapons inspectors were available. We recognize the importance of building a critical mass of public opinion to persuade governments to follow policies of reason and nonviolence. Never before have so many marched so calmly and passionately to say "No" to war. We did not fail. Not only did the six states refuse to vote for war, but we demonstrated our power, our intelligence, and our ability to be outraged when conditions become outrageous, to ourselves and to the world. The media could not ignore us. The *New York Times*

---

[3] Refer to the book *Armageddon or Brave New World? Reflections on the Hostilities in Iraq*, by C. G. Weeramantry, published by the Weeramantry International Centre for Peace Education and Research, Sri Lanka (2003).

labeled us civil society's organized public opinion, the world's second superpower.

For those who are not pacifists, the issue of going to war became acute when the world entered the nuclear age and nuclear bombs were actually dropped. The United Nations and the atomic age were born at the same time and in a sense have been competing for dominance ever since.

The UN is only as good as its member states. But it has over the past 57 years built a body of law, created a record of experiences and successes, and produced a talented body of experts, demonstrating the capacity for dialogue, for negotiation, for investigation, and for reason. With all its warts, it remains the one hope for humanity to be able to sit together and talk, not fight. Its capacity for success will now depend on an increased role for civil society about which there has been a lot of talk. Clearly governments alone cannot produce and sustain change, nor can international organizations alone. But if we put the power of people together with decent governments and international organizations, and create a new democratic diplomacy, as we call it, we would have a better chance at designing more creative approaches to reach peace and justice for everyone, and a better chance of implementing those ideas.

Unless people whose lives will be affected are at the tables where the fate of humanity is at stake, agreements reached will not succeed in being carried out. It can no longer be acceptable that only the "sides" (the opposing warring parties) reach a peace agreement. Victims, youth, women, teachers, the UN, as well as the sides must work out peace agreements.

Thus, the IPB was one of the four founders of the Hague Appeal for Peace, along with the International Association of Lawyers Against Nuclear Arms, (IALANA), International Physicians for the Prevention of Nuclear War (IPPNW) and the World Federalist Movement. The founders elected me President of the new network which would quickly expand to include thousands of organizations from over a hundred countries. Together we held a conference in May 1999 on the centennial of the 1899 historic first

Hague Peace congress. It was deemed the largest peace conference in history. The purpose was to sow the seeds for the abolition of war and make peace a human right. Out of the conference came a number of campaigns, including one to stop child soldiers; to support the International Criminal Court; to ban land mines; to create an international action network on small arms; and others, including one to promote peace education.

The Hague Appeal for Peace adopted the Global Campaign for Peace Education as its principal program. The International Peace Bureau, active on the Board of the HAP, worked to enlist ministries of education to endorse the Campaign. The Youth Coordinator of the Hague Appeal for Peace worked out of the IPB's Geneva office, demonstrating the close collaboration between the two networks.

Let us look at both the agenda of the IPB and the work of the Hague Appeal for Peace.

The IPB is the oldest peace federation, covering issues from nuclear weapons to small arms, from human rights to peace education. It maintains an extensive electronic list serve to keep its over 200-member organizations equally informed about each others news as well as world events; publishes a regular newsletter and a practical handbook, "From War to Peace", based on an analysis of nine different conflicts. "Peace is Possible" provides 35 accounts of positive success in peacemaking.

The IPB awards an annual Sean MacBride[4] Prize to the individual or organization that best exemplifies the life and contributions of the great Irish peace and human rights statesman, himself a laureate. The 2003 MacBride Prize went to the Japanese Hibakushas' Nihon Hidankyo Organization, whose few remaining survivors are unrelenting in reminding the world of the danger of nuclear weapons. Recent previous recipients include: the U.S. Member of Congress, Barbara Lee, (D.CA) for her sole vote against the bombing of Afghanistan (2002); Rosalie Bertell of Canada's International Institute of Public Health for her work on the effects

---

[4] Sean MacBride was IPB's president from 1974 to 1985.

of nuclear radiation to health (2001) and to Praful Bidwai and Achin Vanaik, Indian journalists writing against the nuclearization of South Asia (2000). Ireland's John Hume (Nobel Peace Prize, 1998), and the Mayor of Tuzla, Bosnia, were also prize winners.

International meetings and conferences organized by the IPB and which were scheduled for Athens, October 23–26, 2003, and for Barcelona as part of Barcelona Forum '04, from 23–27 June 04, entitled "Towards a World Without Violence", offer opportunities for member organizations and the public to bring their power to bear on the continuing critical struggle to reduce violence, accelerate disarmament, and create a culture of peace.

The IPB has decided to concentrate one part of its work on the human security approach. When we put people and their basic needs at the center of our concerns we can more easily understand the root causes of violence and apply our experience to its prevention. There is now a Commission on Human Security (CHS)[5] co-chaired by Mrs. Sadako Ogata (former UN High Commissioner for Refugees) and Prof. Amartya Sen (Nobel laureate in Economics, 1998 and Master of Trinity College, Cambridge), as well as a Network of countries devoted to Human Security. Now, if civil society organizations begin to promote the needs of people for clean water, jobs, literacy, participation in decision making, etc., all of which are readily fundable and doable, maybe we can begin to refocus our priorities

---

[5] Adversities such as conflict, poverty, infectious diseases and human rights violations threaten the survival and dignity of millions of people today. Communities and individuals are unevenly affected by the challenges of globalization. These problems are not adequately addressed by conventional approaches alone. The UN Secretary-General has called the world community to advance the twin goals of "freedom from want" and "freedom from fear". A new human-centered approach has to be developed if these issues are to be addressed in an effective and comprehensive way.

As a contribution to this effort and inspired by the UN Secretary-General's call at the 2000 Millennium Summit, the Commission on Human Security (CHS) was established in January, 2001, with the initiative of the Government of Japan. It benefits from the participation of ten distinguished Commissioners from around the world. Members of the Human Security Network include Austria, Canada, Chile, Greece, Ireland, Jordan, Mali, The Netherlands, Norway, Slovenia, South Africa (as an observer), Switzerland and Thailand.

and reduce bloated military budgets to make resources available for human needs. This is not rhetoric. Human security will not eliminate the insatiable appetite of those in power for more power, but it very well may reduce the willingness of ordinary people to go along with military adventures. It may demonstrate to law makers that people who are in good health, and contribute to the productivity of their national economies, are less apt to fall into fundamentalist misadventures. It is true that the men who took over the planes that were turned into bombs and destroyed the World Trade Center on September 11th, were well educated and middle class. Were they exceptions to this analysis? Perhaps we also need a world committed to the rule of law; where nations do not impose their will on other nations, and where militarism is rejected as a way of life and a solution to problems. Dreams? Nothing happens unless there is first a dream, said our great poet, Carl Sandburg. And even the Irish poet, W. Butler Yeats thought that "In dreams begins responsibility". The presence and potential use of omnicidal weaponry makes it all the more urgent for thoughtful people to promote and insist on nonmilitary solutions to conflict.

Toward this end, the IPB has joined with the Hague Appeal for Peace to urge national ministries of education to incorporate and integrate peace education into their school systems as a means of preparing young people for participatory democracy and offering alternatives to violent behavior.

Teachers, parent and grandparents are faced with a huge challenge. Do we teach our children to make money or to make a difference? Does teaching for testing allow any space to encourage young people to ask, "Why? Why are there foreign troops in Iraq?" or "Why did the U.S. and the UK invade Iraq if the Security Council did not authorize such an action?"

Ariel Dorfman, the great playwright and a survivor of Pinochet's Chile, speaks of the "secret education" children get from cartoons and movies. The role of the media is of considerable concern. How will children learn about the values and beliefs of Muslims, Christians, Jews, Shiites or Buddhists when the press thinks of all terrorists as Arabs and Muslims?

While many schools teach conflict resolution and promote nonviolence for the classroom and the home, they do not apply this to the world. Young people are no longer just born into their family, or village: they are born into the world. They see that children are child soldiers and are told that countries invade each other with little objection. We teach children to obey laws, not to walk against the red light, or smoke in school, yet they see law breaking by the very governments they are asked to respect.

We hope to educate young people to put the institution of war on the table for de legitimation, for abolition, just as generations before us looked at the cost of slavery, colonialism and apartheid and passed laws to make it illegal to own a slave or discriminate on the basis of color.

Barbara Erenreich reminds us that wars create warlike societies, that fighting abroad camouflages social and economic ills at home. "The only way to abolish war is to make peace heroic," said the great educator, John Dewey. And heroes have been plenty, especially when recognized with the Nobel Peace Prize, including Martin Luther King, Jr. who said, "Through violence you can murder a murderer, but you cannot murder murder; Through violence you may murder a hater, but you cannot murder hate; Darkness cannot put out darkness, only light can do that." So, too, we cannot respond to terrorism with terror. We need to study and remove the conditions that give rise to fundamentalist behavior and to terrorism.

We believe that we need to help our young people learn to dream, to imagine a world without war. We can nurture compassion, imagination and insight. We believe that the safety of our children's future depends on how much we, as teachers in the family, the classroom, or the community can infuse into our work the values of democracy, of cooperation, of disarmament, human rights, respect for law, and for gender equality. We can teach our children to respect and care for our fragile environment and to study alternatives to violence. We can teach the importance of a strengthened United Nations, of the skills of negotiation. We can teach human security, not national security.

Perhaps most important for a future of peace and reconciliation is a new approach to reaching peace agreements. Traditionally, the "sides" have been at the peace table following violent conflict. We propose that negotiating tables must now include the people whose lives will be affected by the peace agreement, who will be responsible for implementing the agreement. Thus, not only should the warring factions be represented, but victims, youth, women, teachers, and significant civil society elders. Teachers will have to teach about the war and the agreement reached. Peace Education should be part of peace agreements, required for every school and community following violence. If there are no women present, there can be no peace. And one woman does not represent women in general. We have an extraordinary opportunity to create a model peace table to resolve the North Korean issue and to promote reunification with South Korea as well as a nuclear free North East Asia. This parallel peace table can play a significant role in influencing the "official" negotiations. One day, our model table, which will be inclusive of civil society, will become the norm.

Until then, we need to prevent the world from "slipping deeper into a thick cover of dark clouds that they fear at any minute could become mushroom clouds spilling black rain", if we do not abolish nuclear weapons and war, as Hiroshima's Mayor, Tadatoshi Akiba declared on the 58th anniversary of the bombing of his city, August 6, 2003.

Christian Dominicé
INSTITUTE OF INTERNATIONAL LAW 1904

Emeritus of the University of Geneva, Prof. Dominicé is the Secretary-General of the Institut de Droit International (Institute of International Law). Founded in 1873 in Ghent by international jurists, the organization — made up of the best international legal talents of the world — attempts to "formulate the general principles of the science of international law 'in a way to respond to the juridical conscience of the civilized world'". Both the League of Nations and the United Nations have considered its proposals on critical issues such as extradition, human rights law and the problems of pollution of international waters and of the air.

Some Legal Aspects of the Military Operation in Iraq[1]

For international lawyers, it is evident that the military operation in Iraq gives rise to fundamental questions concerning the rules regulating peace and security.

Being an exclusively learned society, the Institute of International Law has, as its purpose, to promote the progress of international law.

If international law is seen — and indeed it is — as a necessary set of rules to maintain order and justice in international relations, particularly within a society basically composed of states and some other groups or entities, then the regulation of the use of military force takes a paramount importance and lies at the root of the international legal system.

---

[1] The present article, written in July 2003, expresses the personal opinion of its author and not that of the Institute.

The regulation of the use of force in international law includes the scope of the right to resort to force (*ius ad bellum* or *ius contra bellum*) and the rules governing the military operations (*ius in bello*), in other words, the law of armed conflicts. The law of armed conflicts stipulates permitted and prohibited means of warfare, regulates military occupations of territories, etc.

In the case of Iraq, three main sets of questions ought to be considered. First, the question of the legality of the invasion of Iraq; second, the question of the respect of the law of armed conflicts, particularly the rules of international humanitarian law during the military operation; and third, the various questions arising in the context of the lasting occupation of the territory — and, consequently, the population — of Iraq.

The present article deals only with the first question: the legality of the military attack, by U.S. and UK military forces, against Iraq, starting on March 21st 2003, and terminating at the end of April with a total conquest.

The right to resort to force is regulated since 1945 by the Charter of the United Nations (Article 2, para. 4):

> "All Members shall refrain in their international relations from the threat or use of force against the territorial integrity or political independence of any State, or in any other manner inconsistent with the Purposes of the United Nations."

It is now admitted that this prohibition of the use of force has become a rule of customary international law. However, it is well recognized that two important exceptions do exist and must be taken into consideration. The first exception is self-defense, as provided for by Article 51 of the UN Charter. The second exception to the prohibition of the use of force is an authorization by the Security Council.

To answer the question of the legality of the attack against Iraq, it must first be examined if it meets the requirements of one of those exceptions. Since other arguments have also been put forward, they must also be considered.

The "inherent right of individual or collective self-defense" in the meaning of Article 51 of the UN Charter is actually conferred to the victim of an "armed attack". Without such an attack, there is no right of self-defense.

In the Iraqi situation, there was manifestly no armed attack against the United States, or even one of its allies. Article 51 of the Charter was not a legal basis for the invasion of Iraq. However, some attempts have been made to give an extensive interpretation of that provision. It is argued that a serious threat of an attack may be a case of self-defense.

It must be stressed that such an interpretation cannot be accepted. It has not been confirmed by practice, and even in the doctrine only isolated voices can be found supporting it. Furthermore, it would be a very dangerous course to take. Self-defense is a unilateral reaction — at least until the Security Council takes action. That reaction would depend upon a unilateral decision made by the State "threatened". This could be the pretext for arbitrary intervention.

Such a line of reasoning — preventive self-defense as it has been argued — must be rejected without hesitation. One can add that in the case of Iraq, even if such a doctrine would have been applicable, the war was illegal. It cannot be contended that the threat of an armed attack was real and imminent. Against the United States? Against one of its allies (but a request for help would have been needed)? No sign of such a threat has been found.

The first exception to the prohibition of the use of force — self-defense — is no justification for the invasion of Iraq.

The use of force can be legal under international law if it is authorized by the Security Council. According to the Charter, when the Security Council determined "the existence of any threat to the peace, breach of the peace, or act of aggression ..." (Article 39), it can take various types of measures.

According to Chapter VII of the Charter, those measures include military action (Article 42) by the Security Council itself. It was supposed that some military forces would be made available to it, according to agreements which were to be concluded (Article 43 of the Charter). This, however, never occurred. The substitute which has been found is a kind of a delegation. The Security Council may authorize Member States to resort to military forces in specific circumstances. That practice was inaugurated on the occasion of the invasion of Kuwait by Iraq (1990). In order to liberate that country, States were authorized to use "all necessary means" (Resolution 678), which clearly included military action. That is a procedure which, since then, has been resorted to by the Security Council in various cases.

As to Iraq, the United States attempted, particularly during the first months of 2003, to convince the Members of the Security Council to adopt a Resolution authorizing the use of force against Iraq, but without success. The main opponents, France, Germany, and Russia, argued that the disarmament of Iraq was to be achieved through the work of UN inspectors, as stipulated by CS Resolution 1441 (2001). Without an expressed authorization by the Security Council, the invasion of Iraq was manifestedly contrary to the Charter, hence illegal. However, it has been argued that an implied authorization could be deduced from previous CS Resolutions.

For example, Resolution 1441, which has been so much discussed, was invoked. It is a text which, *inter alia*, decides that Iraq "has been and remains in material breach of its obligations under relevant resolutions, including resolution 687 (1991), in particular through Iraq's failure to cooperate with United Nations inspectors and the IAEA [International Atomic Energy Agency] ...". It imposes on Iraq various obligations concerning inspections and cooperation with UN inspectors. It then concludes with the paragraph: "Recalls, in that context, that the Council has repeatedly warned Iraq that it will face serious consequences as a result of its continued violations of its obligations".

Neither the decision that Iraq is in material breach of its obligation, nor the warning at the end of the Resolution, can really be considered as constituting an authorization given to any Member State to go to war against Iraq. Resolution 1441 is no argument. The "serious consequences" are measures to be decided by the Security Council.

It has also been attempted, but with no convincing force, to argue that Resolution 678 (1990), which authorized the use of force to restore Kuwait's Sovereignty, or Resolution 687 (1991), which imposed a set of obligations on Iraq — with its agreement — afforded a legal basis for the war against Iraq. The purpose for which the use of force had been authorized by the first one had been achieved in 1991, and the second one did not authorize the use of force against Iraq.

Our conclusion is that the invasion of Iraq was not justified by either of the two exceptions to the prohibition of the use of force. It was illegal.

It has been suggested that the Charter can be reinterpreted by subsequent practice. This is true to some extent, provided there is consensus.

Concerning Chapter VII, the idea is that specific facts or circumstances should be considered as threat to the peace sufficient to justify the use of force. The examples given are grave and systematic violations of human rights in a country, or evidence of clear intentions to aggress other nations, or perhaps also the possession of weapons of mass destruction.

It is now admitted, and confirmed by practice, that the Security Council has a rather broad discretionary power when interpreting Article 39 of the Charter. It has already decided that some types of internal situations constitute a "threat to the peace". It is a pragmatic approach, which can take into consideration situations such as those described above. However, it is clear that there must be a determination by the Security Council, and that it is the only body entitled to take measures following such a determination. A unilateral determination that there exists a threat to the peace, not to speak of unilaterally decided military actions, is a totally unacceptable procedure.

The unilateral and illegal military invasion of Iraq by the so-called coalition, is a challenge for the system of collective security instituted by the Charter of the United Nations. Some commentators have even concluded that the system has broken down and that the world, the international society, is entering a new era, the era of unilateralism with one dominant Power.

Whether that is true or not, it is perhaps too early to determine. At the present stage, some remarks and questions come to everybody's mind.

As demonstrated by practice since the United Nations Charter is in force, it is not the first time that the prohibition of the use of force (Article 2, para. 4) is violated. Many cases of illegal use of force have actually occurred, and the system has survived.

What can be considered as new in the Iraqi case, is the amplitude and the nature of the invasion. It resulted in the total conquest of a large sovereign country with more than 20 million people. This is quite different from another important transgression of the Charter, the British and French military operation in 1956 on the Suez Canal. In that case, the operation was stopped by the firm common attitude of the United States and the Soviet Union.

However, in the opinion of the present author, a final appraisal cannot be made, and definitive conclusions may not be drawn, until the eventual outcome of the Iraqi adventure is known. The military victory was the easiest part of the operation, and the main problems, which do not seem to have been seriously envisaged in Washington, are still to come.

Nobody can tell precisely how the situation will evolve over the next months or years. Some indications can be found in history and in the analysis of the nature and objective of the invasion of Iraq.

In historical and geo-political perspective, the invasion and conquest of Iraq, whatever the pretexts or alibis, appears as a new and modern form of colonial expansion. A massive and evident military superiority is used to take control over the resources of a foreign country, the oil factor being decisive. Furthermore, some evident strategic interests are at stake.

It is different from the old forms of colonialism. There is no acquisition of territory or title of sovereignty. Administration of the country, possibly through local authorities, and free disposal of the oil resources are the main characteristics, and they cannot be maintained without military occupation.

This is the point where the lessons of the past may be of some interest. No population having a normal feeling of dignity and of national identity can accept a colonial or colonial-type foreign domination. Resistance, violent actions, even movements of national liberation, are likely to become part of life. The American people is for sure well aware of this, remembering the historical circumstances of the independence of the United States. Such an analysis may be wrong. But, if it is right, it means that the postwar situation, as it is since May 2003, will not last for very long. But what else is there to consider?

The United States — and Britain — could of course retreat from Iraq. This is not likely to occur. It would signify that unilateralism does not necessarily succeed. Thus the value of the collective system of the Charter would be indirectly strengthened.

If an enlarged multilateral military alliance or coalition, but with the United States having the predominant role, takes over the administration of Iraq, there will not be much change. It will still be resented as a foreign occupation.

On the other hand, if the power to administer Iraq is fully entrusted to the United Nations, with a clear indication that it is temporary and that Iraq's sovereignty must be restored, then this outcome could be seen as a recognition of the indispensable role of the United Nations. It could be interpreted as a sign that the collective security system, whatever its weakness and shortcomings, still has its value and must be respected.

It is too early to know if it is right or wrong to predict that the UN system is dead. We can hope that it will survive. There are some good reasons to expect such an evolution, provided the Member States are aware of their responsibilities for the international order.

PART II

CONTRIBUTIONS FROM
EMINENT SCHOLARS

Wars of Terror[1]

Noam Chomsky

A renowned Professor of Linguistics at Massachusetts Institute of Technology and one of America's most prominent political dissidents, Prof. Chomsky has authored over 30 political books dissecting issues such as U.S. interventionism in the developing world, the political economy of human rights and the propaganda role of corporate media.

It is widely argued that the September 11 terrorist attacks have change the world dramatically, that nothing will be the same as the world enters into a new and frightening "age of terror" — the title of a collection of academic essays by Yale University scholars and others, which regards the anthrax attack as even more ominous.[2]

It had been recognized for some time that with new technology, the industrial powers would probably lose their virtual monopoly of violence, retaining only an enormous preponderance. Well before 9/11, technical studies had concluded that "a well-planned operation to smuggle WMD (weapons of mass destruction) into the United States would have at least a 90 percent probability of success — much higher than ICBM delivery even in the absence of [National Missile Defense]." That has become "America's Achilles Heel", a study with that title concluded several years ago. Surely the dangers were evident after the 1993 attempt to blow up

---

[1] This article is a reprint from *New Political Science*, Vol. 25, No. 1, 2003.

[2] Strobe Talbott and Nayan Chanda (eds.), *The Age of Terror*. New York: Basic Books (2001). The editors write that with the anthrax attacks, which they attribute to bin Laden, "anxiety became a certainty".

the World Trade Center, which came close to succeeding along with much more ambitious plans, and might have killed tens of thousands of people with better planning, the WTC building engineers reported.[3]

On September 11, the threats were realized: with "wickedness and awesome cruelty", to recall Robert Fisk's memorable words, capturing the world reaction of shock and horror, and sympathy for the innocent victims. For the first time in modern history, Europe and its offshoots were subjected, on home soil, to atrocities of the kind that are all too familiar elsewhere. The history should be unnecessary to review, and though the West may choose to disregard it, the victims do not. The sharp break in the traditional pattern surely qualifies 9/11 as an historic event, and the repercussions are sure to be significant. The consequences will, of course, be determined substantially by policy choices made within the United States. In this case, the target of the terrorist attack is not Cuba or Lebanon or Chechnya or a long list of others, but a state with an awesome potential for shaping the future. Any sensible attempt to assess the likely consequences will naturally begin with an investigation of U.S. power, how it has been exercised, particularly in the very recent past, and how it is interpreted within the political culture.

At this point there are two choices: we can approach these questions with the rational standards we apply to others, or we can dismiss the historical and contemporary record on some grounds or other.

One familiar device is miraculous conversion: true, there have been flaws in the past, but they have now been overcome so we can

---

[3] Study cited by Charles Glaser and Steve Fetter, "National Missile Defense and the Future of U.S. Nuclear Weapons Policy," *International Security* 261 (2001). Richard Falkenrath, Robert Newman and Bradley Thayer, *America's Achilles Heel: Nuclear, Biological and Chemical Terrorism and Covert Attack*. Cambridge, MA: MIT Press (1998). Barton Gellman, "Broad Effort Launched after '98 Attacks," *Washington Post*, December 20, 2001. ISSN 0739-3148 print/ISSN 1469-9931 online/03/010113–15 ÆÉ 2003 Caucus for a New Political Science DOI: 10.1080/0739314032000071253.

forget those boring and now-irrelevant topics and march on to a bright future. This useful doctrine of "change of course" has been invoked frequently over the years, in ways that are instructive when we look closely. To take a current example, a few months ago Bill Clinton attended the independence day celebration of the world's newest country, East Timor. He informed the press that "I don't believe America and any of the other countries were sufficiently sensitive in the beginning ... and for a long time before 1999, going way back to the '70s, to the suffering of the people of East Timor", but "when it became obvious to me what was really going on ... I tried to make sure we had the right policy".

We can identify the timing of the conversion with some precision. Clearly, it was after September 8, 1999, when the Secretary of Defense reiterated the official position that "it is the responsibility of the Government of Indonesia, and we don't want to take that responsibility away from them". They had fulfilled their responsibility by killing hundreds of thousands of people with firm U.S. and British support since the 1970s, then thousands more in the early months of 1999, finally destroying most of the country and driving out the population when they voted the wrong way in the August 30 referendum — fulfilling not only their responsibilities but also their promises, as Washington and London surely had known well before.

The U.S. "never tried to sanction or support the oppression of the East Timorese," Clinton explained, referring to the 25 years of crucial military and diplomatic support for Indonesian atrocities, continuing through the last paroxysm of fury in September. But we should not "look backward," he advised, because America did finally become sensitive to the "oppression" sometime between September 8 and September 11, when, under severe domestic and international pressure, Clinton informed the Indonesian generals that the game is over and they quickly withdrew, allowing an Australian-led UN peacekeeping force to enter unopposed.

The course of events revealed with great clarity how some of the worst crimes of the late 20th century could have been ended very easily, simply by withdrawing crucial participation. That is hardly the only case, and Clinton was not alone in his interpretation of what scholarship now depicts as another inspiring achievement of the new era of humanitarianism.[4]

There is a new and highly regarded literary genre inquiring into the cultural defects that keep us from responding properly to the crimes of others.

An interesting question no doubt, though by any reasonable standards it ranks well below a different one: why do we and our allies persist in our own substantial crimes, either directly or through crucial support for murderous clients? That remains unasked, and if raised at the margins, arouses shivers of horror.

Another familiar way to evade rational standards is to dismiss the historical record as merely "the abuse of reality", not "reality itself", which is "the unachieved national purpose". In this version of the traditional "city on a hill" conception, formulated by the founder of realist IR (International Relations) theory, America has a "transcendent purpose", "the establishment of equality in freedom", and American politics is designed to achieve this "national purpose", however flawed it may be in execution. In a current version, published shortly before 9/11 by a prominent scholar, there is a guiding principle that "defines the parameters within which the policy debate occurs", a spectrum that excludes only "tattered remnants" on the right and left and is "so authoritative as to be virtually immune to challenge". The principle is that America is an "historical vanguard". "History has a discernible direction and destination. Uniquely among all the nations of the world, the United States comprehends and manifests history's purpose". It follows that U.S. "hegemony" is the realization of history's purpose

---

[4] Joseph Nevins, "First the Butchery, Then the Flowers: Clinton and Holbrooke in East Timor," *Counterpunch*, May 16–31, 2002. On the background, see Richard Tanter, Mark Selden and Stephen Shalom (eds.), *Bitter Flowers. Sweet Flowers: East Timor, Indonesia, and the World Community*. Lanham, MD: Rowman & Littlefield (2001); Chomsky, *A New Generation Draws the Line*. London, New York: Verso (2001).

and its application is therefore for the common good, a truism that renders empirical evaluation irrelevant.[5]

That stance too has a distinguished pedigree. A century before Rumsfeld and Cheney, Woodrow Wilson called for conquest of the Philippines because "[o]ur interest must march forward, altruists though we are; other nations must see to it that they stand off, and do not seek to stay us". And he was borrowing from admired sources, among them John Stuart Mill in a remarkable essay.[6] That is one choice. The other is to understand "reality" as reality, and to ask whether its unpleasant features are "flaws" in the pursuit of history's purpose or have more mundane causes, as in the case of every other power system of past and present. If we adopt that stance, joining the tattered remnants outside the authoritative spectrum, we will be led to conclude, I think, that policy choices are likely to remain within a framework that is well entrenched, enhanced perhaps in important ways but not fundamentally changed: much as after the collapse of the USSR, I believe. There are a number of reasons to anticipate essential continuity, among them the stability of the basic institutions in which policy decisions are rooted, but also narrower ones that merit some attention.

The "war on terror" re-declared on 9/11 had been declared 20 years earlier, with much the same rhetoric and many of the same people in high-level positions.[7] The Reagan administration came into office announcing that a primary concern of U.S. foreign policy

---

[5] Hans Morgenthau, *The Purpose of American Politics*. New York: Vintage (1964); Andrew Bacevich, "Different Drummers, Same Drum," *National Interest*, Summer 2001. Greatly to his credit, Morgenthau took the highly unusual step of abandoning this conventional stance, forcefully, in the early days of the Vietnam War.

[6] Wilson, "Democracy and Efficiency," *Atlantic Monthly*, 1901, cited by Ido Oren, *Our Enemies and Us: America's Rivalries and the Making of Political Science*. Ithaca, NY: Cornell University Press (2002). For some discussion of Mill's classic essay on intervention, see my *Peering into the Abyss of the Future*. Delhi: Institute of Social Sciences (2002, Fifth Lakdawala Memorial Lecture).

[7] For further detail on the first phase of the "war on terror", and sources here and below, see Alexander George (ed.), *Western State Terrorism*. Cambridge, UK: Polity—Blackwell (1991), and sources cited.

would be a "war on terror", particularly state-supported international terrorism, the most virulent form of the plague spread by "depraved opponents of civilization itself" in "a return to barbarism in the modern age", in the words of the Administration moderate George Shultz. The war to eradicate the plague was to focus on two regions where it was raging with unusual virulence: Central America and West Asia/North Africa. Shultz was particularly exercised by the "cancer, right here in our land mass", which was openly renewing the goals of Hitler's Mein Kampf, he informed Congress. The President declared a national emergency, renewed annually, because "the policies and actions of the Government of Nicaragua constitute an unusual and extraordinary threat to the national security and foreign policy of the United States". Explaining the bombing of Libya, Reagan announced that the mad dog Qaddafi was sending arms and advisers to Nicaragua "to bring his war home to the United States", part of the campaign "to expel America from the world", Reagan lamented. Scholarship has explored still deeper roots for that ambitious enterprise. One prominent academic terrorologist finds that contemporary terrorism can be traced to South Vietnam, where "the effectiveness of Vietcong terror against the American Goliath armed with modern technology kindled hopes that the Western heartland was vulnerable too".[8]

More ominous still, by the 1980s, was the swamp from which the plague was spreading. It was drained just in time by the U.S. army, which helped to "defeat liberation theology", the School of the Americas now proclaims with pride.[9] In the second locus of the war, the threat was no less dreadful: Mideast/Mediterranean terror was selected as the peak story of the year in 1985 in the annual AP poll of editors, and ranked high in others. As the worst year of terror ended, Reagan and Israeli Prime Minister Peres condemned "the evil scourge of terrorism" in a news conference in Washington.

[8] David Rapoport, "The Fourth Wave," *Current History*, December 2001.
[9] 999, cited by Adam Isacson and Joy Olson, *Just the Facts*. Washington, DC: Latin America Working Group and Center for International Policy (1999), p. ix.

A few days before Peres had sent his bombers to Tunis, where they killed 75 people on no credible pretext, a mission expedited by Washington and praised by Secretary of State Shultz, though he chose silence after the Security Council condemned the attack as an "act of armed aggression" (U.S. abstaining). That was only one of the contenders for the prize of major terrorist atrocity in the peak year of terror. A second was a carbomb outside a mosque in Beirut that killed 80 people and wounded 250 others, timed to explode as people were leaving, killing mostly women and girls, traced back to the CIA and British intelligence. The third contender is Peres's Iron Fist operations in southern Lebanon, fought against "terrorist villagers," the high command explained, and "reaching new depths of calculated brutality and arbitrary murder," according to a Western diplomat familiar with the area, a judgment amply supported by direct coverage.

Scholarship too recognizes 1985 to be a peak year of Middle East terrorism, but does not cite these events, but rather, two terrorist atrocities in which a single person was murdered, in each case an American.[10] But the victims do not so easily forget.

Shultz demanded resort to violence to destroy "the evil scourge of terrorism", particularly in Central America. He bitterly condemned advocates of "utopian, legalistic means like outside mediation, the United Nations, and the World Court, while ignoring the power element of the equation". His administration succumbed to no such weaknesses, and should be praised for its foresight by sober scholars who now explain that international law and institutions of world order must be swept aside by the enlightened hegemon, in a new era of dedication to human rights.

In both regions of primary concern, the commanders of the "war on terror" compiled a record of "state-supported international terrorism" that vastly exceeded anything that could be attributed to their targets. And that hardly exhausts the record. During the Reagan years Washington's South African ally had primary responsibility for over 1.5 million dead and $60 billion in damage in

---

[10] See *Current History*, op. cit.

neighboring countries, while the administration found ways to evade congressional sanctions and substantially increase trade. A UNICEF study estimated the death toll of infants and young children at 850,000, with 150,000 in the single year 1988, reversing gains of the early post-independence years primarily by the weapon of "mass terrorism". That is putting aside South Africa's practices within, where it was defending civilization against the onslaughts of the ANC, one of the "more notorious terrorist groups", according to a 1988 Pentagon report.[11]

For such reasons the U.S. and Israel voted alone against a 1987 UN resolution condemning terrorism in the strongest terms and calling on all nations to combat the plague, passed 153–2, with Honduras abstaining. The two opponents identified the offending passage: it recognized "the right to self-determination, freedom, and independence, as derived from the Charter of the United Nations, of people forcibly deprived of that right ... particularly peoples under colonial and racist regimes and foreign occupation" — understood to refer to South Africa and the Israeli-occupied territories, therefore unacceptable.

The base for U.S. operations in Central America was Honduras, where the U.S. Ambassador during the worst years of terror was John Negroponte, who is now in charge of the diplomatic component of the new phase of the "war on terror" at the UN. Reagan's special envoy to the Middle East was Donald Rumsfeld, who now presides over its military component, as well as the new wars that have been announced.

Rumsfeld is joined by others who were prominent figures in the Reagan administration. Their thinking and goals have not changed,

---

[11] 1980–1988 record; see "Inter-Agency Task Force, Africa Recovery Program/ Economic Commission," in *South African Destabilization: The Economic Cost of Frontline Resistance to Apartheid*. New York: UN (1989), p. 13, cited by Merle Bowen, Fletcher Forum, Winter 1991. *Children on the Front Line*. New York and Geneva: UNICEF (1989). ANC, Joseba Zulaika and William Douglass, *Terror and Taboo*. New York and London: Routledge (1996), p. 12. On expansion of U.S. trade with South Africa after Congress authorized sanctions in 1985 (overriding Reagan's veto), see Gay McDougall and Richard Knight, in Robert Edgar (ed.), *Sanctioning Apartheid*. Trenton, NJ: Africa World Press (1990).

and although they may represent an extreme position on the policy spectrum, it is worth bearing in mind that they are by no means isolated. There is considerable continuity of doctrine, assumptions, and actions, persisting for many years until today. Careful investigation of this very recent history should be a particularly high priority for those who hold that "global security" requires "a respected and legitimate law-enforcer", in Brzezinski's words. He is referring of course to the sole power capable of undertaking this critical role: "the idealistic new world bent on ending inhumanity", as the world's leading newspaper describes it, dedicated to "principles and values" rather than crass and narrow ends, mobilizing its reluctant allies to join it in a new epoch of moral rectitude.[12]

The concept "respected and legitimate law-enforcer" is an important one. The term "legitimate" begs the question, so we can drop it. Perhaps some question arises about the respect for law of the chosen "law-enforcer", and about its reputation outside of narrow elite circles. But such questions aside, the concept again reflects the emerging doctrine that we must discard the efforts of the past century to construct an international order in which the powerful are not free to resort to violence at will. Instead, we must institute a new principle — which is in fact a venerable principle: the self-anointed "enlightened states" will serve as global enforcers, no impolite questions asked.

The scrupulous avoidance of the events of the recent past is easy to understand, given what inquiry will quickly reveal. That includes not only the terrorist crimes of the 1980s and what came before, but also those of the 1990s, right to the present. A comparison of leading beneficiaries of U.S. military assistance and the record of state terror should shame honest people, and would, if it were not so effectively removed from the public eye. It suffices to look at the two countries that have been vying for leadership in this competition: Turkey and Colombia. As a personal aside I happened to visit both recently,

---

[12] Zbigniew Brzezinski, "If We Fight, It Must Be in a Way to Legitimize Global U.S. Role," *Guardian Weekly*, August 22–28, 2002. Michael Wines, "The World: Double Vision; Two Views of Inhumanity Split the World, Even in Victory," *New York Times*, June 13, 1999.

including scenes of some of the worst crimes of the 1990s, adding
some vivid personal experience to what is horrifying enough in the
printed record. I am putting aside Israel and Egypt, a separate
category.

To repeat the obvious, we basically have two choices. Either
history is bunk, including current history, and we can march forward
with confidence that the global enforcer will drive evil from the
world much as the President's speech writers declare, plagiarizing
ancient epics and children's tales. Or we can subject the doctrines
of the proclaimed grand new era to scrutiny, drawing rational
conclusions, perhaps gaining some sense of the emerging reality. If
there is a third way, I do not see it.

The wars that are contemplated in the renewed "war on terror"
are to go on for a long time. "There's no telling how many wars
it will take to secure freedom in the homeland," the President
announced. That's fair enough. Potential threats are virtually limit-
less, everywhere, even at home, as the anthrax attack illustrates. We
should also be able to appreciate recent comments on the matter by
the 1996–2000 head of Israel's General Security Service (Shabak),
Ami Ayalon. He observed realistically that "those who want victory"
against terror without addressing underlying grievances "want an
unending war". He was speaking of Israel-Palestine, where the only
"solution of the problem of terrorism [is] to offer an honorable
solution to the Palestinians respecting their right to self-
determination", as former head of Israeli military intelligence
Yehoshaphat Harkabi, also a leading Arabist, observed 20 years ago,
at a time when Israel still retained its immunity from retaliation from
within the occupied territories to its harsh and brutal practices
there.[13]

---

[13] Anthony Shadid Bush, "U.S. Rebuffs Second Iraq Offer on Arms Inspection,"
Boston Globe, August 6, 2002. Ami Ayalon, director of Shabak, 1996–2000,
interview, Le Monde, December 22, 2001; reprinted in Roane Carey and Jonathan
Shanin, *The Other Israel*. New York: New Press (2002). Harkabi, cited by Israeli
journalist Amnon Kapeliouk, Le Monde diplomatique, February 1986.

The observations generalize in obvious ways. In serious scholarship, at least, it is recognized that "unless the social, political, and economic conditions that spawned Al-Qaeda and other associated groups are addressed, the United States and its allies in Western Europe and elsewhere will continue to be targeted by Islamist terrorists".[14]

In proclaiming the right of attack against perceived potential threats, the President is once again echoing the principles of the first phase of the "war on terror". The Reagan–Shultz doctrine held that the UN Charter entitles the U.S. to resort to force in "self-defense against future attack". That interpretation of Article 51 was offered in justification of the bombing of Libya, eliciting praise from commentators who were impressed by the reliance "on a legal argument that violence against the perpetrators of repeated violence is justified as an act of self-defense"; I am quoting *New York Times* legal specialist Anthony Lewis.

The doctrine was amplified by the Bush 1 administration, which justified the invasion of Panama, vetoing two Security Council resolutions, on the grounds that Article 51 "provides for the use of armed force to defend a country, to defend our interests and our people", and entitles the U.S. to invade another country to prevent its "territory from being used as a base for smuggling drugs into the United States". In the light of that expansive interpretation of the Charter, it is not surprising that James Baker suggested a few days ago that Washington could now appeal to Article 51 to authorize conquest and occupation of Iraq, because Iraq may someday threaten the U.S. with WMD, or threaten others while the U.S. stands helplessly by.[15]

Quite apart from the plain meaning of the Charter, the argument offered by Baker's State Department in 1989 was not too convincing on other grounds. *Operation Just Cause* reinstated in

---

[14] Sumit Ganguly, *Current History*, op. cit.

[15] James Baker, op-ed, *New York Times*, August 25, 2002. On Panama, see my *Deterring Democracy*. New York and London: Verso (1991); New York: Hill & Wang (1992, extended edn.), Chapters 4 and 5.

power the white elite of bankers and businessmen, many suspected of narcotrafficking and money laundering, who soon lived up to their reputation; drug trafficking "may have doubled" and money laundering "flourished" in the months after the invasion, the GAO reported, while USAID found that narcotics use in Panama had gone up by 400%, reaching the highest level in Latin America, all without eliciting notable concern, except in Latin America and Panama itself, where the invasion was harshly condemned.[16]

Clinton's Strategic Command also advocated "preemptive response", with nuclear weapons if deemed appropriate.[17] Clinton himself forged some new paths in implementing the doctrine, though his major contributions to international terrorism lie elsewhere.

The doctrine of preemptive strike has much earlier origins, even in words. Forty years ago Dean Acheson informed the American Society of International Law that legal issues do not arise in the case of a U.S. response to a "challenge [to its] power, position, and prestige". He was referring to Washington's response to what it regarded as Cuba's "successful defiance" of the United States. That included Cuba's resistance to the Bay of Pigs invasion, but also much more serious crimes. When Kennedy ordered his staff to subject Cubans to the "terrors of the earth" until Castro is eliminated, his planners advised that "The very existence of his regime ... represents a successful defiance of the U.S., a negation of our whole hemispheric policy of almost a century and a half", based on the principle of subordination to U.S. will. Worse yet, Castro's regime was providing an "example and general stimulus" that might "encourage agitation and radical change" in other parts of Latin America, where "social and economic conditions ... invite opposition to ruling authority" and susceptibility to "the Castro idea of taking matters into one's own hands". These are grave dangers,

---

[16] *Ibid.*, and my *Year 501*. Boston: South End (1993), Chapter 3.

[17] STRATCOM, "Essentials of Post-Cold War Deterrence," 1995, partially declassified. For quotes and sources, see my *New Military Humanism*. Monroe, Maine: Common Courage (1999), Chapter 6.

Kennedy planners recognized, when "distribution of land and other forms of national wealth greatly favors the propertied classes ... [and] The poor and underprivileged, stimulated by the example of the Cuban revolution, are now demanding opportunities for a decent living". These threats were only compounded by successful resistance to invasion, an intolerable threat to credibility, warranting the "terrors of the earth" and destructive economic warfare to excise that earlier "cancer".[18]

Cuba's crimes became still more immense when it served as the instrument of Russia's crusade to dominate the world in 1975, Washington proclaimed. "If Soviet neocolonialism succeeds" in Angola, UN Ambassador Daniel Patrick Moynihan thundered, "the world will not be the same in the aftermath. Europe's oil routes will be under Soviet control as will the strategic South Atlantic, with the next target on the Kremlin's list being Brazil." Washington's fury was caused by another Cuban act of "successful defiance". When a U.S.-backed South African invasion was coming close to conquering newly independent Angola, Cuba sent troops on its own initiative, scarcely even notifying Russia, and beat back the invaders. In the major scholarly study, Piero Gleijeses observes that "Kissinger did his best to smash the one movement that represented any hope for the future of Angola" — the MPLA. And though the MPLA "bears a grave responsibility for its country's plight" in later years, it was "the relentless hostility of the United States [that] forced it into an unhealthy dependence on the Soviet bloc and encouraged South Africa to launch devastating military raids in the 1980s".[19] These further crimes of Cuba could not be forgiven; those years saw some of the worst terrorist attacks against Cuba, with no slight U.S. role. After any pretense of a Soviet threat collapsed in 1989, the U.S. tightened its stranglehold on Cuba on new pretexts, notably the alleged role in terrorism of the prime target of U.S.-based terrorism

---

[18] Acheson, see *ibid.*, Chapter 7. Piero Gleijeses, *Conflicting Missions: Havana, Washington, and Africa, 1959–1976.* Chapel Hill, NC: University of North Carolina (2002); my *Profit over People.* New York: Seven Stories (1999).

[19] Gleijeses, op. cit.

for 40 years. The level of fanaticism is illustrated by minor incidents. For example, as we meet, a visa is being withheld for a young Cuban woman artist who was offered an art fellowship, apparently because Cuba has been declared a "terrorist state" by Colin Powell's State Department.[20] It should be unnecessary to review how the "terrors of the earth" were unleashed against Cuba since 1962. "No laughing matter," Jorge Domý́nguez points out with considerable under-statement, discussing newly-released documents.[21] Of particular interest and contemporary import are the internal perceptions of the planners. Domý́nguez observes that "only once in these nearly thousand pages of documentation did a U.S. official raise something that resembled a faint moral objection to U.S.-government spon-sored terrorism": a member of the NSC staff suggested that it might lead to some Russian reaction; furthermore, raids that are "haphazard and kill innocents ... might mean a bad press in some friendly countries". Scholarship on terrorism rarely goes even that far.

Little new ground is broken when one has to turn to House Majority leader Dick Armey to find a voice in the mainstream questioning "an unprovoked attack against Iraq" not on grounds of cost to us, but because it "would violate international law" and "would not be consistent with what we have been or what we should be as a nation".[22]

What we or others "have been" is a separate story.

Much more should be said about continuity and its institutional roots. But let's turn instead to some of the immediate questions posed by the crimes of 9/11:

(1) Who is responsible?
(2) What are the reasons?
(3) What is the proper reaction?
(4) What are the longer-term consequences?

---

[20] Alix Ritchie, "Cuban Artist Program May Get Bush-whacked," *Provincetown Banner*, August 29, 2002.

[21] "Cuba and the Missile Crisis," *Diplomatic History*, 242 (2000).

[22] Eric Schmitt, "House G.O.P. Leader Warns Against Iraq Attack," *New York Times*, August 9, 2002.

As for (1), it was assumed, plausibly, that the guilty parties were bin Laden and his Al-Qaeda network. No one knows more about them than the CIA, which, together with U.S. allies, recruited radical Islamists from many countries and organized them into a military and terrorist force that Reagan anointed "the moral equivalent of the founding fathers", joining Jonas Savimbi and similar dignitaries in that Pantheon.[23] The goal was not to help Afghans resist Russian aggression, which would have been a legitimate objective, but rather normal reasons of state, with grim consequences for Afghans when the moral equivalents finally took control.

U.S. intelligence has surely been following the exploits of these networks closely ever since they assassinated President Sadat of Egypt 20 years ago, and more intensively since their failed terrorist efforts in New York in 1993. Nevertheless, despite what must be the most intensive international intelligence investigation in history, evidence about the perpetrators of 9/11 has been elusive. Eight months after the bombing, FBI director Robert Mueller could only inform a Senate Committee that U.S. intelligence now "believes" the plot was hatched in Afghanistan, though planned and implemented elsewhere.[24] And well after the source of the anthrax attack was localized to government weapons laboratories, it has still not been identified. These are indications of how hard it may be to counter acts of terror targeting the rich and powerful in the future. Nevertheless, despite the thin evidence, the initial conclusion about 9/11 is presumably correct.

Turning to (2), scholarship is virtually unanimous in taking the terrorists at their word, which matches their deeds for the past

---

[23] Reagan, cited by Samina Amin, International Security 265 (2001/2002). Savimbi was "one of the few authentic heroes of our times," Jeane Kirkpatrick declared at a Conservative Political Action convention, where he "received enthusiastic applause after vowing to attack American oil installations in *his country.*" Colin Nickerson, "Sarimbi Finds Support on the Right," *Boston Globe*, February 3, 1986.

[24] Walter Pincus, "The 9–11 Masterminds may have been in Afghanistan," *Washington Post Weekly*, June 10–16.

20 years: their goal, in their terms, is to drive the infidels from Muslim lands, to overthrow the corrupt governments they impose and sustain, and to institute an extremist version of Islam. They despise the Russians, but ceased their terrorist attacks against Russia based in Afghanistan — which were quite serious — when Russia withdrew. And "the call to wage war against America was made [when it sent] tens of thousands of its troops to the land of the two Holy Mosques over and above ... its support of the oppressive, corrupt and tyrannical regime that is in control," so bin Laden announced well before 9/11.

More significant, at least for those who hope to reduce the likelihood of further crimes of a similar nature, are the background conditions from which the terrorist organizations arose, and that provide a reservoir of sympathetic understanding for at least parts of their message, even among those who despise and fear them. In George Bush's plaintive phrase, "Why do they hate us?"

The question is wrongly put: they do not "hate us", but rather the policies of the U.S. government, which is something quite different. If the question is properly formulated, however, answers to it are not hard to find. Forty-four years ago President Eisenhower and his staff discussed what he called the "campaign of hatred against us" in the Arab world, "not by the governments but by the people". The basic reason, the NSC advised, is the recognition that the U.S. supports corrupt and brutal governments and is "opposing political or economic progress", in order "to protect its interest in Near East oil". The *Wall Street Journal* and others found much the same when they investigated attitudes of wealthy westernized Muslims after 9/11, feelings now exacerbated by U.S. policies with regard to Israel-Palestine and Iraq.[25]

These are attitudes of people who like Americans and admire much about the United States, including its freedoms. What they

---

[25] For sources and background discussion, see my *World Orders Old and New*. New York: Columbia University Press (1994, extended edn. 1996), p. 79, 201f.; New York: Seven Stories (2001), 9–11.

hate is official policies that deny them the freedoms to which they too aspire for.

Many commentators prefer a more comforting answer: their anger is rooted in resentment of our freedom and democracy, their cultural failings tracing back many centuries, their inability to take part in the form of "globalization" in which they happily participate, and other such deficiencies. More comforting, perhaps, but not too wise.

These issues are very much alive. Just in the past few weeks, Asia correspondent Ahmed Rashid reported that in Pakistan, "there is growing anger that U.S. support is allowing [Musharraf's] military regime to delay the promise of democracy". And a well-known Egyptian academic told the BBC that Arab and Islamic people were opposed to the U.S. because it has "supported every possible anti-democratic government in the Arab-Islamic world ... When we hear American officials speaking of freedom, democracy and such values, they make terms like these sound obscene". An Egyptian writer added, "Living in a country with an atrocious human rights record that also happens to be strategically vital to U.S. interests is an illuminating lesson in moral hypocrisy and political double standards." Terrorism, he said, is "a reaction to the injustice in the region's domestic politics, inflicted in large part by the U.S.". The director of the terrorism program at the Council of Foreign Relations agreed that "Backing repressive regimes like Egypt and Saudi Arabia is certainly a leading cause of anti-Americanism in the Arab world", but warned that "in both cases the likely alternatives are even nastier".

There is a long and illuminating history of the problems in supporting democratic forms while ensuring that they will lead to preferred outcomes, not just in this region. And it doesn't win many friends.[26]

---

[26] Rashid, "Is Terror Worse than Oppression?" *Far Eastern Economic Review*, August 1, 2002. AUC professor El-Lozy, writer Azizuddin El-Kaissouni, and Warren Bass of the CFR, quoted by Joyce Koh, " 'Two-faced' U.S. policy blamed for Arab hatred," *Straits Times* (Singapore), August 14, 2002.

What about proper reaction in question (3)? Answers are doubtless contentious, but at least the reaction should meet the most elementary moral standards: specifically, if an action is right for us, it is right for others; and if it is wrong for others, it is wrong for us. Those who reject that standard can be ignored in any discussion of appropriateness of action, of right or wrong. One might ask what remains of the flood of commentary on proper reaction — thoughts about "just war", for example — if this simple criterion is adopted.

Suppose we adopt the criterion, thus entering the arena of moral discourse. We can then ask, for example, how Cuba has been entitled to react after "the terrors of the earth" were unleashed against it 40 years ago. Or Nicaragua, after Washington rejected the orders of the World Court and Security Council to terminate its "unlawful use of force", choosing instead to escalate its terrorist war and issue the first official orders to its forces to attack undefended civilian "soft targets", leaving tens of thousands dead and the country ruined perhaps beyond recovery. No one believes that Cuba or Nicaragua had the right to set off bombs in Washington or New York or to kill U.S. political leaders or send them to prison camps. And it is all too easy to add far more severe cases in those years, and others to the present.

Accordingly, those who accept elementary moral standards have some work to do to show that the U.S. and Britain were justified in bombing Afghans in order to compel them to turn over people whom the U.S. suspected of criminal atrocities, the official war aim announced by the President as the bombing began. Or that the enforcers were justified in informing Afghans that they would be bombed until they brought about "regime change", the war aim announced several weeks later, as the war was approaching its end.

The same moral standard holds of more nuanced proposals about an appropriate response to terrorist atrocities. Military historian Michael Howard advocated "a police operation conducted under the auspices of the United Nations ... against a criminal conspiracy whose members should be hunted down and brought before an international court, where they would receive a fair trial and, if found guilty, be awarded an appropriate sentence".[27] That seems reasonable, though we may ask what the reaction would be to the suggestion that the proposal should be applied universally. That is unthinkable, and if the suggestion were to be made, it would elicit outrage and horror.

Similar questions arise with regard to the doctrine of "preemptive strike" against suspected threats, not new, though its bold assertion is novel. There is no doubt about the address. The standard of universality, therefore, would appear to justify Iraqi preemptive terror against the U.S. Of course, the conclusion is outlandish. The burden of proof again lies on those who advocate or tolerate the selective version that grants the right to those powerful enough to exercise it. And the burden is not light, as is always true when the threat or use of violence is advocated or tolerated.

There is, of course, an easy counter to such elementary observations: WE are good, and THEY are evil. That doctrine trumps virtually any argument. Analysis of commentary and much of scholarship reveals that its roots commonly lie in that crucial principle, which is not argued but asserted. None of this, of course, is an invention of contemporary power centers and the dominant intellectual culture, but it is, nevertheless, instructive to observe the means employed to protect the doctrine from the heretical challenge that seeks to confront it with the factual record, including such intriguing notions as "moral equivalence", "moral relativism", "anti-Americanism", and others.

One useful barrier against heresy, already mentioned, is the principle that questions about the state's resort to violence simply do not arise among sane people. That is a common refrain in the current debate over the modalities of the invasion of Iraq. To select an example at the liberal end of the spectrum, *New York Times* columnist Bill Keller remarks that "the last time America dispatched soldiers in the cause of 'regime change', less than a year ago in

---

[27] "What's in a Name? How to Fight Terrorism," *Foreign Affairs*, January/February 2002; talk of October 30, 2001. Tania Branigan, *Guardian*, October 31.

Afghanistan, the opposition was mostly limited to the people who are reflexively against the American use of power", either timid supporters or "isolationists, the doctrinaire left and the soft-headed types Christopher Hitchens described as people who, 'discovering a viper in the bed of their child, would place the first call to People for the Ethical Treatment of Animals'". To borrow the words of a noted predecessor, "We went to war, not because we wanted to, but because humanity demanded it"; President McKinley, in this case, as he ordered his armies to "carry the burden, whatever it may be, in the interest of civilization, humanity, and liberty" in the Philippines.[28]

Let's ignore the fact that "regime change" was not "the cause" in Afghanistan — rather, an afterthought late in the game — and look more closely at the lunatic fringe. We have some information about them. In late September 2001, the Gallup organization surveyed international opinion on the announced U.S. bombing. The lead question was whether, "once the identity of the terrorists is known, should the American government launch a military attack on the country or countries where the terrorists are based or should the American government seek to extradite the terrorists to stand trial?" As we recently learned, the identity of the terrorists was only surmised eight months later, and the countries where they were based are presumed to be Germany, the UAE, and elsewhere, but let's ignore that too. The poll revealed that opinion strongly favored judicial over military action, in Europe overwhelmingly. The only exceptions were India and Israel, where Afghanistan was a surrogate for something quite different. Follow-up questions revealed that support for the military attack that was actually carried out was very slight.

Support for military action was least in Latin America, the region that has the most experience with U.S. intervention. It ranged from 2% in Mexico to 11% in Colombia and Venezuela,

---

[28] Keller, op-ed, *New York Times*, August 24, 2002. McKinley and many others; see Louis A. Pe'rez, *The War of 1898*. Chapel Hill, NC: University of North Carolina (1998).

where 85% preferred extradition and trial; whether that was feasible is known only to ideologues. The sole exception was Panama, where only 80% preferred judicial means and 16% advocated military attack; and even there, correspondents recalled the death of perhaps thousands of poor people (western crimes, therefore unexamined) in the course of *Operation Just Cause*, undertaken to kidnap a disobedient thug who was sentenced to life imprisonment in Florida for crimes mostly committed while he was on the CIA payroll. One remarked, "how much alike [the victims of 9/11] are to the boys and girls, to those who are unable to be born that December 20 [1989] that they imposed on us in Chorrillo; how much alike they seem to the mothers, the grandfathers and the little old grandmothers, all of them also innocent and anonymous deaths, whose terror was called Just Cause and the terrorist called liberator."[29]

I suspect that the director of Human Rights Watch Africa (1993–1995), now a Professor of Law at Emory University, may have spoken for many others around the world when he addressed the International Council on Human Rights Policy in Geneva in January 2002, saying, "I am unable to appreciate any moral, political or legal difference between this jihad by the United States against those it deems to be its enemies and the jihad by Islamic groups against those they deem to be their enemies."[30]

What about Afghan opinion? Here information is scanty, but not entirely lacking. In late October, 1000 Afghan leaders gathered in Peshawar, some exiles, some coming from within Afghanistan, all committed to overthrowing the Taliban regime. It was "a rare display of unity among tribal elders, Islamic scholars, fractious politicians, and former guerrilla commanders", the press reported. They unanimously "urged the U.S. to stop the air raids", appealed to the international media to call for an end to the "bombing of

---

[29] Ricardo Stevens, October 19, cited in NACLA Report on the Americas XXXV:3 (2001).

[30] Abdullahi Ahmed An-Na'im, "Upholding International Legality Against Islamic and American Jihad," in Ken Booth and Tim Dunne (eds.), *Worlds in Collision: Terror and the Future of Global Order*. New York: Palgrave (2002).

innocent people", and "demanded an end to the U.S. bombing of Afghanistan". They urged that other means be adopted to over-throw the hated Taliban regime, a goal they believed could be achieved without further death and destruction.

A similar message was conveyed by Afghan opposition leader Abdul Haq, who was highly regarded in Washington, and received special praise as a martyr during the Loya Jirga, his memory bringing tears to the eyes of President Hamid Karzai. Just before he entered Afghanistan, apparently without U.S. support, and was then captured and killed, he condemned the bombing and criticized the U.S. for refusing to support efforts of his and of others "to create a revolt within the Taliban". The bombing was "a big setback for these efforts," he said, outlining his efforts and calling on the U.S. to assist them with funding and other support instead of undermining them with bombs. The U.S., he said, "is trying to show its muscle, score a victory and scare everyone in the world. They don't care about the suffering of the Afghans or how many people we will lose." The prominent women's organization RAWA, which received some belated recognition in the course of the war, also bitterly condemned the bombing.

In short, the lunatic fringe of "soft-headed types who are reflexively against the American use of power" was not insubstantial as the bombing was undertaken and proceeded. But since virtually no word of any of this was published in the U.S., we can continue to comfort ourselves that "humanity demanded" the bombing.[31]

---

[31] A media review by Jeff Nygaard found one reference to the Gallup poll, a brief notice in the *Omaha World-Herald* that "completely misrepresented the findings". *Nygaard Notes Independent Weekly News and Analysis,* November 16, 2001, reprinted in Counterpoise 53/4 (2001). Karzai on Abdul Haq, Elizabeth Rubin, *New Republic,* July 8, 2002. Abdul Haq, interview with Anatol Lieven, *Guardian,* November 2, 2001. Peshawar gathering, Barry Bearak, *New York Times,* October 25, 2001; John Thornhill and Farhan Bokhari, *Financial Times,* October 25, 26, 2001; John Burns, *New York Times,* October 26, 2001; Indira Laskhmanan, *Boston Globe,* October 25, 26, 2001. RAWA website. The information was available throughout in independent ("alternative") journals, published and electronic, including Znet (www.zmag.org).

There is, obviously, a great deal more to say about all of these topics, but let us turn briefly to question (4).

In the longer term, I suspect that the crimes of 9/11 will accelerate tendencies that were already underway: the Bush doctrine on preemption is an illustration. As was predicted at once, governments throughout the world seized upon 9/11 as a "window of opportunity" to institute or escalate harsh and repressive programs. Russia eagerly joined the "coalition against terror", expecting to receive tacit authorization for its shocking atrocities in Chechnya, and was not disappointed. China happily joined for similar reasons. Turkey was the first country to offer troops for the new phase of the U.S. "war on terror", in gratitude, as the Prime Minister explained, for the U.S. contribution to Turkey's campaign against its miserably-repressed Kurdish population, waged with extreme savagery and relying crucially on a huge flow of U.S. arms, peaking in 1997; in that single year arms transfers exceeded the entire postwar period combined up to the onset of the counterinsurgency campaign. Turkey is highly praised for these achievements and was rewarded by grant of authority to protect Kabul from terror, funded by the same superpower that provided the means for its recent acts of state terror, including some of the major atrocities of the grisly 1990s. Israel recognized that it would be able to crush Palestinians even more brutally, with even firmer U.S. support. The situation goes on throughout much of the world.

Many governments, including the U.S., instituted measures to discipline the domestic population and to carry forward unpopular measures under the guise of "combating terror", exploiting the atmosphere of fear and the demand for "patriotism" — which in practice means: "You shut up and I'll pursue my own agenda relentlessly". The Bush administration used the opportunity to advance its assault against most of the population, and future generations, serving the narrow corporate interests that dominate the administration to an extent even beyond the norm.

One major outcome is that the U.S., for the first time, has major military bases in Central Asia. These help to position U.S. corporate interests favorably in the current "great game" to control the resources of the region, but also to complete the encirclement of the world's major energy resources, in the Gulf region. The U.S. base system targeting the Gulf extends from the Pacific to the Azores, but the closest reliable base before the Afghan war was Diego Garcia. Now that situation is much improved and forceful intervention should be facilitated.

The Bush administration also exploited the new phase of the "war on terror" to expand its overwhelming military advantages over the rest of the world, and to move on to other methods to ensure global dominance. Government thinking was clarified by high officials when Prince Abdullah of Saudi Arabia visited the U.S. in April to urge the administration to pay more attention to the reaction in the Arab world to its strong support for Israeli terror and repression. He was told, in effect, that the U.S. did not care what he or other Arabs think. A high official explained that "if he thought we were strong in Desert Storm, we're 10 times as strong today. This was to give him some idea what Afghanistan demonstrated about our capabilities". A senior defense analyst gave a simple gloss: others will "respect us for our toughness and won't mess with us". That stand has many precedents too, but in the post-9/11 world it gains new force. It is reasonable to speculate that such consequences were one goal of the bombing of Afghanistan: to warn the world of what the "legitimate enforcer" can do if someone steps out of line. The bombing of Serbia was undertaken for similar reasons: to "ensure NATO's credibility", as Blair and Clinton explained — not referring to the credibility of Norway or Italy. That is a common theme of statecraft. And with some reason, as history amply reveals. Without continuing, the basic issues of international society seem to me to remain much as they were, but 9/11 surely has induced changes, in some cases, with significant and not very attractive implications.

Rumors of War

Joseph Stiglitz

A winner of the 2001 Nobel Prize in Economics and Professor of Economics and Finance at Columbia University, he has made seminal and fundamental contributions to every subfield of economic theory, and is the recipient of the prestigious John Bates Clark Medal, awarded every two years to the American economist under the age of 40 who has made the most significant contributions to the subject. Joseph Stiglitz is also author of Globalization and its Discontents, *published by W.W. Norton (the German edition,* Die Schatten Der Globalisierung, *was published by Siedler; the French edition,* La Grande Désillusion, *by Fayard).*

War is widely thought to be linked to economic good times. World War II is often said to have brought the world out of the Great Depression, and war has since enhanced its reputation as a spur to economic growth. Some even suggest that capitalism needs wars, that without them, recession would always lurk on the horizon.

Today, we know that these propositions are nonsense. The 1990s boom showed that peace is economically far better than war. The Gulf War of 1991 demonstrated that wars can actually be bad for an economy. That conflict contributed mightily to the onset of the recession of 1991 (which, it should be remembered, was probably the key factor in denying the first President Bush re-election in 1992).

The current situation is far more akin to the Gulf War than to wars that may have contributed to economic growth. Indeed, the economic effects of a second war against Iraq would probably be far more adverse. WWII called for total mobilization, and it was that total mobilization, requiring a country's total resources, that wiped out unemployment. Total war means total employment.

By contrast, the direct costs of a military attack on Saddam Hussein's regime will be minuscule in terms of total U.S. government spending. Most analysts put the total costs of the war at less than 0.1% of GDP, the highest at 0.2% of GDP. Much of that, moreover, includes the usage of munitions that already exist, implying that little or no stimulus will be provided to today's economy.

The Bush administration's (admittedly wavering) commitment to fiscal prudence means that much, perhaps most, of the war costs will be offset by expenditure cuts elsewhere. Investments in education, health, research, and the environment will almost inevitably be crowded out. Accordingly, war will be unambiguously bad in terms of what really counts: the standard of living of ordinary people.

America will thus be poorer, both now and the future. Obviously, if this military adventure were in fact necessary to maintain security or to preserve freedom, as its advocates and promoters proclaim — and if it were to prove as successful as its boosters hope — then the cost might still be worth it. But that is another matter. I want to debunk the idea that it is possible both to achieve the war's ends and benefit the economy.

There is also the uncertainty factor. Of course, resolving uncertainty is no reason to invade Iraq prematurely, for the costs of any war are high, and are not to be measured only, or primarily, in economic terms. Innocent lives will be lost — possibly far more than were lost on September 11, 2001. But the wait for war adds to uncertainties that already weigh on the American (and the global) economy: uncertainties arising from America's looming fiscal deficit, due to macroeconomic mismanagement and a tax cut that the country cannot afford; uncertainties arising from the unfinished "war on terrorism"; uncertainties associated with the massive corporate accounting and banking scandals, and the Bush Administration's half-hearted efforts at reform, as a result of which no one knows what America's corporations are worth; and uncertainties connected to America's massive trade deficit, which has reached all-time records. Will foreigners be willing to continue to lend to the U.S., with all of its problems, at a rate in excess of a billion dollars a day? Uncertainties associated with Europe's stability pact: will it survive, and will it be good for Europe if it does? Finally, the uncertainties associated with Japan: will it at long last fix its banking system, and if it does, how negative will be the short-term impact?

Some suggest that the U.S. may be going to war to maintain steady oil supplies, or to advance its oil interests. Few can doubt the influence that oil interests have on President Bush — witness the administration's energy policy, with its emphasis on expanding oil production rather than conservation. But even from the perspective of oil interests, war against Iraq is a risky venture: not only is the impact on price, and therefore on oil company prices, highly uncertain, but other oil producers, including Russian and European interests, will not easily be ignored.

Indeed, should the U.S. go to war, no one can predict the effect on oil supplies. A peaceful, democratic Iraqi regime could be established. Desperate for funds for reconstruction, that new regime could sell large amounts of oil, lowering global oil prices. Domestic U.S. oil producers, as well as those in allied countries, such as Mexico and Russia, would be devastated, though users of oil around the world would benefit enormously.

Or the turmoil throughout the Muslim world could lead to disruptions of oil supplies, with high prices the result. This will please oil producers in other parts of the world, but will have enormously adverse consequences for the global economy, akin to those resulting from the oil price hikes in 1973.

Whichever way one looks at it, the economic effects of war with Iraq will not be good. Markets loathe uncertainty and volatility. War, and anticipation of war, bring both. We should be prepared for them.

The Hidden Costs of War: How the Bush Doctrine is Undermining Democracy in Iraq And Democracy in America

William D. Hartung with Ceara Donnelley[1]

Senior Research Fellow at World Policy Institute in New York and Director for Institute's Arms Trade Resource Center, his articles on military spending, nuclear policy and the arms trade have appeared in The New York Times, The Washington Post, *and* The Nation *and he has been featured as an expert on NBC Nightly News, CBS 60 Minutes, The Newshour with Jim Lehrer, Fox News, the BBC and MSNBC. His books and essays on security issues include* Desperately Seeking Dominance: The Bush Administration's Military Strategy *in Power Trip,* John Feffer, editor *(Seven Stories Press, 2003) and* How Much Are You Making on the War, Daddy? — A Quick and Dirty Guide to War Profiteering in the Bush Administration *(Nation Books/ Thunder's Mouth Press, forthcoming, 2004).*

Introduction: A Privatized Occupation

When the Bush administration decided to invade Iraq without the approval of the United Nations Security Council in March of 2003,

---

[1] Ceara Donnelley was a research intern at the World Policy Institute during the summer of 2003. William D. Hartung directs the Institute's arms project. This chapter is an expanded and updated version of a World Policy Institute research report that Ms. Donnelley wrote and released in August of 2003. The original report can be accessed at www.worldpolicy.org/projects/arms, under "reports".

the Pentagon optimistically named the action "Operation Iraqi Freedom". Prior to the intervention, Deputy Secretary of Defense Paul Wolfowitz, one of the strongest advocates for intervention within the administration, told a reporter for the *New York Times* magazine that overthrowing Saddam Hussein's regime would be the hard part, and that spreading democracy in Iraq and throughout the Middle East would be the easy part. A number of Wolfowitz's neo-conservative colleagues even chimed in to suggest that even the "hard part" — overthrowing the Baathist regime in Baghdad — would not be all that hard. Kenneth Adelman, the former head of the U.S. Arms Control and Disarmament Agency in the Reagan administration, wrote an op-ed suggesting that the Iraqi intervention would be "a cakewalk". Neo-conservative officials like Richard Perle, then chairman of an influential Pentagon advisory panel known as the Defense Policy Board, reinforced the notion that the Iraqi people would rise up spontaneously in support of U.S. interventionary forces, making their job far easier than it would be if they had to fight a hostile population.

As this goes to press, in the fall of 2003, it is painfully clear that Wolfowitz and his neo-conservative colleagues were wrong, wrong, and wrong again in their optimistic views of how a unilateral U.S. invasion of Iraq would play out. The "hard part" — overthrowing Saddam Hussein's regime and stabilizing Iraq — is far from over. By the end of the summer of 2003, U.S. forces had suffered as many casualties since the start of the "peacekeeping" phase of the war in Iraq as they had suffered in the combat phase that resulted in the displacement of Saddam Hussein's regime. High-profile suicide bombings against the United Nations complex in Baghdad and the main mosque of an Islamic cleric who had shown qualified support for the U.S. occupying administration made it clear that the task of securing Iraq was far from over. A growing number of families of military personnel based in Iraq had begun to call for a U.S. withdrawal after hearing horror stories of the difficult and dangerous conditions faced by U.S. forces there. Also, the costs of the occupation were skyrocketing, as the Bush administration was forced to go to Congress for its second supplemental appropriation to pay for the war, with a price tag of roughly $87 billion.

While the Bush administration Secretary of Defense Donald Rumsfeld tried to argue that the disorder in Iraq represented the growing pains of a society moving from tyranny to democracy, his own policies put the lie to that rose-colored view of Iraqi realities. To the extent that Iraqis had any input into the rebuilding of their own nation, it was through a hand-picked Iraqi governing council, composed primarily of Iraqi exiles with close ties to neo-conservatives in the United States. Ahmed Chalabi, the man who was selected to serve as the first chairman of the group, has longstanding ties to the American Enterprise Institute, the think tank that Bush Vice-President Dick Cheney and rabid right-wing State Department official John Bolton worked with prior to joining the Bush administration. Chalabi had not been inside Iraq for 45 years prior to the March 2003 U.S. invasion, and his reputation as a playboy and a corrupt businessman made him an extremely unlikely choice to lead Iraq into a new democratic era. Nonetheless, Rumsfeld and his cronies at the Pentagon have taken every opportunity to push for more power for Chalabi, because they see him as "their man in Baghdad" — a pliable leader who will accommodate himself to U.S. military and economic interests in Iraq, even if his pro-U.S. stance ends up selling out the needs and aspirations of the Iraqi people. Even the more legitimate members of the Iraqi Governing Council suffer from a major problem — since the head of the U.S. occupation, Paul Bremer, has veto power over any decision they may make, or try to make, even as of this writing the Pentagon and U.S. military forces are still making virtually all of the major decisions about Iraq's future. As a result, many Iraqis, and many foreign observers, view the council as a U.S. "puppet" operation, not the seedbed for a new democratic system in Iraq. And even if the governing council does start to attain some real power, it will lack legitimacy in many quarters for two main reasons: 1) Its members were hand-picked by Donald Rumsfeld's Pentagon cronies and the U.S. occupying authority; and 2) Much of the power to determine the future of Iraq's security, economy, and government is being handed over to private U.S. companies like Halliburton, Bechtel, and Dyncorps — companies that are involved in everything from running Iraq's oil operations to designing its criminal justice system.

Back in the United States, most Americans realize that something has gone seriously wrong in Iraq, but they may or may not blame the unfolding fiasco that is "Operation Iraqi Freedom" on decisions made by the Bush administration. Your average CNN-watching American may be able to report the latest on soldiers killed or Iraqis successfully "found, killed or captured", but you would be hard pressed to find an average American who could tell you how the scene is really unfolding. How many Americans know who supplied the war, who is in charge of reconstruction, how much they are being paid for it, and how they were hired? And if Americans do not know what is being done in their name, what does that say about the quality of *American* democracy? It could be that there will not be an opportunity for real democracy to emerge in Iraq until such time as democracy has been restored and revitalized in America. And that will mean, first and foremost, asserting control over what the late, great U.S. President Dwight Eisenhower described as the "military-industrial complex" — the network of arms company executives, White House and military officials, and members of Congress that profit politically and financially from keeping the United States on a permanent war footing. Taking the rebuilding of Iraq out of the hands of private corporations and putting it back in the hands of the international community offers the best hope of building a true democracy in Iraq, and of opening the way to a restoration and revitalization of democracy in America. If the Bush/ Cheney/Rumsfeld approach of turning America into an aggressive, unilateralist garrison state is not resisted, there would not be much of a democracy left worth talking about in America in the years and decades to come. Building a true democracy in Iraq is part and parcel of restoring a true democracy in America, and making America a responsible global partner rather than an over-militarized global bully. The next few years will be critical in determining which direction America takes — militarization, occupation, and war, or cooperative diplomacy, democratic rebuilding, and peace. The Bush administration's approach thus far has been far too militaristic. It remains to be seen whether its September 2003 decision to seek a larger United Nations role in Iraq will mark a genuine step towards a more cooperative foreign policy, or just another tactical retreat in the service of the administration's aggressive global agenda.

The answer to the question of who is currently in charge in Iraq is not quite so simple as a predictable response — "the military". Few know the real details: how the projects and personnel planning post-war Iraq come from private American corporations making world class lemonade out of the sour situation in the Persian Gulf.

From providing the weapons and tanks that took us to Baghdad, to the personnel rebuilding dams and bridges or operating ports, to the pencils and lesson plans revamping the education system for young Iraqis, private American corporations are spearheading U.S. campaigns in Iraq and reaping the financial rewards of warfare.

Private corporations have played an unprecedented role in the Second Gulf War, and from the looks of just one key number — $680 million, the projected contract with Bechtel Group Inc. for its reconstructive work in Iraq — they will continue to do so.

Some of jobs undertaken by the Bechtels and the Halliburtons — such as rebuilding water and electrical systems for instance are necessary and important. Yet as a nation and a democracy we must ponder seriously whether such private corporations, with firm connections to our leadership, are necessarily the ones who should be handed these jobs. The privatization of the United States military is not a new controversy. P. W. Singer's new book *Corporate Warriors: The Rise of the Privatized Military Industry* (Ithaca, New York: Cornell University Press, 2003) offers insights into the questions that should be asked about the unprecedented levels of privatization of military planning, training, construction, and services that were pursued during the Clinton/Gore administration and have been accelerated under the Bush/Cheney administration. If the experience thus far in Iraq is any indication, we clearly have a long way to go before we establish the appropriate balance between profits and patriotism in the use of private corporations to implement our national security strategy.

From the perspective of U.S. taxpayers, the most important question is how many billions of dollars has the Bush administration paid private corporations to secure a U.S. "victory" in Iraq — whatever victory means in the context of an unstable, open-ended military occupation of another nation.

What follows is a breakdown of the major corporations involved in Iraq from the incipient days of U.S. military action to the forthcoming years of rebuilding.

Run-up to War: Who Put the Shock in "Shock and Awe"

Long before the Bush Administration could sufficiently sell its case to the United Nations, Congress, and the American people, it was planning for war against Saddam and his Republican Guard. For companies like Lockheed Martin, Boeing, and Raytheon this meant a big boom in business in exchange for the big booms their weapons and bombs showered on Iraq months later. Though the ties that bind these companies to the Bush administration are not quite as controversial as those linking rebuilding and private military companies such as Halliburton and Bechtel, it is still clear, by tracing overlapping personnel, that far from being a relic of the Cold War, the military-industrial complex is alive and well and thriving in George W. Bush's Washington.

Lockheed Martin

The Pentagon's No. 1 contractor has certainly benefited from military action in Iraq. The company reports 80% of its business is with the U.S. Department of Defense and the U.S. federal government agencies. It is also the largest provider of information technology (IT) services, systems integration, and training to the U.S. government. Such business has grown substantially during the Bush tenure, especially in fiscal year 2002, as plans for war were formulated and expenditures in weapons and dollars calculated.

- The company was awarded $17 billion in defense contracts in 2002, up from $14.7 billion in 2001.[2]
- First quarter sales for 2003 were $7.1 billion, an 18% increase from the corresponding quarter in 2002.
- In March of 2003, as the first bombs rained on Baghdad, the U.S. Air Force awarded Lockheed Martin a $106.6 million contract for Paveway II GBU-12 and -16 Laser Guided Bomb (LGB) kits, as part of a $281 million contract characterized by "indefinite delivery, indefinite quantity" — a fancy term for an open-ended, cost-plus contract. The majority of the kits, also known as "smart bombs" (when fitted on warheads) were ordered to restock diminishing U.S. Navy inventories.

Also in March of 2003, Lockheed Martin received a $4 billion multi-year contract with the U.S. Air Force and the Marine Corps for the acquisition of C-130J Super Hercules Aircraft, to deliver the additional planes (the two departments combined already own 41) from 2003 to 2008.

Lockheed Martin's good fortune is no accident — it has close ties to President Bush and his inner circle. Former Lockheed Martin Vice-President Bruce Jackson was a finance chair for the Bush President Campaign; Vice-Presidential spouse Lynne Cheney is a former board member of Lockheed Martin, and used to receive $120,000 per year from the company for attending a handful of semi-annual board meetings.[3] Chris Williams, lobbyist for Johnston & Associates, is one among nine members of the Defense Policy Board to have ties to defense companies. His firms represent Lockheed Martin, Boeing, TRW and Northrop Grumman.[4]

---

[2] "War in Iraq: We foot the billing, Corporations make a killing," www.citizensworks.org.

[3] *Ibid.*

[4] "Advisors of Influence: Nine Members of the Defense Policy Board Have Ties to Defense Contractors," report by the Center for Public Integrity, www.publici.org.

Boeing

Boeing is the Pentagon's No. 2 contractor as a supplier of war materials ranging from information technology, to planes, to the bombs that drop from them. The B-52, the aircraft made famous during the Korean War, remained the "workhorse" in Operation Iraqi Freedom. It has been upgraded to modern technological heights by "smart bombs" and precision-guided weapons like those produced by Lockheed Martin, as well as those devised by Boeing itself. In fact, Boeing's Joint Direct Attack Munitions (JDAMs) are the majority of the military's smart bomb arsenal, because they are cheap and effective: a $22,000 kit makes almost any bomb a precision munition.

In 2002, Boeing received $16.6 billion in Pentagon contracts — up from $13 billion in 2001, $12 billion in 2000.

While the Air Force originally ordered 87,000 JDAM kits, it expanded that order to more than 230,000 sometime before the March invasion. The contract was for $378 million.[5]

The company recently won a $9.7 billion contract from the DoD to build 60 additional C-17 transport planes, praised as the only aircraft capable of lifting the Army's heavy tanks, in addition to Apache helicopters, Humvees, and Bradley fighting vehicles. In a deployment that began in January 2003, the C-17s were operating constantly delivering equipment to staging spots in the Persian Gulf.

Other recent Boeing contracts include $60.3 million for additional production of 120 Standoff Land Attack Missiles Expanded Response (SLAM-ER) and $3.3 billion for the sale of 40 F-15K aircraft and weapons support for the Republic of Korea.

Boeing has also cultivated influential friends with clout in the Bush administration. Richard Perle, former Chairman of the Defense Policy Board (now he is a mere member) is a managing partner at venture-capital company Trireme Partners, L.P., which invests in homeland security and defense companies. Half of the $45 million

---

[5] *Ibid.*

in capital thus far comes from Boeing.[6] Over 58% of the $1.5 million in soft money and PAC contributions Boeing made during the 2000 campaign went to the Republican candidates. And when Bush was declared victor, Boeing gave $100,000 to help pay for the festivities surrounding his inauguration.

Raytheon

The fourth largest defense contractor in the United States, Raytheon boasts involvement in over 4,000 weapons programs. The defense electronics company is best known for the publicity garnered during the 1991 Gulf conflict by its Patriot Air Defense missile that intercepted Iraqi Scud missiles. Since 1991 the Pentagon has spent $3 billion improving the accuracy of the weapon, which studies subsequent to Desert Storm revealed to be far less than perfect.

Raytheon also manufactures the Tomahawk land attack missile, another familiar name in times of combat. Raytheon's website morbidly celebrates its popularity: "Over 300 Tomahawks were used in Operation Desert Storm alone. Since Desert Storm in 1991, more than 1,000 Tomahawks have been fired". Estimates of the weapon's use the second time around predicted that 800 would be fired in just the first hours of war. In addition to these two well-known weapons of war, Raytheon produces a wide range of popular missile systems, radar and surveillance systems, and bombs. As a major arms exporter to countries including Israel, Egypt, Saudi Arabia, Turkey, and South Korea, the company is likely to doubly benefit from the militarization of world politics as nations clamor to bolster defense systems.

Raytheon CEO Daniel Burnham is content with the course set by Bush and company, applauding the fact that "the market is higher today than we thought a year ago", and boasting that "We are perfectly aligned with the defense department's priorities". Also there's no question that Burnham's company has thrived under the

---

[6] For more details on Boeing's role in Iraq and its connections to Washington, see ATRC's April 4, 2003 update.

Bush/Cheney/Rumsfeld "war without end" policies. The Navy recently contracted a $1.2 billion deal to develop future ships like the DDX destroyer, for which Raytheon integrates electronics. The Air Force raised its request from $12.2 million to $80 million worth of 901 Javelin anti-tank missiles, co-produced by Raytheon and Lockheed Martin.

Like its brethren in the weapons industry, Raytheon is making sure it has friends in high places. Since 1996, the company has donated more than $3.3 million in soft money and PAC donations, which places it fourth in donations among major defense contractors in the 2002 midterm electoral campaigns. Despite a traditional relationship with Massachusetts Democrats, Raytheon's contributions have increasingly leaned towards the Republican party culminating in a 58%/42% split, R/D, in the 2002 midterm Congressional elections.[7]

Alliant Tech Systems

Lesser known than defense giants like Boeing, Lockheed Martin, and Raytheon, Alliant nonetheless may be the defense company that profits most consistently from the war in Iraq and for the wars for "regime change" that may be yet to come under the Bush administration's first-strike military doctrine. Alliant Tech supplies all of the Army's small arms munitions, used in rifles and machine guns, and approximately half of the medium-caliber rounds fired by tanks and antitank chain guns in attack helicopters. War strategies may change, favoring tanks over aircraft or vice versa, but soldiers will always need ammo and they will always need more ammo in times of combat. Alliant's recent 16% increase in sales reflects that bottom line.

Alliant's sales rose from $1.8 to $2.1 billion in FY 2002, a 16% increase. Last year the Army awarded Alliant a $92 million dollar contract for 265 million rounds of small-caliber ammunition, notably including cartridges for M-16 rifles. In February, Alliant received

---

[7] For additional information on Raytheon, see ATRC's March 24, 2003 update.

another \$113 million in contracts to make ammunition for the Abrams battle tank.[8]

Cleaning up the Mess: Rebuilding Contracts

P. W. Singer calls it the "service side" of war. Private military companies are on the rise as the purported defenders of freedom. During "Operation Iraqi Freedom", the United States deployed one private military worker for every ten soldiers — a tenfold increase since the 1991 Gulf War.

Between 1994 and 2002 the Pentagon entered into more than 3,000 contracts with private military companies of varying notoriety.[9] Worldwide, private military contractors constitute a \$100 billion annual business. And with the war on terrorism being described as the "endless war", there will be more money to be made in the years ahead.

Many Americans now know the link between private military contractor Halliburton and Vice President Cheney, yet the morally ambiguous relationships between military-industrial giants and the Washington elite do not end there. Mainstream news reports have also focused on the role played by Bechtel, another corporation that enjoys close ties with the Republican administration and is reaping billions as it rebuilds Iraq.

Along with these familiar examples, we should add Dyncorp, MPRI, Vinnell, Logicon, AirScan: these names should become familiar because their employees are being paid to do the dirty work alongside U.S. soldiers in Iraq. One wonders whose salaries are higher.

---

[8] "Quiet, but Central, Role for Ammunition Maker," by Amy Cortese, *New York Times*, March 23, 2003.

[9] "Have Guns, Will Travel," by P. W. Singer, *New York Times*, July 21, 2003.

Halliburton

Halliburton first made headlines in this war, when it won the very first rebuilding contract without bidding and before U.S. tanks even made it to Baghdad. In the shadow of Enron and seemingly ubiquitous corporate scandal, the relationship between Halliburton and its former CEO, Vice President Dick Cheney, raised a red flag.

In March 2003, Halliburton subsidiary Kellogg, Brown, and Root (KBR) was awarded the main contract to control oil fires and stabilize oil fields under U.S. command; no limit was placed on the duration or dollars involved in this venture.

Halliburton is not all about oil; its profit from the war on Iraq runs deeper than the oil wells. Cheney's former company provides a wide range of services and is correspondingly contracted to perform them in private bidding sessions that exclude most competitors.

Since September 11, the Bush administration has doled out over $2.2 billion in defense-related contracts to Cheney's former company.[10] Halliburton's contract to secure and protect oil fields in Iraq, secretly awarded by the Army without any competitive bidding, could be worth up to $1 billion.[11] From September 2002 to April 2003, Halliburton received over $443 million in defense related contracts to provide services ranging from logistical support to building enemy prisoner of war camps and refueling military tanks. From 1999 to 2002, Halliburton donated $708,770 in soft money and PAC contributions, 95% of that total going to Republicans.

A recent *Newsweek* article reports that as "Defense secretary in the first Bush administration, Cheney awarded KBR the Army's first private contract to manage troop tent cities. During the Clinton years Halliburton lost that contract after KBR came under fire for allegedly overcharging the government. But after Cheney was elected, KBR was again awarded that Army contract and has rung up

---

[10] "The World According to Halliburton," by Michael Scherer, www.motherjones.org.

[11] "Fanning the Flames: Cheney's Halliburton ties," by Keith Naughton and Michael Hirsch, *Newsweek*, April 7, 2003.

$1.15 billion so far on the 10-year deal."[12] Due to a decision he made upon leaving Halliburton, Cheney still receives annual deferred compensation of $140,000 to $160,000 from his former company.

Bechtel

Though contracts for rebuilding Iraq were awarded as soon as war was underway, if not sooner, as late as mid-April the big question was regarding who would win the grand prize, the jackpot in the current round in bidding — a wide ranging $600 million reconstruction contract awarded by USAID to cover the cost of rebuilding critical infrastructure: airports, roads, water and power systems, schools and hospitals.

After a secretive bidding process, Bechtel Group of San Francisco was announced as the winner, sparking a flurry of attention from the media and those who know of Bechtel's intricate ties to the Bush Administration. As one *New York Times* article aptly put it: "Awarding the first major contract for reconstruction in Iraq to a politically connected American company under restricted business procedures sends a deplorable message to a skeptical world… the award of a contract worth up to $680 million to the Bechtel Group of San Francisco in a competition limited to a handful of American companies can only add to the impression that the United States seeks to profit from the war it waged."[13]

Bechtel was widely regarded as a highly capable contender for the $600 million plus contract, yet its ties to Washington are so intricately and firmly woven that it is nearly impossible not to imagine that pressure was applied to those making the contracting decision.

As Secretary of State for Reagan (and former president of Bechtel), George Schultz in 1983 sent Donald Rumsfeld as a Middle East peace envoy to the city of Baghdad to meet with Saddam Hussein. Rumsfeld was instructed to ask for the leader's support in Bechtel's bid on construction of an oil pipeline from Iraq to the

---

[12] *Ibid.*

[13] "And the Winner is Bechtel," *New York Times*, April 19, 2003.

port of Aqaba. Twenty years later, Rumsfeld and his cohorts were in the position to once again launch Bechtel into a position of power in the Middle East, and they did so.[14]

Bechtel's political connections in Bush's Washington are as strong as any of its rivals. Jack Sheehan, a senior Vice President at Bechtel, is a member of the Defense Policy Board.[15] USAID administrator Andrew Natsios, the overseer of bidding contracts in Iraq, also has close ties to Bechtel; he headed Boston's massive "Big Dig" construction process, a disastrous $14 billion boondoggle that accounted for some of the biggest cost overruns in the history of American municipal public works. Bechtel is one of the main contractors on the "Big Dig" project.[16]

Just two months before war, President Bush appointed multi-billionaire Riley Bechtel (the 104th richest man in the world, thanks to his family's company) to his Export Council to advise the government on how to create markets for American companies overseas.[17] From 1999 to 2001, Bechtel contributed $1.3 million to political campaigns; 58% went to Republican candidates.[18]

Dyncorp

The celebratory images from the fall of Baghdad — giant Saddam statues falling, spontaneous exultation — were quickly replaced with grim reality of the consequences of destroying order in hopes of implementing a better one. Looting ran rampant: much needed medical equipment and supplies disappeared, precious and invaluable artifacts were stolen from museums.

The U.S. military, already stretched thin and committed to the continuing task of stabilizing the region, stood by helplessly.

---

[14] "Bechtel's Friends in High Places," by Pratap Chatterjee, special to Corpwatch, April 24, 2003, www.corpwatch.org.

[15] "Advisors of Influence," www.publici.org.

[16] Chatterjee, April 24, 2003.

[17] *Ibid.*

[18] "Rebuilding Iraq — The Contractors," www.opensecrets.org.

It was clear something had to be done. Enter Dyncorp: a multi-billion dollar military contractor providing personnel that fits the description offered by one Pentagon official to the *New York Times*: "something a little more corporate and more efficient with cleaner lines of authority and responsibility [than United Nations peace-keeping troops]".[19] Corpwatch.org reporter Prattap Chatterjee has accurately characterized this service as rent-a-cop; Dyncorp's website is still advertising lucrative positions to fill the Iraqi police force it has promised to build under contract to the U.S. government. Former servicemen, police officers, and prison guards line up.

In April 2003, the State Department awarded DynCorp a multi-million dollar contract to advise the Iraqi government on setting up effective law enforcement, judicial, and correctional facilities. The company estimates it will send 1,000 American law enforcement experts to Iraq to meet the task. DynCorp projects a return of up to $50 million for the first year of the contract.[20]

DynCorp also knows how to play politics in Washington. The firm contributed 74% of a total $276, 975 to the Republican party from 1999 to 2002.[21]

Critics question whether the company is the right choice to rebuild the Iraqi justice system, given its own long history of alleged human rights violations and fraud. The most well known example appears to be just the tip of the iceberg. Two Dyncorp employees ran an underage sex slave ring in Bosnia while they were there under a U.S. contract. The employees who exposed this crime were fired; the ones responsible were merely transferred.

---

[19] "DynCorp Rent-a-Cops May Head to Post-Saddam Iraq," by Pratap Chatterjee, special to Corpwatch, April 9, 2003, www.corpwatch.org.

[20] "Rebuilding Iraq — The Contractors," www.opensecrets.org.

[21] *Ibid.*

Full Spectrum Privatization: Other Contracts

The U.S. government has not only hired companies to dramatically supplant the duties of the occupying military. American taxpayers are also paying for the specialized rebuilding of other essentials in Iraq. To appreciate fully the cost of the war and its aftermath, these contracts are listed below with brief summaries of tasks for which they were awarded.[22]

USAID has awarded $4.8 million to Stevedoring Services of America for "assessment and management" of the Umm Qasr port on southeastern Iraq.

Abt Associates Inc. has received a $10 million contract from U.S. occupying authorities to reform the Iraqi Ministry of Health and to deliver health services and supplies in the interim.

Skylink Air and Logistic Support (USA) Inc. have received an initial contract of $2.5 million to help reopen and manage Iraq's airports.

The International Resources Group was awarded a $7 million plus contract for the management of relief and rebuilding efforts. That was in addition to the $7.9 million that went to Research Triangle Institute (RTI) to promote Iraqi civic participation in the reconstruction process. RTI will provide technical assistance and training systems in the effort to improve internal administrative skills and understanding of municipal government and services.

Creative Associates International Inc. will get $2.5 million over one year to address "immediate educational needs" of Iraq's primary and secondary schools. The contract provides for school supplies, training teachers, and developing testing methods to track student performance.

---

[22] All statistics provided by the USAID fact sheet on reconstruction contracts for Iraq: www.usaid.gov/press/factsheets/2003/fs030620.html.

Iraqi Oil: The Bottom Line

In the late summer of 2003, the U.S. occupying authority in Iraq lined up long-term oil deals with 12 companies around the world in a hastened effort to gain revenue to pay for reconstruction. According to its senior American advisor, Philip Carroll (a former executive of oil giant Royal Dutch Shell), Iraq's State Oil Marketing Organization plans to supply an average of 725,000 to 750,000 barrels of oil a day to U.S. firms like ExxonMobil, ChevronTexaco, ConocoPhilipps, Marathon and Valero Energy, as well as European giants like Shell, BP, Total, Repsol YPF; the Chinese firm Sinochem; Switzerland-based oil dealer Vitol and Japan's Mitsubishi.[23] The choices of oil contractors seem to be entirely political, with Carroll's former company on the list, along with National Security Advisor Condoleeza Rice's former firm, Chevron. The contract with BP may be a partial payback for the United Kingdom's commitment of combat troops to the U.S.-led war against Hussein's regime, and the Japanese deal has been discussed as "bait" to lure the Japanese government into supplying personnel for security and policing functions in occupied Iraq. And, of course, while Washington's man from Royal Dutch Shell exercises veto power over the decisions of the new Iraqi oil ministry, the money for rebuilding Iraq's devastated oil producing infrastructure goes to Dick Cheney's former company, Halliburton, on a cost-plus basis.

Conclusion: Democracy Demands Accountability

As costs mount for the U.S.-led rebuilding and occupation of Iraq, the profits of companies like Lockheed Martin, Boeing, Raytheon, Bechtel, Halliburton and Dyncorp are likely to rise substantially as a result of contracts steered their way by the Bush administration. In

---

[23] "Iraq Lines Up Long-Term Oil Deals," by Chip Cummins, *Wall Street Journal*, July 29, 2003, company identification provided by *Agence France-Presse*, July 31, 2003.

early August of 2003, the *New York Times* reported yet another example of favoritism that benefited Halliburton (Neela Bannerjee, "Bechtel Ends Move for Work in Iraq, Seeing a Done Deal," August 8, 2003).

After responding to pressure from Rep. Henry Waxman (D-CA) and rival companies to re-bid the longer-term portion of Halliburton's multi-year, multi-billion dollar contract for rebuilding and operating Iraq's oil infrastructure, it now appears that the bidding process is a sham, like so much else about the Bush administration's privatized rebuilding effort in Iraq. After going through the process of recruiting bidders for the contract and holding an all day meeting in Dallas in mid-July with companies interested in competing with Halliburton for the Iraqi oil industry rebuilding contract, the Army Corps of Engineers quietly revised the specs for the new contract so that the vast majority of the $1 billion in work that was supposed to be up for competition was in essence handed back to Halliburton. The work schedules for the alleged $1 billion bid were fixed so that the majority of the work (or at least the majority of the contract dollars) would be issued during calendar year 2003. Given that the bidding process for the second phase of rebuilding Iraq's oil sector will not yield a winner until October 15, 2003, at the earliest, this essentially meant that Halliburton would get the majority of phase two work by default. This led Bechtel, a major potential competitor for the phase two work, to withdraw from the bidding, arguing that, because so much of the work had essentially been handed to Halliburton in a back-door deal with the Army Corps that was not revealed during the initial rounds of bidding, the notion of a true "competition" for the Army Corps' second phase contract was basically a sham.

It is clear that there needs to be more accountability — both to the people of Iraq and the American taxpayers — about how the privatized rebuilding process in Iraq is going to proceed. Contracts should be opened to true competitive bidding, involving not only U.S. firms but competent companies from allied nations. The decisions about which tasks are appropriate for private corporations, as opposed to U.S. government entities or non profit, non governmental organizations, should be made openly and transparently, with appropriate Congressional oversight and public input. Rebuilding contracts should be short-term, limited profit arrangements that do not preempt the ability of a future democratic government in Iraq to choose its own contractors and structure its own industries as the Iraqi people — not Washington bureaucrats or politically-wired companies like Bechtel and Halliburton — see fit.

Companies which are profiting from the rebuilding of Iraq should take a pledge not to make contributions towards the 2004 presidential and Congressional campaigns, to avoid the unseemly appearance of payback, as if firms that have been rewarded by the Bush administration with contracts in Iraq are funneling a percentage of their profits back to Republican candidates. Ideally, if President Bush wants to set an appropriate moral tone, he should agree not to accept contributions for his re-election campaign from any company involved in the rebuilding of Iraq.

At the height of World War II, Senator Harry Truman of Missouri made a name for himself by uncovering profiteering and fraud by companies involved in providing supplies for the war effort. Given the high political and economic stakes in Iraq, a comparable investigation is in order now. Rep. Henry Waxman (D-CA) has been asking all the right questions in his role as the ranking Democrat on the House Committee on Government Reform, but he needs to be joined by prominent colleagues of both parties, and in the Senate as well as the House, in digging up answers about the cost, effectiveness, and propriety of rebuilding Iraq via the secretive, privatized process that the Bush administration and the Pentagon have been pushing thus far.[24]

The alternative to a privatized occupation is clear — a genuine engagement with the United Nations and key allies to share responsibility for rebuilding Iraq's economy, restoring public order,

---

[24] To see Waxman's excellent series of letters to the Army Corp of Engineers and other key Bush administration policy makers, go to the web site of the House Committee on Government Reform, www.house.gov/reform, and find the site for minority caucus.

and building a democracy of, by, and for the Iraqi people. But in order to move in that direction, the Bush administration, or its successor, must discard the stale unilateralist sloganeering that has characterized U.S. policymaking in the early years of the Bush era in favor of a genuine spirit of cooperation. The United States needs allies to extricate itself from the difficult situation that Bush and his hawkish inner circle have gotten American military personnel into in Iraq. It needs them to share the military and economic burden of rebuilding Iraq, but it also needs them for the far more important, albeit intangible task of re-establishing legitimacy for a process that is viewed by many Iraqis — and most citizens of the world — as illegitimate. Unilateral military intervention against nations that do not pose an imminent threat — the concept which is at the heart of the Bush doctrine — should have no place in the global security architecture of the 20th century. The sooner the powers that be in Washington realize that, the better America and the world will be.

What Future for the UN Charter System of War Prevention? Reflections on the Iraq War

Richard Falk

Professor Falk is Albert G. Milbank Professor of International Law and Practice, Emeritus, Princeton University. He has been a Visiting Professor in Global Studies at the University of California at Santa Barbara since 2002. Editor or co-editor of more than twenty books, he is the author of several books, including This Endangered Planet *(Random House, 1971);* Human Rights and State Sovereignty *(Holmes & Meier, 1981);* Reviving the World Court *(University of Virginia, 1986);* The Promise of World Order *(Temple University Press, 1987);* Revolutionaries and Functionaries: The Dual Face of Terrorism *(E.P. Dutton, 1988);* Predatory Globalization *(Polity, 1999); and* The Great Terror War *(Olive Branch, 2003). He has been a Fellow at the Center Advanced Study in the Behavioral Sciences, a Guggenheim Fellow, the Olaf Palme Visiting Professor in Stockholm and Visiting Distinguished Professor at the Mediterranean Academy of Diplomatic Studies, University of Malta, and received his J.S.D. Harvard University.*

The impact of the Iraq War on the future role of the United Nations is a highly speculative matter at this stage. Even the combat phases of the war are far from over despite President George W. Bush's ill-conceived proclamation of victory on May 1, 2003. The war is now assuming the form of resistance to unwanted foreign occupation, and it's unclear whether, as Washington officially contends, its main perpetrators are remnants of Saddam Hussein's regime. Earlier the American leadership was inclined to minimize the UN participation in the restoration of normalcy in Iraq, but as of July 2003, the U.S. Government is beginning to suggest a much expanded set of UN responsibilities, as well as calling upon a wide range of countries to supply troops and share the peacekeeping burdens and risks. Despite this fluidity it does not seem too soon to consider the bearing of the Iraq War upon the future of the United Nations in the area of peace and security.

Framing an Inquiry

President Bush historically challenged the United Nation Security Council when he uttered some memorable words in the course of his September 12, 2002 speech to the General Assembly: "Will the UN serve the purpose of its founding, or will it be irrelevant?"[1] In the aftermath of the Iraq War there are at least two answers to this question. The answer of the U.S. Government would be to suggest that the UN turned out to be irrelevant due to its failure to endorse recourse to war against the Iraq of Saddam Hussein. The answer of those who opposed the war is that the UNSC served the purpose of its founding by its refusal to endorse recourse to a war that could not be persuasively reconciled with the UN Charter and international law. This difference of assessment is not just factual, whether Iraq was a threat and whether the inspection process was succeeding at a reasonable pace, it was also conceptual, even jurisprudential. The resolution of this latter debate is likely to shape the future role of the United Nations, as well as influence the attitude of the most powerful sovereign state as to the relationship between international law generally and the use of force as an instrument of foreign policy.

---

[1] "President's Remarks at the United Nations General Assembly," September 12, 2003, White House Text.

These underlying concerns antedate the recent preoccupation, and were vigorously debated during the Cold War era, especially during the latter stages of the Vietnam War.[2] But the present context of the debate as to the interplay between sovereign discretion as to the use of force and UN authority was framed in the late 1990s around the topic of humanitarian intervention, especially in relation to the Kosovo War. The burning issue in the Kosovo setting was whether "a coalition of the willing" acting under the umbrella of NATO was legally entitled to act as a residual option given the perceived UNSC unwillingness to mandate a use of force despite the urgent humanitarian dangers facing the Albanian Kosovars. In that instance, a formal mandate was sought and provided by NATO, but without what was textually required by Article 53(1) of the UN Charter, that is, lacking some expression of explicit authorization by the UN Security Council. Legal apologists for the initiative insisted that such authorization could be derived from prior UN Security Council resolutions, as well as from the willingness of the UN to manage the post-conflict civil reconstruction of Kosovo that amounted to a tacit assent, providing the undertaking with a retroactive certification of legality. To similar effect were arguments suggesting that the defeat in the Security Council of a resolution of censure introduced by those members opposed to the Kosovo War amounted to an implied acknowledgement of legality, or at the very least a refusal to categorize the war as "illegal" or in violation of the Charter.

But the tension with the Charter rules on the use of force was so clear that these efforts at legalization seemed lame, and what seems a far preferable approach was adopted by the Independent International Commission on Kosovo, which concluded that the intervention in Kosovo was "illegal, but legitimate".[3] The trouble-

---

[2] For representative contributions see *The Vietnam War and International Law* (Richard Falk, ed., 4 vols., 1968, 1969, 1972, 1976).

[3] The *Kosovo Report: Conflict, International Response, Lessons Learned* (2002) 185–198; it should be mentioned that I was a member of the commission.

some elasticity of this doctrine was qualified in two ways: by suggesting the need for the intervening side to bear a heavy burden of persuasion as to the necessity of intervention to avoid an impending or ongoing humanitarian catastrophe; and by a checklist of duties that need to be fulfilled by the intervenors to achieve legitimacy, emphasizing the protection of the civilian population, adherence to the international laws of war, and a convincing focus on humanitarian goals, as distinct from economic and strategic aims of benefit to the intervenors. In Kosovo the moral and political case for intervention seemed strong: a vulnerable and long abused majority population facing an imminent prospect of ethnic cleansing by Serb rulers, a scenario for effective intervention with minimal risks of unforeseen negative effects or extensive collateral damage; and the absence of significant non-humanitarian motivations on the intervening side. As such, the foundation for a principled departure under exceptional circumstances from a strict rendering of Charter rules on the use of force seemed present. The legality/legitimacy gap, however, was recognized as unhealthy, eroding the authority of international law over time, and the Commission recommended strongly that it be closed at the earliest possible time by UN initiative. Its report urged, for example, that the Permanent Members of the Security Council consider informally agreeing to refrain from casting adverse votes in the setting of impending humanitarian catastrophes, and thus suspend the operation of the veto despite disagreeing with the initiative under consideration.[4] The adoption of such a practice would have enabled the Kosovo intervention to be approved by the Security Council even in the face of Russian and Chinese opposition, which would have been registered in the debate, and by way of veto-avoiding abstentions in the vote.

---

[4] Such a practice could be regarded an an informal and substantive extension of the established practice of treating abstentions by permanent members as not blocking decisions by the Security Council despite the wording of Article 27(3) requiring "the concurring votes of the permanent members." Such a practice shows the degree to which the Security Council was able to contrive ways to overcome a paralysis that would have resulted from an interpretative approach based on textual fidelity, and it is impressive that this approach was established in the midst of the Cold War.

More ambitiously, the Commission proposed a three-step process designed to acknowledge within the United Nations Charter System the enforcement role of the Organization in contexts of severe human rights violations. The first step consists of a framework of principles designed to limit claims of humanitarian intervention to a narrow set of circumstances, and to assure that the dynamics of implementation adhere to international humanitarian law and promote the well-being of the people being protected. The second step is to draft a resolution for adoption by the General Assembly in the form of a Declaration on the Right and Responsibility of Humanitarian Intervention that seeks to reconcile respect for sovereign rights, the duty to implement human rights, and the responsibility to prevent humanitarian catastrophes. The third step would be to amend the Charter to incorporate these changes as they pertain to the role and responsibility of the UN Security Council, and other multilateral frameworks and coalitions that undertake humanitarian interventions.[5] It should be noted that no progress toward closing this legitimacy/legality gap by formal or informal action within the United Nations can be anticipated in the near future. There exists substantial opposition on issues of principle as well as policy, especially among Asian countries, to any expansion of the interventionary mandate of the United Nations and other political actors in the setting of human rights. This opposition has deepened since Kosovo because of the controversial uses of force claimed by the United States in its anti-terrorism campaign that have combined security and human rights arguments in settings where widespread suspicion existed with respect to the geopolitical motives of Washington.

Iraq tested the UN Charter system in a way complementary to that associated with the Kosovo controversy, but more fundamentally. The Iraq test was associated with the overall impact of the September 11 attacks and the challenge of mega-terrorism on the viability of the Charter framework governing the use of interna-

---

[5] These three steps outlined in *Kosovo Report, supra* note 3, 187.

tional force.[6] The initial American military response to the Al-Qaeda attack and continuing threat was directed at Afghanistan, a convenient territorial target because it both seemed to be the nerve center of the terrorist organization and a country ruled by the Taliban, a regime enjoying the most minimal diplomatic stature, and complicit in the attacks by allowing Al-Qaeda to operate extensive terrorist training bases within its territory. As such, Afghanistan, as represented by the Taliban, lacked some crucial attributes needed for full membership in international society, including the failure to obtain widespread diplomatic recognition. The reasonableness of waging war to supplant the Taliban regime and destroy the Al-Qaeda base of operations in Afghanistan was widely accepted by the entire spectrum of countries active in world politics, although there was only the most minimal effort by the U.S. Government to demonstrate that it was acting within the UN framework. The Al-Qaeda responsibility for September 11 was amply demonstrated, although controversy and skepticism persists as to whether the attacks could and should have been prevented. Beyond this assurance about responsibility for September 11, the prospect of future attacks seemed great and possibly imminent, and the American capability to win a war in Afghanistan at a proportional cost seemed convincing. For these reasons, there was no significant international opposition to the American initiation and conduct of the Afghanistan War, and varying levels of support from all of America's traditional allies. International law was successfully stretched in these novel circumstances to provide a major state with the practical option of responding with force to one important territorial source of mega-terrorist warfare, thereby upholding the White House claim that a government that knowingly harbors such transnational terrorists shares in responsibility for the political violence that ensues.

But when the Iraq phase of the September 11 response beyond Afghanistan began to be discussed by American leaders, most reactions around the world were deeply opposed, generating a world-

---

[6] A discussion of this challenge and the U.S. response is the theme of my book, *The Great Terror War*. Massachusetts: Olive Branch (2003).

wide peace movement dedicated to avoiding the war and a variety of efforts by governments normally allied with the United States to urge an alternative to war. The main American justification for proceeding immediately against Iraq was articulated in the form of a claimed right of preemptive warfare, abstractly explained as necessary conduct in view of the alleged interface between weaponry of mass destruction and the extremist tactics of the mega-terrorists.[7] It was argued that it was unacceptable in these circumstances for the United States to wait to be attacked, and that rights of preemptive warfare was essential to uphold the security of the "civilized" portion of the world. Bush in his talk at the United Nations said, "We cannot stand by and do nothing while dangers gather."[8] It was this claim that was essentially rejected by the UN Security Council refusal to go along with U.S./UK demands for a direct endorsement of an enforcement mandate. The precise American contention was more narrowly and multiply framed in relation to the failures of Iraq to cooperate fully with the UN inspectors, the years of non-implementation of earlier Security Council resolutions imposing disarmament obligations on Iraq after the Gulf War, and, above all, by the supposedly heightened threat posed by Iraq's alleged arsenal of weapons of mass destruction.[9]

The Iraq War was initiated, and ended militarily with rapid American battlefield victories. President Bush so declared, "In the battle of Iraq, the United States and our allies have prevailed. And now our coalition is engaged in securing and reconstructing that country."[10] The president carefully described the military operations

---

[7] Initially fully depicted in "Remarks by the President at 2002 Graduation Exercise of the United States Military Academy," June 1, 2002; given a more enduring and authoritative status by their emphasis in the official White House document, The National Security Strategy of the United States of America, September 2002, esp. Chapter V, 13–16.

[8] See *supra*, note 1.

[9] The most important Security Council resolutions were 678 (1990), 687 (1991), and, of course, 1441 (2002).

[10] "President Bush's Prepared Remarks Declaring End to Major Combat in Iraq," text printed in *New York Times*, May 2, 2003, A14.

as "a battle" rather than as "a war", subsuming the attack on Iraq within the wider, ongoing war against global terrorism, and implying that the undertaking should be seen as one element in the anti-terrorism campaign launched in response to the September 11 attacks. Again, as in relation to Kosovo, the UNSC refrained from censuring the United States and its allies, and the UN has seemed fully willing, even eager, to play whatever part is assigned to it during the current period of military occupation and political, economic, and social reconstruction, so far under exclusive U.S./ UK control. Such acquiescence is particularly impressive given the failure of the victorious coalition in the Iraq war to find any evidence of weapons of mass destruction, or to be attacked by such weaponry despite launching a war designed to destroy precisely these capabilities of the regime of Saddam Hussein. It seems reasonable to conclude that either such weaponry does not exist, or if it does exist, then it is of no operational relevance and a strategy of deterrence would be fully able to assure against a future use. That is, if such weapons were not used by Iraq to defend the survival of the regime *in extremis*, then it is highly unlikely that they would ever have been used in circumstances where an annihilating retaliation could be anticipated. If Iraq refrained when it had nothing to lose, why would it use such weaponry when the assured response would be the assured destruction of country and regime? There has never existed any basis for supposing the Baghdad regime to be suicidal, and what evidence exists suggest the opposite, a strong willingness to subordinate other goals to survival. Even in this current occupation phase of the war the impulse to survive as an independent political entity seems to be the primary foundation of fierce Iraqi resistance.

How should such a pattern of circumvention of Charter rules combined with the reluctance of the UNSC to seek censure for such violations be construed from the perspective of the future of international law? There are several overlapping modes of interpretation, each of which illuminates the issue to some extent, but none seems to provide a satisfactory account from the perspective of international law:

- The United States as the dominant state in a unipolar world order enjoys an exemption from legal accountability with respect to uses of force irreconcilable with the UN Charter System; other states, in contrast, would be generally held to account unless directly protected by the U.S. exemption;
- The pattern of behavior confirms a skeptical trend that suggests the Charter System no longer corresponds, or never did correspond, with the realities of world politics, and is not authoritative in relation to the behavior of states;[11]
- The American pattern of behavior is in some tension with the Charter System, but it is a creative tension that suggests respect for the underlying values of the world community, viewing legality as a matter of degree, not either/or, and as requiring continuing adjustment to changing circumstances; as such, the claims of preemption in relation to mega-terrorism provide a reasonable doctrinal explanation for an expanded right of self-defense;
- Acknowledging the behavioral pressures of the world on the Charter guidelines with respect to force, the possibility exists that contested uses of force under the Charter are "illegal, yet legitimate" either by reference to the rationale for initiating action without UNSC approval or on the basis of the beneficial impact of the intervention.[12] From this perspective, the failure to find weapons of mass destruction does not definitively undermine the claim that the intervention is "legitimate". It still could be judged as legitimate due to a series of effects: the emancipation of the Iraqi people from an oppressive regime, reinforced

---

[11] This position is most clearly articulated by Michael J. Glennon, "Why the Security Council Failed," *Foreign Affairs* 82 (No. 3): 16–35 (2003); the overall argument is more fully developed in Glennon's book *Limits of Law, Prerogatives of Power: Interventionism After Kosovo* (2001); also relevant, Anthony C. Arend and Robert J. Beck, *International Law and the Use of Force: Beyond the UN Charter Paradigm* (1993); A. Mark Weisbrud, *Use of Force: The Practice of States Since World War II* (1997).

[12] See Anne-Marie Slaughter, "Good Reasons for Going Around the UN," *New York Times*, March 15, 2003.

by the overwhelming evidence that the Baghdad rulers were guilty of systematic, widespread, and massive Crimes Against Humanity, and an occupation that prepares the Iraqi people for political democracy and economic success.[13]

At this stage, it is impossible to predict how the Iraq War will impact upon the Charter system with respect to the international regulation of force. It will depend on how principal states treat the issue, especially the United States. International law, in this crucial sense, is neither more nor less than what the powerful actors in the system, and to a lesser extent the global community of international jurists, as well as the global jury of public opinion, say it is. International law in the area of the use of force cannot by itself induce consistent compliance because of sovereignty-oriented political attitudes combined with the gross disparities in power that prevent the logic of reciprocity and the benefits of mutuality operating with respect to the security agenda of states. The "realist" school has dominated the foreign policy process of major countries throughout the existence of the modern state system, being only marginally challenged by a Wilsonian approach that is more reliant on legalism and moralism.[14] To the extent that restraint with respect to the use of force is advocated by realists, it is based on cost-benefit assessments, including the diplomatic virtue of prudence and the avoidance of over-extension that has been blamed throughout history for the decline of major states.[15]

---

[13] See Charles Krauthammer, "U.S. cleaning up Hussein's mess in Iraq," *Los Angeles Times*, May 16, 2003; Thomas I. Friedman, "Bored with Baghdad—Already," *New York Times*, May 18, 2003, §4, 13.

[14] For the view that American moralism and legalism has had a detrimental impact on U.S. foreign policy during the first half of the twentieth century see George F. Kennan, *American Diplomacy 1900–1950* (1951); also Henry Kissinger, *Diplomacy* (1994), esp. 218–245, 762–835. For a more general interpretation of the Wilsonian component as a more widely conceived aspect of the overall American foreign policy tradition see Walter Russell Mead, *Special Providence: American Foreign Policy and How It Changed the World* (2001), 132–173.

[15] Paul Kennedy, *The Rise and Fall of Great Power: Economic Change and Military Conflict 1500–2000* (1987).

There are grounds for supposing that the approach of the Bush administration may not fit within the realist paradigm, but rather represents a militant and reactionary version of Wilsonian idealism.[16] President Bush has consistently described the war against terrorism in terms of good and evil, which works against even constraints based on calculations of self-interest and prudence.[17] To the extent that such an orientation shapes the near future of American conduct the UN Charter system will be disregarded except possibly in those circumstances where the Security Council would support an American claim to use force.[18]

The Iraq War and the Future of the Charter System

Against the jurisprudential background depicted in the previous section, an interpretation of the Iraq precedent is necessarily tentative. It depends, in the first analysis, on whether the American battlefield victory in the Iraq War can be converted by reasonable means in a short time period into what is generally interpreted to be a political victory. Such an outcome is best measured in Iraq by such factors as stability, democratization, recovery of Iraqi sovereignty, economic development, and public perceptions. If the American occupation is viewed as successful, then the intervention is likely

---

[16] For an argument along these lines see Max Boot, "George Woodrow Bush: the president is becoming a Wilsonian interventionist," *Wall Street Journal*, July 1, 2002.

[17] Aside from identifying specific states as "the axis of evil" in the global setting of the war against terrorism, in his West Point speech the president includes some strongly moralistic rhetoric of a visionary quality, quite inimical to the realist tradition. The following excerpt is indicative of the tone and message: "We are in a conflict between good and evil, and America will call evil by its name. By confronting evil and lawless regimes, we do not create a problem, we reveal a problem. And we will lead the world in opposing it." See *supra*, note 1.

[18] See Richard Perle, "Thank God for the death of the UN: Its abject failure gave us only anarchy, The World Needs Order," *The Guardian*, March 20, 2003.

to be treated as "legitimate", despite being generally regarded as "illegal". Such a perception will be viewed by some as adding a needed measure of flexibility in the application of the Charter system in a world where the possible interplay of mega-terrorist tactics and weaponry of mass destruction validates recourse to anticipatory self-defense and it will be dismissed by others as an opportunistic and retroactively rationalized repudiation of legal restraints by the world's sole superpower.

There are two main conceptual explanations of this likely divergence of opinion. The first relates to issues of *factual plausibility*. The doctrine of preemption, as such, is less troublesome than its unilateral application in circumstances where the burden of persuasion as to the imminence and severity of the threat is not sustained. The diplomatic repudiation of the United States in the Security Council resulted mainly from the factual unpersuasiveness of the U.S. arguments about the threats associated with Iraqi retention of weaponry of mass destruction and the claims of a purported linkage between the Baghdad regime and the Al-Qaeda network, arguably making reliance on deterrence and containment unacceptable. There was no doubts about the brutality of Saddam Hussein's rule, but there was little support for recourse to an international war on such grounds. This skepticism has been heightened by the failure so far to uncover weaponry of mass destruction in the aftermath of the war, despite unimpeded access to suspicious sites, the cooperation of Iraqi scientists and weapons personnel, and a huge intelligence effort.

The second ground of divergence relates to arguments of *retroactive justification*. Here the focus is on whether a war opposed because its side-effects seemed potentially dangerous and its advance rationale was not convincing enough to justify stretching the Charter System of restraint could be justified after the fact. The justifications combine the quick military victory on the battlefield with relatively low casualty figures, as reinforced by the documentation of Saddam Hussein's criminality as an Iraqi leader. Such an argument would seem more convincing if the American-led coalition forces had been more clearly welcomed as "liberators" rather than viewed as "occupiers", and if the post-combat American presence in Iraq was less marred by continuous and even escalating violent incidents of resistance and further American casualties. It remains too early to reach any sort of judgment as to the political effects of the war and its wider ramifications regionally and globally. If the American occupation turns out to be relatively short, and is generally perceived to benefit the Iraqi people and not the American occupiers, arguments based on retroactive justification are likely to gain support, and the Iraqi precedent would not be viewed so much as destructive of the Charter System, as an extension of it based on the emerging enlargement of the role of the international community to protect societies vulnerable to abusive governments.[19]

Of course, the issue of process is important, as well as the substantive outcome. The Iraq War represented a circumvention of the collective procedures of the Charter System with respect to uses of force in contexts not covered by the Article 51 conception of self-defense. To some extent, a favorable view of the effects of such a use of force weaken objections to unilateralism. Adopting a constructivist view of international law, much depends on the future conduct and attitudes of the United States Government. Constructivism is an assessment of political and legal reality that places decisive emphasis on dominant mental perceptions as to a given set of conditions, whether or not such perceptions are accurate as evaluated from other standpoints.[20] Will the U.S. Government in the future exhibit generally respect for the role of the Security Council or will it feel vindicated by its decision to act unilaterally in conjunction with cooperative allies, and continue to rely on such a model for conflict resolution? If the latter interpretation shapes

---

[19] For influential comprehensive presentation along these lines see *The Responsibility to Protect: Report of the International Commission on Intervention and State Sovereignty* (2001).

[20] Constructivism as an academic approach to the study of international relations is best explained by Alexander Wendt in his *Social Theory of International Politics* (1999).

future American foreign policy, then the Charter System is marginalized, at least with respect to the United States, and because the United States sets the rules of the game, the overall acceptance of the prohibition on recourse to non-defensive force is likely to be seriously weakened.

Can the Charter System work without adherence to its procedures and restraining rules by the dominant state in the world? The constructivist answer is clarifying to a degree. To the extent that other states continue to take the Charter System as authoritative it will certainly heavily influence international responses to challenged uses of force by states other than the United States, and will affect global attitudes toward American leadership. There will be complaints about the degree to which geopolitical realities trump international law restraints and about double standards, but these complaints have been made since the United Nations came into being, and arguably were embedded in the Charter by granting a veto to the permanent members.

The approach taken after the collapse of the Baghdad regime by the Security Council in its Resolution 1483 is indicative of a tension between acquiescence and opposition to the United States/United Kingdom recourse to war against Iraq. The resolution divides responsibility and authority between the occupying powers and the United Nations, granting the U.S./UK predominant control over the most vital concerns of security, economic and political reconstruction, and governance. At the same time, the resolution stops far short of retroactively endorsing recourse to force by the U.S./UK under the factual circumstances that existed. It dodges the issue of legality/legitimacy by avoiding any formal pronouncement, while accepting as a legitimate given the realities of the apparent outcome of the war. As a result, a high degree of ambiguity surrounds the Iraq War as precedent. Undoubtedly, this ambiguity will be reduced, and possibly eliminated, by a clearer sense of the political outcome of the war and by patterns of subsequent UNSC practice in future peace and security contexts.

The Charter System, Mega-terrorism, and Humanitarian Intervention

In the 1990s there was a definite trend toward accepting a more interventionary role for the United Nations with respect to the prevention of ethnic cleansing and genocide. The Security Council, as supported by the last three Secretaries General, reflecting a greater prominence for the international protection of human rights and less anxiety about risks of escalation that were operative during the Cold War, narrowed the degree of deference owed to the territorial supremacy of sovereign governments. As such, the domestic jurisdiction exclusion of UN intervention expressed in Article 2(7) was definitely under challenge from the widespread grassroots and governmental advocacy of humanitarian intervention in the years following the Cold War. Although the pattern of claims and practice remained contested, being resisted especially by China and other Asian countries, there was considerable inter-governmental and grassroots support for humanitarian intervention. The UN was more often and more sharply attacked for doing too little to mitigate human suffering, as in Bosnia and Rwanda, than criticized for doing too much.[21]

A variant on this debate is connected with the instances of uses of force under American leadership in the post-September 11 world. In both Afghanistan and Iraq recourse to force rested on defensive claims against the new threats of mega-terrorism, but the effect in both instances was to liberate captive populations from extremely oppressive regimes, establishing patterns of governance and potential self-determination that seemed virtually impossible for the oppressed citizenry to challenge by normal modes of resistance. Even though the humanitarian *motivations* of the United States are suspect in both instances, due to a past record of collaboration with these regimes while their abusive conduct was

---

[21] For useful overviews of this trend see Sean Murphy, *Humanitarian Intervention: The United Nations in an Evolving World* (1996); Nicholas J. Wheeler, *Saving Strangers: Humanitarian Intervention in International Society* (2000).

at its worst, the effect of the interventions was emancipatory, and the declared intention of the occupation to support human rights and democratization, if implemented, would strengthen the humanitarian argument. Undoubtedly, such forcible liberations would not have taken place without the pressures mounted and the climate created by the September 11 attacks. Nevertheless, to the extent that mega-terrorism is associated with criminal forms of governmental authority, would it not be reasonable to construe uses of force that accomplished "regime change" as part of an enlarged doctrine of humanitarian intervention?

I think not for some obvious reasons. Recourse to war is too serious a matter to allow decisions about it to proceed on the basis of a retroactive rationales that are not fully articulated and debated in advance. For this reason also, prudential considerations alone would rule out humanitarian intervention in all but the most extreme cases, and even in most of these due to the magnitude of the undertaking and the uncertainty of the consequences. Who would be so crazy as to advocate humanitarian intervention by military means on behalf of the Chechens, Tibetans, Kashmiris? Of course, there are many options open to the international community and its member states not involving the use of force that could range from expressions of disapproval to the imposition of comprehensive sanctions. The case for humanitarian intervention relying on force must be treated as a principled, and even then, a rare exception to the generalized prohibition of the Charter with respect to the use of force embodied in Article 2(4).[22] If the Security Council does not mandate the intervention, and a coalition of the willing proceeds, the undertaking could still be substantially vindicated, as in Kosovo,

---

[22] For a well-crafted narrow doctrine of humanitarian intervention see Jack Donnelly, *Universal Human Rights in Theory And Practice* (2nd edn., 2003) 242–260. For a generally skeptical set of reflections about claims of humanitarian intervention see *Humanitarian Intervention: Moral and Philosophical Issues* (Aleksandar Jokic, ed., 2003); for a somewhat more optimistic set of accounts see *Humanitarian Intervention: Ethical, Legal, and Political Dilemmas* (J. L. Holzgrefe and Robert O. Keohane, eds., 2003).

if some sort of collective process was involved and the facts confirmed the imminence of a humanitarian emergency. The Kosovo Commission tackled this issue of principled humanitarian intervention, as have scholars, seeking to provide guidance that preserves the balance between the prohibition on uses of force contained in international law and the moral/political imperatives to mitigate impending or ongoing humanitarian catastrophes by stretching the legal restraints.[23]

A pro-intervention argument should not be treated as acceptable in circumstances where the use of force is associated with alleged security threats posed by the menace of mega-terrorism, but the justification tendered after the fact emphasizes the case for humanitarian intervention. In Afghanistan the security argument was sufficiently convincing as to make the humanitarian benefits of the war a political and moral bonus, but without bearing on the legal case for recourse to force, which was sufficiently convincing on the defensive grounds claimed to satisfy most international law experts. In Iraq, by contrast, the security and related anti-Al-Qaeda arguments were unconvincing, and the claimed humanitarian benefits resulting from the war were emphasized by American officials as a way to circumvent the illegality of the American-led recourse to force. Such post hoc efforts at legalization should not be accorded much respect, especially in the context of a major war where prior efforts to obtain a mandate for the use of force were not endorsed by the Security Council even in the face of major diplomatic pressures mounted by Washington in the several months prior to the Iraq War, and where disclosure suggest that the

---

[23] For important efforts see *Kosovo Report*, note 3; *The Responsibility to Protect*, Report of the International Commission on Intervention and State Sovereignty (2001) 53–57; Lori Fisler Damrosch (ed.), "Concluding Remarks," in *Enforcing Restraint: Collective Intervention in Internal Conflicts* (1993), 348–367; and esp. Damrosch, "The inevitability of selective response? Principles to guide urgent international action," *Kosovo and the Challenge of Humanitarian Intervention* (Albrecht Schnabel and Ramesh Thakur, eds., 2001) 405–419.

supposed threat associated with weapons of mass destruction was deliberately exaggerated.[24]

A Constructivist Future for the UN Charter System

The position favored here is that the United States would be best served by adhering to the UN Charter System, and to international law generally.[25] This system is flexible enough to accommodate new and genuine security imperatives as well as changing values, including a shifting balance between sovereign rights and world community responsibilities.[26] In both settings of humanitarian intervention and responses against mega-terrorism the Charter System can be *legally* vindicated *in appropriate factual circumstances.*

From this perspective recourse to war against Iraq should not have been undertaken without a *prior* mandate from the Security Council, and rather than "a failure" of the United Nations, it represented a responsible exercise of its institutional responsibility to administer a system of constitutional restraints.[27] The facts did not support the case for preemption, as there was neither *imminence* nor *necessity*. As a result, the Iraq War seemed, at best, to qualify as an instance of *preventive war*, but there are strong legal, moral, and political reasons to deny both legality and legitimacy to such a use of force, and even the more remote threat being countered by

---

[24] It may be worth recalling the vigorous U.S. Government objections to the Vietnamese intervention in Cambodia, and subsequent occupation, that disrupted the Khmer Rouge genocide. The American position repudiated the humanitarian considerations, emphasizing the Vietnamese violation of Cambodian sovereignty, urging immediate withdrawal despite the risk of regenerating a genocidal regime.

[25] A more generalized view of the benefits arising from a law-oreinted approach are well explained in *Rule of Power or Rule of Law?* (Nicole Deller, Arjun Makhijani, and John Burroughs, eds., 2003).

[26] See Oscar Schachter, "In Defense of International Rules on the Use of Force," *U. Chi. L. Rev*, 53, p. 113 (1986).

[27] The reference to failure is to challenge the central conclusion of Glennon's analysis, *supra*, note 10.

"prevention" was not factually sustained with respect to Iraq. It is not an acceptable exception to the Charter System, and no effort was made by the U.S. Government to claim a right of preventive war, although the highly abstract and vague phrasing of the preemptive war doctrine in the National Security Strategy of the U.S. would be more accurately formulated and explained as "a preventive war doctrine". But even within this highly dubious doctrinal setting, to be at all convincing the evidence would at least have to demonstrate a credible future Iraqi threat that could not be reliably deterred, and this was never done, or even attempted.

My legal constructivist position is that the United States (and the world) would benefit from a self-imposed discipline of adherence to the UN Charter System governing the use of force. Such a voluntary discipline would overcome the absence of geopolitical limits associated with countervailing power in a unipolar world.[28] It would also work against tendencies by the United States and others to rely too much on military superiority, which encourages the formation of defensive alliances, and possibly arms races. International law is flexible enough to allow the United States, and other countries, to meet novel security needs. Beyond this, neither American values nor strategic goals, should be construed to validate uses of force that cannot win support in the UN Security Council. If one considers the course of American foreign policy over the course of the last half century, adherence to the Charter System with respect to the use of force would have avoided the worst policy failures, including that of Vietnam. Deviations from the Charter system of prohibitions on the use of force can be credited with no clear successes.

It is not the Charter System that is in disarray, providing sensible grounds for declaring the project of regulating recourse to war by states a failed experiment that should now be abandoned. It is

---

[28] My assertion is in direct opposition to the inferences drawn by Robert Kagan in his influential book. See Kagan, *Of Paradise and Power: America and Europe in the New World Order* (2003).

rather leading states, and above all the United States, that need to be persuaded that their interests are served and their values realized by a more diligent pursuit of a law-oriented foreign policy. The Charter System is not a legal prison that presents states with the dilemma of adherence (and defeat) and violation or disregard (and victory). Rather adherence is the best policy, if understood against a jurisprudential background that is neither slavishly legalistic nor cynically nihilistic. The law can be stretched as new necessities arise, but the stretching must to the extent possible be in accord with procedures and norms contained in the Charter System, with a factually and doctrinally persuasive explanation of why a particular instance of stretching is justified.

Such positive constructivist attitudes will renew confidence in the Charter System. It is also true that constructivism can work negatively, and so if the sorts of disregard of the legal framework, public opposition, and governmental resistance present in the Iraq case is repeated in the future, then indeed the Charter System will be in a shambles before much longer.

There is little doubt that the Iraq War and the American occupation that has ensued represents a serious setback for advocates of a law-governed approach to world order, as well as to the procedural effort to give the United Nations Security Council primary authority to mandate exceptions to the Charter prohibition on the non-defensive use of force to resolve international conflicts. But history can be cunning. There exists some possibility that the burdens of occupation in Iraq, as well as the discrediting of the rationale advanced to justify the American recourse to war, will cause a political swing in the United States and elsewhere in the direction of greater respect for the cardinal rules and principles of international law, for the United Nations, and for a peace-oriented public opinion at home and abroad.

Iraq: Educational Renewal for an Arab Renaissance?

Sir John Daniel

A Fellow of the Open University and Assistant Director-General for Education at UNESCO (United Nations Educational, Scientific and Cultural Organisation), he was knighted by Queen Elizabeth for services to higher education in 1994. This honour recognized the leading role that he has played internationally, over three decades, in the development of distance learning in universities. The success of his book, Mega-Universities and Knowledge Media: Technology Strategies for Higher Education *(Kogan Page, 1996), established his reputation in international university circles as a leading thinker about the role of technology in academic communities. Sir John Daniel holds honorary degrees from universities in ten countries.*

Introduction

Great expectations are vested in the reform of Iraq after the overthrow of Saddam Hussein. The coalition that ousted his regime hopes to help the Iraqi people build an exemplary new polity that will inspire change in other Arab countries. A thorough renewal of Iraq's education system, and particularly of its institutions of higher learning, will be vital if these hopes are to become reality.

In 1990 Iraq had the best education system in the Arab world and a decade of sanctions degraded rather than destroyed it. The 2003 war did relatively little damage to educational institutions. The orgy of looting that followed the formal ending of hostilities was more devastating. Nevertheless, given the ambitions of the coalition, the competence of the Iraqi people and the resources available,

215

rebuilding a system comparable to that in place in 1990 should not be difficult.

If, however, the reconstruction of Iraq is to usher in a new era of freedom, democracy and peace for the whole Arab world, simply rebuilding the education system will not suffice. The aim has to be to make Iraq an educational and academic beacon for the region. For this to happen reform must address explicitly the weaknesses that have blighted the Arab world for too long. It also requires institutional renewal that does not merely ape western models. For a new Iraq to win the admiration and envy of other Arab countries that will inspire them to emulate its achievements, it must recover some of the intellectual and educational dynamism that made Arab scholars world leaders for hundreds of years in the first and second millennia.

Is such an ambitious agenda possible? In trying to answer this question we shall make three major — maybe heroic — assumptions about the background to the task of educational reform. The first is that continued progress towards peace between Israel and Palestine will create the conditions for all Arabs to take a more optimistic view of their future. The second is that the coalition and other players, such as the UN system, will stay the course, maintain a secure environment, and carry the majority of Iraqis with them in the overall effort of rebuilding the country and its institutions. The third is that under these conditions Iraq will gradually develop the values of public participation, openness and transparency that have to be the foundation for development.

A hard-hitting diagnosis of the weaknesses and problems of the Arab world has been provided by Arab scholars and specialists in the *Arab Human Development Report 2002* (UNDP, 2002). We shall summarise some of its key conclusions before asking whether the key characteristics of the great historical period of Arab education and scholarship can illuminate and inspire the contemporary effort of reform. This will provide the background for examining the requirements for educational reform in the Arab world generally. Finally we shall review current situation of higher education in Iraq and the work of renewal that is under way.

What Holds the Arab World Back?

The *Arab Human Development Report 2002* takes the Arab world to mean the 22 countries of the Arab League, which are home to 280 million people. This region has the highest proportion of young people in the world. Since nearly 40% of Arabs are under 14, it is estimated that the Arab population will number 400 million in the third decade of this century. This makes educational reform even more urgent. A survey (UNDP, 2002, p. 51) showed that 51% of older youth in the Arab world wish to emigrate to other countries, most of them outside the Arab region. This indicates the dissatisfaction of young people with current conditions and future prospects in their home countries and is a serious indictment of the economic and political environments that governments have created across the region.

The recent development of the Arab world can count some successes. Life expectancy has grown by 15 years since 1970 and infant mortality is down by two-thirds. Income per head is higher than in other developing regions of the world and a smaller proportion of people suffer the abject poverty of less than one dollar per day. However, one in five Arabs lives on less than two dollars a day and economic growth, at an annual 0.5%, is dismal. Unless growth can be accelerated, the current figure of 12 million unemployed could rise to 25 million by 2010.

The Report concludes that the Arab world is not held back by a shortage of resources, but by the lack of three essentials: freedom, knowledge and womanpower. It argues that these three deficits prevent Arabs from achieving their potential and create, in the words of *The Economist* (2002), "a deadly combination of wealth and backwardness".

The deficit of freedom is the central problem. Although the region is rich in the trappings of democracy these Arab authors argue that the wave of democratisation that has swept the globe in recent times has left the Arab world largely untouched. The transfer of power through the ballot box is not a common phenomenon. Furthermore, freedom of expression and freedom of association are very limited. In no Arab country are the media truly free and in only three do they qualify as partly free. Not surprisingly civil society, an important manifestation of freedom, is highly circumscribed, and the social environment is often oppressive. The distinction between the executive and judicial branches of government is usually fuzzy.

The deficit of knowledge that the UNDP report identifies is perhaps surprising, because Arabs spend a higher proportion of GDP on education than any other developing region. However, this expenditure does not yield quality education and the mismatch between what schools teach and what the labour market requires is stark. 10 million children between 6 and 15 years are out of school and, if current trends persist, this number will increase by 40% by 2015. There are still about 70 million illiterates over the age of 15, two-thirds of them women. Although secondary enrolment has increased, it is still below 60% with a high dropout rate (Billeh, 2002).

Against the impressive contributions to knowledge made by the Arab world in earlier times, the current state of Arab research, scholarship and creativity is very weak. This applies as much to science and technology as to literature and the creative industries. Only 0.6% of Arabs use the Internet and 1.2% have personal computers, or, to put it another way, Arabs constitute 5% of the world population but only 0.5% of its Internet users. The report laments a declining film industry, a lack of new writing in Arabic and small availability of foreign authors in translation. The cumulative total of books translated into Arabic over the last thousand years is only 100,000, which is roughly equal to the number translated in Spain every year. This combination of lack of freedom and modest intellectual creativity is captured in the sub-heading "Bridled Minds, Shackled Potential" (UNDP, 2002, p. 3)

The report considers that the deficit of womanpower is a particular handicap in the Arab world. Half the region's productive human potential is sidelined because women usually have inferior legal status and citizenship. The extent of this discrimination is hard to document because only 14 of the 22 countries could supply the data that the UNDP uses to calculate its gender empowerment measure. Some progress is being made, for rates of female literacy have trebled since 1970. Nevertheless, in the region as a whole, 50% of adult women are illiterate.

The report draws a parallel between the discrimination imposed by sexism and the prejudice implied by ageism, because both types of bias curtail the participation of the two majorities in the Arab region: women and the young. It notes that both emanate from patriarchal dominance that exploits divergence with respect to gender and age (UNDP, 2002, p. 10).

Lessons from the Past

Other regions of the world, notably sub-Saharan Africa, share these deficits of freedom, knowledge and womanpower to varying degrees. The question here is whether reform in Iraq can inspire the whole Arab world to address these deficits in a successful and expeditious manner. Are there features of Iraq, or of the Arab world generally, that would make it possible to accelerate the slow and painful processes of development that are being implemented in other under performing countries?

One reason for optimism is that the Arab world does have a history, centuries ago, of being more developed than much of the rest of the world. For a period from the later centuries of the first millennium through the early centuries of the second millennium AD, Arabs led the world in many areas of knowledge. Much of this intellectual leadership came out of the cities of Iraq. What was the nature of their leadership and does it hold lessons for today? We shall comment first on interesting aspects of the Arab education system of those times and then review particular areas of intellectual prowess.

The prophet Muhammad said "it is the duty of every Muslim man and woman to seek education" and founded mosque schools himself. Under his influence Arabs pursued knowledge for its own sake and the use of Arabic, the language of the Koran, spread with Islam. The Arabs translated and preserved teachings from Greece, India and Persia and from these texts a mass revolution in education began during the Abbasid dynasty (750–1258 AD). In the tenth century there were 3,000 mosques in Baghdad alone, and the mosque schools were open to rich and poor and to men and women alike. Although lessons on the Koran and hadith (the science of tradition) were restricted to Muslims, non-Muslims could attend lessons in other subjects such as jurisprudence, philology, poetry and rhetoric.

Today, to many outside the Arab world, the term madrasa (which means place of learning) evokes a narrow, even reactionary, education focused solely on the Koran. History tells a different story. In 1066 the vizier Nizam al-Mulk founded the Nizamiyya Madrasa in Baghdad, which became the forerunner of secondary and college level education in the Arab empire. He not only popularised this type of school but also inspired the early universities in Europe. Each madrasa had its own curriculum, which included religious sciences and intellectual sciences (astronomy, mathematics, music and physics). As particular madrasas grew and attracted scholars from all over the Arab empire the number of disciplines grew. Teachers received good salaries and scholarships were available to students. Funds came from both government and private sources.

In view of the current status of women in much of the Arab world, we note that there were no restrictions on women attending classes — and women also taught classes that included men. At that time Arab women contributed strongly to the economic, political and social life of the empire and excelled in medicine, poetry, oratory and other subjects.

In a phenomenon that was a precursor to the movement of scholars between the universities of medieval Europe, travelling from city to city in search of knowledge was a common practice in the early centuries of Islam. Academies built up impressive collections of books and knowledge was freely shared. As Arab influence spread to Spain and beyond, knowledge transfer based on Arab learning and scholarship helped to advance education in Europe, adding new disciplines to the traditional seven liberal arts, and introducing empirical methods to research. A few examples will show the remarkable impact of this contribution.

From the 7th century onward the Arab world generated a rich literature, which was by no means simply the expression of an elite. The writer considered to be the outstanding genius of Arab prose, al-Jahiz (776–869) was the grandson of a black slave yet received an excellent education in Basra, Iraq. He began a tradition of *belles-lettres*, which later expanded to embrace history. At first this concentrated on biographies of the life of the prophet Muhammad and accounts of events. However, in the 14th century Ibn Khaldun, whom many consider the true father of modern historiography and sociology, showed that historical events depended on a variety of factors. His *Muqaddimah*, which the historian George Sarton called the most important historical work of the Middle Ages, used such lenses as the labour market, social structures and climate to illuminate developments. According to Arnold Toynbee, "Ibn Khaldun has conceived and formulated a philosophy of history which is undoubtedly the greatest work of its kind that has ever been created by any mind in any time". Appropriately, the UNDP report recalls an important chapter in the *Muqaddimah* to argue for a holistic approach to human development, and particularly for the importance of a healthy labour market to a properly functioning society (UNDP, 2002, p. 16.)

George Sarton had similar praise for Arab contributions to other disciplines in his *Introduction to the History of Science* where he states:

"From the second half of the 8th to the end of the 11th century, Arabic was the scientific and progressive language of mankind... When the West was sufficiently mature to feel the need of deeper knowledge, it turned its attention, first of all, not to the Greek sources, but to the Arabic ones."

We note, for example, the outstanding contribution to mathematics of Muhammad ibn Musa al-Khawarazmi, who went to study science in India in the 9th century and, on his return, introduced Hindu numerals — and the concept of zero — into the Arab world. It is difficult to overestimate the importance of zero, whose use was first recorded in Arab writing in 873 and in Hindu work in 876, in opening up mathematical calculation. Although using Roman numerals made the simplest arithmetical calculation complex and tedious, it was 400 years before Europe ceased to ridicule the zero as "a meaningless nothing" and adopted the flexible and powerful decimal system that Al-Khawarazmi had developed. He also invented algebra (*al-jabr*) and thereby influenced medieval mathematical thought more than any other writer, as well as making important contributions to astronomy, geography and music.

Today we think of Omar Khayyam primarily as the author of The Rubaiyat. In the Arab world, however, he was thought of first and foremost as a mathematician. He reformed the Persian calendar to give an error of one day in 5,000 years, which is superior to the Gregorian calendar in use today, whose error is one day in 3,300 years.

In physics the great Arab name was Ibn al-Haytham (965–1030), another native of Basra. Although he contributed to various fields he is best known for his development of the science of optics. His painstaking studies of light established that it travels in straight lines and is subject to universal laws. In studying the refraction of light he realised that light is bent at the interface between two media and that this, rather than any inherent property in glass, explained how lenses work. In his ability both to ask and to answer profound questions that others ignored, Ibn al-Haytham has been compared to Isaac Newton many centuries later. For example, his reflections on the perception of light by the eye, which brought together the notion of the reflection of light by objects and the role of the brain in interpreting the light rays received by the eye, helped the later Italian school of painters to understand perspective.

The insistence on the importance of experimentation had also been made by the 8th century Arab chemist Jabir ibn Hayyan, known in the West as Geber. Jabir detailed the different types of chemical transformations, such as crystallisation, solution and sublimation, as well as describing the processes for steel making and the preparation of hair dyes and illuminating inks. He also discovered a number of chemicals, of which nitric acid was particularly important and useful.

Some notes on the contribution to medicine will complete this brief commentary on the great era of Arab science. Here again, the Arabs were responsible for passing on to Europe, through Arabic translations, the legacy of Greek medicine. Arab medicine itself began to flourish with the creation of the first *bimaristan*, a hospital and medical institution, in Baghdad in the 8th century. These institutions continued to be built throughout the Abbasid Empire and housed some of its most important educational activities. Medical staffs were highly international and believed in treating the whole person. The first great name in Arab medicine was Muhammad Ibn Zakariya al-Razi, who wrote some 200 books one of which, on smallpox, was translated into English as recently as 1948.

Another commanding intellect and physician was Abu Ali al-Hussain Ibn Sina, or Avicenna (980–1037). By the age of 16 he had already mastered Islamic Law, philosophy and mathematics and turned his attention to medicine. By the age of 18 his fame led rulers and princes to seek his services. Of his sixteen books on medicine, the Canun, a million-word encyclopaedia, was the basis for much of the European medical curriculum until the 15th century.

We could add many more Arab names in listing some of the key contributions to the development of modern science and knowledge. However, the examples given will suffice to show how ironic it is that Arabs themselves identify a knowledge deficit as one of their major weaknesses at the beginning of the 21st century. As we have seen, a thousand years ago the Arab contribution was not simply to make discoveries and to codify knowledge, but also to develop the scientific method. In a comment relevant to today's reforms of higher education the *Arab Human Development Report 2002* notes (UNDP, 2002, p. 69):

"Arab scientists pioneered the structured experimentation process (commonly known in Western culture as the scientific method and represented by the concept of algorithms, derived from the Arabic Al-Khwarizmi). Although this is a rudimentary, well understood process, modern Arab curricula have devoted too little time and attention to this central pillar of research and development."

In seeking to harness education to an Arab renaissance it is important to reaffirm the historic importance of knowledge in Arab culture. As long ago as the 6th century Imam Ali bin abi Taleb wrote that "if God were to humiliate a human being, He would deny him knowledge". Some of his other statements are also good texts for educational reform. One is: "Knowledge is superior to wealth. Knowledge guards you, whereas you guard wealth. Wealth decreases with expenditure, whereas knowledge multiplies with dissemination". The other is: "Knowledge is the twin of action. He who is knowledgeable must act. Knowledge calls upon action; if answered, it will stay, otherwise, it will depart".

Education for an Arab Renaissance

Before examining higher education in Iraq it is useful to look more generally at the requirements of educational renewal in the Arab world in the light of the weaknesses that have been identified. This will highlight some of the conditions that the renewal and reconstruction of Iraq will need to create. Then we shall focus on higher education in Iraq because it is through its universities and tertiary institutions that a country stakes out its place in the global knowledge society.

In numerical terms Arab education has made slow if steady progress in recent years, even if a good part of the expansion of school systems has been absorbed by the rapid increase in the population of children. However, the challenge is not merely, indeed not primarily, numerical. All states must reflect on whether the educational systems that they are trying to expand are properly organised to achieve the objectives that they wish to achieve.

The root of an Arabic word for government means "lifting injustice", which nicely encapsulates the goals that Arab states must achieve in developing their education systems. Education is first and foremost a human right and an end in itself for a civilised society. It is also, secondarily, a means to enhance the well-being of society through its effects in improving health, increasing productivity and enhancing the participation of individuals in community affairs.

In order to lift injustice education must have quality. Ensuring the quality of education is the major challenge facing Arab states and, indeed, many other countries. Two key components of educational quality are what is learned (content) and how well it is learned (performance). About performance there is little controversy, which is not the same thing as saying that it is easy to achieve. Countries are increasingly eager to compare the performance and competence of their youngsters with those of other countries, one example being the Programme of International Student Assessment (PISA) that was originated by the OECD and is now being administered, with the help of UNESCO, to some 50 OECD and non-OECD countries. It measures the reading literacy, mathematical literacy and scientific literacy of 15-year olds using tests developed by an international team. To date there has been little participation of Arab countries but the door is open.

More difficult, but also more important, is quality seen through the lens of educational content. This is attracting increasing attention from governments as they realise that school curricula and school organisation may determine whether the future of their country is peaceful and prosperous. The difficulty is that perspectives on content reflect culture, traditions and values, which are seen as a particular problem in the Arab world. However, our brief survey of Arab intellectual history has shown that, over a long period that was much closer to the historical origins of Islam than to our own era, Arab culture was a model of openness, engagement and the search for truth.

These are the values recommended as benchmarks for quality today. Education should inculcate respect for the rights of everyone and appreciation — not merely tolerance — for human diversity. It should celebrate the values of democracy, liberty and justice. It should lead people to treasure a healthy and sustainable environment.

The authors of the *Arab Human Development Report* expand these values as ten principles that should underpin the philosophy of reform in the region (UNDP, 2002 p. 55):

- Put the individual at the centre of the learning process.
- Develop the critical faculties of Arab youth.
- Dialogue is vital. Intellectual and cultural heritage is not immune to criticism.
- Give precedence to creativity and the dignity of productive work.
- Develop the spirit of challenge.
- Make equal opportunities available to all children.
- Promote students' emotional and societal well-being.
- Help students understand their culture in a global context.
- Integrate Arab children into today's scientific world.
- Help the young develop the flexibility to cope with uncertainty.

Such principles are a challenge to existing school systems all over the world, but perhaps especially in the Arab region. The report suggests that to implement them requires action in three main areas (UNDP, 2002, pp. 55–58).

First, human capabilities must be enhanced by achieving 100% completion of 10 years of compulsory education. This will require better use of existing resources and the allocation of more resources. A major problem in many Arab states is that the school system is no longer a means for achieving social advancement but has become instead a way of perpetuating social stratification and poverty. This is because systems are tending to split into poor-quality government education for the majority and expensive private education for the richer minority. The private tuition required to assure success in the public examinations for university entrance is gradually closing, to students from poorer families, the tertiary programmes that lead to the best careers.

The major international bodies such as UNESCO, UNICEF and the World Bank are agreed that basic education should be free and compulsory. To make this achievable it may be necessary to introduce tuition fees for some types of post-basic education, an issue we shall discuss in the context of Iraq.

A second area for action is to create strong synergy between education and the socio-economic system. Embedding schools in society by linking them more strongly to local communities is a feature of many successful educational reforms around the world. Education has to prepare children for the world into which they will grow up. This means that the different components of that world must be involved, which means parents, civil society, business and government as a whole, not just the ministries of education. This will help schools adapt to the demands that society will make on the youngsters they teach. In the Arab world that society is likely to become more market oriented, which requires the strengthening of education as a vehicle for social progress. At present too many Arab school systems are neither adapted to their surrounding socio-economic system, nor geared to promote social equity.

Third, Arab cooperation is a key to development in general and the advancement of education in particular. Islam carried the Arabic language to a large region, which should now take full advantage of the asset of a common language and recover some of the pan-Arab spirit that helped to make the great era of Arab intellectual achievement so dynamic. To the extent that aspects of the necessary reforms will meet resistance in some places it will be helpful for countries to work on them together. Curriculum development, textbooks and teacher training should be particularly fruitful areas for collaboration at the school level and, as we shall see, there are compelling reasons for seeing certain aspects of higher education in a pan-Arab perspective.

Higher Education in Iraq

The current process of renewal of higher education in Iraq provides a unique opportunity to implement reforms that could see Iraq's universities leading a renaissance in Arab intellectual life. We observed at the beginning of this essay that success in those reforms, even within Iraq itself, depends on three ambitious assumptions. Whether they can inspire the wider Arab world is even more uncertain. Nevertheless, this may be the best chance in a generation for higher education in the region to set a new course and attempt to recover some of the intellectual dynamism that once defined Arab scholarship. What is the present situation of Iraqi higher education? What is being done to compensate for the effects of sanctions and war? What kinds of reform are necessary?

UNESCO has published an assessment of the state of Iraq's education system when hostilities started in March 2003 (UNESCO, 2003). It provides a baseline for planning the reconstruction, although it needs to be completed by a further assessment — still being conducted at the time of writing — of the impact of the war and subsequent looting. Here we shall comment only on higher education, even though intensive work is also being carried out in primary and secondary education, including revision of school textbooks for the 2003–04 academic year.

Iraq has 18 universities, 9 technical colleges, 38 technical institutes and 10 specialised research centres. These enrol 300,000 students and count nearly 15,000 academic staff. Mustansiriya University, founded in 1280, was one of the world's earliest universities although its history is not continuous since that date. Prior to the first Gulf War, the Iraqi government allocated funds generously to higher education, some $1,000 per student per year. Institutions were well built and equipped. Many academic staff have degrees from foreign universities, either in the former Soviet bloc or in the West — mainly Germany, the UK and the U.S.

This higher education system began to decline when sanctions were imposed soon after the Gulf War. Equipment became obsolete, library collections stagnated and scientific contact was much reduced. The Oil for Food humanitarian programme attempted to slow the decline by directing some funds to higher education, but this had different effects in the north and south of the country. In the centre/south, which is home to 61 of the 75 tertiary institutions, the programme was run by the Iraqi government and some $263 million worth of supplies were provided. Although an energetic building programme continued, the restrictions — designed to prevent military use — on the equipment that could be imported vitiated much of the effort. Orders for computer equipment, for example, were put on hold for two years, which meant that much of it was obsolete on arrival. Hence, despite some alleviation, the decline of the higher education infrastructure continued.

However, in the 14 institutions in the northern governorates the development of the university system continued under a programme managed by UNESCO. Enrolment increased by 76% over the decade and the institutions were visibly undergoing modernisation with some $176 million of expenditures from the Oil for Food programme. These paid for building rehabilitation, equipment, library materials, technical infrastructure and staff training.

That was the situation prior to the war that overthrew Saddam Hussein. Because the assessment of the state of the institutions after those hostilities had not been completed by July 2003, we can only comment on the current picture in general terms. The war itself did relatively little damage to Iraq's educational infrastructure. More harmful was the looting and wanton destruction that took place in the days after the regime fell. In June 2003 the journal *Science* described the havoc done by looters — encouraged in some instances by coalition troops who took away or destroyed computing equipment from institutions that had been visited by the UN weapons inspectors (Science, 2003).

Mustansiriya University, for example, was seriously looted, although repentant thieves later responded to an appeal and returned some items to a local mosque. In another university a statue of Louis Pasteur was mistaken for Saddam Hussein and destroyed, while other institutions, including many in the north, came out relatively unscathed. At Baghdad's private Al-Mansour University College the Dean and his sons quickly recruited help, as troops arrived in the city, to mount a spirited and successful two-day defence of their institution against repeated attacks by looters.

Although the orgy of looting of educational and public institutions was an unpromising start to the creation of a freer and more democratic regime, the damage can be probably be repaired fairly quickly. As noted above, much of the IT equipment, even that listed as "new" had actually been shipped from manufacturers much earlier. Other laboratory equipment was often in an even more decrepit state and academic libraries had little in the way of recent books and current periodicals. For many institutions the opportunity to re-equip from scratch will be an advantage, provided, of course that funds are available. What help is being offered?

The *Arab Human Development Report 2002* identified deficits of freedom, knowledge and womanpower as major weaknesses in the Arab world. It is therefore a most encouraging symbol that the first substantial offer of assistance to rebuild Iraqi higher education came from a female leader in a relatively democratic Arab country, Her Highness Shaika Mozah Bint Nasser Al-Misnad of Qatar. She has pledged $15 million to a fund for this purpose, which other governments, such as Japan, have agreed to augment. Criteria for the use of this fund are to be established in autumn 2003.

Meanwhile, the Oil for Food programme is processing over $100 million of expenditures that were pledged but not yet delivered. This work will be completed in November 2003. No doubt some successor programme to the Oil for Food arrangements will be set up for higher education but discussions are only beginning. However, given Iraq's own riches and the coalition's commitment to get the country working again, resources will likely be forthcoming from various sources. The real challenge, if the aim is a higher education system that will serve as a beacon for the Arab world, is to identify the appropriate reforms.

The most vital reform, the establishment of a new Iraq with basic human freedoms, is not specific to higher education. Experience elsewhere has shown that no amount of money will put a university in the world league unless it can operate in an environment where freedom of expression, of association and of religion are taken as given.

Following the 1998 World Conference on Higher Education Iraq showed a willingness to undertake the reforms then recommended, although a combination of sanctions and the totalitarian nature of the regime meant that progress was limited. Now the country should be able to press ahead with reforms that encourage a variety of institutional formats within a clear framework of quality assurance and accountability. At present most tertiary institutions in Iraq are so tightly controlled by governments that no significant financial or personnel decisions are made within the institutions themselves. It is time to make them accountable for their own affairs through boards of governors made up of four stakeholder groups: the academic community, government, civil society and business.

Different types of institutions, public, private and for-profit, should co-exist within the overall national framework. The UNDP (UNDP, 2002, p. 61) argues that no new institutions of any type should be created unless they can offer higher standards of quality than what is already there. A solid quality assurance and accreditation framework should be put in place at the national level, in close collaboration with pan-Arab initiatives in this area that are being promoted by UNESCO and the UNDP.

State funding for higher education needs to be increased within this quality assurance framework. This should be accompanied by a regime of tuition fees backed by bursary schemes to make them affordable to all students. There must be an emphasis on accountability and efficiency throughout the system. This will mean comprehensive reforms of personnel policies in the tertiary sector. Faculty training, both within the country and overseas, must be combined with the nurturing of professional and learned societies. Schemes to attract able Arab academics currently working outside the region should be put in place because estimates suggest that one million highly qualified Arabs were working in OECD countries in 2000 (UNDP, 2002, p. 71).

As regards subjects and disciplines it will be important to emphasise areas of particular economic importance for Iraq, such as oil and water. At present the opportunities for studying medicine, at least in northern Iraq, seem disproportionately large in view of the overall balance of needs. Furthermore, while it is important to ensure that higher education supports the economic and industrial base, disciplines such as the humanities, which were seriously underdeveloped during the previous regime, should now take on a new lease of life. Just as some western universities have departments of religious studies that are outside the structures of organised religion, so it would be useful for Iraq to develop similar centres for Islamic studies.

Given the asset of the common language and the hope that the example of Iraq will inspire developments in the wider Arab world, it will be good to foster collaborative academic ventures across the region. The Arab Open University is one very important initiative that is already under way. Quite apart from their power to increase access to higher education, open universities can, as the name implies, be very effective mechanisms for addressing deficits of freedom, knowledge and womanpower. They also make it easier to introduce new types of curriculum quickly and on a large scale.

The UNDP (UNDP, 2002, p. 72) encourages Iraq to set up centres of excellence in collaboration with other Arab states, concentrating especially on what it calls "knowledge sciences". The point here is that in building its research capacity the region should concentrate on research and development that is human-resource intensive rather than capital intensive. At present Iraq is weaker in capital than in brainpower, which argues for giving importance to topics such as information technology, mathematics, theoretical and device physics, and economics. It should concentrate on a small number of specialised centres of excellence that play to its distinctive capabilities and are managed so as to achieve world-class standards.

Reforms such as these could set higher education in Iraq on a new course that would energise the education system at other levels and raise the aspirations of the Iraqi people more generally.

In this essay we have drawn heavily on views and analyses made by Arabs and for Arabs in the *Arab Human Development Report 2002*. They consider that the choice now is:

> "...between continuation of dependency on societies that are leaders in the production of knowledge and building a capacity to belong, from a position of strength, to the global knowledge society by establishing an effective, dynamic knowledge acquisition system. This is one of the main keys to progress in the Arab world."

By renewing its higher education system in this spirit Iraq could unlock the shackles that have held it back and also show the way for its Arab neighbours.

References

Billeh, V. "Educational Reform in the Arab Region", *Newsletter of the Economic Research Forum for the Arab Countries, Iran and Turkey,* 9(2) 2002, 30–32.

Science. *Iraq's Shattered Universities,* Vol. 300, June 2003, pp. 1490–91.

The Economist. *Self-doomed to Failure,* 6 July 2002, 24–25.

UNDP. *Arab Human Development Report.* United Nations Development Programme, New York, 2002.

UNESCO. *Situation Analysis of Education in Iraq 2003,* Paris, April 2003.

Warning from History: Why Iraq is Not Japan[1]

John W. Dower

A Pulitzer Prize winner and Elting E. Morison Professor of History at Massachusetts Institute of Technology, John W. Dower's 1986 book, War Without Mercy: Race and Power in the Pacific War, *won several prizes in the U.S., including the National Book Critics Circle Award for non-fiction, as well as the Masayoshi Ohira Memorial Prize in Japan. His 1999 book* Embracing Defeat: Japan in the Wake of World War II *won the Pulitzer Prize, the Bancroft Prize, and the National Book Award. It has been hailed as a major contribution to studies of the postwar occupation era.*

U.S. Postwar Policies in Japan after WWII and their Relevance to a Possible U.S. Occupation of Iraq

Starting last fall, we began to hear that U.S. policymakers were looking into Japan and Germany after World War II as examples or even models of successful military occupations. In the case of Japan, the imagined analogy with Iraq is probably irresistible. Although Japan was nominally occupied by the victorious "Allied powers" from August 1945 until early 1952, the Americans ran the show and tolerated no disagreement. This was Unilateralism with a capital "U" — much as we are seeing in U.S. global policy in general today. And the occupation was a pronounced success. A repressive

---

[1] The article is written before the actual U.S. war in Iraq.

235

society became democratic, and Japan — like Germany — has posed no military threat for over half a century.

The problem is that few if any of the ingredients that made this success possible are present — or would be present — in the case of Iraq. The lessons we can draw from the occupation of Japan all become warnings where Iraq is concerned.

It is difficult for most people today to imagine what the situation was like in 1945, in the wake of the Second World War. One must remember that Japan had been engaged in aggression in Asia since 1931, when Imperial Army militarists launched a successful takeover of Manchuria. Open war against China began in 1937, and the great and foolhardy "preemptive" strike against Pearl Harbor took place in December 1941 — in the context of a Japanese declaration of war against the United States and European powers with colonies in Southeast Asia. Japan's aggression was as open and audacious as that of its Axis allies Germany and Italy.

Just as is the case with Europe and the Soviet Union, we will never have an exact reckoning of the death toll of the war in Asia. China bore the brunt of Japanese aggression. Estimates vary and have tended to become inflated in recent years, but the number of Chinese who died directly or indirectly as a consequence of the war is probably in the neighborhood of fifteen million. In countries like the Dutch East Indies — known today as Indonesia — estimates of fatalities range from one million to several million. In their final frenzy in the Philippines the emperor's men massacred around one hundred thousand civilians in Manila alone. U.S. battle deaths in the Pacific War also were approximately one hundred thousand. Japan's own war dead numbered around two million servicemen and another one million civilians — roughly four percent of the total population at the time.

This was a charnel house in which the Japanese not only savaged others but were themselves savaged by war and militarism and their own repressive leaders. So, the dream that everyone embraced once Japan had been defeated was of a nation that would never again bring such havoc on its neighbors or, indeed, on its own people. "Demilitarization" became the watchword of the time, and it was argued that this could only be enduring if the country was "democratized" as well, so that irresponsible leaders could not repeat these horrors.

When I say that "everyone" embraced this vision of a demilitarized, democratized Japan, I have in mind not merely the victorious Allied nations but also the Asian peoples who had been so grievously victimized by the Japanese war machine — many of whom remained at war's end colonial subjects of the British, French, Dutch, and Americans. I also have in mind the great majority of the Japanese, who found themselves not only bereaved but also living in a country utterly devastated by a miserable, losing war. Even people who are familiar with the atomic bombings of Hiroshima and Nagasaki that preceded Japan's surrender in August 1945 often are unaware that the U.S. terror-bombing raids that came before them — aimed primarily at destroying civilian morale — had pulverized large portions of 64 other major cities. Tokyo, for example, had been mostly reduced to rubble.

It is important to keep all this in mind when we begin to talk about drawing lessons from Japan that might be applicable to Iraq after any projected U.S. hostilities. The postwar occupation of Japan possessed a great intangible quality that simply will not be present in the event of a U.S. war against Iraq. It enjoyed virtually unquestioned legitimacy — moral as well as legal — in the eyes of not merely the victors but all of Japan's Asian neighbors and most Japanese themselves. Japan had been at war for almost fifteen years. It had declared war on the Allied powers in 1941. It had accepted the somewhat vague terms of surrender "unconditionally" less than four years later. Quite the opposite can be anticipated if the United States attacks and then occupies Iraq. The United States will find the legitimacy of its actions widely challenged — within Iraq, throughout the Middle East and much of the rest of the world, and even among many of its erstwhile supporters and allies.

What made the occupation of Japan a success was two years or so of genuine reformist idealism before U.S. policy became consumed by the Cold War, coupled with a real Japanese embrace of the opportunity to start over. There are moments in history —

fleeting occasions of opportunity — when people actually sit down and ask, "What is a good society? How can we bring this about?" Winners in war do not ask this of themselves. Winners tend to say "we won, we're good, we're righteous, what we did was just, now it's time to get back to business and build on our strengths." But losers — certainly in the case of Japan — are under more compulsion to ask what went wrong and what they might do to make sure they don't fall into the same disasters again.

American policy toward defeated Japan meshed with this Japanese sense of failure and the necessity of starting over. The Americans may not have been self-critical, but they had definite ideas about what needed to be done to make Japan democratic. Much of this thinking came from liberals and leftists who had been associated with Franklin D. Roosevelt's progressive New Deal policies — policies that were already falling out of favor in Washington before the war ended. One might say that the last great exercise of New Deal idealism was carried out by Americans in defeated Japan. It was this combination of the Americans using their "unconditional" authority to crack open the old authoritarian system and Japanese at all levels seizing this opportunity to make the reforms work that accounts for the success of the occupation.

The reforms that were introduced in the opening year and a half or so of the occupation were quite stunning. They amounted to a sweeping commitment to what we now call "nation-building" — the sort of hands-on commitment that George W. Bush explicitly repudiated in his presidential campaign. The Americans introduced in Japan a major land reform, for example, that essentially took land from rich landlords, eliminated widespread tenancy, and created a class of small rural landowners. The argument for this was that rural oppression had kept the countryside poor, thwarted democracy, constricted the domestic market, and fueled the drive to control overseas markets. We introduced labor laws that guaranteed the right to organize, bargain collectively, and strike, on the grounds that a viable labor movement is essential to any viable democracy. We encouraged the passage of a strong labor standards law to prevent exploitation of workers including women and children. We revamped both the content and structure of the educational system. In all this the input of Japanese bureaucrats and technocrats was essential to implement such reforms, and serious grass-roots support was basic to their survival.

One of our major initiatives was to create an entirely new constitution. There were no citizens in Japan in 1945. There was no popular sovereignty. Under the existing constitution, sovereignty was vested in the emperor and all Japanese were his "subjects". So, the Americans drafted — but the Japanese translated, debated, tinkered with, and adopted — a new national charter that remains one of the most progressive constitutions in the world. The emperor became a "symbol" of the state. An extensive range of human and civil rights was guaranteed — including an explicit guarantee of gender equality. Belligerency of the state was repudiated. Changing the constitution meant, moreover, that much of the civil code had to be rewritten to conform to these new strictures concerning equality and guaranteed rights. Although the occupation ended in 1952 and there are no restrictions on amending the constitution, not a word of it has been changed.

There will be revisions in the near future, I would predict, primarily to clarify the legal status of Japan's present-day military forces. But it is inconceivable that they will undo the principles of popular sovereignty and extensive guarantee of democracy rights. And, in one way or another, whatever revision takes place, we should expect to see reaffirmation of the fundamental ideals of anti-militarism.

I have no doubt that huge numbers of Iraqis would welcome the end of repression and establishment of a democratic society, but any number of considerations make the situation there very different than it was in Japan. Apart from lacking the moral legitimacy and internal and global support that buttressed its occupation of Japan, the United States is not in the business of nation-building any more — just look at Afghanistan. And we certainly are not in the business of promoting radical democratic reform. Even liberal ideals are anathema in the conservative circles that shape U.S. policy today. And beyond this, many of the conditions that contributed to the success of the occupation of Japan are simply absent in Iraq.

Unique Conditions that Contributed to Success in Japan but which are Absent in Iraq

John Stuart Mill has a wonderful line somewhere to the effect that a country can be laid waste by fire and sword, but in and of itself this really doesn't matter where recovery is concerned. What matters is not so much what is destroyed but rather what human resources survive. Even though Japan had been laid to ruin by the terror-bombing of its cities, what survived was an exceptionally literate populace whose long war effort had, in fact, contributed to great and widespread advances in technological and technocratic skills. At the same time this was an essentially homogeneous populace that had been mobilized behind a common national cause.

The failure and discredit of the cause did not destroy this general sense of collective national purpose. It meant, however, that these great human resources were available to be mobilized to new ends that were more peaceful and progressive. Put simply, one of the reasons the reformist agenda succeeded is that Japan was spared the type of fierce tribal, religious, and political factionalism that exists in countries like Iraq today.

Particularly in the early stages of effecting a smooth surrender Japan also possessed an unusually flexible — some would say chameleonlike — leader in the person of Emperor Hirohito. The emperor had certainly been the symbol of presurrender militarism, and no innocent bystander to wartime policymaking. He was not, however, a hands-on dictator akin to Hitler or Mussolini — or to Saddam Hussein. Once surrender became unavoidable the emperor adroitly metamorphosed into a symbol of cooperation with the conquerors. He came quietly, and for reasons of pure expediency the Americans happily whitewashed and welcomed him. He became, as it were, a beacon of continuity in the midst of drastic change. We cannot, of course, imagine anything of the sort taking place in a post-hostilities Iraq.

Much the same sort of continuity took place at the levels of both national and local government. Certain important reforms were introduced at the national level — most notably the abolition of the War (army) and Navy ministries and the breakup and gutting of the once-powerful Home Ministry, which had controlled the police and dictated policies at the level of the prefectures or states. But for all practical purposes the bureaucracy remained intact, top to bottom. And to a far greater extent than anyone really anticipated, bureaucrats and civil servants cooperated in implementing the early reformist agendas. "Democratization" of the structure and content of the educational system, to take but one example, required and received enormous input from bureaucrats and teachers at every level. The skills and education levels of the Iraqi people are substantial, but it is nonetheless difficult to imagine a comparably swift, smooth, and substantial redirection of existing administrative and institutional structures in a post-hostilities Iraq.

We should also keep in mind what defeated Japan did not possess. Japan is notoriously poor in natural resources. A desperate quest for control of raw materials as well as markets was one of the major considerations that drove Japanese imperialism and aggression in the first place. That, after all, is why the emperor's men deemed it necessary to invade Southeast Asia and — once that decision had been made — attempted to forestall American retaliation by launching a preemptive strike at the U.S. fleet at Pearl Harbor. In the wake of Japan's shattering defeat, no one ever imagined that it would ever again become a major power, and there were no resources within Japan itself to covet. And so the reformers — Americans and Japanese alike — had a brief breathing space in which to push their ambitious agendas without being hammered by special economic interests. Iraq, of course, with its great oil resources, will not be spared such interference.

Lessons to be Drawn from that Earlier War and
U.S. Occupation of Japan

The occupation of Japan offers no model whatsoever for any projected occupation of Iraq. On the contrary, it should stand as a warning that we are lurching toward war with no idea of what we are really getting into. What is presented as hard-nosed realism by the advocates of a preemptive strike against Iraq is really — what? I have concluded after much thought that our so-called realism is simply a terrible hubris.

But to an historian of the United States and Japan and World War II there are also terrible ironies in these recent developments. Part of the irony is that Americans — certainly Americans in the current administration — have no sense of irony. "September 11" has become our terrible new "Pearl Harbor", and at the very same time we are touting "preemptive strikes" as a moral and practical *modus operandi*. In the name of curbing weapons of mass destruction we have embarked on a massive program of producing new arsenals of mass destruction and have announced that we may resort to first-use of nuclear weapons. We express moral repulsion and horror at the terror-bombing of civilians, and rightly so; and then an endless stream of politicians and pundits explains how this is peculiar to Islamic fundamentalists who do not value human life as we do. But "terror-bombing" has been everyone's game since World War II. This is the term historians routinely use to describe the U.S. bombing campaign against Japan that began with the destruction, in a single air raid, of fourteen square miles of downtown Tokyo in March 1945 and continued through Hiroshima and Nagasaki. There is nothing cultural or religious or unique about this.

There is one "lesson" from my own field of Japanese history that I find increasingly difficult to put out of mind these days, and that concerns the road to war that began in the early 1930s for Japan and only ended in 1945. Until recently, historians used to explain this disaster in terms of Japan's "backwardness" and "semifeudal" nature. The country had all these old warrior traditions. It wasn't a democracy — and, of course, democracies don't wage aggressive war.

More recent studies, however, cast Japan's road to war in a different and more terrifying light.

Why "terrifying"? First, much recent scholarship suggests that it was the modern rather than "backward" aspects of Japanese society and culture that enabled a hawkish leadership to mobilize the country for all-out war. Modern mass communications enabled politicians and ideologues to whip up war sentiment and castigate those who criticized the move to war as traitors. Modern concerns about external markets and resources drove Japan into Manchuria, China, and Southeast Asia. Modern weaponry carried its own technological imperatives. Top-level planners advanced up-to-date theories about mobilizing the entire resources of the country (and surrounding areas) for "total war". Sophisticated phrasemakers pumped out propaganda about defending the homeland and promoting "coexistence and co-prosperity" throughout Asia. Cultures of violence, cultures of militarism, cultures of unquestioning obedience to supreme authority in the face of national crisis — all of this was nurtured by sophisticated organs of propaganda and control. And, in retrospect, none of this seems peculiarly dated or peculiarly "Japanese" today.

The other aspect that is so terrifying to contemplate is that virtually every step of the way, the Japanese leaders who concluded that military solutions had become unavoidable were very smart and very proud of their technical expertise, their special knowledge, their unsentimental "realism" in a threatening world. Many of these planners were, in our own phrase, "the best and the brightest". We have detailed records of their deliberations and planning papers, and most are couched in highly rational terms. Each new escalation, each new extension of the empire, was deemed essential to the national interest. And even in retrospect, it is difficult to say at what point this so-called realism crossed the border into madness. But it was, in the end, madness.

Kirkuk: An Eyewitness Account[1]

Eric Stover

The Director of the Human Rights Center and Adjunct Professor of Public Health at UC Berkeley, Stover was the Executive Director of Physicians for Human Rights (PHR) until December 1995. Since 1993, he has served on several medicolegal investigations as an "Expert on Mission" to the International Criminal Tribunal *for the former Yugoslavia in* The Hague. *He is the author of numerous books, reports, and articles on medicine and human rights.*

Ethnic tensions in the oil-rich Kirkuk region could quickly spin out of control. As members of a Human Rights Watch investigation team in northern Iraq, we witnessed a confrontation that suggests just how that may happen.

At approximately 7 pm on April 13, a vehicle pulled up in front of the headquarters of the Iraqi Turkoman Front (ITF) where dozens of its members, many of them bearing arms, had gathered. A man descended from the vehicle carrying the body of a young boy in his arms. The left side of the boy's head was shattered revealing brain matter and his left leg bore what appeared to be a gunshot wound.

Holding the dead body aloft for all to see, the man swung through crowd shouting, "Look! Look! This is what the Kurds have

---

[1] The account is written by Eric Stover and Hania Mufti, Human Rights Watch investigation team in northern Iraq, on April 14, 2003.

done!" Within seconds, the crowd began calling for revenge and for the Turks to intervene to take control of the city. Once the man placed the boy's body on the pavement, we came forward with a sheet we'd brought from a nearby hotel to cover the boy's body.

However, despite our repeated attempts to conceal the body, several men pushed us away and draped a small Turkoman flag across the body, calling on photographers who had gathered at the scene to photograph it. Men in the crowd prevented medical personnel who arrived with an ambulance from removing the body. Later in the evening, members of the Turkoman Front removed the body and put it on display in front of a hotel housing foreign journalists.

The following morning, we set out to investigate the incident. Having learned the night before that the boy's father and several other men had also been wounded in the same attack, we went to the recently renamed Azadi Hospital (formerly Saddam Hospital) where the boy's father, who was suffering from gunshot wounds and a broken arm, had been admitted.

The boy's father, Muhsin Jalal Tahsin, 35, told us that on the afternoon of the day before, armed men wearing traditional Kurdish clothes and driving five pickup trucks had drawn up near a crowd of people trying to retrieve petrol from a depot left behind at a government building. He said the armed men fired over the heads of the crowd. When he confronted them they threatened to kill him. He was frightened and returned to his car and drove away from the scene.

His eight-year-old son, Hussain, was with him, sitting in the back of the car. The father said he was then pursued by two of the pickup trucks until they caught up with him on the Baghdad Road near a sweet shop. His car skidded and he thought one of the tires may have burst since the armed men were shooting in his direction. He then got out of the car and started running. He told us, "I don't know what happened to my son. They say he is dead."

At the reported scene of the shooting, we found the father's car, a Toyota Corona, parked outside a branch office of the Iraqi Turkoman Front, a short distance away from the sweet shop. The rear left tire was punctured and there were four bullet holes in the rear window. There was what appeared to be blood and brain tissue splattered across the back seat. We photographed the car. One eyewitness told us that at around 7 pm the previous day, two pickup trucks without license plates had driven past the ITF office and the passengers of the first car sprayed bullets in the direction of the office.

He, and others we met, told us that the incident had continued into the next day. At 2 pm that afternoon, representatives of the Kurdistan Democratic Party (KDP), some of them bearing arms, had served them with an eviction notice, giving them until 7 pm to vacate the premises. Indeed, one of these KDP officials arrived while we were there. He confirmed that there was indeed a dispute over the property, and that he had come to find out whether the ITF had left the premises, and told us that if they did not, there would be "further trouble". Soon thereafter we had to leave because of an altercation at the scene, in which weapons were brandished, and were unable to complete our investigation.

When we first got to Kirkuk on April 10, Kurdish peshmerga were patrolling the city streets and an uneasy peace prevailed. Those Kurdish fighters have now withdrawn. But U.S. forces have not taken their place: no one seems to be in charge.

In this vacuum, serious ethnic clashes could easily break out. We have seen with our own eyes how this begins. We don't want to see how it ends.

Lifting the Fog of War[1]

While hundreds of journalists traveled with U.S.-led coalition troops, there were only two human-rights investigators in all of Iraq during the war. And as the journalists bombarded the world with reports filed seemingly every 30 seconds about ambushes and heroic rescues, these two researchers focused on one issue for days at a time, interviewing multiple people to make sure they painted an accurate picture.

"It's very easy to write about the bang-bang of war," says veteran human-rights researcher Eric Stover, one of the two investigators in Iraq. "It's much harder to find out what's actually happening on the ground and analyze it."

But that is exactly what Stover, director of the Human Rights Center at UC Berkeley and an adjunct professor of public health, does. For more than two decades, working with nongovernmental organizations (NGOs) like Physicians for Human Rights and Human Rights Watch, Stover as immersed himself in the kind of things that make many of us turn off our televisions after a few seconds. He has waded into mass graves in Bosnia and Croatia and surveyed them in Rwanda; documented the social and medical consequences of the land mines that have claimed children's limbs in Cambodia and other war-torn countries; and tracked disappearances and torture in Latin America.

Last month, Stover crossed the Syria-Iraq border to work as a researcher in northern Iraq for Human Rights Watch. By then, the

---

[1] The article was written by Bonnie Azab Powell, Public Affairs, UC Berkeley, on April 29, 2003, from her interview with Eric Stover on chaos and lawlessness in Iraq.

United Nations and many other NGOs had pulled out of the country. Stover was joined by Hania Mufti, the London director of the group's Middle East and North Africa division. Mufti, who is Jordanian, speaks fluent Arabic and English and has two decades of experience documenting human rights in the Middle East.

Undertaking a campaign that cried out for a legion of human rights workers, Stover and Mufti assessed the situation of displaced persons in Iraqi Kurdistan; investigated Kurdish treatment of Iraqi prisoners of war there; and once the coalition forces succeeded in taking Kirkuk, monitored whether U.S.-led forces were obeying the Geneva Convention's prescription to restore and ensure public order. In addition to these primary goals, Stover and Mufti also tried to ascertain the extent of civilian casualties.

Not Enough Tents

Before the U.S. even began its bombing campaign, several thousand Iraqis had already fled government-held areas along the border with Kurdistan for the Kurdish-controlled region, while thousands of civilians in Kurdish cities had fled to the countryside fearing chemical weapon attacks by the Iraqi military. Although the UN and other aid agencies had had months to anticipate the refugee flood, little had been done before they pulled out of Iraq. When Stover and Mufti arrived in Iraqi Kurdistan in mid-March, only 100 tents had been erected in a muddy camp with no sanitation facilities. (Such people are called "internally displaced persons" rather than "refugees" because they have not crossed international borders.) Most of the displaced persons were being housed in schools and townspeoples' homes, depending for food on what citizens shared with them. The medical facilities were woefully inadequate.

Through a Human Rights Watch press release, Stover and Mufti raised a red flag, warning of the potential humanitarian crisis should thousands more internally displaced persons swarm across the border into Kurdistan. Fortunately, the crisis did not materialize, as the Iraqi government did not resort to chemical weapons and the numbers did not spike as expected.

POW Protection

Turning their attention to prisoners of war, Stover and Mufti interviewed captives to find out if they were being treated in accordance with the Geneva Convention. Although the Kurdish forces are not signatories to the Convention, by fighting under the direction of the United States they become subject to its guidelines.

Stover and Mufti interviewed 35 prisoners of war, access that was initially denied to journalists. "We had a very different role from journalists," explains Stover. "They were writing a story on a different topic every day, while we would take one issue like the treatment of POWs and work it for four to five days, interviewing prisoners to find the inconsistencies and the consistencies in their accounts."

They found that overall, the Kurdish forces were treating captured and surrendered Iraqi soldiers humanely, giving them food and medical treatment. Some Iraqi soldiers, however, were locked up with other prisoners, including suspected spies and terrorists. The Geneva Convention specifies that POWs should be housed separately for their own protection. One Iraqi officer told Stover that he was in a cell with 30 Kurds who did not speak Arabic; he was afraid to speak for the quite legitimate fear of being beaten.

"Imagine how the U.S. or Britain would feel if our soldiers were being held in cells with Iraqi criminals," points out Stover.

Saddam's 4-by-4-foot Cells

The real challenge for Stover and Mufti came when the Kurdish forces, aided by U.S. air support and 1,000 paratroopers who seemingly arrived overnight, succeeded in breaking through the Iraqi front line in northern Iraq and retaking Kirkuk.

The two human-rights researchers accompanied the Kurdish forces into Kirkuk, a city unique in Iraq for its ethnic diversity. It is home to Kurds, Turkmen (the ethnic group making up Turkmenistan), Assyrians, and Arabs, both Muslims and Christians — a volatile mix in the aftermath of the Iraqi government's fall.

Stover and Mufti interviewed Kirkuk residents and visited hospital morgues to discover the extent of civilian casualties. They found that at least in Kirkuk, U.S. bombs had struck government and military targets with surgical accuracy, resulting in few accidental deaths.

They visited one of those targets, Saddam's security headquarters in Kirkuk, which had been gutted by bombs. Valuable records were strewn everywhere, whether by bombs, fleeing government officials, or looters Stover did not know. "It is the occupying forces' duty to protect these records," he explained, "to preserve what they may reveal about the whereabouts of missing persons and of crimes committed by the government."

But there were also human witnesses to such crimes. Former prisoners who had been held and tortured in the security headquarters had flocked to the bombed-out site. "They'd come back like iron filings to a magnet to see their cells," says Stover, and they were eager to tell their stories. One man had been imprisoned with five other people in a 4-by-4-foot cell for more than a year. They had barely enough room to squat on the ground, their knees and backs touching. He showed Stover and Mufti where he had scratched his name and drawings into the plaster of the now roofless cell, a space the size of a large broom closet.

The Home Front

It was not the first time that Stover had been to Kirkuk. In 1991, when the city was still under Kurdish control, he led a forensic team there to exhume the graves of Kurds executed by the Iraqi government. In what is known as the Anfal Campaign of the late 1980s, tens of thousands of mostly male Kurdish civilians were forced onto trucks and driven away, never to be seen alive again. The Anfal Campaign is just a small part of the brutal history of the Kurds' treatment under Saddam Hussein. The 1991 report that Stover cowrote for Human Rights Watch states that "both the government of Saddam Hussein and his Baath party are responsible not only for gassing, deporting, and massacring Kurds but for destroying some 4,000 Kurdish villages."

Now, with the fall of Saddam Hussein, Stover and Mufti feared that the 130,000 Kurds who had fled or been expelled into Iraqi Kurdistan in 1992 would return to Kirkuk to reclaim their homes. Under the Geneva Convention, forcibly displaced persons have a right to repossess their private property, but that right must be balanced against any rights the current occupants may have in domestic or international law.

"We recommended that a commission be established to oversee the gradual and orderly return of internally displaced persons to Kirkuk," says Stover. "In the new Iraq there has to be new behavior. You can't just go back and force people out of their homes with guns because you were forced out."

Stover and Mufti's fears materialized when they found four vacant villages just south of Kirkuk, on the way to Baghdad. Approximately 2,000 residents (from the villages of al-Muntasir, Khalid, al-Wahda and Umar Ibn al-Khattab) had been given official "eviction notices" by the Patriotic Union of Kurdistan (PUK) and told to pack up and leave immediately. The residents were Arabs from the al-Shummar tribe in southern Iraq who Saddam Hussein had either moved forcibly or enticed to occupy Kurdish homes as part of his Arabization campaign beginning in the mid-1970s. And now the Kurds wanted the territory back on which these homes sat.

Stover and Mufti heard reports that the al-Shummar refugees had been forced from their homes at gunpoint, while their possessions, including cars, tractors, and household goods, were taken away. "Many of the homes we saw had been spray-painted with the names of Kurdish families," Stover says — the families who planned to move into them.

The two investigators confronted the local PUK officials, who claimed that the resettlement policy had been approved by U.S. coalition forces. But Stover and Mufti could not confirm that any such approval had ever been granted. "We caught them red-handed," says Stover. "We said to them, 'We understand your grievances, but you're doing exactly what the Baathists and Saddam did. This isn't right.'"

Iraq's Future

The al-Shummar residents were still homeless, camped in a fifth village, when Stover returned April 20 to the States. "It's going to take a U.S. commander standing there with [PUK leader Jalal] Talabani and publicly announcing, 'We will not tolerate this behavior,'" says Stover. "And that hasn't happened yet."

Several other Human Rights Watch representatives have arrived to take up the work in both southern and northern Iraq. Disconcertingly, Mufti has reported that civilian casualties have increased in northern Iraq since hostilities stopped, due to general lawlessness and the amount of unexploded ordinance that children have picked up unwittingly.

Stover reports that throughout the war, in cities across Iraq, the U.S.-led coalition failed to contain the lawlessness that arose in the vacuum left by the Iraqi government. He believes that at least in northern Iraq, this failure was due to a shortage of troops caused by Turkey's refusal to let the U.S. invade across its border. "We were troubled that the U.S. forces seemed to have no plan as to how they would secure Kirkuk," says Stover. "There were guns everywhere, and so many factions. Kirkuk needs not just short-term security but long-range plans to maintain order."

Currently, Iraqis are out searching for the mass graves of missing loved ones. Stover cautions that unless the mass graves are exhumed methodically, critical nformation could be lost that would help to identify the bodies and preserve evidence of when and how they were killed. Likewise, if government records that bear witness to the past are to be recovered, the remains of government buildings also must be protected.

There is much to be done, and much that remains uncertain. Iraq requires not just physical reconstruction, but emotional. "What's important now is the question of justice for past crimes, which no one is thinking of with any alacrity," says Stover. "Will there be a Truth Commission, like in South Africa? How will Iraq deal with this past? More than 300,000 people disappeared; there was genocide and crimes against humanity." Without the involvement of the United Nations and other international relief organization, Stover warns, Iraq's wounds may never heal.

Is the Human Rights Era Over? Reflections on the Asia-Pacific Post-September 11th[1]

Rosemary Foot, Ph.D.

Delivered on October 16, 2002 at the Lone Mountain Campus of the University of San Francisco, the lecture featured Foot, Kiriyama Distinguished Visiting Professor at the USF Center for the Pacific Rim in Fall 2002 and professor of international relations and John Swire Senior Research Fellow in the International Relations of East Asia at St. Antony's College, Oxford University. Foot is the author most recently of Rights Beyond Borders: The Global Community and the Struggle over Human Rights in China *(Oxford University Press, 2000). She has also published* The Practice of Power: U.S. Relations with China Since 1949 *(Oxford University Press, 1995), and* A Substitute for Victory: The Politics of Peacemaking at the Korean Armistice Talks *(Cornell University Press 1990) among others. Her many scholarly articles and book chapters include "A Buttress Not a Pillar: The UN System as a Pathway to Security in Asia", in* Asian Security Order *(Stanford University Press, 2002), "The ASEAN Regional Forum and China" (in* Asia in the New Millennium: Geopolitics, Security and Foreign Policy, *Berkeley IEAS, 2000), and "Whatever Happened to the Pacific Century?" (with Andrew Walter,* Review of International Studies, *Vol. 25, December 1999).*

[1] This Pacific Rim Report records the 2002 Kiriyama Distinguished Lecture. It was first published as a University of San Francisco Pacific Rim Report, number 16, January 2003. Grateful acknowledgement is given to the Kiriyama Chair for Pacific Rim Studies at the USF Center for the Pacific Rim for funding this issue of Pacific Rim Report.

Is the human rights era over, especially when we compare the current state to the 1990s during which there was a particularly vigorous interest in the promotion of human rights?[2]

In this lecture, I want to outline why this matter has become such an acute concern in recent months; and then to explore the proposition in greater depth, drawing on examples from U.S. policy towards three states in the Asia-Pacific. Even though I shall conclude that it is an exaggeration to state that the human rights era is over, clearly the human rights idea is under challenge in ways that I shall illustrate at the start and at the close of my talk.

Introduction

This question — is the human rights era over — is being asked because many involved with the theory and practice of international relations have argued that, post-September 11th, international — and especially U.S. — concern with human rights abuses in other countries has given way to an overwhelming concern with security relations, reminiscent of the Cold War era.

How is this argument put? As Michael Ignatieff wrote at the start of 2002, "the new element in determining American foreign policy" towards particular countries is no longer where you stand on the human rights/democracy index, but what assets you have in the struggle against terrorism. What "bases, intelligence, and diplomatic leverage" can you "bring to bear against Al-Qaeda?"[3] Mary Robinson, said something similar in the week that she signed

---

[2] I would like to thank Rita Kernacs of the USF Master of Arts in Asia Pacific Studies program for invaluable research assistance for this lecture.

[3] Ignatieff, *International Herald Tribune*, February 6, 2002; and see too the *Far Eastern Economic Review*, October 25, 2001 — "United States policy toward Asia has undergone a radical realignment since the September 11 terrorist attacks on New York and Washington. Suddenly, all other priorities have become secondary to the overriding focus that redefines foes and friends on the basis of whether they support the U.S. in the new war against terrorism."

off as the UN High Commissioner for Human Rights: "everything is justified by the T-word".

Robinson is right of course, up to a point. There are many examples to draw on which would show that the human rights idea is under threat or in danger of being sidelined.

With respect to Indonesia, for example, the U.S. administration, and especially the Pentagon, searches strenuously for ways to restore full relations with a military that, while it is probably the strongest institutional ally in the country in the fight against terrorists, has also been and remains the source of extensive human rights violations that only help to swell the ranks of the desperate.

In China, the Bush administration has been accused of turning a blind eye to the Chinese crack-down on separatist forces in Xinjiang. Moreover, it recently came closer to agreeing with the Chinese leadership that Xinjiang should be thought of less as a region that has good reason to strive for independence or autonomy, and more as a center of terrorist activity — a place that houses groups with links to Al-Qaeda.

The Prime Minister of Malaysia, Mahathir Mohamad, at the time of his visit to the United States in May 2002, apparently was no longer seen as a man who wields the Internal Security Act (ISA) and manipulates other aspects of the judicial system to imprison his political opponents — such as his former deputy Anwar Ibrahim — but instead is spoken of as a respected leader from a country that is a "beacon of stability" and that "plays an important role in the global war on terror". The examples could go on.

At least as relevant to this argument is U.S. domestic legislation enacted since September 11th that represents a serious constraint on civil liberties. With the U.S. detaining many, mostly Arab or Muslim men, refusing to reveal who is being held, and re-fusing public access to their trials; and with new laws that can compel disclosure of all kinds of personal records, then it seems that the balance between national security and civil liberties has shifted sharply in favor of the former. As the American International Lawyer, Harold Hongju Koh has argued, these initiatives reject three principles by which the U.S. has balanced national security and civil liberties since World War II:

1) the separation of "domestic law enforcement from foreign intelligence", to keep the government from spying on Americans and "to guarantee the constitutional rights of the accused";
2) the granting of civil rights to lawfully admitted aliens comparable to the rights of other citizens, "rejecting the notion that foreign born Americans or immigrants have only second class rights";
3) the acknowledgement of the executive branch's lead on national security issues, but the insistence "that its actions be subject to congressional oversight and judicial review."[4]

And if the United States, as well as other consolidated democracies in the world, are scaling back on civil liberties, how can these countries comment negatively on some of the oppressive national security laws that are in operation elsewhere in the world? Everything is justified by the T-word.

Or so it seems. I want to suggest that, while the prominent place that the human rights idea enjoyed in the 1990s has come under challenge, to argue that it no longer imposes any constraints on U.S. policy (and it is U.S. policy that I am going to concentrate on in this lecture) is an exaggeration. Two main arguments will be made in support of this.

1) The first rests on the notion that ideas and institutions matter, and the human rights idea over the course of the post-1945 era has become embedded and codified. Inside the U.S. government, the United Nations, and in global and local civil society, many remain committed to the advancement of human rights protections.
2) But, in addition to this, what we have heard argued over the last few years is that human rights promotion and the promotion of security are not either-or propositions, but can be thought of as complementary, and this understanding too helps to

---

[4] Harold Hongju Koh, article in *The Nation*, accessed via *TIME.com* on October 10, 2002.

maintain attention to rights.[5] In this post-September 11th era, we are seeing some evidence that human rights and anti-terrorism programs are being brought together in particular ways to try to satisfy both the demands for security as well as for rights protection.

The difficult part is to determine when that linkage between human rights and security is being made for instrumental purposes without any genuine commitment to rights promotion, or when the means adopted for the promotion of human rights and security don't justify the ends, or when there is a genuine acceptance of the idea that the two concepts are indeed inextricably and beneficially linked.

The Institutionalization of the Human Rights Idea Post-1945

In the period since 1945, and especially since the 1980s, we have witnessed the growth and deepening of two bodies of law — human rights law and international humanitarian law. Despite the lack of an effective enforcement mechanism for human rights, the protection of rights has become built into the policy frameworks of democratic states, of multilateral lending institutions, and into the UN itself, and this in turn has prompted the development of civil society groupings devoted to the cause of promoting adherence to human rights.

---

[5] "Where human rights are ignored, experience shows that criminals and terrorists thrive, and regional and global security are at risk, because chaos spreads," speech by the UK Foreign Secretary, Jack Straw, to the United Nations Commission on Human Rights, April 18, 2002. *www.fco.gov.uk/*.

U.S. Congressional Initiatives

It was initiatives within the U.S. Congress in the early 1970s that led to the development of commitments to promote rights protections — action that has been attributed to the burgeoning civil rights movement, the character and outcome of the Vietnam War, and the amoral aspects of the Nixon administration's behavior.[6] To put this in summary form, Congressional legislation sought to deny aid to those countries that engaged in gross violations of internationally recognized human rights. Although this might have been applied inconsistently, it had the overall affect of raising awareness because it required investigation of human rights conditions inside many countries before decisions could be reached.

The Carter presidency gave an enormous fillip to these developments. It was during his administration that the post of human rights coordinator within the State Department was upgraded to the level of Assistant Secretary. Between the years 1977 and 1979, the staff of two associated with the Bureau of Human Rights went up to 29. In subsequent years, the annual Country Reports on Human Rights Practices produced by the Department of State became recognized as generally accurate, unbiased, and useful sources of information about human rights violations.

When some Nongovernmental organizations (NGOs), as well as the U.S. Congress, began to publish their critiques of these reports, these criticisms were sent to U.S. embassies for use in constructing reports the following year. The embassies and their human rights personnel recognized that, in order to comply with the Congressional legislation and to satisfy or even shield from criticism high officials within the State Department, they would have to obtain better quality information. This led them to establish links with local human rights organizations, if there were any, and with opposition groups, thus deepening U.S. understanding of the countries in

---

[6] For further detail and references see Foot, *Rights Beyond Borders: the Global Community and the Struggle over Human Rights in China*. Oxford: Oxford University Press (2000) esp. pp. 42–45.

question. Overall, levels of awareness about and of resources devoted to human rights matters increased within the U.S. Congress, and in the bureaucracy, especially in the Department of State.

Turning more directly to the NGOs, both those that operate transnationally, as well as locally, these have increased substantially in number: for example, international NGOs have expanded five-fold between 1950 and 1993, with a doubling between 1983 and 1993.[7] Many have established offices in New York and Washington, DC, because of the lobbying opportunities this affords. The UN and individual governments have become highly dependent on the information that these NGOs provide, and these NGOs have become major contributors to policy development in the field of human rights. This has had the effect of tightening the bonds between the NGO and the policymaker and making them a recognized, often valued, part of the landscape in this issue area.

I mention these developments because they provide an illustration of the constraining environment that is in place when states seek — or at least democratic states — seek to circumvent human rights promotion in their foreign policy. To quote Mary Robinson again: "human rights are now firmly on the agenda of the international community. ...Most governments today will at least acknowledge that human rights have a role to play [in international relations]. Unfortunately that does not necessarily mean that they will observe human rights standards. You will often still hear governments arguing that they must place other factors first. The difference is that today those sorts of claims go against the tide of opinion".[8]

---

[7] Margaret E. Keck and Kathryn Sikkink, *Activists Beyond Borders: Advocacy Networks in International Politics.* Ithaca, NY: Cornell University Press (1998), pp. 10–11.

[8] Mary Robinson's Farewell Speech, September 12, 2002. Jack Donnelly had put it in a similar way in 1998: "In contrast to the 1970s and early 1980s, when debate often focused on whether human rights should be an active foreign policy concern, today the question is usually which rights to emphasize in which particular cases." *International Human Rights.* Boulder, CO: Westview Press (1998).

Human Rights and International Peace and Security

My second argument relates to the intertwining of the concepts of rights and security. Since the 1990s, in particular, there has been increased attention to the concept of humanitarian intervention and the circumstances under which it is appropriate to intervene — including militarily — in support of populations that are experiencing gross violations of their human rights, actions that have been depicted as representing threats to international peace and security. Between 1991 and 1999, for example, the question of whether or not external institutions should organize or authorize military action within a state on humanitarian grounds has arisen on at least nine occasions within the UN Security Council. In these nine cases humanitarian considerations were cited as a basis for action. As Adam Roberts has argued, these were never the only reasons cited as the basis for action, and it is unlikely that humanitarian motives will ever stand alone, but nevertheless it was striking how frequently humanitarian concerns were referred to.[9]

Indeed, we have witnessed this even in the case of President George W. Bush and his description of the war against the Taliban. Those that have tracked Bush's speeches argue that he moved from emphasizing a "retributive strike", to statements that claimed that the action was in support of the broader humanitarian goal of "helping transform Afghanistan into a stable member of the international community", through the building of its capacity to maintain the Bush definition of human dignity.[10] And the argument runs that Bush was forced to develop this rhetoric in order to maintain both local Afghan and international support for the policy.

Other examples that show the intertwining of rights and security involve the implementation of policies that help to reform the

---

[9] Adam Roberts, "The So-called 'Right' of Humanitarian Intervention", in *Yearbook of International Humanitarian Law*, vol. 3, Spring 2002.

[10] Simon Chesterman, "Humanitarian Intervention and Afghanistan", in Jennifer Welsh (ed.), *Humanitarian Intervention and International Relations: Theory and Practice* (forthcoming).

security sector in countries where large-scale abuses of human rights have taken place. The U.S. and UK governments, for example, have provided aid designed to reform the security apparatus of a variety of countries because this apparatus — that is the armed forces and police, paramilitary and intelligence — has been heavily associated with human rights abuses. Thus, U.S. AID among others have developed policies that are designed to strengthen civilian management of the security forces and their accountability; and to create a climate in which civil society can monitor the security sector and be consulted regularly on defense policy, resource allocation and related issues.

Both the debates over humanitarian intervention and security sector reform are responses to the argument that international order "cannot rest solely on the sovereignty" and inviolability of state boundaries, but depends as well on building an individual's "own sense of security".[11] The idea of human security has entered the lexicon. Human security places the individual not the state as the point of reference, and as a paradigm assumes that the safety of individuals is the key to global security — the protection of basic human rights stands as a crucial component and, for some, the sole component of what we mean by human security.

In laying out this case for the deepening over time of international attention to human rights issues, I do not mean to suggest that it is not still a huge struggle to get governments to behave consistently and in a principled manner when it comes to human rights promotion. All I mean to say, is that it has become more difficult to ignore the commitments that numerous governments have made in terms of domestic legislation and international law, and that human rights concerns have filtered out from the foreign ministries into other agencies of governments (particularly the development agencies). In the case of the United States, the legislative branch has also long played an active if selective role.

---

[11] Fen Osler Hampson and John B. Hay, "Human Security: A Review of the Scholarly Literature" produced for the University of British Columbia, Vancouver, *Human Security Index* project, October 2002.

Bodies such as these have embraced the human rights idea and brought that idea to bear on their own particular concerns.

Application

Let me now try to apply some of these ideas to the Asia Pacific states I referred to at the start of this lecture: namely China, Indonesia and Malaysia, and in particular examine U.S. policy towards these countries, post-September 11th.

China

Lowell Dittmer is surely right when he argues that America and other governments have always found it difficult to formulate a coherent and consistent human rights policy towards China, constrained by the fact that, only under the most exceptional circumstances, would either the international community or the U.S. intervene forcefully in such a country to protect the abused. Trade and investment sanctions as an alternative also impose sacrifices on the enforcing country, especially with respect to a country with the size and potential of China. Moreover, at the time of the Most-Favored-Nation/human rights debates in the United States, many in Hong Kong and elsewhere argued that economic sanctions against China were likely to have their greatest impact on the more cosmopolitan within the targeted country.[12]

Apart from the immediate post-Tiananmen period, the U.S. human rights promotion policy has relied primarily on two main avenues: verbal shaming of China either at the UN Commission on Human Rights, or in bilateral meetings between U.S. and Chinese officials, or through reports of special U.S. Commissions set up for monitoring purposes; and through some "subcontracting" of the issue via funding of NGOs, for example, that carry out "rule of law"

---

[12] Lowell Dittmer, "Chinese Human Rights and American Foreign Policy: A Realist Approach," *The Review of Politics*, 63(3), 2001.

initiatives, or trying to persuade U.S. businesses to adopt codes of conduct in the workplace that seek to advance health and labor rights.

In broad terms, there is not much difference between the Clinton and current Bush administrations in the human rights promotion policy towards Beijing. One change is that there is greater rhetorical emphasis under Bush on the need for enhancing religious freedom in China. Bush's speech at Qinghua university in February 2002 (carried live on Chinese TV, but heavily edited by the Xinhua News Agency) gave considerable attention to religious faith and freedom. And Bush has also given greater support to the Tibetan struggle. For example, where Clinton received the Dalai Lama on an unscheduled basis, Bush broke with this in May 2001 in a scheduled and well-publicized "private" meeting — the date was particularly significant because it marked the 50th anniversary of the signature of the 17 Point Agreement of 1951, "an agreement Beijing claims as the legal basis for its take over of Tibet, and which the Dalai Lama's government in exile insists has been grossly violated by Beijing."[13]

The Bush administration's recently published National Security Strategy (September 22, 2002) in its sections on China also gives some prominence to human rights matters: it stresses the need for Chinese people to be able "to think, assemble, and worship freely" and records "profound disagreement" over three issues — Taiwan, weapons proliferation commitments, and human rights. With that language on record in this document and in many previous ones, it is difficult if not impossible for the Bush administration to lay the matter aside. And should Bush seek to do so, the pluralist nature of the political system ensures that there is continuing attention to China's human rights record, especially from China's critics in the U.S. Congress (operating either for political or strategic reasons or out of genuine concern), the Human Rights NGOs, and the media.

---

[13] John W. Garver, "Sino-American Relations in 2001: the Difficult Accommodation of Two Great Powers," *International Journal*, March 2002, p. 3 in internet edition.

These particular forces are relevant to the human rights issue that has received most attention post-September 11th: that is, the apparent U.S. closing of its eyes to the Chinese crackdown in Xinjiang, and the U.S. labeling of the East Turkestan Islamic Movement operating in Xinjiang as a terrorist organization. Two reasons have been advanced as to why the U.S. agreed to the Chinese designation of this group as terrorist in late August 2002:

1) In order to get the Chinese to promulgate and implement missile-related export control regulations, particularly important in the age of terror; and
2) to get China to soften its attitude to the likely military action against Iraq (an abstention rather than a veto in the UN Security Council).

It seems to me that the timing of the designation of this group as terrorist might well be explained by these two related issues, but that the actual designation of a group in Xinjiang as terrorist was probable anyway. As early as March 2002 U.S. officials were on record as stating that there was no question "that at least some members of the Uighur population who are Chinese citizens were trained at the Al-Qaeda camps." Chinese Uighurs were picked up in Afghanistan during the fighting against the Taliban and some are still being held in the U.S. camps in Guantanamo bay. Moreover, prior to September 11th, the Chinese government had been trying to persuade the Taliban to stop its support of certain groupings in Xinjiang.

However, U.S. officials in March and on subsequent occasions always add to their statements, there are "also peaceful Uighur dissidents and the United States is concerned that" the struggle against terrorism not be used as a tool to "persecute...particular religious and ethnic minorities".[14] And in terms of the broader point

---

[14] Thus, when the U.S. embassy in Beijing made a sloppy statement that parroted the Chinese description to the effect that ETIM was responsible for more than 200 acts of terrorism in China, the U.S. press and the NGOs were immediately on to this, demanding proof and criticizing that statement for its inaccuracies and simplistic tone.

about turning a blind eye to China's crackdown on the Uighurs, it is notable that U.S. administrations have always paid less attention to that Uighur struggle for independence than to the actions of those in Tibet fighting for a similar cause. Tibet has been the minority issue of concern to the U.S. Congress, the attentive public, and administration — not the Uighur struggle.

Thus, the human rights issue will remain important in bilateral relations. Although the actual policy influence of human rights ideas will remain limited as it has in the past, human rights groups in Congress and outside of it have put this matter firmly on the domestic agenda and this sets limits on the U.S. relationship with China. A stable and cooperative relationship between the U.S. and China is difficult to maintain and human rights issues remain an important component of that.

Indonesia

Undoubtedly there is a strong desire within parts of the Bush administration to restore ties with the Indonesian military in order to step up the level of cooperation in the fight against terrorist groupings in the country that are linked to Al-Qaeda forces. This has been pressed with particular vigor by the Pentagon since April 2002, and is likely to get stronger still as a result of the recent terrible events in Bali in October 2002. Arrayed against the Department of Defense are certain U.S. Senators, international NGOs, and NGOs inside Indonesia who have been watching these efforts closely. The Bush administration is also constrained by its recent discourse stressing that those in the military responsible for past atrocities have to be held to account before military to military ties can be fully restored.

The links between the U.S. and Indonesian militaries were severed in the first place because of two serious instances of human rights abuse, both involving East Timor, first in 1991 and then again in 1999. In reaction to the Santa Cruz massacre in Dili in November 1991, the U.S. Congress stopped all American training of Indonesian officers under the IMET (the International Military and Education Training) program. Further restrictions were added in 1994 and 1998. The violence that accompanied East Timor's move towards independence in September 1999 was severe enough that UN Secretary-General Kofi Annan spoke of the need to establish an international tribunal for war crimes. At that point, President Clinton cut off most remaining ties.

The most powerful legislative constraint on the restoration of these ties is the amendment put forward by Senator Leahy that has made assistance and contact with the Indonesian military contingent on evidence that the Indonesian government is holding military officers accountable for major human rights abuses. This legislation has served as an obstacle to restoration of full ties and it has to be overcome by those who seek to deepen U.S. relations once again with the Indonesian military.

At the beginning of August this year, Secretary of State Colin Powell announced new aid to Indonesia ($50million+), but over 93% of that is to go to the police, and the bulk of the rest is to fund so called regional counter terrorism fellowships to provide training to the Indonesian military, with $400,000 to go to IMET (still blocked in Congress at the time of writing). Money to the police is designed to help develop a civilian institution that will take over a number of the roles that have in the past been carried out by the Indonesian military. The so-called regional counter terrorism fellowships are to go to military officers, and thus this looks like a breach of current restrictions on military to military ties. But supposedly those fellowships are only to go to officers that are not prime suspects in human rights cases. This promise will be monitored closely, again by NGOs, local and transnational, and by some in the U.S. Congress.

Beyond some congressional and NGO oversight on this activity, U.S. officials and the U.S. ambassador to Indonesia are on record as saying at the time this funding was announced that the matter of accountability had to be addressed before full normalization of relations could be realized. The trials of Indonesian army officers were described as "an important litmus test" of Indonesia's serious-ness about accountability. A week later, the Indonesian judiciary demonstrated it was not serious about accountability when its human rights tribunal acquitted six army officers, and the last Indonesian-appointed governor of East Timor received a sentence of only three years, despite being found guilty of crimes against humanity. U.S. officials described the outcome of these trials as a "disappointment" — a serious understatement since the administration knows that in order to circumvent the Congressional legislation and its prior verbal commitments it needs to demonstrate that the military in Indonesia has indeed been held to account for its past abuses.

This is an ongoing story, but again it shows that human rights matters have been imposing some constraints on what the U.S. executive seeks to achieve, even in an important second front country in the struggle against terrorism.

Malaysia

My third example is Malaysia, a country whose human rights record does not concern the United States as much as the records of Indonesia and China. Nevertheless, relations had been frosty for many years related generally to a dislike of Mahathir, and more specifically to Malaysia's liberal use of its Internal Security Act, together with the arrest, trial and sentencing of Mahathir's former deputy, Anwar Ibrahim, who had many supporters in the United States.

U.S. relations with Malaysia began to improve markedly from April 2002[15] with U.S. officials praising Malaysia's support for the struggle against terrorism, and in particular for the detention of a former army captain who had been linked to some of the September 11th highjackers. There has also been some discussion about establishing a regional center to coordinate anti-terrorism activities.

---

[15] According to a report in the *Far Eastern Economic Review*, the Bush administration had "rebuffed at least three envoys sent to Washington by Malaysian Prime Minister Mahathir Mohamad" before September 11, 2001. *Far East Economic Review*, October 25, 2001.

However, despite the success of Mahathir's meetings in Washington with Bush administration officials in May this year, human rights concerns have not been laid to rest. In this case, it is not the U.S. Congress that has been especially active but the media, as well as the human rights organizations. CNN, for example, ran an interview with Mahathir that was focused largely on the illiberal way in which Mahathir treats his domestic political opponents. And during each of the meetings with the press during that May visit and in the course of subsequent meetings in Kuala Lumpur, the matter of the Anwar trials was raised. All U.S. officials, entrapped by previous statements they had made about the Anwar trial, use similar language to describe the current U.S. position on this episode: the "trials were flawed".

During Colin Powell's last visit to Malaysia at the end of July 2002, he reported to the press that human rights issues had been raised on every occasion that he met with Malaysian officials, and that his Assistant Secretary of State had met with Anwar's wife, Dr Wan Azizah Wan Ismail. Powell also raised concerns about the detention of six reform activists under the ISA, including five leaders from the opposition National Justice Party. A full coming together has been denied therefore and human rights matters plays some, not insubstantial, role in preventing that.

Conclusion

While all three Asia Pacific states have become important in new ways to the U.S. in the struggle against terrorism, my point in discussing these three cases in some detail is to illustrate a number of things:

1) We must realize that words matter — there is discursive entrapment at work here. Past verbal commitments to the protection of rights do constrain: we document these things more fully than in the past, in part because of the NGOs — both local and transnational. (As Michael Ignatieff reminds us, human rights has gone global by going local — "imbedding itself in the soil of

cultures and world views independent of the West".)[16] There is too a media in the Western world and elsewhere that is more skeptical of politicians and more investigative in its methods. It too has taken up the cause of rights.

2) There have also been a number of legislative commitments made in the United States, and these can be difficult to circumvent.

3) There has been a coming together in the thinking about human rights, development, and security — an acceptance of the idea that the security apparatus can often produce much insecurity in its abuse of human rights.

The Bush administration's National Security Strategy document picks up this latter idea. As it puts it: "poverty, weak institutions, and corruption can make weak states vulnerable to terrorist networks". Prosperity and a stable peace belong only to those "nations that share a commitment to protecting basic human rights and guaranteeing political and economic freedom".

Having mentioned this national security document again brings me to my final and in some ways most troubling points. The University of San Francisco is devoted to making a better world and sees human rights promotion as a vital part of that. It is one of the reasons why I have enjoyed being a part of this community. But as many have recognized — and particularly as a result of the military intervention in Kosovo — all those concerned about human rights promotion face serious moral questions, for one thing because human rights and security issues have come together in a way that is both logical and intellectually defensible. But it can also be a dangerous coming together.

The U.S. National Security Strategy makes reference to failed states that might host terrorist or other criminal networks and that invariably abuse the human rights of their citizens. But it speaks too of the doctrine of preemption — the right to take preemptive military action against terrorists and their state sponsors, unilaterally if necessary. Iraq, of course, comes to mind in all this. There is no

---

[16] Michael Ignatieff, *Human Rights as Politics and Idolatry*. Princeton, NJ: Princeton University Press (2001), p. 7.

doubt that in calling for regime change in Iraq the Bush administration — in support of its case — can point to credible instances of human rights abuse on the part of this odious government in Baghdad, along with the more strictly national security case that it has been making.

Nevertheless, Iraq and a number of other cases raise the question of whether we want military action to be used in support of human rights in this and other instances. And if we don't, what are we left with except some of the policies I have mentioned: verbal shaming of abusers, occasionally economic and diplomatic sanctions, and sometimes policies that engage the abuser and focus on reform efforts.

Despite the lack of strong legal enforcement mechanisms associated with the human rights regime, I think the answer has to be that rarely, and only under very exceptional circumstances, should force be contemplated on human rights grounds. And even then, only when all possible attempts at peaceful resolution have been exhausted. If force is used then the just war tradition has to be appealed to: it has to be proportionate. Crucially for me it also has to have attracted the legitimacy that multilateral endorsement brings along with it.

While in certain respects it is of some credit to the current U.S. administration that it places stress on the need to protect "human dignity" as it puts it, it is necessary as ever to weigh the consequences of the policies that appear to be about to flow from its ideas of protection, especially the likelihood of their truly bettering the conditions of those human beings inside the abusive state. It is also necessary to ponder the consequences of its portrayal of human rights promotion as an imposition rather than a negotiation. That tone of imposition will also have negative consequences for those in America who are interested in rights promotion abroad.[17]

---

[17] The United States has always been problematic in this regard, because, while it is a leading norm entrepreneur in this field, it is reluctant to ratify a number of the major human rights instruments. The recent debate over the International Criminal Court is illustrative of this.

So, the human rights era is not over but it is a troubled time for it. If you're an activist, it is necessary to keep on with the struggle; if an oppressor don't think that matters are going all your own way; and if an academic, then watch, document, and try to expose what it all might mean for the future of the human rights idea.

Audience Questions

Do you think the anti-globalization movement should be considered a legitimate part of the human rights movement and, if so, do you think it will continue to be so regarded?

The "anti-globalization movement" is a rather rough and ready term for many different groupings bringing together a huge variety of different interests. If one can generalize, these groupings are indeed something of a response to the inequalities that globalization has brought in its wake. Although some countries or some sectors of some countries have enriched themselves as a result of the phenomenon of globalization, there are many countries, communities, and individuals that feel totally left out of that. So, in this generalized sense the anti-globalization movement includes voices that say we should think about the negative consequences, about people whose livelihoods have been destroyed, about some of the basic issues such as opening rich economies to trade from poor countries. So I think this movement is important for putting human rights ideas on the agenda. I also think that it will continue because those inequalities and injustices are still present.

Australia and a number of other countries in the developed world have toughened their refugee asylum laws. Doesn't this represent something of a setback for human rights in the post-September 11th world?

I think you are absolutely right. This is a huge problem with something like 18 million refugees in the world at the moment. We know, for example, that people have been returned to countries where they can be expected to undergo torture, certainly imprisonment. This is a particularly difficult issue, and I would have to think about qualifying my argument; I would be perfectly willing to give ground on that one. Refugees have always had a pretty rough time. It would be worth actually looking over a longer time period to see whether there has in fact been a dramatic recent increase in the intolerance which immigrants are subject to, or whether that intolerance has been growing rather steadily in recent years for different reasons. Certainly that has been the case in the UK well before September 11th. I would like to look into that a bit further but I am perfectly willing to acknowledge that you have made a very good point.

Migrant workers have suffered badly in Southeast Asia post-September 11th. How can their rights be protected?

This helps me to say something about local NGOs. I am sure you know better than I do that inside these countries there has been a vast increase in the number of groups that have tried to bring about some recognition of the rights of these kinds of workers. Malaysia is a very good case in point. It is also interesting that groups in that country find it necessary to discuss this rights issue not so much with reference to an international human rights regime but in relation to their own local language of and cultural perspective on human rights. They draw much less on the idea that there is indeed an international refugee asylum law, that there are things like the International Labor Organization with its rules and regulations, and try instead to find indigenous ways in which they can promote their message and get it to the people involved. This is a huge issue inside these countries particularly after the Asian financial crisis, and it is one that local NGOs are taking up with some vigor.

What about the issue of human rights violations within the United States?

There are several possible responses to this question. Some of the United Nations special rapporteurs and monitors have been to this country and looked at prisons and other issues and made various negative comments about what they have found here: about the disproportionate number of minority groups, for example, inside prisons, and about the use of the death penalty. The death penalty, and in particular its use on those below the age of 18, is a major issue internationally and it is one of the issues that has sometimes made it difficult for the Europeans and the U.S. to come together inside bodies like the UN Commission on Human Rights.

One of the small things that the U.S. could do that I think would be enormously beneficial would be to actually add itself into its own Country Reports on Human Rights Practices. It is something that the Europeans have done only recently with their own reports. Although European states were extraordinarily reluctant to do so they came under extreme pressure from human rights organizations to be more introspective. So in their own reports they do talk a bit more about themselves, especially about things like the issue of racism in Europe. I think this is a very healthy development, not because I think that there is a kind of moral equivalence wherever you look around the world, but because we all need to be more introspective in this issue area.

There is international monitoring of the United States, but as you probably know it has taken a long time for the U.S. to sign up to international human rights covenants and when it does it often adds reservations, and "understandings" which some human rights organizations claim strike at the core of these agreements. The United States still has not ratified the International Covenant on Economic, Social and Cultural Rights, for example. This gets thrown back at the U.S. when it tries to promote its human rights policies. The argument used in the United States is an interesting one. It is said that the U.S. Constitution is the "supreme document"; it guarantees democracy in this country, and it alone represents the people's opinions, and rights, and ideas, and so on. Therefore, it is sometimes argued that imposition of international law is just not appropriate. One can see something in that type of argument, but it does not play well internationally.

Is it possible that the U.S. can work to prevent human rights violations in places like Asia without appearing to be the overbearing international policeman?

It is extraordinarily difficult. One always has to listen to local views and try to get a better understanding of what people on the ground are saying. Of course a bit of humility is not a bad thing. It is interesting that when Bush gave his speech at Qinghua University [in Beijing] it played very well in China's press and Chinese commentators were more receptive to it because he did put it in a reasonably modest, humble way: that problems existed in the United States, and he gave reasons why he held to his own beliefs, etc. He wanted to appear to be more sensitive and not to impose his ideas, and it seemed to play extremely well.

That does seem one way of achieving greater receptivity. Reform efforts and rule of law programs seem to be another way in that local groupings desire these sources of support. Inside China, many local lawyers look to these international standards and to outsiders as ways of introducing the ideas that they themselves support and to argue that there is an international consensus on the nature of legal reform. So, local people sometimes help find avenues through which outsiders that are concerned with human rights can promote those goals without seeming to be overbearing.

Dealing with Rights-Abusing Regimes Without Going to War

Helena Cobban

A Senior Global Affairs Fellow at the University of Virginia, Ms. Cobban is a writer and researcher who has contributed a column on global affairs to The Christian Science Monitor *since 1990. In mid-2002 she was a member of an International Quaker Working Party on the Israel-Palestine Conflict. She is a long-time member of the International Institute for Strategic Studies, and sits on the Middle East advisory committee of Human Rights Watch. In addition to her five books, Ms. Cobban has published numerous essays, reviews, and scholarly articles. She wrote* The Moral Architecture of World Peace: Nobel Laureates Discuss Our Global Future *(Charlottesville and London: University Press of Virginia, 2000), which was based on a conference eight Laureates held at the University of Virginia in 1998. She is the owner and author of the weblog <www.justworldnews.org>.*

The U.S.-Iraq War of 2003 was a tragedy. People acting from honorable motivations launched a war that, like all wars in the history of humankind, inflicted harm, suffering, and therefore gross human-rights violations of all those living in the war zone. I know a little about such harms, since I lived and worked as a journalist in Beirut from 1974 through 1981; and unlike most of my colleagues there from the global media I was part of the local community by marriage, and struggled alongside my neighbors to raise two small children and run a household amidst the uncertainties and horrors of the unfolding strife.

War always harms civilian communities. That much is clear to me, as it can be clear to anyone who has read the International

279

Committee of the Red Cross's excellent studies of "People on War" or conducted other serious investigations into the phenomenon of war.

I don't know how familiar the people in the U.S. administration who launched the war of March-April 2003 were or are with this irreducible fact about war. But I assume that when they launched the war they were acting from righteous motivations. Were their actual motivations the same as the reasons they articulated in public to bolster their case for going to war? We cannot know the answer to that. What we do know is that many of the "reasons" they adduced in the pre-March 2003 period for going to war turned out to have a very shaky basis in reality. That includes the information they claimed to have regarding Iraq's then-existing weapons of mass destruction (WMDs) and its "programs" for future developments in the WMD field, as well as the information they claimed to have about the Saddam Hussein regime's ties to Al-Qaeda.

In the period after President George W. Bush declared the end of major combat (May 1, 2003), the reasoning that he and members of his administration started to articulate in retrospect around the question of why the war had been justified started to change significantly. Neither the alleged WMDs nor any persuasive evidence about the existence of advanced programs to develop such weapons were found inside Iraq, despite the U.S./UK military's investment of considerable time, energy, and other resources in the search for them. Similarly, despite the access to archives, informants, and other sources of evidence that the U.S./UK occupation of Iraq allowed, no persuasive evidence about close ties between Saddam Hussein and Al-Qaeda were found, either. As these failures of evidence production became increasingly evident, and as the casualty toll among the occupation forces (and the Iraqis) continued to mount in the weeks after May 1, the President and his advisors increasingly resorted to the argument that regardless of these failures, the war had been a good thing anyway, since it succeeded in ridding the Iraqi people (and the world) of the blight of Saddamist rule.

I know from my 30 years of study of the Middle East that this development in the lives of Iraqis is a substantial and very welcome one. I say that, even though it is not yet clear in mid-2003 whether the longer-term effects on the welfare of Iraqi families of the decision to launch the war will turn out to better, about the same, or possibly even worse than one could have reasonably expected from a continuation of the "Saddam ruling but tightly contained" situation that preceded the war. My time in Lebanon and my intense study of chronic war situations elsewhere in the world have taught me that war and violence are creatures that are relatively easy to unleash, but whose course once unleashed is unpredictable and always harmful to human wellbeing.

Nevertheless, two aspects of the war's outcome were in my view indubitably good. One was the fall of the Saddam regime. The other, the ending of the UN's unintendedly lethal sanctions regime. The fact that these significant good outcomes grew out of a war whose launching and conduct I all along opposed has caused me to reflect deeply, once again, on the nature of war, and more especially on the urgency of the need to develop effective alternatives to it.

The main product of these reflections so far has come in the form of a question that can be asked regarding both the challenge posed by Saddamist rule in the pre-2003 period and the issue of how the global community could appropriately deal with other similar tyrants elsewhere, now or in the future. The question is this: Are there mechanisms the global community could have used to bring an end to Saddam's human-rights abuses, or that it could use in analogous situations in the future, that do not involve going to war?

I would like to sketch one possible answer to this question. It grows out of the experience the UN actually had in dealing with allegations of Saddamist abuses — but abuses in the field of WMDs, rather than human rights. Could we not request that the UN respond to international concerns about grave human-rights abuse with the same kind of very robust "monitoring, verification and inspection" mechanism that was deployed in Iraq in response to concerns about WMD contraventions?

People may have a number of different responses to this proposal. "But the UN has never done anything like that before," might be one. Well, that is true. But then, the UN had never put together anything nearly as intrusive and thorough as UNMOVIC (UN monitoring, Verification and Inspection Commission) in Iraq, prior to its inception, but once the Security Council had ruled in 1999 that UNMOVIC should be established, and in 2002 that it be deployed, the UN bureaucracy was able to make it happen.

This objection is linked to one of political feasibility. Much of the UN's work in the field of human rights, after all, comes up hard against the notion and practice of state sovereignty. How, such questioners might ask, could we expect this Security Council, including this present roster of permanent, veto-wielding members, ever to agree to the establishment of such a deeply sovereignty-challenging body as a "human rights UNMOVIC"?

The answer to this question might once again look at precedent. Fifteen years ago, could we have expected that this same Security Council would, in April 1991, create UNMOVIC's strongly sovereignty-challenging predecessor organization, UNSCOM (UN Special Commission), and then insist on Iraqi compliance with it? Or that eight years later, the Security Council would create the even more intrusive UNMOVIC? No, those large steps toward challenging Iraq's sovereignty on the WMD issue would have been almost unimaginable from the Security Council any time prior to 1990. It is true that when the Security Council took the first of these steps, in its resolution 687 of 3 April 1991, it did so in the context of a significant Iraqi military defeat, and both then and eleven years later, when it insisted on the deployment of UNMOVIC in November 2002 it acted at the strong urging of the United States. But we should note that all of the Council's permanent members supported resolution 687, and all the Council's members — permanent as well as rotating — supported resolution 1441 of November 2002. So why should we think that the creation of a human-rights UNMOVIC might not within just a few years similarly become "politically feasible"? Why should we think that only the shock of a major war (like that of 1991) would be sufficient to budge permanent members like Russia or China? Surely, if enough people, civil-society groups, and governments around the world care enough about allegations of gross human-rights abuse, then we should be able to bring enough suasion to bear on the governments of even the permanent members that a human-rights UNMOVIC can become a real-world possibility.

Another possible objection might look at the distinctly disappointing record of the UN's creaky existing human-rights apparatus, and conclude that human rights monitoring is something that the UN cannot do very well. Here again, the assumption of stasis needs to be challenged. In this context, it is worth recalling that back in April 1991, the Security Council passed not one but two resolutions that called for a global response to bad behavior by the Iraqi regime. The second of those resolutions was number 688, passed on 5 April 1991. Passed while the Saddam regime was still continuing its extremely brutal crackdown on dissidents who had risen up in response to a specific appeal from U.S. President George H.W. Bush for an internal insurrection against the regime, resolution 688 expressed the Council's grave concern at "the repression of the Iraqi civilian population in many parts of Iraq". It demanded that Iraq "immediately end this repression, and in the same context express[ed] the hope that an open dialogue will take place to ensure that the human and political rights of all Iraqi civilians are respected." All the Council's permanent members except China supported resolution 688; and even China did not oppose it but merely abstained. But the Council did not, alas, follow up these fine words with the creation of any kind of monitoring mechanism at all — let alone, one with the "bite" of an UNSCOM or an UNMOVIC.

I believe that the work of a robust, UNMOVIC-style body dedicated to following up determinedly on allegations of rights abuse could — whether it is established on an *ad hoc* basis or, more helpfully, on a semi-permanent basis so long as it is needed — make a real difference in the behavior of governments around the world that until now have fallen too easily into the habits of gross rights abuse. It would empower local rights activists at all levels. It would not necessarily have the high-profile, extremely accusatory and polarizing aspect of the International Criminal Court (ICC); but for that very reason it would have, in my view, a much greater chance than the ICC of actually changing the situation of those communities around the world that suffer gross abuse at the hands of their supposed "leaders". In addition, crucially, it would provide a mechanism in the area of human rights performance to monitor situations, establish goals for their improvement, and verify the implementation of those goals that could be far more successful at effecting long-term improvements than any attempt at forceful intervention, that is, war.

I would also like to note that despite the evidently tragic nature of the events of early 2003 in Iraq, it now seems neither glib, Pollyanna-ish, nor inappropriate to suggest that the longer-term global trend regarding the attempt to use force to resolve human differences seems to be a hopeful one. I live, work, and have my citizenship in the U.S., a country with just four percent of the world's population that wields a totally disproportionate amount of power in world affairs. That fact saddens me deeply, most especially because it has allowed far too many of my fellow-citizens to remain unaware of the essential fact of global interdependence to which the U.S. citizenry is subject just as much as are any of the 96 percent of the world's people who are citizens of other countries.

I have known ever since I first came to this country in 1982 that there has been a strong set of assumptions embedded in the public discourse here that takes as a given that war and the military goods and military establishment with which it is waged are good for something. That assumption was very widespread throughout the Cold War, which was the first time in history when the U.S. has maintained a sizeable standing army for such a lengthy period. And through a process of inertia — aided by the ever-expert lobbying of the military-industrial complex — this notion still continued to be widely held even after the end of the Cold War. Thus in 2001, out of a total global expenditure on military goods of $835 billion, no less than $322 billion (38.6 percent) was spent by the U.S. taxpayers.[1] Then, in the period between September 2001 and April

---

[1] International Institute for Strategic Studies, *The Military Balance, 2002–2003.* London: IISS (2002), pp. 332 and 337.

2003, we saw the U.S. administration reacting to the heinous attack of 9/11/2001 by launching not one but two wars. The idea that the military was good for something seemed to gain enormous ground in U.S. public opinion in those months. (As did U.S. military spending.) Along the way there, too, September 2002 saw the President's adoption of a "National Security Strategy" that openly endorsed the idea not just of preemptive war but also of preventive war.

By contrast, in the months that followed the "end of major combat" in Iraq, support for the view that military approaches provide the most effective response to security challenges seems to have become questioned by increasing numbers of U.S. citizens. In Iraq, a large-scale U.S. military force configured largely along the "rapid intervention" lines advocated by Defense Secretary Donald Rumsfeld won the expected military victory over the long-battered forces of the Saddam regime fairly easily and quickly. But they proved ill-suited to the tasks of physical, social, and political reconstruction with which they were immediately thereafter faced. As the casualty toll mounted, the U.S. public seemed to start recognizing with increasing clarity that the nation needed many more tools than merely the military one in its "international intervention" toolkit. So the hunt for means of intervening other than that of unilateral military action will, I am confident, be expanded. At the same time, though, much of the U.S. public agrees with President Bush that "it is a good thing that Saddam Hussein is no longer in power."

Personally, I am extremely wary of any desire to effect "regime change" in countries other than one's own. I do not see the issue as being predominantly one of personalities — far less, of dichoto-mized forces of "good" and "evil". I see the central issue in Saddamist Iraq, or in Burma, or Chechnya, or tens of other places around the globe, as being one of leaders behaving abusively toward the people under their control. For me, the central challenge is to end that abuse — an outcome that is by no means assured if all that happens with "regime change" is the replacement of one abusive leader by another. And I am convinced that there are numerous ways other than war by which this desired behavior change may be brought about. Supporting the human-rights and democratization efforts of the relevant (and preferably still-resident) citizenry is one essential means to this end. Investigating the possibilities for having the UN establish a robust, UNMOVIC-style body to monitor improvements in a regime's human-rights behavior might well be another. Either of these steps, or others of a similar nature, certainly are enactable — provided enough of us around the world care deeply enough to get the relevant governments to move. And if fully enacted, they could provide a credible and effective alternative for nations to use, in place of that tragic and always unpredictable phenomenon, war.

Alternatives to War on Iraq, North Korea and Iran[1]

Frank N. von Hippel

Professor of Public and International Affairs, Woodrow Wilson School at Princeton University and Co-Director of the Program on Science and Global Security, he is a former assistant director for national security in the White House Office of Science and Technology. Frank von Hippel's areas of policy research include nuclear arms control and nonproliferation, energy, and checks and balances in policymaking for technology. He has written extensively on the technical basis for nuclear nonproliferation and disarmament initiatives, the future of nuclear energy, and improved automobile fuel economy. He won a 1993 MacArthur fellowship in recognition of his outstanding contributions to his fields of research.

I will speak first briefly about the U.S. invasion of Iraq, which most of us believe is imminent. Then I will turn to another war that may be only a little further down the road. That war could start at any time with a U.S. bombing of North Korea's nuclear sites.

Iraq

Let me first recap how we have gotten to where we are with Iraq. Four months ago,[2] as a result of Colin Powell's skillful

---

[1] The following text is based on a speech delivered by von Hippel at the Princeton Unitarian Church on March 16, 2003.

[2] November 8, 2002.

diplomacy, the UN Security Council voted unanimously to "set up an enhanced inspection regime [in Iraq] with the aim of bringing to full and verified completion the disarmament process" there. Three weeks later, the first inspections began.

Ten weeks later, at the beginning of February,[3] however, President Bush sent Colin Powell to the UN Security Council to inform it that Iraq was successfully hiding its weapons of mass destruction programs from the inspectors. Powell also informed the Security Council that "leaving Saddam Hussein in possession of weapons of mass destruction for [even] a few more months...is not an option, not in a post-September 11th world."

However, Prime Minister Blair persuaded the Bush Administration to go back to the Security Council with a resolution that would give Iraq until March 17th (tomorrow) to demonstrate compliance, Then, if the U.S. and Britain are not satisfied, the resolution would allow them to invade Iraq without further UN Security Council action. Two days ago the Bush Administration rebuffed a compromise proposal from the six undecided states on the Security Council that would have delayed the deadline by three weeks and then required an additional Security Council resolution.

In response to the Bush Administration's relentless drive toward war, there have been huge demonstrations in cities around the world and public warnings from a myriad of respected experts.

President Bush, Prime Minister Blair and Prime Minister Aznar are meeting on an isolated island today to decide what to do next. However, it is generally assumed that the U.S. will — perhaps within days — invade Iraq with the moral support of an *ad hoc* group of countries, possibly not even including Britain.

Why are We Doing This?

The UN Charter only permits a country to attack another without Security Council authorization if it does so in self defense. President Bush argues that an invasion of Iraq would be self defense. As a

---

[3] February 5, 2003.

result of September 11, 2001, he says, we have learned that we can't take any chances when someone like Saddam Hussein shows an interest in weapons of mass destruction.

President Bush has conflated September 11 with Iraq so often that, according some polls, half the U.S population thinks that Saddam was behind the attack on the World Trade Center. The U.S. intelligence community has not been able to find any significant evidence of such a connection. In fact, Saddam has not attacked any other country since the UN put him in quarantine in 12 years ago.

But the Bush Administration argues that Saddam's behavior during the 1980s shows that he could use weapons of mass destruction at any time. It cites in particular his use of poison gas against Iran and against Iraq's rebellious Kurds during the Iraq-Iran War.

But the U.S. did not oppose Saddam's use of chemical weapons in the 1980s. At that time Iraq was our ally against Iran, which we saw as the chief threat to stability in the Persian Gulf region. According to reports in *New York Times*, the U.S. provided targeting information to Iraq even when we knew that it was going to use chemical weapons against Iran's Army. And even after Iraq gassed the town of Halabja in 1988, killing 5,000 Kurds, the Reagan Administration and first Bush Administration blocked legislation proposed by Senate Democrats to impose sanctions on Iraq.[4] That blocking effort was led by high-level officials who now serve in this Bush Administration.

Iraq's Nuclear-Weapons Program

In any case, Iraq's chemical and biological weapons are not the Bush Administration's primary concern. It says that its biggest worry is that Saddam has renewed his efforts to acquire nuclear weapons. Plastic suits and gas masks can't protect soldiers against a nuclear bomb.

---

[4] According to Patrick Tyler, officers say U.S. aided Iraq in war despite use of gas, *New York Times*, August 18, 2002, p. 1; "Iraq Chemical Arms Condemned, but West Once Looked the Other Way" by Elaine Sciolino, *New York Times*, February 13, 2003, A18.

However, the evidence that Colin Powell brought to the UN in February about alleged efforts by Iraq to acquire uranium and aluminum tubes and magnets for centrifuges has not held up. Indeed, when the documents that the U.S. provided to the UN as evidence for Iraqi efforts to purchase uranium were revealed to be crude forgeries, an embarrassed CIA leaked out the word that it had been suspicious of those documents all along.

The Mission of Overthrowing Tyrants

The final argument for an invasion of Iraq is that Saddam is a tyrant, a murderer and torturer. There is do doubt that he is. Unfortunately, there are a quite a few tyrants in the world. In a number of cases — as with Saddam — the U.S. helped install them.

It would be wonderful if the U.S. decided to work systematically with the UN to rid the world of tyrants. However, the Bush Administration is not arguing at the UN that Saddam should be removed because he is a tyrant. That argument is purely for domestic consumption.

Indeed, the Administration has been trying to prevent the establishment of an International Criminal Court that would be able to bring tyrants to justice for genocide and other crimes against humanity, including the crime of aggression. The Administration is concerned that U.S. officials and military officers might be brought before such a Court for war crimes.

Most people think that concern is exaggerated. But in the present case it may not be. Two weeks ago, a group of eminent Australian jurists warned the Australian Prime Minister that he and Australian military officers could be prosecuted for war crimes in the International Criminal Court if Australia joins the U.S. in an invasion of Iraq.[5]

---

[5] "Coalition of the willing? Make that war criminals. A preemptive strike on Iraq would constitute a crime against humanity," write 43 experts on law and human rights, *Sydney Morning Herald*, February 26, 2003.

Unfortunately, before the November elections, Congress wrote the President a blank check authorizing war on Iraq without United Nations Security Council authorization. The President has dismissed the millions who have demonstrated worldwide against an invasion. And he is ready to dismiss the UN Security Council as "irrelevant" to international security if it does not agree with the U.S. Whether we go to war or not is now up to the whim of one man and the small circle of hardliners who advise him.

So, having told you what you mostly knew already about Iraq, I would like to talk about what might be the location of the next U.S. war after Iraq: the Korean Peninsula.

A Renewed Korean War?

We now know that President Bush gave the go ahead for planning an invasion of Iraq the day after the Al-Qaeda attack on September 11th 2001. This shows that how deeply rooted in his mind the connection of Iraq to September 11th is — even if there is no real connection.

A few months later, however, in his State of the Union speech, he publicly added Iran and North Korea to what he called "the Axis of Evil". He said about all three that "The United States of America will not permit the world's most dangerous regimes to threaten us with the world's most destructive weapons".

President Bush had already questioned South Korea's new policy of reconciliation toward North Korea and had terminated the negotiations that the Clinton Administration had been pursuing to shut down North Korea's long-range missile program.

In January 2002, North Korea learned that the Pentagon had put it back on the U.S. nuclear target list, along with Iraq, Iran, Syria and Libya. This contravened the 25-year-old commitment the U.S. had made not to threaten non-nuclear-weapon states with nuclear weapons and is profoundly undermining of the nuclear Nonproliferation Treaty.

Things came to a head, however, last October when North Korea admitted that it had an uranium-enrichment program. It said that it would be willing to give up that program if the Bush Administration would sign a non-aggression pact. The Bush Administration's response has been "we won't negotiate with you until after you get rid of your nuclear weapons program." From North Korea's point of view, its nuclear-weapons program is its only bargaining chip — and it certainly needs a bargaining chip. Even paranoids have enemies.

Resumption of North Korean Plutonium Production

In November, the Bush Administration cut off the supply of heavy fuel oil that the U.S. had been providing to North Korea since 1994. The oil was fuel for power plants to replace the electricity that North Korea lost by shutting down its small dual-purpose plutonium- and electricity production reactor and by not completing the construction of two larger dual-purpose reactors. Not surprisingly, North Korea has restarted the reactor that it had shut down as a result of that 1994 agreement with the Clinton Administration.

Of more immediate concern, however, is the possibility that North Korea might begin to separate out the several bombs worth of the plutonium in spent fuel that, under its 1994 agreement with the Clinton Administration, has been stored under International Atomic Energy Agency seals. At the end of December, North Korea kicked out the international inspectors who were monitoring the spent fuel.

A week ago, Secretary of Defense Rumsfeld responded by moving two dozen heavy bombers to Guam within range of North Korea. The U.S. also announced that, if North Korea begins plutonium separation, it will be making a serious mistake.

Israel bombed Iraq's nuclear reactor in 1981 and set back its nuclear-weapons program for a decade. The situation is different for North Korea, however. Iraq's nuclear reactor had not yet operated when Israel bombed it. North Korea's reactor has already produced in spent fuel enough plutonium for several Nagasaki-type bombs.

We could bomb both the reactor and facility that North Korea built to separate plutonium from its spent fuel. But North Korea could still haul the spent fuel off to a cave, improvise a chemical separation facility there, and separate the plutonium in a year or so. If we want to solve the North Korean nuclear problem permanently and by force, therefore, we will have to invade North Korea after we bomb it.

The coalition of the willing to help us do that is going to be pretty small.

Iran

As if this weren't enough, we have just learned that Iran is building a uranium enrichment plant and probably a plutonium-production reactor. Iran, seeing what the U.S. is about to do to Iraq, and seeing itself on the U.S. target list wants a nuclear deterrent in a hurry. Are we going to bomb Iran too?

Summary

To summarize on all these prospective wars:

- We have not yet exhausted the alternatives to a unilateral invasion of Iraq.
- There may still be an alternative to war in the case of North Korea — but we won't find out if we continue to refuse to talk to North Korea.
- And there may be reassurances that we can give to Iran that will convince it that it doesn't need a bomb — at least not in the near term.

President Bush would like to establish democracy in Iraq. It would also be a good idea to reestablish a democratic process of foreign-policy making in the U.S. According to our Constitution, issues of war and peace should not be the decision of the President alone.

It was a mistake for the Congress to give President Bush a blank check to go to war with Iraq because of the national trauma of

September 11 — just as it was a mistake for Congress to give President Johnson a blank check in the form of the Tonkin Gulf resolution to go to war with North Vietnam.

The only recourse left to people who believe in international law is to work for political change in Washington. I am encouraged that so many have been seized by the seriousness of what is going on. I hope that the result is a political movement strong enough to influence the course of the next elections and restore function to our system of checks and balances.

Missing in Action: The Iraq Museum and the Human Past

Benjamin R. Foster

Professor of Assyriology and Curator of the Yale Babylonian Collection at Yale University, Foster's research interests focus on two main areas: Mesopotamian, especially Akkadian, literature, and the social and economic history of Mesopotamia. He is author of Before the Muses *(1993, 1996), a two-volume anthology of annotated translations from Akkadian literature of all periods (revised edition in preparation, to appear 2004).*

Mesopotamia, as understood today, refers to the land on both sides and between the Euphrates and Tigris rivers, bounded on the north by the Anatolian plateau, on the east by the Zagros mountains, on the south by the Arab/Persian gulf and the Arabian desert, and on the west by the Syrian and Arabian deserts. In ancient times, Mesopotamia included Assyria (the northern half of Iraq) and Babylonia (the southern half of Iraq). Babylonia was divided into Sumer (southern Babylonia) and Akkad (northern Babylonia). The term "Iraq", the etymology of which is disputed, is associated with the settlement of Arabs in the region, first peacefully along the Euphrates river in the fourth to sixth centuries CE, then by invasion from Arabia, with the Muslim conquest in the seventh century CE. From the ninth until the thirteenth century, Iraq was the seat of the Abbasid caliphate and so one of the major political and cultural centers of the world in the Middle Ages. From the sixteenth century until the British occupation of Baghdad in 1918, Iraq was part of the Ottoman Empire ruled from Constantinople. Iraq was made a

British mandate by the League of Nations in 1921 and became a fully independent state in 1932.

Early European explorers and adventurers in Iraq had long been intrigued by the potential of the numerous ruins that dotted the landscape. Beginning in the 1840s, excavation of ancient sites in Iraq yielded architecture, sculpture, inscriptions, pottery, jewelry, metalwork and clay tablets inscribed in the cuneiform ("wedge-shaped") writing system. It had been written in damp clay with stylus, which made distinctive wedge-shaped impressions. The wedge-shaped appearance of the script was reproduced when it was carved into stone, metal, or other media. By 1860, scholars had succeeded in deciphering one of the languages written in cuneiform script, now called by its ancient name "Akkadian". This language, also referred to by its two main dialects, Babylonian and Assyrian, belongs to the same family of languages as Hebrew and Arabic, so could be rapidly reconstructed. An older Mesopotamian language, Sumerian, which is not related to any other known language, was not deciphered until later in the nineteenth century, but can now be understood. Cuneiform was also used to write several other languages elsewhere in the ancient Near East. This writing system was first invented in Mesopotamia about 3300 BCE and went out of use early in the Christian era.

By the end of the nineteenth century, scholars and members of the educated general public were excited to learn that Mesopotamian clay tablets contained historical and cultural information directly related to the European sense of its own past, as known from Classical sources and the Bible. Two cite just two examples, cuneiform tablets told a story of a universal deluge that was unmistakably the same as that in the Bible, but far older; the so-called Pythagorean theorem was in use in Mesopotamia centuries before Pythagoras. It became clear that traditional European and American concepts of "ancient history" had to be revised to take account of the more than three thousand years of documented history from ancient Mesopotamia that preceded the Christian era. Furthermore, historians recognized that the written evidence from ancient Mesopotamia was larger, in sheer bulk, than that of all the rest of the ancient world combined. Interest in exploring Mesopotamia intensified, as no one knew what discoveries might tell of the early history of the human race or of its hitherto unsuspected cultural achievements. European and American archaeologists excavated many sites in Iraq, taking back to their own museums what they found, with the exception of some artifacts turned over to the Imperial Ottoman Museum in Constantinople, since Iraq was still then part of the Ottoman Empire.

After World War I, the British occupying forces and administration in Iraq included people keenly interested in the ancient history of that country and eager to promote its exploration. Gertrude Bell, an Englishwoman closely involved with creating the new kingdom of Iraq, threw her considerable energies into creating an Iraqi antiquities service, backed up by an antiquities law, to protect historical sites and to supervise scientific exploration of them. She was also instrumental in founding the Iraq Museum in 1923. This was to be a great national museum, like those in London, Paris, or Berlin, but, unlike the European museums, was to concentrate on the heritage of one country, Iraq, rather than gather objects from all over the world. According to the Iraqi antiquities law of 1924, foreign excavations were to divide their finds with the Iraq Museum as evenly as possible, though exceptional pieces were to remain in Iraq. This law was modified in 1936 and again in 1974 to require that all excavated antiquities remain in Iraq.

For some Iraqi politicians and intellectuals involved in building the new nation, its most ancient past offered a common ground for national pride that transcended the many religious, social, and ethnic divisions of the country: all Iraqis could claim ancient Mesopotamia as their past, just as modern Egyptians were claiming pharaonic Egypt as their past. The major disadvantage of this strategy was that the Mesopotamian past had been largely reconstructed by European and American scholars, so was associated by some thinkers with colonialism. A native cadre of professional scholars and archaeologists was needed.

To this end, an American Assyriologist, Albert T. Clay of Yale University, sought to create a school in Baghdad, under the auspices of the American Schools for Oriental Research, a consortium of American colleges, seminaries, and universities. The school was to be a residence for foreign scholars, a research center, and a training institute for Iraqi scholars until such time as the University of Baghdad could take up the ancient languages and civilizations of Mesopotamia in its curriculum. Clay acquired and brought to Iraq in 1923 a superb scholarly library in ancient Near Eastern languages, art and archaeology, and history. This remains today the best of its kind in the Arab world and is housed in the Iraq Museum. It is said to have survived the recent looting of the Museum without major damage. Iraqi universities, especially Baghdad and Mosul, but in provincial centers as well, added ancient Mesopotamian studies to their curricula and today there are undergraduate and graduate students in Iraq eager to pursue these studies professionally.

In the years between the British creation of the kingdom of Iraq in 1921 and the outbreak of World War II, dozens of important archaeological excavations were carried out at ancient Mesopotamian, Classical, and medieval sites in all parts of Iraq. American archaeologists developed methods of regional survey, in order to reconstruct the settlement and cultural history of a wide area by surveying its surface remains, in preference to digging intensively in one place. Research focused as well on important developments in universal human history: the transition from a hunting and gathering way of life to animal husbandry and agriculture, from seasonal encampments to villages, towns, and cities; the creation and redistribution of surplus production; and the growth of trade, business, social stratification, city states, and empires. Mesopotamia often provided the first and clearest evidence for these transitions and developments. Mesopotamia also provided some of the first and best evidence for early arts and technologies, such as pottery, textiles, ivory and wood carving, and the production, casting, and working of metals, as well as for man-made substances such as glass. The past as known from ancient Mesopotamia is therefore exemplary of the past of the entire human race, not just of the ancient peoples who lived in Iraq, and so Mesopotamia is often referred to as the "cradle of civilization".

Historians of arts and letters found in Mesopotamia the beginnings of representational art and monumental architecture, and, closely associated with these, the earliest symbolic communication, especially the invention of writing. The world's oldest literature gradually yielded its secrets. This included the poetry of the first author in history known by name and specific work: a woman, whose passionate and highly personal lyrics spoke over a gap of four thousand years. Narrative poems, such as the Epic of Gilgamesh, told of kingly deeds a millennium before Homer. Hymns, prayers, and myths revealed a long-forgotten spirituality of the human race. School books told of ancient education; inscriptions told of war, peace, and great public works; folktales told of talking animals and wicked sorcerers. Treatises on such varied subjects as astronomy, mathematics, production of perfumes, training of horses, the meaning of words, human sickness, psychology, and sexual behavior, opened entirely unexpected vistas into the mind, person, and spirit of ancient human beings. Contracts of sale and loans, records of birth, marriage, child-bearing, and death, gave details on social life unavailable for most of the ancient world. Law collections, court cases, and documents from the practice of law pushed the history of law 1500 years before the earliest legislation known from Europe. Tens of thousands of administrative records opened up concepts of ancient management and provided massive data for quantitative analysis. Musical instruments, treatises on theory, and performance indications in manuscripts added two millennia to the knowledge of human music. Recipes fifteen hundred years older than any others known from the ancient world revealed unexpected information on diet and elaborate cookery. Indeed, the potential of Mesopotamian written evidence remains today as great as the potential and creativity of the human mind allows. No one knows what the next tablet or the next turn of the shovel is going to reveal.

After World War II, Iraqi archaeologists developed their own program under Naji al-Asil, director-general of antiquities. Iraq's senior archaeologist, Fuad Safar, began excavations in 1946 at the site of Eridu, reputed to be the primeval cult city of Sumer. Many other Iraqi excavations followed, for example at Dur Kurigalzu, an important capital city of the second millennium BCE, and at Tell Harmal, a small early second millennium town near Baghdad. Over 10,000 archaeological sites were eventually listed in an official survey. The Iraqi archaeological journal Sumer commenced publication in 1945, with articles in both Arabic and European languages. For cuneiform tablets, a series Texts in the Iraq Museum presented work by both Iraqi and foreign scholars. Numerous other serials and monographs established the worldwide reputation of the Iraq Museum, Baghdad and Mosul universities, and the Antiquities Service for high professional standards and excellent wardenship of many aspects of Iraq's ancient and medieval heritage.

The collections of the Iraq Museum grew rapidly. A survey of the tablet collections in 1947 inventoried 20,000 cuneiform tablets and fragments from twenty or more archaeological sites, some from Iraqi excavations, some from foreign expeditions. Prior to World War II, the Museum allowed large discoveries of tablets to be taken out of the country for study, against a promise to return half of them to Iraq. Thus important groups were sent for long-term study to the British Museum, the Harvard Semitic Museum, and the Berlin Museum. Most of these loans had been returned by the early 1980s. No precise count of the tablets in the Iraq Museum is available from recent years, but 80,000 may be offered as a rough estimate.

Although a network of thirteen regional museums, plus museums at archaeological sites, was created in Iraq, the most important finds and records were kept in the Iraq Museum in Baghdad, for which a new building was opened in 1966. This contained public galleries, displaying material from earliest times through the medieval period, including celebrated objects that can be seen in any book on the history of art. In addition, there were large storerooms and vaults to house study collections, records of excavations, and the overwhelming majority of the museum's holdings that could not be shown in cases. Ongoing public works programs in Iraq, such as construction of highways and dams and development of agriculture, often posed an immediate threat to archaeological sites, so the Department of Antiquities sent out salvage expeditions, the finds from which were stored in the Museum awaiting further study.

During the 1970s and 1980s, the Department's staff grew apace, with 1600 site guards, plus archaeologists, curators, conservators, and office staff. Work at long-studied sites, such as Nimrud, continued; the scholarly world was astonished to learn in 1989 of the discovery there by Iraqi archaeologists of tombs of Assyrian royal women containing exquisite gold jewelry that had miraculously escaped looting in antiquity. In 1987, discovery by an Iraqi team of a well-preserved scholarly library of about 800 cuneiform tablets at Sippar was announced, the oldest library known in which the materials were still shelved in their original sequence. Among other compositions, this contained a set of tablets giving a fuller version of the same story of the creation of the human race and the primeval flood that had captured the imagination of European and American readers a century previous. These tablets, as well as other important finds, were housed in the Iraq Museum. In addition, the Iraqi Antiquities Service confiscated for the museum objects taken illeglly from ancient sites and also purchased pieces from people who found them by chance.

The Gulf War in 1991 effectively removed the tight control the Iraqi Antiquities Service had exercised over most sites and museum collections. Nine of the local museums were plundered and of 2000 objects whose loss could be documented, scarcely a dozen had been recovered more than a decade later. Large-scale, organized looting of unprotected sites began, using teams of armed men with cavalcades of vehicles and heavy earth-moving equipment. The antiquities market became replete with objects, large and small, from Iraq, including architectural fragments, statuary, seals, ceramics, jewelry, and tens of thousands of cuneiform tablets, often discovered in large groups but divided by dealers among various purchasers. This looting was driven by the high prices paid by dealers and collectors for important pieces, sometimes more than $5 million for a single object. An Assyrian relief of legitimate origin sold at

Christie's in July, 1994 for $11.9 million; numerous fragments of such reliefs were stolen from storerooms and sites in the Mosul region. These have been hammered and sawed into saleable pieces and have been scattered on the trade. Small routine tablets usually sell for $150 or so apiece, collections of related documents $50,000 or more, and high quality cylinder seals may begin at around $5000 apiece. More interesting inscriptions and literary documents may run much higher.

Neither the purchasers nor the dealers were concerned enough about the irreparable damage done by this looting of ancient sites to curb their appetite for more. Collectors are mostly people of wealth with the means and will to use their prestige and influence to justify their collecting. They present themselves as friends of the arts and as connoisseurs; they have access to first-rate legal and scholarly advice. They include leading donors to American and Israeli museums, which, unlike their European counterparts, rely largely on philanthropy to sustain themselves. Museums are eager to court these prominent collectors and often compete with each other to acquire and display objects whose dubious provenience they prefer to ignore, insisting that the burden of proof lies on those who would impugn their collecting policies. The UNESCO convention of 1970, ratified by 96 countries, prohibits traffic in cultural property that has been taken out of a country in contravention of its laws, but has left the burden of proof of illegitimacy on the country of origin. This is difficult, because of the clandestine nature of the trade. Despite a few high-profile victories over dealers in stolen, or "recently excavated" artifacts, the flood of objects looted from Iraq continues unabated.

The Iraq Museum closed for a decade after the Gulf War. Cutbacks in its budget in 1995, allegedly because of the effects of United Nations sanctions, made conservation work difficult and only a few scholars had access to its collections. The staff of the Antiquities Service was greatly reduced and most sites were left unguarded. Some museum holdings were said to have been taken for safekeeping to banks and other repositories; others were said to have been taken to the palaces constructed for the ruling clique;

what was left in some of the provincial museums was transferred to Baghdad. Some leading Iraqi scholars of ancient Mesopotamia had gone into seclusion or left the country for political reasons during the years Iraq was dominated by the Baath party and Saddam Hussein, so only a few professionals remained active. Hussein compared himself to Nebuchadnezzar II and even built a palace at ancient Babylon, so discussion of Iraq's past gained unwelcome political overtones. Promising foreign excavations came to a halt, and contacts between Iraqi scholars and foreigners could endanger them, so tended to be few and tentative. In anticipation of an American attack, Iraq Museum staff rehearsed evacuation procedures for the major pieces in the collection.

During Allied and American planning for the invasion of Iraq in 2003, some attention was given to protecting archaeological sites. There was ample precedent for this, as during World War II, the American armed forces had relied on cultural officers to advise them what to protect. A section of monuments, fine arts, and archives personnel had regularly briefed combat troops and after the war had assumed an active role in repatriating stolen and looted goods, disbanding only in 1951. Although the United States and Britain were not signatories to the 1954 Hague Convention, which required combatants to protect cultural property, they routinely claimed prior to the invasion of Iraq that they would observe its provisions. American learned societies and archaeologists sought to brief military planners on the necessity of preserving the archaeological heritage of Iraq, but had limited success in finding a hearing.

To their dismay, more ready access was granted to a low-profile but influential group of museum officials and collectors of antiquities calling themselves the American Council for Cultural Policy. Some scholars were concerned that this group was seeking to enhance their collections and trade by changing the Iraqi antiquities law after American occupation, and their fears seemed confirmed when the group's attorney, William Pearlman, referred to Iraqi law as excessively "retentionist". Although the president of the group, Ashley Hunter, later said that Iraqi antiquites laws had not been raised in meetings with the military, and that Pearlman was speaking only for himself, Philippe de Montebello, director of the Metropolitan Museum of Art in New York, suggested that future American museum excavations in Iraq should be able seek export licenses for their finds. The *Wall Street Journal* ran a piece by a prominent buyer of antiquities arguing that "retentionist" policies of archaeologically rich countries should be reconsidered in favor of dealers and private collectors. Airing of such views served only to fuel suspicion in the academic community, which has long opposed commerce in antiquities and favors strengthening existing antiquities laws, rather than relaxing them. Their position is based on the reality that the antiquities trade is sustained by and encourages looting of archaeological sites and stealing from museums.

Meetings of these "experts", including, however, at least one qualified archaeologist unaffiliated with the group, with military officials took place in January and February, 2003, but no formal commitments were made by military planners. On March 26, a five-page memo from the Pentagon's Office of Reconstruction and Humanitarian Assistance to the Coalition Forces Land Component Command listed sixteen sites in Iraq to be protected, in order of preference. Of these, site no. 1 was the Iraqi Central Bank and site no. 2 was the Iraq Museum. Later, critics pointed out that site no. 16 on the list, the Iraqi oil ministry, was fully protected, but neither the bank nor the museum. The March 26 memo identified the Iraq Museum as a "prime target for looters". On April 5, U.S. Major Christopher Varbola, a cultural anthropologist, gave a formal press briefing in Kuwait, in which he referred to the threat of looting and "in particular the National Museum of Baghdad". He further stated that "the U.S. military is eager to cooperate with any organization dedicated to the task of preservation, which transcends military and operational necessity". However, in an April 15 briefing, General Vincent Brooks, United States Central Command deputy director of operations, would claim, "I don't think that anyone anticipated that the riches of Iraq would be looted by the Iraqi people."

At dawn on Thursday, April 10, 2003, large crowds of people descended upon the Iraq Museum, where, according to some accounts, four staff members remained, and came and went freely until sunset the next day, and possibly for much of the next day as well. Eyewitness accounts, published immediately after the events, stated that the crowd was a mixture of men, women, and children from poorer neighborhoods of Baghdad, armed with guns, clubs, and knives, and what looked to museum staff like professional thieves, armed with glass cutters of a type said not to be commercially available in Iraq. Of 451 exhibit cases, 27 were smashed or cut open; the other exhibit cases were largely empty because, prior to the invasion, the museum staff had removed many objects for safekeeping elsewhere in the city. Looters also made their way to the locked storerooms and vaults. Some mystery surrounds the whereabouts of the keys to the vaults. One set was said to have been in the museum director's safe but disappeared; two vaults were said to have been opened with keys, while a third was forced. Keys to storage cabinets for the large numismatic collection were taken by thieves from hiding places but accidentally dropped on the floor and lost in the debris and darkness, so that collection was not rifled. For two days or more, the crowds rushed from the museum with boxes, pushcarts, bicycles, wheelbarrows, and pockets full of loot. Some large, heavy objects, such as a copper statue weighing about 160 kilograms, were carted away by teams, others were smashed and the fragments trampled on the floor. Early in the afternoon of the 10th, a museum staff member located an American tank and four marines not far from the museum. At his urging, they came to the museum and dispersed the looters by firing a few shots over their heads, but left about half an hour later and did not return. Appeals by museum staff to the coalition command to protect the museum were unsuccessful. Five days later, the museum was still open to anyone who wished to walk around, and an American newspaper reporter who walked through the galleries stated that there was nothing left there to be seen.

This event became worldwide front page news, along with photographs and TV coverage of the looted and vandalized galleries and the ransacked offices. Editorial comment laid the blame on the American military for not protecting the museum and other destroyed facilities, such as the National Library, a major collection of Koranic manuscripts, and a museum of Islamic legal documents and manuscripts. U.S. Government spokesmen were at first inclined to trivialize the catastrophe. Secretary of Defense Donald Rumsfeld was in the forefront of this, referring to the "untidiness of war", and even quipped, "how many vases could they have in that country, anyway?" White House spokesman Ari Fleischer called the looting "a reaction to oppression". General Richard Myers, chairman of the Joint Chiefs of Staff, dismissed American inaction as a "matter of priorities".

On April 16, an American tank platoon was finally stationed at the museum and a thirteen-member team began to work on recovering the looted museum objects. On April 17, an international group of archaeologists and museum directors met at the Paris headquarters of UNESCO. A petition, initiated at Yale and Oxford Universities, was presented through the UN headquarters in New York, calling for safeguarding Iraqi antiquities "for the future of the Iraqi people and for the world". UNESCO's director general, Koichiro Matsuura, supported this appeal in a request that the UN Security Council impose an embargo for a "limited period" on acquisition of all Iraqi cultural property. A similar approach was advocated by the American Council for Cultural Policy and the National Association of Dealers in Ancient, Oriental and Primitive Art. Three members of the President's Advisory Committee on Cultural Property, Richard S. Lanier, director of the Trust for Mutual Understanding, a New York cultural foundation; Gary Vikan, director of the Walters Art Museum in Baltimore, and Martin E. Sullivan, director of the Historic St. Mary's City Museum (Maryland) and chairman of the committee, resigned in protest at the government's failure to preserve the Iraq Museum and the several libraries and archives that were looted and burned.

Gradually American government officials saw that the destruction of Iraqi cultural material had captured worldwide attention, so damage control appeared necessary. Secretary of State Colin Powell said, "The United States understands its obligations and will be taking a leading role with respect to antiquities in general but this museum in particular." He named an American diplomat,

John W. Limbert, to coordinate efforts to recover stolen property, and sent a representative to confer with UNESCO. Robert S. Mueller III, director of the FBI, said, "We are firmly committed to doing whatever we can in order to secure the return of these treasures to the people of Iraq" and sent agents to Iraq. A Marine lieutenant colonel with background in American law enforcement, Matthew Bogdanos, was stationed at the museum. He stated initially that he knew of only twenty-five missing objects, in his words, "a long way from 170,000". He complained that he did not have reliable lists and photographs of missing objects and suggested that the Iraqi antiquities staff were not fully cooperating with his efforts to recover items from the museum. Stories went out that looters had taken only old guns and office equipment and light fixtures, but not antiquities, even as more than nine hundred stolen objects were being returned voluntarily or confiscated. Some inspections were made at Jordanian border stations, in which most of the antiquities found were in the possession of western newsmen, but American forces made no significant effort to impede outgoing traffic in antiquities, much of which moves through the desert to Saudi Arabia and Jordan, some to Iran as well.

By early May, major museums in Europe and the United States had begun to offer technical support. Promises of funding were received, the first offer being $1 million from the Italian government, but these were dwarfed into insignificance compared to the funding immediately available to restore other installations, such as $62 million from the U.S. government to resume Iraqi TV broadcasting. Visits to Iraq, news stories, and telephone calls to museum officials still had not given a clear picture as to what was still safe in the museum or elsewhere or what was stolen, though the loss of a few major pieces, such as the Uruk vase and head and the Bassetki bronze statue, was confirmed. The American Attorney General, John Ashcroft, in a speech to a May 6 meeting of Interpol in Lyon, France, reconfirmed that the United States would help find plundered objects and referred to "organized criminal groups". The U.S. State Department committed $2 million to restore the museum and establish a conservation laboratory in it.

The American academic community was divided as to what steps should be taken next and under whose auspices. Some American archaeologists with experience in Iraq wanted to take leading positions in coordinating a response, but other members of the academic community preferred broader consultation and leadership. Two organizations, the American Schools of Oriental Research, which had maintained a Baghdad School or Committee since 1923, but because of its presence in Israel had political liabilities in Iraq, and a newer one called the American Association for Research in Baghdad, under the auspices of the Council of American Overseas Research Centers, claimed competitively the allegiance of the American orientalist and archaeological communities. At a meeting in New York on May 6, a new umbrella organization of major American museums and universities was formed called the American Coordinating Committee for Iraqi Cultural Heritage, headed by Robert Mc. Adams, America's senior Mesopotamian archaeologist. This hoped to present a unified position for the American academic community to the U.S. government. Major American philanthropic foundations, while considering the possibilities of support for restoring the Museum, preferred to take a cautious approach, waiting to see if stability could be established in Iraq and what mechanism could be developed for responsible management of their funds.

The U.S. government's response was hampered by its ignorance as to the very nature of museum collections in general and of Mesopotamian antiquities in particular, little hard data on the antiquities trade, and an ongoing desire to minimize a public relations disaster. Genuine investigative efforts were counterpointed with official statements implying that the losses were not so great as feared, that the Iraqis were withholding needed information, and that members of the antiquities staff had stolen objects themselves. At the same time, the American academic community had virtually no access to senior administration or military officials and was divided by what some saw as the personal vanity and ambition of their colleagues. The academic community viewed with continuing suspicion the motives of American dealers in antiquities, collectors, and of major museums well known for accepting material of dubious provenance, despite their joining the rising call for a moratorium on the sale of Iraqi antiquities. To the archaeologists and scholars, this seemed like a cynical effort to legitimize their commerce by making it appear as if they normally dealt in legitimately imported artifacts. The events of the Iraqi looting of the Kuwait National Museum during the Gulf War, and the active role of Iraqi antiquities and museum staff in that looting, were reviewed in the press. Various websites were developed, devoted to recording facts or opinion on the damage to the museum and libraries, as well as sites providing lists and imagery of stolen objects. The Iraqi libraries and archives attracted far less attention in the American press than the museums. Predictably, a month after the event, stories appeared purporting to be eyewitness accounts, in which it was said that American soldiers had forced open the museum gate and doors and urged on the looters with such idiomatic usage as "This is your treasure! Get in!" These were too absurd to be given serious consideration.

The cultural and historical consequences of the American invasion of Iraq will long outlast the political and economic ones. No one remembers who won or even participated in the street battle that led to the burning of the library of Alexandria, for example, but nearly two millennia later the event is still mourned by educated people as a purposeless act of vandalism with universal and perpetual consequences. The damage to Iraqi museums and libraries will also live in history as another example of the extent to which supposedly civilized human beings are capable of utter folly.

The American government's preparation for attacks on the museum showed the ignorance and indifference of the coalition command. The looting could easily have been prevented with the forces to hand and its prevention was a stated goal of American military planning. The American response to the attack on the Museum was at first inadequate, then tended to focus on the Iraq Museum while ignoring the ongoing attacks on archaeological sites and museums elsewhere in the country. Yet it was obvious that American policy makers were stung by the harsh and continuing international condemnation of their failure, so efforts were undertaken to repair the damage.

Most recently, the American government's interest in the antiquities trade has been stimulated by the reality that traffic in one illegal commodity is often connected to traffic in others. Furthermore, looting of ancient sites is a very effective way to launder money and for local radical groups to raise substantial funds in cash. There is, moreover, an opportunity for the American government to garner international good will by investigating the trade in stolen cultural property. Countries that have suffered the most from theft and looting, such as Greece, Cyprus, Egypt, Turkey, Italy, and China, as well as various countries in Latin America, have varied widely in their efforts to enlist American support for curtailing sales of stolen and looted antiquities, but some will see in the enormous public scrutiny of the issue, following the Iraq Museum catastrophe, a chance to recover choice pieces they have a reasonable hope of documenting. Since the Iraqi antiquities laws were so strict, one can reasonably assume that most valuable objects of Mesopotamian origin on the trade today have been stolen or looted from Iraq, dealers' protestations notwithstanding.

Although the looting of the Iraq Museum was in and of itself a heinous crime, it stands also as a dramatic symbol for the looting and destruction of cultural property and archaeological heritage throughout Iraq and worldwide, merely to gratify collectors and enrich dealers. Objects stolen from museums may often have some information about their cultural context, but objects looted from archaeological sites have been torn from their context and nearly everything that could be learned from them has been wantonly destroyed. Under American occupation, nothing has been done to stem the wholesale looting of sites in the Iraqi countryside. Even if the best-known objects from the Iraq Museum are eventually recovered, the ongoing loss of the other Iraqi museums and the destruction of archaeological sites throughout the country is wiping out our richest sources for the human past, solely in the interests of greed and the vanity of ownership.

The known losses are staggering; the unknown losses must remain unimaginable. The future of the human past, both in Iraq and worldwide, is bleak.

Suggestions For Further Reading[1]

Ancient Mesopotamia

Sasson, J. M. (ed.). *Civilizations of the Ancient Near East*. New York: Scribners, 1995.

Van de Mieroop, M. *A History of the Ancient Near East, ca. 3000–323 BC*. London: Blackwell, 2004.

Antiquities and the Kingdom and Republic of Iraq

Bernhardsson, M. *Reclaiming a Plundered Past: Archaeology and Nationalism in Iraq, 1921–1941*. Austin: University of Texas Press, 2004.

Farchakh, J. "The Specter of War," *Archaeology*, May/June, 2003, 14–15.

Antiquites issues in general

Brodie, N., J. Doole and C. Renfrew. *Trade in Illicit Antiquities: The Destruction of the World's Archaeological Heritage*. Cambridge, UK: McDonald Institute Monographs, 2001.

Norman, K. "The Retrieval of Kuwait National Museum's Collections from Iraq: An Assessment of the Operation and Lessons Learned," *Journal for the American Institute for Conservation*, 39(1), 2000.

Tubb, K. W. *Antiquities Trade or Betrayed, Legal, Ethical and Conservation Issues*. London: Archetype, 1995.

The looting of the museum and its aftermath

(This list, spanning approximately a month after the looting, is the basis for the narrative above, and will give an idea of the publicity and comment on the event.)

Burns, John F. "Pillagers Strip Iraqi Museum of Its Treasure," *New York Times*, April 13, 2003.

Campbell, Matthew. "Iraq Museum Chief Accused of Looting Plot," *The Times* (UK), May 11, 2003.

---

[1] I thank Constance T. Foster for her assistance, Karen Polinger Foster for writing the captions and Patrick Arrasmith for the three drawings.

Coleman, Joseph. "Looting Throws Spotlight on Illicit Art Trafficking," *Meriden* (CT) *Record-Journal*, April 17, 2003 (Associated Press dispatch).

Duffy, Robert W. "Number of Objects Looted Still Eludes Experts," *St Louis* (MO) *Post-Dispatch*, May 10, 2003.

Emmerich, Andre. "Let the Market Preserve Art, What Were All Those Antiquities Doing in Iraq Anyway?" *Wall Street Journal*, April 24, 2003.

"FBI Sends Team to Help Recover Iraqi Artifacts," *Hamilton* (Ontario) *Spectator*, April 19, 2003.

Fisher, Ian. "Museum Pillage Described as Devastating but Not Total," *New York Times*, April 17, 2003.

Foster, Benjamin R. and Karen Polinger Foster. "Missing in Action: The Coalition is Responsible for Iraq's Treasures," *New York Times*, April 18, 2003.

Goodheart, Adam. "Missing: A Vase, a Book, a Bird and 10,000 Years of History," *New York Times*, April 20, 2003.

Gottlieb, Martin. "Ashcroft Says U.S. Will Aid Effort to Save Iraq Treasures," *New York Times*, May 7, 2003.

Gottlieb, Martin. "Campaign Starts to Help Iraq Rebuild Cultural Institutions," *New York Times*, April 30, 2003.

Gottlieb, Marvin and Barry Meier. "Of 2,000 Treasures Stolen in Gulf War of 1991, Only 12 Have Been Recovered," *New York Times*, May 1, 2003.

Gugliotta, Guy. "Looters May Have Destroyed Priceless Cuneiform Archive," *Washington Post*, April 18, 2003.

Hundley, Tom. "Experts Revise Scope of Theft from Museum, Iraqi Curators Hid Some Antiquities," *Chicago Tribune*, May 16, 2003.

Jehl, Douglas and Elizabeth Becker. "Experts' Pleas to Pentagon Didn't Save Museum," *New York Times*, April 16, 2003.

Jenkins, S. "A Shameful Theft of the Crown Jewels of Memory," *The Times* (UK), May 2, 2003.

MacAskill, Ewen. "Marines Accuse Baghdad Thieves of Hampering Hunt for Treasures," *The Guardian* (UK), May 6, 2003.

Manguel, Alberto. "Our First Words, Written in Clay, in an Accountant's Hand," *New York Times*, April 20, 2003.

Martin, Paul. "Troops Were Told to Guard Treasures: Two Weeks After the Memo Was Sent, US Forces Took Baghdad and Iraqi Looters Hit Museum," *Washington Times*, April 20, 2003.

Meier, Barry. "Most Iraqi Treasures Are Said to Be Kept Safe," *New York Times*, May 6, 2003.

New York Times News Service: "Museum: Losses May Not Be As Severe As Once Thought," *Meriden* (CT) *Record-Journal*, May 1, 2003.

O'Leary, Mary E. "Yale-driven Petition Aims to Protect Iraqi Antiquities," *New Haven* (CT) *Register*, April 16, 2003.

Rich, Frank. "And Now: 'Operation Iraqi Looting'," *New York Times News Service*, April 27, 2003.

_____ "Kitsch and Oil Secure; Museums Looted, Books Burned," *Meriden* (CT) *Record-Journal*, April 29, 2003 (*New York Times News Service*).

Riding, Alan. "Art Experts Mobilize Team to Recover Stolen Treasure and Salvage Iraqi Museums," *New York Times*, April 18, 2003.

_____ "Experts Despair of Iraq's Stopping Loss of Relics," *New York Times*, May 3, 2003.

_____ "Loss Estimates are Cut on Iraqi Artifacts, but Questions Remain," *New York Times*, May 1, 2003.

Sam Dillon, "Islamic World Less Welcoming to American Scholars," *New York Times*, April 18, 2002.

Shenon, Philip. "U.S. Says It Has Recovered Hundreds of Artifacts and Thousands of Manuscripts in Iraq," *New York Times*, May 7, 2003.

Sommerfeld, W. "Go In, Ali Baba! It's All Yours," *Süddeutsche Zeitung* (Germany) *News Service*, May 8, 2003.

Tierney, John. "Did Lord Elgin Do Something Right?" *New York Times*, April 20, 2003.

Waldbaum, Jane and Patty Gerstenblith. "Tracing Iraq's Lost Treasures," *Washington Post*, April 27, 2003.

Weinraub, Bernard. "Recovery of Looted Treasures Is a Slow, Agonizing Process," *New York Times*, April 24, 2003.

Weir, William. "Yale Scholars Battle For Artifacts, Give Petition to UN, Seek Ban on Sales," *Hartford* (CT) *Courant*, April 18, 2003.

Wilford, John N. "Art Experts Fear Worst In the Plunder of a Museum," *New York Times*, April 13, 2003.

———— "Curators Appeal for a Ban on Purchase of Iraqi Artifacts," *New York Times*, April 16, 2003.

Winter, Irene J. "The Next Threat: Complacency," Martin Sullivan, "The Next Deterrent: Laws with Muscle," Richard Zettler, "The Next Step: Reconstruct Records," *Washington Post*, April 27, 2003.

Zimansky, Paul and Elizabeth Stone. "Iraq's Lost Cultural Treasures," *Boston Globe*, April 16, 2003.

Looting under American occupation

Andrews, Edmund L. "Global Network Aids Theft of Iraqi Artifacts," *New York Times* international edition, May 28, 2003.

———— "Iraqi Looters Tearing Up Archaeological Sites," *New York Times*, May 23, 2003.

Addendum

On July 11, 2003, Colonel Bogdanos gave a briefing at the Rencontre Assyriologique Internationale at the British Museum. He stated that there had been professional, selective theft from the public galleries, for a total of 40 objects, of which 10 had been recovered; random theft from the conservation rooms, 199 objects taken, of which 30 had been recovered; random theft from the magazines on the ground floor, 2939 objects taken, of which 2060 had been recovered; and an insider attempt on the basement storage by someone with access to the hidden keys, 10,337 objects stolen, including 4795 cylinder seals, of which 671 had been recovered. The estimated total loss was about 10,500 objects. The tablet collection was mostly intact. The Nimrud gold was found in sealed cases in a flooded bank vault.

Appendix 1A

Fig. 1.   Limestone statue from Eshnunna, ca. 2500 B.C.

Votive figures, such as the one shown here, were placed in Sumerian temples to perpetuate prayers for the life of their donors. Often, they possessed over-size lapis lazuli eyes, thought to indicate awe at the sight of the temple's resident deity. This figure was part of a large group found in a temple cache at Eshnunna, most of which had remained together as an integral unit in the Iraq Museum.

Appendix 1B

Fig. 2.   Copper head from Nineveh, ca. 2300 B.C.
The last third of the third millennium witnessed the rise of the world's earliest
empire, founded by Sargon of Akkad. This life-size head represents one of the
Akkadian kings, perhaps Sargon's grandson, Naram-Sin, who vigorously enlarged
his realm. Seventeen hundred years later, the sculpture was venerated in a temple at
Nineveh, the Assyrian capital in the seventh century B.C. When the Medes sacked
Nineveh in 512 B.C., they seem to have deliberatly mutilated the head. Twenty-six
hundred years later, what has now befallen this Akkadian masterpiece?

Appendix 1C

Fig. 3.   Gold wristlet from Nimrud, ca. 875 B.C.

The city of Nimrud served as the capital of Assyria during the ninth and eighth centuries B.C. In the southern part of the palace of Assurnasirpal II, Iraqi archaeologists recently discovered the intact tombs of at least two Assyrian queens. This gold wristlet, inlaid with semiprecious stones, was among thousands of items of jewelry, crowns, and other royal accouterments. No other unplundered Assyrian graves are known. All of the finds were in the Iraq Museum.

Reflections on the Looting of the Iraqi National Museum in Baghdad

Colin Renfrew (Lord Renfrew of Kaimsthorn)

Colin Renfrew is the Disney Professor of Archaeology and Director of the McDonald Institute for Archaeological Research in the University of Cambridge, UK. Among Lord Renfrew's many books are Archaeology: Theories, Methods and Practice; Archaeology and Language: The Puzzle of Indo-European Origins; The Prehistory of Orkney *(Editor);* Approaches to Social Archaeology; Towards an Archaeology of Mind; Figuring It Out; The Emergence of Civilization, the Cyclades and the Aegean in the Third Millennium B.C.

When the history of the Iraq war of 2003 comes to be written, the failure of the Coalition Forces to anticipate, prevent or interrupt the looting of the Iraqi National Museum in Baghdad will constitute perhaps one of those interesting chapters which serve to illuminate the values and priorities of the participants. Or if that turns out to be too harsh a judgement, it will certainly serve as a touchstone by which to measure the success or failure of the early days of their enterprise. For the loss of some of the most notable relics of the world's first urban and literature civilization (such as the Warka Vase: later returned) and the destruction of some of the most interesting art from the land of Mesopotamia and the deserts to the west (such as the statuary of Hatra) has scandalised the civilised world. Belatedly senior members of both Coalition governments took an interest in the problem but only some days after the damage was done. The United States Attorney General John Ashcroft travelled to an Interpol meeting in Lyon at the very end of April, but the Secretary of Defense Donald Rumsfeld was dismissive in the more immediate aftermath of the looting, referring to the looted antiquities as "stuff", and offering the analytical observation that in the course of war "things happen". The United Kingdom Secretary of State for Culture Tessa Jowell spoke at the British Museum meeting of April 29th to give assurance of the wish of the Government to alleviate the disaster, but no interest in the problems from herself or her colleagues could be aroused in the months before it happened. For this is a disaster that was easily foreseeable. Moreover it was foreseen.

The following may serve as a small footnote to the chapter on the subject of the looting which will one day be written in the History of the 2003 Iraq War. It can only give a single, personal perspective. There are others in Baghdad who can give an informed account of what actually happened. And there are others again, for instance Professor McGuire Gibson of the University of Chicago, who can document the warnings about possible looting, which were transmitted to the United States Government. But I believe it is relevant to set on record the correspondence with representatives of the United Kingdom Government, in advance of the event, undertaken by one professional archaeologist who also happens to be, since 1991 a member (appointed) of the House of Lords, the second chamber in the United Kingdom's bicameral parliamentary system.

I am anxious, also, that this documentation should not be taken as a more general criticism of the War and its causes. During the months before the war, like many others in Britain, I accepted the force of the advocacy of the British Prime Minister Tony Blair that it was time to seek military enforcement of the relevant resolutions of the United Nations Security Council which over the years Saddam Hussein had failed to follow. It seemed clear that no significant links between Saddam Hussein's regime and Al-Qaeda had been demonstrated, so that there was no coherent logic to the attempts to relate the Iraqi regime to the events of the 11th September 2001 in New York and Washington. But in a general sense I agreed with Tony Blair and the Conservative Opposition Leader Ian Duncan Smith that those events had made it more urgent to combat international terrorism, and I agreed that Saddam Hussein's flaunting of the various Security Council resolutions and the inconclusive outcome of the UN arms inspections made military intervention appropriate. These points are made here since my remarks are not intended as a critique of the War as such, but of the catastrophic failure of its implementation in the matter under discussion. Nor is my standpoint in any sense anti-American. I have enjoyed close links with United States archaeologists and anthropologists over the years (and have the honour to be a Foreign Member of the National Academy of Sciences of the United States of America). So while there have certainly been moments when I have felt unease at some of the statements of Dick Cheney or Donald Rumsfeld, and while I have been surprised at what sometimes seems the unquestioning support of the United States for the state of Israel in its own disregard of Security Council resolutions concerning Palestine, I support the general position of the United Kingdom Government in the matter of the Coalition. Certainly I am unimpressed by the grand-standing of President Chirac in the days preceding the War.

It is well documented (Lawler, 2003) that the distinguished specialist in Mesopotamian civilisation Professor McGuire Gibson and others met with U.S. Defense Department Officials on 24th January 2003 to warn of the risks of the looting of ancient sites and museums in Iraq in the event of war, and there was a second later meeting with State Department officials. I attach herewith the text of the letter which I wrote on 11th February to the Prime Minister on behalf of the United Kingdom All-Party Parliamentary Group on Archaeology — a group composed of more than 100 Members of Parliament (the elected chamber) and of Peers (members of the appointed chamber) — to warn of the risks of looting and offering to meet to provide further information. The letter was also signed by the Secretary of the Group Lord Redesdale (a member of the

Liberal-Democrat Party) and by Lord Lea of Crondall (a member of the Labour Party), giving a political balance since I am myself a member of the Conservative Party. It was accompanied by a short memorandum from the Chairman of the British School of Archaeology at Iraq, Dr. Harriet Crawford, giving further details. As the correspondence shows, a reply dated 18th February was sent by the Prime Minister's Office saying that the matter would be dealt with by a Minister at the Foreign and Commonwealth Office. But no reply was sent until the letter from the Foreign Office by Michael O'Brien MP on 16th April, which was, of course, after the looting had taken place. The looting, according to the account given by Donny George of the Iraqi National Museum to the British Museum Symposium on 29th April, took place in the week beginning Tuesday 8th April. On that day he and his colleagues felt obliged at 11 am, to leave the Museum, which they had been hoping to protect, since the area around it had become one of conflict. Later that day he went to the provisional Headquarters of the U.S. Marine Corps to request that guards be sent to the Museum. But in the event no United States guards were sent until Wednesday 16th April. During the intervening week the Museum had been extensively looted. He felt that a single United States tank with a party of armed soldiers could have prevented or stopped this process. In his view there were two kinds of looters. First there were the destructive and casual mob who had trashed many government buildings, taking office furniture etc. as well as antiquities, and causing deliberate damage to the exhibited collections. Secondly there were those who came armed with glass-cutters and who had access to the storerooms with the use of keys. It seemed reasonable to infer that these looters were much better informed, knew what they wanted, and presumably had plans in place to sell on the looted material.

In view of the looting which took place in Baghdad in the course of the first Gulf War of 1991, these events were to be anticipated. Indeed they *were* anticipated, and it is this fact which makes the week-long delay to do anything to retrieve the situation so reprehensible. In the Appendix below will be found the other documentation which indicates my own personal and frustrating experience, as a Member of the House of Lords, in failing to elicit any significant response from the British Government until well after the looting had taken place. There are other archaeologists, notably Dr. Harriet Crawford, Chair of the British School of Archaeology at Iraq, who could tell a similar story.

Baghdad was occupied in early April by American not by British troops, whose sphere of activity was further south, in and around Basra. But one does have the feeling that if the British Government, as a partner in the Coalition, had made strong and early representations to the United States Government, during February or March, it is perfectly possible that the protection of the Museum might have been placed higher on the list of priorities. That it was on such a list is documented by a report in *The Washington Post* (Martin, 2003):

> " 'Coalition forces must secure these facilities in order to prevent looting and the resulting loss of cultural treasures,' says the March 26 memo. The Pentagon's Office of Reconstruction and Humanitarian Assistance (ORHA) led by retired Lt. Gen. Jay Garner sent the five-page memo to senior commanders at the Coalition Forces Land Component Command (CFLCC). The museum was No. 2 on a list of 16 sites that ORHA deemed crucial to protect. 'We asked for just a few soldiers at each building, or if they feared snipers, then just one or two tanks,' said an angry ORHA official. At a meeting on April 10, the ORHA staff were aghast when told that the document had not even been read, the official said."

It seems reasonably clear from this documentation that the looting was anticipated by the ORHA, but that the matter had not been accorded any significant priority in the orders given to the United States military in Baghdad until 16th April, when a military force did arrive at the Museum, eight days after Museum officials had actively requested it.

Subsequent events, including the replacement of General Garner, have indeed documented that the Defense Department was not well prepared for the situation in Iraq following the occupation of Baghdad, and it has been suggested that differences and disputes between the Defense Department and the State Department played a role in the confusion which continued to prevail. But as Mr. Kevin Chamberlain, a lawyer formerly on the staff of the British Department of Culture, Media and Sport, points out in his letter to *The Times*, printed in the Appendix, an occupying power (in this case the Coalition) has clear responsibilities under the Geneva Convention to maintain order and to preserve cultural property. It is of course unfortunate (and to me inexplicable) that neither the United States nor the United Kingdom are parties to The Hague Convention and its Protocols. In any case it is difficult to feel that their responsibilities under the Geneva Convention (to which they are indeed party) were adequately discharged.

The general problem of the looting of archaeological sites to provide antiquities for unscrupulous collectors and museums is well known (see Renfrew, 2000), and it is to be anticipated that when the full story is known, other Iraqi museums and indeed various archaeological sites will also prove to have been looted. Indeed to prevent the looting of archaeological sites in the open country during or following armed conflict can be no easy task. Even with proper planning and execution this would have been a difficult project for the occupying Coalition Forces. One accepts also that the first need in a military campaign is to achieve military objectives. But to allow more than seven days to elapse before the most obvious protective measures were undertaken, measures explicitly formulated in General Garner's Memorandum, seems a clear abnegation of the obligations of an occupying power. It is evident that the United States military were in the front line and bear much of the responsibility. But it seems clear also that the British Government fell far short of its own responsibilities in this matter. I have seen no evidence that high-level representations were made by the British to the United States Government in the light of representations which they themselves had received, such as those documented in the Appendix. And the failure even adequately to acknowledge these until well after the looting had taken place (and caused an international scandal) would seem to carry its own implication.

Members of the archaeological community in the United Kingdom naturally deplore what happened to the Museum in Baghdad. They also feel that the voice of the academic community, which did speak clearly in the months before the conflict began, was not heard by the United Kingdom Government. Subsequent attempts by senior Ministers to take remedial action in the aftermath no doubt have some merit in themselves. But they do not change what appears to be the reality, namely that this was a disaster which was foreseen and which could quite readily have been prevented. Many of us who felt that the War had coherent objectives, and indeed who may still believe that to be the case, feel also a sense of shame that our Government and its allies in the Coalition failed to prevent so predictable a catastrophe.

References

Lawler A. "Impending war stokes battle over fate of Iraqi antiquities," *Science*, 299, January 31, 2003, 643.

Martin P. "Troops were told to guard treasure," *Washington Post*, April 20, 2003.

Renfrew C. *Loot, Legitimacy and Ownership, the Ethical Crisis in Archaeology*. London: Duckworth, 2000.

Appendix

The McDonald Institute for Archaeological Research

Colin Renfrew:
Looting of the Iraqi National Museum in
Baghdad was foreseeable and foreseen.

During January 2003 Professor McGuire Gibson had discussions with officials of the U.S. Defense Department in Washington and drew to their attention the risk of looting at the Baghdad Museum and at other museums and archaeological sites in the event of armed conflict.

In Britain, representatives of the British School of Archaeology in Iraq, including the Chairperson, Dr. Harriet Crawford, and Dr. Eleanor Robson of All Soul's College Oxford, made several representations to UK Ministers without receiving reply or acknowledgement.

The looting was foreseeable and it was foreseen. It may be relevant to place on record the following pieces of correspondence:

---

1. Letter from Professor Lord Renfrew of Kaimsthorn, Lord Redesdale and Lord Lea of Crondall on behalf of the All Party Parliamentary Group on Archaeology to the Prime Minister, dated February 11, 2003 (with attachment prepared by Dr. Harriet Crawford).

2. Reply to the above from the Direct Communications Unit, 10 Downing Street, dated February 18, 2003.

3. Letter from Lord Renfrew to the Prime Minister, dated April 2, 2003.

4. Letter from Mr. Mike O' Brien, Minister responsible for relations with Iraq, Foreign & Commonwealth Office dated April 16, 2003, in response to Letter from Professor Lord Renfrew of Kaimsthorn, Lord Redesdale and Lord Lea of Crondall on behalf of the All Party Parliamentary Group on Archaeology to the Prime Minister, dated February 11, 2003 (see above 1).

5. Letter from Lord Renfrew to *The Times*, published Thursday, April 24, 2003.

6. Letter to *The Times*, from Kevin Chamberlain, published April 29, 2003.

Correspondence 1

All Party Parliamentary Group on Archaeology

Professor Lord Renfrew of Kaimsthorn FBA FSA (Chair)
Lord Redesdale (Secretary)
Lord Lea of Crondall OBE

Rt. Hon. Tony Blair MP
Prime Minister
10 Downing Street
London SW1   11ᵗʰ February 2003

Dear Prime Minister

Archaeological Sites in Iraq

We are writing to ask that, in the event of military intervention, some attention be given
to the problem of archaeological sites and museums in Iraq. We understand of course that
military considerations will be the top priority, along with humanitarian concerns. But
there are many archaeological sites in Iraq, many of which date back to the earliest roots
of our civilisation in Mesopotamia, which may be at risk, as well as important museums
vulnerable to looting in the event of civil disorder.

We enclose a note from the Chairman of the British School of Archaeology in Iraq, Dr.
Harriet Crawford, currently based in London, which summarises the range of points we
should wish to make.

We should be glad to discuss this further either at Ministerial or official level, along with
Dr. Crawford.

Yours sincerely

Colin Renfrew   Rupert Redesdale   David Lea

Correspondence 1 (Continued): The note from the Chairman of the British School of Archaeology in Iraq, Dr. Harriet Crawford.

The reconstruction of Iraq

- The heritage of Iraq has considerable potential for the crucial task of forging national unity in Iraq, a country with no natural borders and an extremely disparate population which is in severe danger of splitting into a number of warring segments. All these groups do however share a common pride in their past, a pride which was successfully exploited by Saddam Hussein.
- The history and archaeology of the country are of major global significance: Iraq is the source of many aspects of Western culture as we know it today.
- The archaeological and historical remains are a non-renewable resource.

For all these reasons it is extremely desirable that any reconstruction plans include some provision for safeguarding the archaeological sites, the standing monuments and the artefacts in museums and private collections.

The immediate need
Guards to be placed on major monuments and museums to prevent looting and illicit digging. The former was a major problem at the end of the Gulf war.

It will also be necessary to alert border patrols and border guards to the possibility of large-scale smuggling of illicitly obtained antiquities. Such activities are currently well documented.

Structural assessments may need to be carried out on any damaged monuments to ensure their safety.

The National Museum already has a desperate need for materials to allow them to carry out essential conservation on extremely important items in their collections which have suffered badly from twelve years of sanctions when even the most basic chemicals and equipment were unavailable.

The medium term needs.
A major new dam on the upper Tigris is threatening a minimum of 60 sites which include the major Assyrian sites of Ashur and Kar-Tikulti-Ninurta. An independent feasibility study needs to be undertaken to determine to country's real need for irrigation water and to minimise the damage to the heritage. Consideration might be given to setting up an international rescue operation to examine as many sites as possible before they are flooded.

Great damage has been done to the marshes of southern Iraq by major drainage projects thus virtually wiping out a unique ecological niche and a unique way of life. A study is needed to assess the possibility of reversing this process.

In the longer term the antiquities of Iraq could become an important economic asset as tourism and especially Arab tourism begins to expand.

Correspondence 2

1O DOWNING STREET
LONDON SW1A 2AA

From the Direct Communications Unit   18 February 2003

Dear Lord Renfrew

   I am writing on behalf of the Prime Minister to
thank you and your co-signatories for your letter of
11 February.

   The Prime Minister has asked me to arrange for
a Minister in the Foreign and Commonwealth Office
to reply to you direct.

                    Yours sincerely

                    LUCY RACKHAM

Professor Lord Colin Renfrew of Kaimsthorn

Correspondence 3

The Rt. Hon. Tony Blair MP
Prime Minister
10 Downing Street
London
SW1A 2AA   2nd April 2003

Dear Prime Minister

On 11th February 2003, I wrote to you on the subject of archaeological sites in Iraq on behalf of the All-Party Parliamentary Group on Archaeology, and received a prompt reply from the Direct Communications Unit (18th February) indicating that you had arranged for a Minister in the Foreign & Commonwealth Office to reply to me directly. Having heard nothing, I contacted the FCO on 24th March, receiving a somewhat garbled reply and have received no further response to my own reply to that of the same day.

Subsequently, I have been approached by journalists asking whether I know anything about steps the Government may be making to safeguard museums and archaeological sites in Iraq. Unfortunately, I have had to reply that so far as I am aware, the matter has not received the attention which it merits. I would be very grateful for any information that could indicate otherwise, which I would be happy to pass on to journalists who may enquire in the future.

Yours sincerely

Renfrew of Kaimsthorn

Cc: Baroness Symons of Vernham Dean, Foreign & Commonwealth Office
       Baroness Blackstone, Department of Culture, Media & Sport

Correspondence 4

**Foreign &
Commonwealth
Office**

\6April 2003

London SW1A 2AH

Professor Lord Renfrew of Kaimsthorn FBA FSA
All Party Parliamentary Group on Archaeology
House of Lords
London
SW1A 0PW

From the Parliamentary Under Secretary of State

Our reference: 159738/03

Re: Archaeological Sites in Iraq

Thank you for your Group's letter and enclosure of 11 February to the Prime Minister about archaeological sites and antiquities in Iraq. I am replying as Minister responsible for our relations with Iraq and apologise for the delay in doing so.

We share your concerns about the importance of protecting and preserving archaeological sites and museums in Iraq and note the work done by the Iraqi Antiquities Service and the expertise available in UK through Dr Harriet Crawford, Chair of the British School in Iraq and Professor Nicholas Postgate, former Director.

We are naturally concerned about the looting and damage that has recently affected some sites in Iraq.

Coalition forces continue to take law and order very seriously and have started patrols with local police to crack down further on looting, which already shows signs of diminishing. Local communities are themselves beginning to take responsibility for stopping the looting, and coalition forces will provide support to them where they can. Out latest evidence is that looters are largely avoiding sites of religious or historical sensitivity. It is, however, imperative that archaeological sites and museums are sealed as a matter of urgency and we are assessing how best to achieve this. In Basra, British Forces have already secured the museum to prevent further looting.

Now that military action is drawing to a close the Department for Culture, Media and Sport (DCMS) has started and will continue to take the lead on archaeological issues, in close liaison with the British Museum, UNESCO, the Ministry of Defence and the FCO.

Correspondence 4 *(Continued)*

Neil MacGregor of the British Museum is already taking a lead alongside international colleagues from Europe and the US to ensure a coordinated response from the professional archaelogical fraternity. British Museum staff do, of course, command respect and support from a wide range of other professional, including those from Iraq, Iran and Syria.

It is important in all this that we work closely with UNESCO. The British Museum, with UNESCO, will be hosting a symposium of international colleagues on 29 April. We are also working to ensure that UK administrators and professionals are part of the US Organisation for Reconstruction and Humanitarian Affairs (ORHA). Officials from DCMS will be joining ORHA in the next few days.

We are taking measures to ensure that antiquities looted from Iraq are returned if they reach the international art market. A UN sanction currently requires state parties to the UN to impose import controls on objects from Iraq, including antiquities. This means that no objects could reach the UK legally without an import licence. There is absolutely no intention to issue such licences. We are confident that the legitimate art market will cooperate fully, and Tessa Jowell has written to the British Art Market Federation and other key bodies.

This leaves, though, the substantial market in illicit trade. The Private Members Bill "Dealing in Cultural Objects (Offences) Bill" has just had its second reading. It has all party support and we are looking for ways of ensuring its speedy progress through its remaining stages.

I agree that Iraq's antiquities could play an important economic role as tourism begins to expand. Our immediate priority is to ensure a peaceful and stable Iraq that can play a full role in the international community. This environment will ultimately enhance prospects for tourism. We note the suggestions you make about sites affected by the new dam on the Upper Tigris and in the southern marshes and have passed them to DCMS.

Yours sincerely

Mike O'Brien

Correspondence 5

Letters to the Editor
The Times, Thursday 24 April 2003

FCO was warned of Iraqi looting

From Professor Lord Renfrew of Kaimsthorn, FBA

Sir, The catastrophic loss to the world's cultural heritage from the looting of the Iraqi National Museum in Baghdad may yet prove to exceed any archaeological damage suffered anywhere during the 20th century. This was clearly foreseen on both sides of the Atlantic. It is time to ask why the warnings were not acted upon.

On January 24 Professor McGuire Gibson, of the University of Chicago, drew to the attention of US Defence Department officials in Washington the risk of looting. On February 11 I, Lord Redesdale and Lord Lea of Crondall wrote to the Prime Minister on behalf of the All-Party Parliamentary Archaeological Group, indicating the likelihood of looting in the event of military action.

A reply, dated February 18, stated that the matter had been passed to the Foreign and Commonwealth Office and that a minister would be in touch. On March 24, the FCO indicated that Mr Michael O'Brien was not available since "the situation was changing from day to day". Officials of the British School of Archaeology in Iraq made similar representations, likewise with no response from officials or ministers.

Who was responsible in the FCO for gathering and assessing this information? Why were warnings not heeded and the obvious risks assessed? What happened to the parliamentary archaeological group's letter after it left the Prime Minister's office? What contacts were there with United States colleagues responsible for planning the capture and subsequent administration of Baghdad?

In a written reply on March 26 to my question in the House of Lords the minister, Lord Bach, referred to the provisions of the Geneva Conventions. It will be interesting to learn how the Government and the US State Department view the responsibilities of an occupying power under those conventions and whether they feel those responsibilities have been fulfilled.

I was one of those persuaded by the arguments of the Prime Minister that military action against Saddam Hussein was justifiable; but I doubt whether this incalculable loss to the historic and artistic heritage of Iraq can be justified. I shall certainly be interested to hear.

Yours, etc,
COLIN RENFREW,
British School of
Archaeology at Athens,
Souedias 52, 10676 Athens.
April 22.

Correspondence 6

TIMES ONLINE
April 29, 2003

Coalition responsibilities and prevention of looting in Iraq

FROM MR KEVIN CHAMBERLAIN

Sir, Professor Lord Renfrew of Kaimsthorn (letter, April 24) says that it would be interesting to learn how the Government and the US State Department view the responsibilities of an occupying power under the Geneva Conventions and whether they feel those responsibilities have been fulfilled.

Article 53 of Additional Protocol I to the Geneva Conventions prohibits:

any acts of hostility directed against the historic monuments, works of art and places of worship which constitute the cultural or spiritual heritage of peoples.

However, this provision is directed primarily at the Armed Forces of a high contracting party. However deplorable may have been the looting of the Iraqi National Museum in Baghdad, it is difficult to see how this would constitute a violation of Article 53, unless it can be shown that the coalition forces deliberately encouraged the looting as an act of hostility, as opposed to merely failing to take steps to prevent it.

On the other hand, an occupying force does have an obligation under general international law to maintain law and order in the territory that it occupies. In particular, Article 43 of the 1907 Hague Regulations requires an occupant:

to take all the measures in his power to restore, and ensure, as far as possible, public order and safety, while respecting, unless absolutely prevented, the laws in force in the country.

In addition, Article 4 (3) of the 1954 Hague Convention for the Protection of Cultural Property in the event of Armed Conflict obliges the contracting parties:

to prohibit, prevent and, if necessary, put a stop to any form of theft, pillage or misappropriation of, and any acts of vandalism directed against, cultural property.

Correspondence 6 (Continued)

Although the US and the UK are not parties to this convention (Iraq is a party), the obligation to prevent the looting and pillage of cultural property must be regarded as an aspect of the general obligation of an occupying force to maintain law and order in the territory that it occupies.

By making no apparent effort to prevent the widespread looting, not just of museums but of hospitals public utilities and private property, the British and US forces bear a heavy responsibility, the more so since such looting was clearly foreseeable.

Yours faithfully,
KEVIN CHAMBERLAIN
(Deputy Legal Adviser, Foreign and Commonwealth Office, 1990-99),
Fairfield, Warren Drive,
Kingswood, Surrey KT20 6PY.
chamberlain.fairfield@virgin.net
April 24.

End of a Dictator

Faleh A. Jabar

An Iraqi specialist and Research Fellow at the School of Politics and Sociology, Birkbeck College, University of London, his recent publications include Ayatollahs, Sufis, and Ideologues: State, Religion, and Social Movements in Iraq, *and* Tribes and Power in the Middle East, *both from Saqi Books, London, 2002. His latest book is* The Shi'a Movement of Iraq, *London, Saqi Books, 2003.*

This is the fourth time Baghdad has fallen to foreign troops. The Mongol conquest of 1258 went down in the annals of history; the 1917 British occupation was recorded in photographs; the 1941 British re-invasion was kept alive in the memories of my parents. Now, by dint of that modern crystal ball, the television, I can watch the fourth, and hopefully last, invasion live, as it unfolds in real time.

Since day one of the American campaign, I had been tormented by conflicting feelings: agony, fear, concern and hope. Agony for the civilian casualties; fear of the future; concern over the innocent, the unarmed and ordinary conscripts; and hope that out of this mayhem at least one good thing may emerge: the end of the rapacious Leviathan.

"Why they are so passive?" my wife, who fled Baghdad in 1979 a few months after I did, asked me as we watched the scenes around Basra in the early days of the campaign. There was a reproachful tone in her voice, as if I were responsible for this passivity. I heard the same anger in her observations a few days later when Saddam appeared in Baghdad's Mansour neighbourhood: "He is still there, and smiling!"

"He is putting on a show. Look at the people, they are worried and stern looking. Besides, he glanced quickly at the skies, fearing a missile," I replied, trying to reassure her.

And now, after those early days of anxiety, Saddam Hussein's regime has collapsed. Like my wife, like our fellow exiles, the world is now asking: Why did the Ba'ath party fail? In my view, the reason lies in the nature of the political system Saddam created in his own image. The Russian novelist Fyodor Dostoyevsky once described how, after years of living together, a man and his dog come to look like one another. Never in modern sociological history has a political order resembled creator as closely as modern Iraq grew to mirror Saddam Hussein.

The tyrant who styled himself a 20th century Saladin was born in a small village organised around its tribe. An orphan, Saddam was brought up by his maternal uncle, a disgrace according to Iraqi tribal norms, which cherish paternal descent. In his adolescence, he embraced a form of Arabist ideology, influenced by Nazi ideals, which was advocated by his uncle. As a young man, he developed terrorist skills and took part in the attempt on the life of the Iraqi premier-general Abdul Kareem Qassim in 1959; next he mastered clandestine and mass politics; and finally he worshipped Stalin and his iron rule.

Once in power, Saddam Hussein fashioned state and society in his own image, though the process followed his own personal trajectory in reverse. As the head of the Iraqi state, he began with radical "socialism", moved to Arabism and ended up with tribalism. He instituted a single party system, tightened the grip of the command economy, created a formidable network of secret police and intelligence services, and placed his own tribal allies in strategic positions. Finally, he ensured that his "house" emerged as the ultimate seat of power. The oil boom of the 1970s enabled him to bribe vast swathes of society into allegiance or acquiescence. This was a totalitarian regime par excellence. Iraq's mix of party, tribe, oil and secret police was embedded in the politics of fear, the politics of the gift and the politics of patriarchy. Saddam was the leader, the president, the ideologue and the father of the tribe, all in one. If this mix was what made the political system seemingly invincible, it was also its Achilles heel.

Undoubtedly, military adventurism was the Ba'ath party's greatest folly. But totalitarianism is a flawed system; it constantly produces its own antithesis. It starts by constructing impersonal institutions but ends up by personalising power and promoting personality cults. It strives to homogenise the nation but its assimilative techniques deepen ethnic and cultural divides, ripping the fabric of the nation apart. A command economy claims egalitarianism as its ideal, but it actually widens the gap between the rich and the poor, creating crony capitalism. It claims to embrace the lofty ideal of progress, yet it destroys civil associations and strives to revive outdated traditional value-systems. It gives obsessive priority to regime security but actually endangers national security. Such is the story of Iraqi totalitarianism.

There is another question the world, especially the western world, is asking this week about Iraq and its people: Why would a massive silent majority long for a successful invasion of its country? Lack of patriotism? Far from it. Iraqi nationalism has always been and will continue to be a vibrant force. The reason Iraqis have yearned for liberation from abroad is because of the enormous gulf that has developed between official state nationalism (Ba'athist ideology) and popular patriotism. The bulk of the nation has been gradually disconnected from the ruling class. Far from being a small group at the helm, Iraq's state-party elites constitute a relatively large core allied to a larger tribal and business grouping. I call it clan-class. Blood ties, inter-marriages, ideological bonds, economic interests, and communality of guilt unite this elite.

This clan-class permeates the army, the party, the bureaucracy and the business classes. The core is Saddam's own tribal domain. The latter comprise 85 percent of the highest ranking officers in the Republican Guard, Special Republican Guard and the presidential security service. To judge by the experience of the second world war, this elite will continue to fight the way non-German Nazis did in Berlin in 1945. They were wanted dead rather than alive. The majority of Iraqis, by contrast, have and will look much more like the anti-Mussolini Italians.

The scenes of the still timid crowds in Baghdad are just the tip of the iceberg. These are people from the lower and middle classes, the very social groups that were pauperised throughout the sanctions era. They are the vanguard of the vanguard. We will have to wait before we see the rest of Iraqi society take to the streets. Iraq's still silent majority is like an old hospital inmate who has been in bed too long to remember how to stand on his or her own feet, let alone to walk or run. At some point, though, these Iraqis will emerge to attack the public symbols of Saddam's power. His physical legacy is so grotesque as to be almost comic: 2,400 statues and murals, roughly one for every 1,000 Iraqis. His photographs number 50 million, two for every Iraqi. It will take time to have them removed from public squares and offices. More importantly, they must be removed from a traumatised collective memory.

Watching the first scenes of demolition this week, my wife burst into tears, fits of laughter and cries of joy. Her screaming was like the howl of a wounded animal. So were the fits of joy in Baghdad. The chest-beating Iraqis seemed bizarre to the western observer. Their fierce gestures were a coded display of protest, a physical statement to convey past grief. Pain is a medium of catharsis. It purifies the physical body, it releases trapped agonies — and it also holds a promise of happiness to come.

Watching the crowds, I cried, too. Their political language was so mute. In the Republic of Silence you need to learn how to speak. The crowd I saw on Wednesday in Baghdad could not utter even one political slogan. Instead the people on the streets deployed mute cultural artefacts to speak for them. They hoisted aloft clay tablets, dry date palm leaves, and green banners. These are representations of identity, declarations of freedom, pronouncements of the unutterable. They are all borrowed from popular religion. This ceremonial ritualism was the ultimate statement of defiance of a nation that has been systematically raped for more than 34 years.

The plinth supporting Saddam's statue resembles the pedestal of Hamourabi, the first lawgiver in ancient Mesopotamia. The irony is that a lawbreaker has replaced the lawmaker. Iraqis will correct this flagrant error.

As news of the collapse of the Iraqi regime was broadcast on the world's television screens, I was in the BBC's Bush House studios in central London. I had to collect my emotions and answer my interviewers in a festive but calm manner. At home it was a different story. The moment the statue crashed down, a hysterical ecstasy overwhelmed my wife, Fatima. She screamed, laughed, and wept, all in a matter of seconds.

I phoned her the moment I left the studio.

"Is it final?" she asked.

"Finito," I replied joyfully.

Every 10 minutes or so, I would hear painful screaming coming from the living room. She is painfully joyful. Tears and laughter. She may have remembered her 21 days under torture in the cellar of the General Directorate of the Security Service in Baghdad. Castro, she recalled, decorated Saddam with a José Marti medal when she was released. They wanted her to sign a confession and a pledge to serve the Ba'ath party. She never signed.

For years, she wept and screamed in her dreams. Spiritual scars never heal. Now she is screaming out her agony, purging herself of it. Curing rituals are as varied as fingerprints.

That evening, we were joined by a dozen or so fellow Iraqis for a mad, impromptu party. Our laughter was delirious; our joy was feverish. I received countless telephone calls from Iraqi exiles. One just shouted: "Faleh, He is Gooooooooone! Do you understand? Goooooooone." We laughed, cried and congratulated one another late into the night.

I have my own misgivings, worries and angst. I look at the social map of raq and reflect on Saddam's legacy: tribalisation of our urban civil space, Islamisation of our secular society. Extremism breeds violence. Fundamentalism has been creeping from our southern and eastern neighbours. Neither will welcome a secular Iraq. A democratic Iraq is a nuisance to Saudi Arabia. Federalism is suspect in the eyes of the Turks.

I am a born pessimist, but I am hopeful.

Iraq: Collective Punishment in War and Peace[1]

Mahmood Mamdani

Herbert Lehman Professor of Government in the Departments of International Affairs, Anthropology and Political Science, and Director of the Institute of African Studies at Columbia University, Prof. Mamdani is one of the world's most respected Africa scholars. His book Citizen and Subject: Contemporary Africa and the Legacy of Late Colonialism *(1996) has won three prizes: (a) it was acclaimed in 2002 as "one of Africa's Best 100 Books of the 20th Century" by an All-African Jury in Cape Town; (b) it was awarded the Herskovitz Prize of the African Studies Association of USA for "the best book published in the English language on Africa in 1996"; and (c) it won the University of Cape Town Book Award for the year 1999. He was President of CODESRIA (Council for the Development of Social Research in Africa) for 1999–2002, a member of the African Academy of Sciences, and taught at the University of Dar-es-Salaam (1973–79), Makerere University (1980–91) and the University of Cape Town (1996–99), and was Executive Director of Center for Basic Research in Kampala from 1987 to 1996. His latest book* Good Muslim, Bad Muslim *will be published by Pantheon in April, 2004.*

In this essay, I look at two decades of proxy war, from the Iraq-Iran War in the 1980s to the regime of UN sanctions. Besides providing a background to the invasion of Iraq, this period highlights a novel development in U.S. strategy in the region. If U.S. attitude to the

---

[1] This article is excerpted from a forthcoming book *Good Muslim, Bad Muslim: America, the Cold War and the Roots of Terror*. New York: Pantheon, Random House (2004).

Iraq-Iran War recalls a time-tested strategy of big powers fuelling and sustaining a local conflict to weaken both sides, the regime of sanctions that followed the Gulf War was a remarkable development in the history of low intensity conflict: for the first time, the proxy was not bilateral but multilateral. If the sanctions regime demonstrated the success with which the U.S. turned the UN into a multilateral proxy, the invasion of Iraq demonstrated its limits and, ultimately, failure.

To understand how Iraq became central to U.S. strategy in the Middle East, we need to return to Iran 24 years ago. Postwar U.S. foreign policy operated on the simple assumption that Islam was an anti-communist and anti-nationalist force. The Iranian Revolution of 1979 changed this simple world by giving the U.S. the taste of a nationalist Islamist regime. To contain Iranian nationalism and the force of its example, the U.S. turned to Iraq. Neither the brutal domestic dictatorship that Saddam Hussein ran at home, nor his determination to create a modern and independent state, made much difference at the time. The relationship between the U.S. and Iraq was marked by three phases in the two decades that followed. The first phase was an alliance in which the U.S. supported Iraq in the war against Iran, but it was also a setup, designed to keep the war going than to bring it to a swift conclusion. The second phase, the Gulf War that followed Saddam's occupation of Kuwait, was a war of vengeance. The third phase was a vicious low-intensity, high casualty, campaign conducted through the offices of the UN; in reality, this was nothing short of an officially-conducted and officially-sanctioned genocide whose core victims were young children, mostly under five.

On September 22, 1980, Saddam Hussein invaded Iran, with enthusiastic U.S. support. This war saw the first use of chemical weapons after the U.S. invasion of Vietnam. Nicholas D. Kristof of *The New York Times* reported that "the United States shipped seven strains of anthrax to Iraq from 1978 to 1988".[2] Training for using chemical and biological agents had been provided for the Iraqi

---

[2] Nicholas D. Kristof, "Cheney Didn't Mind Saddam," *International Herald Tribune*, October 12–13, 2002, p. 8.

military officers as early as the 1960s. An official army letter published in the late 1960s noted that "the U.S. army trained 19 Iraqi military officers in the United States in offensive and defensive chemical, biological and radiological warfare from 1957 to 1967".[3] At the time when Iraq got access to U.S. chemical and biological weaponry, the U.S. military was advertising these weapons not only as less expensive but also as more humane. Harvard professor Mathew Meselson, co-director of the Harvard-Sussex Program on Chemical-Biological Warfare Armament and Arms Limitation, explained: "The argument was you would lose fewer American lives if you fought a war because you would knock the enemy out right away." A report in the February 2003 issue of *Foreign Policy* magazine says the U.S. provided Iraq satellite imagery of Kurds and Iranian troops so the Iraqis could target both more effectively. A central figure in Reagan's effort to court Saddam was the person who was one of the most hawkish on Iraq after Nine Eleven — Defence Secretary Donald Rumsfeld who, as Reagan's envoy, met Saddam Hussein in December 1983, and Tariq Aziz, then the Foreign Minister, on March 24, 1984, the very day the UN released its report on Iraq's use of poison gases against Iranian troops.[4]

American assistance to Saddam Hussein ranged from commercial credits to political protection. When Hussein began gassing the Kurdish minority in Iraq with chemical weapons in May 1987, the U.S. was already providing Iraq with commercial credits worth $500 million a year. In spite of public revelations about the use of chemical weapons, the U.S. doubled commercial credits to the Iraqi regime to a billion dollars for 1989.[5] When the use of chemical weapons against Kurds first got known in 1987, the U.S. blocked

---

[3] Both the U.S. Army letter and Meselson cited in David Ruppe, "Army Gave Chem-Bio Warfare Training to Iraqis," *Global Security Newswire*, http://www.govexec.com/dailyfed/0103/012803gsn.htm.

[4] Charles Glass, "Iraq Must Go!" *London Review of Books*, October 3, 2002, p. 13.

[5] Samantha Power, "A Problem from Hell," *America and the Age of Genocide*. Basic Books (2002). For details on U.S. loans and credits, see pp. 173, 176–77, 236. For details on U.S. diplomatic protection to the Iraqi regime during the time of the first and the second chemical gas attacks, see pp. 191, 195, 200–201, 210, 230–31, 234.

attempts to raise this question in the UN Security Council. But when Saddam Hussein's forces gassed Iraqi Kurds for a second time, *after* the September 1988 ceasefire with Iran, the brutality received wide publicity, including in the American press. Compelled to acknowledge the crime, the U.S. asked that the UN response be limited to no more than appointing a fact-finding team to confirm it!

To understand the nature of the alliance between the U.S. and Saddam Hussein, one needs to understand the nature of the Baathist and the Islamist regime in Baghdad and Tehran. Two forms of nationalism, one secular and the other religious, they represented the more successful attempts at state-building in the region. If Washington decided to support Baghdad in the war, it was an indication of its judgment as to who was the greater danger. But Washington's strategic objective was to bleed both to death. Kissinger is famously quoted to have said in the middle of the Iraq-Iran War: "We hope they kill one another."

Saddam Hussein's invasion of Kuwait ended the alliance. Now, Hussein became an example of the price that must be paid by any regime that violates the terms of its alliance with the U.S. The 1991 Gulf War was literally a punishment. It is the first time the U.S. applied the military doctrine it had forged in Laos during the long war from 1964 to 1974. Alfred McCoy has argued that the war in Laos "was in retrospect the laboratory where the U.S. discovered a new military doctrine that became central to its foreign policy: to compensate for the absence of ground forces by an aerial bombardment of unprecedented intensity, without regard to the 'collateral damage'." The political pre-requisite was that collateral damage must not become public. In Laos, it did become public. As it "panned the Ho Chi Minh trail in the jungles of the south" and "the heavily populated areas of the Plain of Jars in the north", the bombing aroused great concern in antiwar circles in the U.S. A group of Cornell University scientists pointed out that the bombing violated the principle of proportionality — "that a reasonable proportionality exists between the damage caused and the military gain sought" — under international law. In his introduction to their report, the Pulitzer-prize winning *New York Times* journalist Neil Sheehan concluded: "The air war may constitute a massive war crime by the American government and its leaders."[6] It is this doctrine of aerial bombing, without regard to the principle of proportionality or to consequences for the civilian population, that the U.S. applied during the Gulf War in Iraq, after it, in Kosovo, and then in Afghanistan.

The Gulf War was waged with little restraint and involved the U.S. in the commission of numerous war crimes. Former Attorney General Ramsey Clark charged that the Administration used "all kinds of weapons in violation of international law", from explosives to depleted uranium to cluster bombs.[7] As Iraq's infrastructure was comprehensively targeted, little thought was given to civilian casualties, which were explained away as "collateral damage". Eric Hoskins, a Canadian doctor who was also coordinator of a Harvard team on Iraq, reported of the Allied bombardment of 1991 that it had "effectively terminated everything vital to human survival in Iraq — electricity, water, sewage systems, agriculture, industry and health care".[8] But George Bush Senior hesitated to replace Saddam Hussein, uncertain of what consequences a regime change would have for the region. Bush Senior faced a double dilemma. On the one hand, the Kurdish minority were the best organized among the Iraqis to take advantage of Saddam's overthrow, but their objective was a Kurdish state that would also include parts of Turkey, a close U.S. ally in the region. On the other hand, there was also the possibility that, if Iraq's majority Shia population with religious and cultural ties to Iran asserted itself, the outcome would surely dim

---

[6] For a discussion, see Alfred W. McCoy, "'Fallout': The Interplay of CIA Cover Warfare and the Global Narcotics Traffic," mimeo, paper presented to the conference on "Cold War and Civil War," Institute of African Studies, Columbia University, November 14–15, 2002, p. 3.

[7] Ramsay Clark, interview with Rasha Saad in *Al-Ahram*, Cairo, December 26, 2002, p. 7.

[8] Cited in David Edwards and David Cromwell, "The British Liberal Press target Iraq," Third World Network Features, *Sunday News*, Dar-es-Salaam, July 14, 2002, p. 3.

America's hopes of isolating Iran. So Bush Senior feared a regime change that would bring even a semblance of democracy to Iraq. The alternative to a regime change was to continue punishing Iraq in peace time, so as to keep the regime from arming effectively against anyone but its own population.

Even after this punishing war, the notion that Iraq was a |danger to the region and to the world was sustained. This fiction provided the argument for why Iraq must be policed and punished, simultaneously. That combined policing and punishing, carried out by the U.S. and Britain, was the intermittent aerial bombardment that continued even after the Gulf War ended. By the time the second edition of the war against Iraq in 2003, the peacetime bombing of Iraq had lasted longer than did the U.S. invasion of Vietnam or the war in Laos. By October of 1999, U.S. officials were already telling the Wall Street Journal they would soon be running out of targets: "We're down to the last outhouse."[9] That was two months before Clinton, bedeviled by the Monica Lewinsky scandal and faced with a vote in the House of Representatives indicting him for perjury and obstruction of justice, decided to unleash a round-the-clock bombing of Iraq.

The intermittent bombing of Iraq ran parallel with an indefinite regime of economic sanctions. The Security Council imposed comprehensive multilateral economic sanctions in resolution 661 of August 6, 1990. All imports, including imports to and from Iraq, were banned, with exemptions for medical supplies and, in some instances, foodstuffs. Resolutions 665 (1990) and 670 (1990) imposed a marine and air blockade to enforce the sanctions. The sanctions regime was renewed, with the same humanitarian caveats, in resolution 687 (1991). A further set of resolutions in 1991 permitted the sale of petroleum and petroleum products, up to $1.6 billion every six months, but it was never implemented, not until

---

[9] Cited in Tariq Ali, *The Clash of Fundamentalisms*, p. 145; see Anthony Arnove, *The Siege of Iraq*. London (2000), pp. 9–20. Also, see Alex de Waal, "US war crimes in Somalia," *New Left Review*, I, 230, July/August, 1998.

resolution 986 (1995) set up the "oil-for-food" program.[10] This regime signified a truly novel and sinister development in the history of low intensity conflict. Waged as a human rights campaign, it claimed to soften a punishment meted out according to a rule of law with provisions for "humanitarian goods" supervised by on-the-ground "UN Humanitarian Aid Coordinators", when in reality it unleashed a mass murder of hundreds of thousands, mainly children, in the full and callous knowledge that the "victims" were not the "target", and a cynical acceptance that the sanctions regime so effectively centralized the official export-import trade that it put the surviving population at the mercy of the very regime that was its supposed target. Done in the name of the UN, it also turned the UN into an American proxy in this latest phase of low intensity conflict.

The UN adopted economic sanctions as part of its 1945 Charter, as a means of maintaining global order. Since then, sanctions have been used fourteen times, twelve of those since the collapse of the Soviet Union. But the Iraqi case is the first time a country has been comprehensively sanctioned since World War II, meaning that virtually every aspect of its exports and imports was controlled by the UN, but subject to a U.S. veto. The rationale for sanctions kept on shifting. First, it was meant as a lever to get Iraq to withdraw from Kuwait. When Iraq withdrew, the rationale shifted to the need to disarm Iraq, particularly of chemical and biological weapons of mass destruction. The real objective was to compromise its sovereignty. When a proposal was floated as early as 1991 that UN-controlled Iraqi oil sales be used to purchase humanitarian goods, Iraq objected on the grounds that the proposal would undercut the sovereignty of the Iraqi state and reduce the government to an internal civil administration. But the sanctions regime continued longer than the Iraqis had expected. As the humanitarian

---

[10] Marc Bossuyt, "The Adverse Consequences of Economic Sanctions on the Enjoyment of Human Rights," Working Paper for UN Sub-Commission on the Promotion of Human Rights, http://www.scn.org/ecpi/UNreport-excerpt.html. I am thankful to Adam Branch for bringing this report to my attention.

crisis deepened, Iraq and the UN finally came to Agreement on the Oil-for-Food Program in 1996.

Since no foreign loans or foreign investment — and no access to foreign exchange — were permitted, this is how the Program worked: Iraq was allowed to sell a set amount of oil over six months (initially $1.2 billion net, later $3 billion net). The revenues went directly into a UN account. The U.S. and the UK required that nearly a third of this (30% from 1996–2000, 25% thereafter) be diverted into a compensation fund to pay outsiders for losses allegedly incurred because of Iraq's invasion of Kuwait. Another 10% went to pay for UN operating expenses in Iraq. The remainder, 60%, was controlled solely by the UN Controller who disbursed funds to contractors and suppliers of foodstuffs and basic medicines approved by the sanctions committee. But as a Working paper prepared for the UN Subcommission on the Promotion and Protection of Human Rights noted, "of the revenue from sale, only about half ended up going towards the purchase of humanitarian goods, the majority of the rest going towards reparations and administrative costs."[11] Finally, the sanctions regime treated the northern Kurdish part of Iraq preferentially — both in the funds provided and the degree of autonomy allowed its Kurdish administrators — in contrast to the central and southern parts. We shall see that whereas child mortality *decreased* in the three Northern governorates during the period of the sanctions regime, it *increased* in the 15 governorates of central and southern Iraq.[12]

---

[11] Marc Bossuyt, "The Adverse Consequences of Economic Sanctions on the Enjoyment of Human Rights," para 62, p. 2; for further information on how the Oil-for-Food Program operated, see Denis J. Halliday (former head of the Oil-for-Food Program), "Iraq and the UN's Weapon of Mass Destruction," *Current History*, February 1999, Vol. 98, Issue 625, pp. 65–68; interview with Hans von Sponeck and Denis Haliday in *The Guardian*, London, November 29, 2001; Hans von Sponeck, "Too Much Collateral Damage: 'Smart Sanctions' Hurt Innocent Iraqis," *Toronto Globe & Mail*, July 2, 2002.

[12] Not only did the North receive 22% more per capita in dollar value goods than does the centre and the south from the Oil-for-Food Program, 10% of the value going into the northern autonomous region was in the form of cash — allowing for greater local participation — whereas no cash, only goods, went into the centre and the south.

The effect of comprehensive sanctions was deadly. Because they followed on the heels of a war which had targeted and destroyed its physical infrastructure, the effect was a veritable social and demographic disaster. Yet, public knowledge of the humanitarian crisis was slow in coming. Part of the reason lay in that the UN Human Rights Rapporteur on Iraq was limited to identifying human rights violations by the Government of Iraq; the Rapporteur was prohibited by mandate to look at human rights violations as a result of the sanctions. At the same time, the Oil-for-Food program lacked an evaluation component, and therefore a trigger mechanism that would require the sanctioning power to respond if conditions deteriorated. As the dimensions of the humanitarian crisis got known, two non-permanent members of the Security Council, Canada and Brazil, pushed through a resolution in 1998 mandating the UN to assess humanitarian conditions in Iraq. The result was the 1999 UNICEF demographic survey, which, for the first time, brought to light comprehensive and credible evidence of the human tragedy wrought by the sanctions regime.

Before 1999, there had been two kinds of studies. On the one hand, there were 43 independent studies on the nutritional status of Iraqi children carried out over fifteen years; on the other, there were data on the number of deaths in hospitals, compiled by the Iraqi Ministry of Health from 1993. These studies and claims were evaluated by Richard Garfield, professor of Clinical International Nursing at Columbia University and chair of the Human Rights Committee of the American Public Health Association. Professor Garfield considered the Iraqi Minister's statistics highly unreliable both because most deaths are not reported to hospitals and because not all deaths in hospitals can be attributed to sanctions. When it came to independent studies, he found that, though reliable, they were of local significance. But Professor Garfield acknowledged that the demographic survey run by UNICEF in 1999 "provides the first reliable mortality estimates for Iraq since 1991".

UNICEF data "confirmed that the rate of mortality more than doubled" among children under five years in the fifteen governorates of central and southern Iraq, from 56 per 1000 births in 1984–89 to 131 per 1000 during 1995–99". The survey findings went on to confirm the worst of fears: of those alive, more than 22 percent of young children were chronically malnourished, and one child in seven died before the age of five, the result being an estimated 5000 "excess child deaths" every month above the 1989 pre-sanctions rate.[13] Writing in the summer of 2000, Professor Garfield gave the figure 300,000 as "a conservative estimate of 'excess deaths' among children under five".[14]

Even in this age of mass murder, the gravity of these figures should not escape our attention. Noting that "even in cases of extreme economic decline like the Great Depression in the United States, there was no increase in the rate of mortality", Professor Garfield underlined the gravity of the Iraqi disaster as *"the only instance of a sustained, large increase in mortality in a stable population of more than 2 million in the last two hundred years* (emphasis mine)".[15] Where death stalked, life too was miserable: Iraq's ranking in the UNDP Human Development Index fell from 96 in 1990 to 126 in 2000. By 2000, there was a consensus in both the UN and the human rights community about 'excess child deaths' directly linked to sanctions: the June, 2000 report to the UN Subcommission on the Promotion and Protection of Human Rights acknowledged that the total deaths "directly attributable to the sanctions" ranged "from half a million to a million and a half, with the majority of the dead being children".[16] Even the minimum

---

[13] Cited in Hans von Sponeck, "Too Much Collateral Damage: 'Smart Sanctions' Hurt Innocent Iraqis."

[14] Richard Garfield, "The Public Health Impact of Sanctions: Contrasting Responses of Iraq and Cuba," *Middle East Report*, 215, Summer 2000, pp. 16-17.

[15] Richard Garfield, "Changes in Health and Well-Being in Iraq during the 1990s," in *Sanctions on Iraq: Background, Consequences, Strategies*, Proceedings of the Conference hosted by the Campaign Against Sanctions on Iraq, November 13–14, 1999, Cambridge, ISBN 1-903488-22-2, pp. 36, 50–51; Richard Garfield, "The Public Health Impact of Sanctions: Contrasting Responses of Iraq and Cuba," *Middle East Report*, 215, Summer 2000, pp. 16–17.

[16] Marc Bossuyt, "The Adverse Consequences of Economic Sanctions on the Enjoyment of Human Rights," para 63, p. 2.

estimate was three times the number of Japanese killed during the U.S. atomic bomb attacks.

How, and by whom, was such a death toll justified for so long? This question was the subject of a research by Joy Gordon, professor of philosophy at Fairfield University, "an academic who studies the ethics of international relations". She described both her research experience and its findings in a cover story that explores "economic sanctions as a weapon of mass destruction" in the American monthly magazine, *Harper's*.[17]

The simple fact was that the U.S. consistently used its veto to minimize the humanitarian goods entering the country. Since it was not required to give a reason for the veto, it gave a reason only when it felt up to it. The reason it gave most often was the possibility of dual-use, civilian and military, claiming that the goods in question — those necessary to provide electricity, telephone service, transportation, even clean water — could also be used to enhance Iraq's military capabilities.

Professor Gordon found that, as of September, 2001, the U.S. had blocked 1051 applications involving "nearly 200 humanitarian contracts" including "contracts that the UN's own agency charged with weapons inspections did not object to". The most notorious were those needed to repair the damaged water and sanitation systems, given that most excess child deaths were "a direct or indirect result of contaminated water". Yet, U.S. officials blocked contracts for water tankers, "on the grounds that they might be used to haul chemical weapons instead". As of September 2001, "nearly a billion dollars' worth of medical-equipment contracts — for which all the information sought had been provided — was still on hold".[18] The U.S. was able to block even contracts approved by UN monitors on the ground because UN procedure allowed it to do so: the U.S. held a veto on Security Council's 661 Committee,

---

[17] Joy Gordon, "Cool War: Economic Sanctions as a Weapon of Mass Destruction," *Harper's Magazine*, November, 2002, pp. 43–49.

[18] Joy Gordon, "Cool War: Economic Sanctions as a Weapon of Mass Destruction," *Harper's Magazine*, November, 2002, p. 47.

the body "generally responsible for both enforcing the sanctions and granting humanitarian exemptions". The only time the U.S. felt compelled to justify its veto was when it was forced to do so by publicity within the U.S., as indeed happened in March, 2001, when Washington Post and Reuters reported that the U.S. had placed a hold on $280 million of "medical supplies, including vaccines to treat infant hepatitis, tetanus, and diphtheria, as well as incubators and cardiac equipment". Washington's rationale was "that the vaccines contained live cultures, albeit highly weakened one", and that the Iraqi government "could conceivably extract these, and eventually grow a virulent fatal strain". The veto persisted in spite of testimony from European biological experts "that such a feat was in fact flatly impossible", and "pressure behind the scenes from the UN and from members of the Security Council. Only when confronted with adverse publicity did the United States abruptly announce it was lifting the veto in this specific instance.[19]

UN administrators on the ground argued that they had developed an aggressive monitoring system to guard against dual use of imports such as gas cylinders, and there was no reason the same system could not be used for other goods. In a 1999 interview, the former UN Humanitarian Aid Coordinator in Baghdad, Hans von Sponeck, pointed out: "We have to control every gas cylinder that comes into this country. We have a number and we must make sure that 'gas cylinder 765' is there and the other one is over there. If you can do it with that detail, surely you can also do it with computers that are necessary for high school or university students that need to learn how to interact with modern technology."[20]

Forced to take responsibility for a policy they could neither defend nor had the power to influence, many of those in charge of implementing Iraq policy at the UN opted to resign, one after

---

[19] Joy Gordon, "Cool War: Economic Sanctions as a Weapon of Mass Destruction," *Harper's Magazine*, November, 2002, p. 47.

[20] Hans Von Sponeck, *Interview*, recorded by Grant Wakefield and Miriam Ryle at the UN Building, Baghdad, April 5, 1999, http://www.firethistime.org/sponeckinterview.htm.

another. The first to resign was Dennis Haliday, an Irishman who was the UN Assistant Secretary General and Humanitarian Coordinator in Iraq for thirteen months. He resigned in September, 1998, declaring: "We are in the process of destroying an entire society. It is as simple and terrifying as that. It is illegal and immoral." His successor, Hans von Sponeck, who served as Humanitarian Coordinator for Iraq from October 1998 to March 2000, was "driven out by U.S. charges of turning soft on sanctions-hit Iraq," a UN official told *Agence France-Presse*. The resignation followed Sponeck's warning in a CNN interview that the UN program was failing to meet even the "minimum requirements" for Iraq's 22 million people: "How long should the civilian population, which is totally innocent on all this, be exposed to such punishment for something they have never done? As a UN official, I should not be expected to be silent to that which I recognize as a true human tragedy that needs to be ended." Two days later, Jutta Burghardt, head of the World Food Program in Iraq, also resigned, stating: "I fully support what Mr. von Sponeck is saying." [21]

The more the scale of human carnage in Iraq became public knowledge, the more there was outrage in the human rights community. Human Rights Watch wrote of the sanctions: "The continued imposition of comprehensive economic sanctions (against Iraq) is undermining the basic rights of children and the civilian population generally," calling on the UN Security Council to "recognize that the sanctions have contributed in a major way to persistent life threatening conditions in the country." Save the Children Fund UK described the economic sanctions as "a silent war against Iraq's children". [22]

---

[21] Marc Bossuyt, "The Adverse Consequences of Economic Sanctions on the Enjoyment of Human Rights," para 68, p. 3; Denis J. Halliday, "Iraq and the UN's Weapon of Mass Destruction," *Current History*, February 1999, Vol. 98, Issue 625, pp. 67; For Hans von Sponeck's remarks, see *Agence France-Presse*, "UN Aid Coordinator Quits Under U.S. Pressure Over Iraqi Sanctions," February 14, 2000, http://www.commondreams.org/headlines/021400-01.htm.

[22] Cited in David Edwards and David Cromwell, "The British Liberal Press target Iraq," Third World Network Features, *Sunday News*, Dar-es-Salaam, July 14, 2002, p. 3.

The moral indefensibility of the sanctions regime became clear as early as 1996, when Madeleine Albright, U.S. Ambassador to the UN, was asked by Lesley Stahl on the T.V. program "60 Minutes" whether the price of "containing" Saddam was worth the deaths of more children than were killed in Hiroshima. The exchange was reproduced in the Working Paper prepared for the UN Sub-commission on the Promotion and Protection of Human Rights. "We have heard that half a million children have died. I mean, that is more than the number who died in Hiroshima. And, as you know, is the price worth it?" Madeleine Albright responded: "I think this is a very hard choice, but the price, we think the price is worth it."[23]

We have seen that the rationale for sanctions shifted over the years. Initially justified to leverage Iraq's withdrawal from occupied Kuwait, they were later said to be necessary to force it to disarm, particularly as regards chemical and biological weapons. Now, the fact was that Iraq armed with weapons of mass destruction during the period of its military collaboration with the U.S. which ended with the Gulf War. There followed a period of disarmament and a debate on how effective the disarmament had been. Among those with hard facts that could help answer this question were the weapons inspectors. Scott Ritter, a marine intelligence officer who became the chief weapons inspector from 1991 to 1998, was the most doubtful that the Saddam Hussein regime any longer represented a significant, let alone an imminent, threat. Ritter resigned in protest that the U.S. government had sabotaged his mission, placing nine American intelligence officers on the inspection team as far back as 1992. Ritter told CNN on July 17, 2002: "As of December 1998 we had accounted for 90 to 95 percent of Iraq's weapons of mass destruction capability. We destroyed all the factories, all the means of production and we could not account for some of the weaponry, but chemical weapons have a shelf-life of five years. Biological weapons have a shelf-life of three years. To have weapons today, they would have had to rebuild the factories and start the process of producing these

---

[23] Marc Bossuyt, "The Adverse Consequences of Economic Sanctions on the Enjoyment of Human Rights," footnote 59, p. 5.

weapons since December 1998" which is, in his view, a remote possibility, since "no one has substantiated the allegations that Iraq possesses weapons of mass destruction or is attempting to acquire weapons of mass destruction".[24] Hans Blix, the last of the Chief Weapons Inspectors, also confirmed that there was no evidence that Iraq possessed weapons of mass destruction. Iraq claimed it had destroyed all its prohibited weapons between 1991 and 1994, either unilaterally or in cooperation with the inspectors. The inspectors were able to verify that unilateral destruction had taken place on a large scale but could not quantify the amounts destroyed. So they recorded the material as unaccounted for, "neither verified destroyed nor believed to still exist", an ambiguity that the U.S. and UK governments seized on to claim the existence of "stockpiles" Iraq was hiding from the inspectors. During the war, no evidence came forth, of stockpiles or use. This meant either that the regime had no such weapons or that, if it did, it was responsible enough not to use them, even in the face of certain defeat. One wondered which fact would be more damning for the invaders. Soon after the war, the Deputy Defense Secretary, Paul Wolfowitz, said in an interview in the magazine *Vanity Fair* that focus on alleged weapons of mass destruction as the primary justification for invading Iraq was politically the most convenient: "For bureaucratic reasons we settled on one issue, weapons of mass destruction, because it was the one reason everybody could agree on."[25]

Why, then, the war? If the Hussein regime was not an imminent threat in military terms, why then did the U.S. target Saddam Hussein? Was oil the answer? Oil helps. Iraq has the world's second largest proven stocks of oil, after Saudi Arabia. But oil cannot provide the full or even the bulk of the explanation. Iraq's real significance is political. Just as after 1991 Iraq was turned into an example of the punishment that can be meted to a regime that dares go outside the framework of a U.S.-defined alliance, so the significance of Iraq after

---

[24] Scott Ritter, "Facts Needed Before Iraq Attack," *CNN Access*, July 17, 2002.

[25] David Usborne, "WMD Just a Convenient Excuse for War, Admits Wolfowitz," *The Independent*, May 30, 2003.

Nine Eleven is once again larger than itself. In attacking Iraq the the Bush administration hopes to achieve more than just a regime change. For the U.S., Iraq presents another chance to redraw the political map of the entire region, something it has tried several times before, the highlights being the Israeli invasion of Lebanon which failed to create a buffer Christian state, the alliance with Iraq against Iran in the 1980s, and the war in Afghanistan. The overthrow of the Saddam Hussein regime is meant to change the balance of forces in the Middle East. Writing in April under the auspices of the Jerusalam Centre for Public Affairs, Israeli Major-General Ya'akov Amidror, put the point forthrightly: "Iraq is not the ultimate goal. The ultimate goal is the Middle East, the Arab world and the Muslim world. Iraq will be the first step in this direction; winning the war against terrorism means structurally changing the entire area."[26] As the U.S. seeks to replace defiant regimes and intimidate the rest, it aims to impose a new regional order by creating pro-American regimes, first in Iraq, and then in a Bantustan-like state of Palestine, presenting regime change as a strategy for "democratization". And yet, the thrust of this administration's policy shift is global, not just regional, in spite of the sometimes shrill rhetoric that equates terrorism with Islam. The policy shift is driven by two tendencies. Only one of these — Protestant fundamentalism — has a parochial orientation. The other — neo-conservatism — is marked by global ambitions. Its target is militant nationalism, whether or not in the Middle East. Whereas methods have changed after Nine Eleven, with proxy war giving way to outright invasion, the objective remains the same as under the Reagan administration: to target and liquidate militant nationalism through "regime change".

---

[26] Cited in Anatol Lieven, "A Trap of Their Own Making," *London Review of Books*, May 8, 2003.

Multilateral Organizations After the U.S.-Iraq War

Lisa L. Martin

Professor of Government at Harvard University. She has received fellowships from the Guggenheim Foundation, MacArthur Foundation, and Hoover Institution. Her major research interests involve international institutions and cooperation, domestic institutions and international cooperation, the international financial institutions, and the political economy of tourism. Her most recent book, Democratic Commitments: Legislatures and International Cooperation, *focuses on the impact of legislative involvement on bargaining and implementation of agreements in the United States and the European Union.*

At the end of World War II, the United States found itself in a situation of unprecedented power. The economy of the former hegemonic state, Britain, was decimated by the war. So were the economies of the rest of Western Europe, including Britain's foremost European economic challenger, Germany. While the Soviet Union presented a growing military threat, in economic terms U.S. power was unchallenged, leaving the United States in a position of hegemony.

Washington responded to this new position by adopting policies of multilateralism. Drawing lessons from the economic catastrophes of the interwar years, leaders in the United States determined that the only way to safeguard U.S. interests was to remain deeply engaged with the rest of the world, rather than turning inwards as after World War I. A major mechanism

Washington used to implement this policy of engagement was the creation of multilateral organizations, including the United Nations, the Bretton Woods institutions, NATO, and others.

As the new millennium gets underway, the United States finds itself unexpectedly in a position of unipolarity, with no serious military challengers and economic challengers all facing serious problems of their own. A student of international relations who somehow missed the decades of the 1980s and 1990s would be startled at this turn of events. In the late 1970s and early 1980s, the discussion centered around how declining U.S. power might translate into instability in the international system. The assumption that the United States would continue its relative decline was challenged by some,[1] but widespread.[2]

Anyone comparing U.S. policy in 2003 to that in, say, 1948, would be struck by the contrast. In both periods American power was immense, creating a situation of hegemony or unipolarity. Yet U.S. policy in 2003 did not reflect the multilateralism of the late 1940s and early 1950s. Rather than creating and strengthening multilateral institutions, the United States turned to unilateral policies, denigrated the entire notion of multilateralism as a principle, and refused to participate in numerous new multilateral ventures such as the International Criminal Court.

This paper begins with the observation of this paradox and builds on it to analyze the future of multilateral organizations. I begin by examining the concept of multilateralism, both in theory and in history. I then turn to an analysis of multilateralism, asking why the United States turned to multilateralism after World War II and evaluating its payoffs. The final section applies the insights

---

[1] Joseph S. Nye, *Bound to Lead: The Changing Nature of American Power*. New York: Basic Books (1990); Duncan Snidal, "The Limits of Hegemonic Stability Theory," *International Organization*, 39(4), Autumn 1985, 579–614.

[2] Robert O. Keohane, *After Hegemony: Cooperation and Discord in the World Political Economy*. Princeton, NJ: Princeton University Press (1984); Paul Kennedy, *The Rise and Fall of the Great Powers: Economic Change and Military Conflict 1500–2000*. New York: Random House (1987).

developed in the rest of the paper to the future of multilateral organizations. It concludes that the current policy of "*ad hoc* multilateralism", or turning to multilateral organizations opportunistically, fundamentally misunderstands the nature and motivation for multilateralism. Such a policy is therefore likely to fail, leaving the United States with a stark choice between expensive unilateralism and needing to rebuild its reputation as a reliable participant in multilateral endeavors.

Multilateralism in Theory and History. What is multilateralism, and what is its relationship to multilateral organizations? Many writers use "multilateral" simply to mean any organization or pattern of cooperation involving more than two states.[3] Others, most notably John Ruggie, have identified an "institution of multilateralism" that is defined by basic principles of behavior. According to this definition, "multilateralism is an institutional form that coordinates relations among three or more states on the basis of generalized principles of conduct".[4] If an institution is based on generalized principles of conduct, appropriate behavior is specified without attention to particularistic interests. Important norms that express generalized principles of conduct include non-discrimination, indivisibility with respect to appropriate behavior, and diffuse reciprocity. These norms contrast sharply, for example, with bilateralism as an organizing principle. In bilateralism, special deals are struck for each participant and reciprocity is specific rather than being based on the assumption that costs and benefits roughly balance out over time.

This elaboration of multilateralism as an institution is useful because it helps us to see what was distinctive about the multilateral organizations created by the United States after World War II. The trade regime of the GATT, for example, was premised on the norm

---

[3] Robert O. Keohane, "Multilateralism: An Agenda for Research," *International Journal*, 45, Autumn 1990, 731–64.

[4] John Gerard Ruggie, "Multilateralism: The Anatomy of an Institution," in John Gerard Ruggie (ed.), *Multilateralism Matters: The Theory and Praxis of an Institutional Form.* New York: Columbia University Press (1993), p. 11.

of non-discrimination. Negotiations took place between the major suppliers of certain goods, but the deals they struck were then extended via the Most-Favored-Nation principle to all other members of the regime. NATO illustrates how indivisibility might work in practice, with an attack on one member of the alliance considered an attack on all. The UN Security Council might seem an important exception to the norms of multilateralism, since the five permanent members have special status in that they can veto resolutions. However, even here at least the five permanent members are treated as equals, rather than giving the United States a privileged position, representing a scaled-down version of multilateralism.

While some earlier international institutions exhibited characteristics of multilateralism, the U.S. emphasis on multilateral norms and its efforts in building multilateral organizations marked a "discontinuity", in Ruggie's terms.[5] Not all organizations reflected multilateral norms perfectly. The Bretton Woods monetary regime, for example, gave a privileged place to the United States with the dollar accepted as equivalent to gold. Nevertheless, even institutions that diverged from multilateralism to some extent reflected multilateral principles in their other aspects.

The U.S. support of multilateralism extended to the creation of organizations in which it would not be a major player. One condition of European states' receiving Marshall Plan aid, for example, was that they create multilateral systems of cooperation among themselves. This led to the creation of the European Payments Union, which settled debts among European states much more effectively than the former bilateral system.[6] American support of the creation of the European Coal and Steel Community (which has now evolved into the European Union) was similarly premised on the belief that multilateral principles would address many of the problems that had led to war in Europe in the preceding centuries.

---

[5] *Ibid.*, p. 23.

[6] Thomas H. Oatley, "Multilateralizing Trade and Payments in Postwar Europe," *International Organization*, 55(4), Autumn 2001, 949–69.

Far from seeing creation of a cooperative European economic entity as a threat, the United States actively supported these efforts as in the interests of peace and stability.

Through these efforts, the United States did not seek to maximize its short-term benefits. As the preeminent power of the time, it could have imposed institutions that inhibited the economic and military advancement of others, attempting to assure that it faced no serious competitors in the foreseeable future.[7] Instead it put in place institutions designed to facilitate the economic recovery and political stability of its allies and former enemies. In fact, it did so using a particularly "demanding" institutional form. Multilateralism is remarkable in that it does not give a privileged position to the hegemon. If generalized operating principles are put into place, the hegemon is subject to the same rules as others. As noted above, multilateral principles were not respected fully. Yet it is striking that this immensely powerful state championed principles and norms that served to bind itself; it created institutions that were premised on the notion that even the United States would play by the rules it asked others to accept. Why so? The following section turns to explanations of this puzzle and evaluation of the consequences of this commitment.

Why Multilateralism? Why would a powerful state choose to create institutions that would bind itself? Scholars have approached this question from different analytical perspectives. Some have traced U.S. behavior to the power of ideas. Ruggie finds that "[f]or American postwar planners, multilateralism in its generic sense served as a foundational architectural principle on the basis of which to reconstruct the postwar world".[8] He attributes this to a set of beliefs that earlier had their expression in the creation of the New Deal on the domestic level. Hegemony fostered multilateralism in this period because it was *American* hegemony, rooted in specific

---

[7] Indeed, other victors throughout history have done so. See Robert Gilpin, *War and Change in World Politics*. New York: Cambridge University Press (1981).

[8] Ruggie, "Multilateralism," p. 25.

American experiences. Anne-Marie Slaughter elaborates this insight by examining the "regulatory state" that grew in the United States during the New Deal and was projected into the international realm.[9] Another twist on this theme is apparent in studies of the creation of the trade regime, which actually began in the 1930s with the passage of the Reciprocal Trade Agreements Act (RTAA). The RTAA delegated negotiating authority from Congress to the president, and so provided the foundation for the multilateral regime that grew in the 1950s.[10] It is common to trace the roots of the RTAA to a belief that the previous trade regime had led to the economic disasters of the 1930s, just as the inadequate security arrangements in Europe had led to two World Wars.

Other analysts focus less on beliefs, ideas, and the lessons of history than on the strategic situation in which the United States found itself at the end of the war.[11] While the norms of multi-lateralism can be useful for resolving coordination problems, for example, they seem less well-suited to situations in which states have strong temptations to renege on deals if they can do so unobserved. However, other features of multilateral organizations, such as strong monitoring powers and clear provisions for enforcement, address such problems. What is most relevant to the strategic situation after World War II is that the United States was able to take a long-term perspective, as it was relatively free from immediate threats (the Soviet Union did not become a serious threat until the 1950s). American policymakers realized that their situation of preeminence was a temporary one. History taught that hegemons declined relative to other powers; challengers were sure to arise. Just as

---

[9] Anne-Marie Slaughter (Burley), "Regulating the World: Multilateralism, International Law, and the Projection of the New Deal Regulatory State," in Ruggie, ed. (1993), pp. 125–56.

[10] Michael A. Bailey, Judith Goldstein, and Barry R. Weingast, "The Institutional Roots of American Trade Policy," *World Politics*, 49(3), April 1997, 309–38.

[11] Lisa L. Martin, "Interests, Power, and Multilateralism," *International Organization*, 46(4), Autumn 1992, pp. 765–92.

importantly, decisionmakers did not believe that a situation of unipolarity was desirable, as it would lead to constant threats and instability. Better to encourage the growth of allies who could in the future undertake cooperative endeavors against emerging threats than to attempt to keep them down indefinitely.

Thus multilateralism was designed with an eye to the future. It put into place structures that were in the long-term interest of the United States as well as others, rather than attempting to maximize short-term gains at their expense. A powerful state attempting to create such a system faces a major strategic dilemma, however.[12] On the one hand, it wants to create integrated systems of rules and norms that will persist in the face of an inevitably changing distribution of power. (This goes to the heart of multilateralism.) On the other hand, creating such a system requires that the rules put in place bind the hegemon as well as other states. It is difficult, however, for a hegemon credibly to bind itself. The United States had to build a reputation for multilateralism. It needed to demonstrate that, although it could maximize its immediate payoffs by rejecting the rules that bound others, it instead would play by the rules. It did so by its commitment to multilateralism throughout the economic and security realms, by investing significant resources in the creation of multilateral regimes and organizations, and by (most of the time) living up to its commitments within those regimes.

"Self-binding" therefore describes the U.S. strategy at the heart of the multilateral organizations it created after World War II. By demonstrating that it would not constantly flex its muscles to derive the maximum immediate payoffs from all situations, it succeeded in building a reliable, stable set of multilateral organizations. In fact, the regimes created in the early postwar years did persist even in the face of rapid economic recovery in Europe and Japan. By the 1980s, analysts were puzzling about the persistence of cooperation

---

[12] See also G. John Ikenberry, *After Victory: Institutions, Strategic Restraint, and the Rebuilding of Order after Major Wars*. Princeton, NJ: Princeton University Press (2001).

"after hegemony", and attributing this phenomenon to the institutions created by the United States throughout the postwar era.[13]

By almost any measure, this U.S. strategy of multilateralism was a striking success, both for the United States and for most of the world. On the security side, the goal of preventing the major-power wars that had devastated Europe for centuries has been achieved. NATO also succeeded in preventing war between the United States and Soviet Union, although wars, both international and civil, have plagued other regions of the world. The EU has both deepened and widened, using its own terminology, so that it now covers nearly all issue-areas in which governments make policy, and will expand to 25 members in this decade.

On the economic side, the multilateral trade regime has been highly successful, in spite of recurrent challenges and complaints of backsliding. Tariffs within the developed world are at negligible levels, and in the rest of the world they have seen a steady downward slide. Levels of trade have correspondingly risen. While some dispute whether the GATT and now WTO have, as organizations, been directly responsible for this trend,[14] there is little doubt that the norms embodied in these organizations have contributed to the growth of trade. While the Bretton Woods monetary regime did not survive the 1970s, the organizations associated with Bretton Woods, especially the International Monetary Fund (IMF) and World Bank, have persisted and taken on new functions in the globalized economy. The international financial system has seen very rapid increases in the level of integration, so that the term "globalization" is an apt description of at least this realm. Globalization has brought with it its discontents, and the IMF and World Bank have made mistakes. Yet prosperity has generally increased, and increased most quickly among those states most deeply integrated into the multilateral institutions. Regions that have stagnated and declined,

---

[13] Keohane, 1984.

[14] Andrew K. Rose, "Do WTO Members have More Liberal Trade Policy?" NBER Working Paper, w9347, November 2002.

such as much of Sub-Saharan Africa, are those that have not participated fully in multilateralism, and governments in these regions are increasingly looking to partake of some of the benefits of globalization for themselves. Criticisms of some dimensions of globalization, such as its homogenization of culture, are well-taken. But these problems should not prevent us from seeing the tremendous gains that multilateral cooperation has achieved.

The United States has prospered under multilateralism. The calculated risk of investing in multilateral organizations in the hope of achieving long-term stability and progress rather than seeking short-term rents has paid off handsomely. In both economic and military terms, self-binding has proven to enhance American power rather than to diminish it. Self-binding means that at times a powerful state will have to make concessions, engage in protracted and frustrating negotiations, or comply with inconvenient restrictions on its freedom of maneuver. But in the long term, these restrictions on action have not in any demonstrable way harmed U.S. economic growth or security. In fact, the greatest challenge to security today — global terrorism — can only be addressed with global cooperation, as even the multilateralism-adverse Bush administration has acknowledged.

The postwar system of multilateralism fostered by the United States rested on a foundation of the principles of multilateralism. U.S. policymakers chose to implement these principles because they believed that they would be in the long-term interests of the United States, in spite of the restrictions on freedom of action that they implied. The multilateral world is no nirvana, but it has been remarkably successful in generating stable patterns of international cooperation that have led to security and prosperity and allowed the United States to achieve the position of power in which it finds itself today.

Implications for the Future of Multilateral Organizations. The contrast between U.S. behavior after World War II and at the turn of the twenty-first century is stark. Many of the postwar organizations remain with us, although modified in form and content. One might have expected the United States, after defeating its Cold

War nemesis and facing no challengers on the immediate horizon, to reinvigorate these organizations or invest in building new ones. Whether out of habit, the lessons of history, or a strict calculation of long-term benefits and opportunities, this would have seemed the natural course of behavior.

Instead, we have seen a distinctive turn away from the self-binding strategy at the heart of multilateralism. The policies pursued by the Bush administration, and exemplified in the U.S.-Iraq war, might be labeled "*ad hoc* multilateralism" or "opportunistic multi-lateralism". Senior administration officials, including the National Security Advisor, have publicly and explicitly rejected the principle of investing in new multilateral organizations. The United States has refused to sign a number of accords seen as important by the rest of the world, such as the Kyoto Protocol and the International Criminal Court (ICC). The turn from multilateralism is especially notable in the case of the ICC, where the United States is specifically demanding special treatment in a series of bilateral deals, demanding exemption from the ICC's procedures. This rejects the essence of multilateralism, the "generalized operating principles" that prevent one state from assuming a privileged position. Instead, the United States claims that its unique power requires it to have a privileged position.

The United States thus has rejected the "self-binding" that characterizes multilateralism. The rejection of multilateral constraints was of course most apparent, and perhaps most damaging, in the case of the Iraq war. Here, under intense pressure from its allies, the United States did go through the motions of attempting to gain support for its planned invasion of Iraq from the UN Security Council. But throughout these efforts the administration made it clear that it would act unilaterally if necessary, and in the end failed to gain UN authority for its invasion. The United States did not end up having to act purely unilaterally. It gained firm and valuable support from Britain, and describes a "coalition of the willing" that offers rhetorical, if not always practical, support for the war effort.

Now that the Iraq effort has shifted from full-scale hostilities to reconstruction and a drawn-out battle with determined resistors, the

United States is returning to multilateral settings. Peacekeeping and reconstruction will be serious challenges, perhaps even greater than anticipated. They will be a major drain on U.S. resources for years to come. In appreciation of this, the United States is calling on others to provide resources for these efforts. In response to their demands to work through the UN, we see some renewed willingness by the Bush administration to consider this forum.

Some analysts have seen the occasional attempts to work within the UN as evidence that the administration remains committed, perhaps against its instincts, to multilateralism. I would instead characterize its approach to multilateral organizations as "opportunistic multilateralism" or "*ad hoc* multilateralism". When the situation demands it, we see some willingness to attempt to operate within the constraints and rules of multilateral organizations. However, this is done as a last resort and on a purely opportunistic basis. There is a strong preference for *ad hoc* coalitions of the willing that allow the United States to operate largely without constraints. In no sense does this pattern of behavior reflect the multilateral principles that animated postwar policy.

As argued above, states with the immense power of the United States face immense strategic challenges. In order to gain the sustained cooperation of others, powerful states need to make commitments to play by the rules themselves. Self-binding is a necessary component of long-term cooperation, and multilateral organizations were designed to encourage and facilitate such self-binding by the United States. Today, in contrast, we see an explicit rejection of self-binding as a strategy. Multilateral organizations will be used under duress or when convenient, but not if they put any significant constraints on U.S. behavior.

History and logic suggest that opportunistic multilateralism is a short-sighted strategy. Operating without the inconveniences of multilateral constraints is a tremendous temptation for the powerful. It allows unfettered expression of power, and may maximize immediate payoffs (although one has to wonder if even this is true in the case of the Iraq war). But the long-term costs can be immense. One of the most valuable aspects of U.S. postwar policy is that the United States developed a reputation for multilateralism. It demonstrated that it would often (if not always) forgo the temptation to act unilaterally in the interest of achieving long-term stability and prosperity. This reputation, in turn, contributed to the success of multilateral organizations.

Reputations can be squandered quickly, and the reputation for multilateralism surely has been. Turning to multilateral organizations only under duress and when it appears convenient demonstrates a lack of commitment, even explicit rejection, of the principles of multilateralism. This in turn leads other states to expect the United States to renege on agreements or operate outside the constraints of multilateral organizations when it is convenient to do so. This hollows out the core of such organizations, as they no longer provide the self-binding function they once did. Multilateral organizations become marginalized, and cannot produce the international agreements and plans of action that provided long-term stability and prosperity in the late twentieth century.

Thus, those who see multilateral organizations as a tool to be used or discarded on a day-to-day basis, or who demand that the United States be given a privileged position within them and not be subject to the rules that constrain others, fundamentally misunderstand the basic premises of multilateralism. Without self-binding by the hegemon, multilateral organizations become empty shells.

What does this analysis imply about the future of multilateral organizations, such as the UN? From a purely explanatory perspective, the short- to medium-term outlook is bleak. There is little doubt that the U.S. reputation for self-binding has been largely destroyed and will need to be rebuilt if these organizations are to regain their effectiveness. From a normative perspective, the functions that such organizations can perform remain vital. They provide forums for negotiation and coordination of policies. They share information and generate expectations about appropriate behavior, sometimes setting in motion enforcement activities. Concretely, it is difficult to imagine an effective and efficient battle against global terrorism without a framework of multilateral cooperation. On the economic side, the momentum in global trade talks has stalled, threatening some of the gains achieved over the last sixty years and the access of the poorest countries to these gains.

Thus the question is whether there is any likelihood of a reversal in U.S. policy, moving toward a willingness to invest resources in rebuilding a reputation for self-binding. One way to approach this question might be to look for factors that differentiate 2003 from 1950, attempting to identify the underlying factors giving rise to such disparate policies. Ideology may be an important factor, but we need to ask why decisionmakers with particular ideologies are influential at certain periods in history. One objective factor that distinguishes the two eras is the distinction between unipolarity and bipolarity in the military realm. In the postwar era, the Soviet Union was a growing military threat and became a serious threat in the early 1950s. We thus had a situation of bipolarity. In 2003, in contrast, U.S. military might is unchallenged. While security threats are everywhere, they are nebulous and hard to target, in contrast to the straightforward military competition of the Cold War. Unipolarity more accurately characterizes the military distribution of power today.

Can this shift from bipolarity to unipolarity explain the U.S. movement away from multilateralism? Perhaps, at least to some extent. The anticipated, and then real, challenge of the Soviet Union focused U.S. efforts in the early postwar era. It led to a desire to gain allies that were strong economically, stable politically, and had adequate military resources. The long-term perspective that characterized U.S. policy during this era, and led to implementation of multilateral principles, was based on this desire. In contrast, the lack of a single state that represents a major military threat today may have led to a discounting of the value of allies. Why invest in a multilateral organization such as NATO, designed in the past to counter a specific threat, if the threat itself is constantly shifting shape and hard to pin down? Just which allies do we need, and what capabilities should they have? These questions are much more complex today than they were in 1950. Thus a strategy of maintaining a preponderance of power, instead of encouraging the strengthening of allies, may seem a reasonable choice in today's world. Without a Soviet Union looming on the horizon, it may appear more realistic to aspire to long-term unipolarity, shedding the unwelcome constraints of multilateralism.

I would argue that this inference is mistaken; that multilateralism is as valuable today as it was earlier. Unipolarity, as we are rapidly learning in Iraq, is immensely expensive to sustain. Talk has quickly shifted from using Iraq's own oil revenues for rebuilding to "burdensharing" and generating contributions from others for rebuilding and peacekeeping. While the Iraq case is the most pressing and immediate example, the high costs of unilateralism are likely to become apparent in other areas as well. Our long, successful experience with multilateralism may have led decisionmakers to expect stable cooperation from other states to continue, without appreciating that such cooperation was contingent on the United States itself playing by the rules. When cooperation that was taken for granted fails to materialize in various issue-areas — trade, finance, peacekeeping, sharing of intelligence — we may find that the expected short-term payoff of unilateralism was vastly inflated. In fact, the costs of multilateralism, annoying as they may often be, are likely to pale in comparison to the vast resources needed to sustain unipolarity or, even more grandly, empire.

It will take time and resources to rebuild the U.S. reputation for multilateralism. It will require making concessions and accepting compromises on a wide range of issues on which we might prefer to go it alone or to impose our most-favored solution. But a growing appreciation of the costs of empire can lead to a recalculation of the long-term costs and benefits of multilateralism. If such a recalculation occurs, either by this administration or by the public as elections approach, the future of multilateral organizations will significantly brighten.

Conclusion. What does the U.S.-Iraq war imply for the future of multilateral organizations such as the UN? This paper has approached this question by considering the concept of multilateralism, how it has been applied in history, and the logic of a strategy of multilateralism. The multilateral organizations created in the postwar era were based on the principles of multilateralism. The United States championed these principles, although they imposed constraints on U.S. exercise of power, because they promised long-term benefits. These benefits materialized.

In contrast, U.S. policy toward multilateral organizations today is one of opportunistic or *ad hoc* multilateralism. Principles of multilateralism, implying self-binding, have been rejected. Instead, multilateral organizations are treated as tools of convenience, to be used when they promise immediate payoffs and minimal restrictions on freedom of action, but in general to be kept marginal and treated with deep distrust.

This paper has argued that a policy of opportunistic multilateralism will gut multilateral organizations and therefore prove costly for the United States. Such a policy misunderstands the logic of multilateralism, which requires the powerful to bind themselves. In order for multilateral organizations to live up to their potential, the United States will have to rebuild a reputation for respecting the limitations of multilateralism. We see little sign of an appreciation this today, but there is some chance that a growing awareness of the very high long-term costs of unilateralism will lead to a renewed appreciation of the benefits of multilateralism.

War Talk

Robin Tolmach Lakoff

Robin T. Lakoff is Professor of Linguistics at UC Berkeley. She is well-known for linguistics research on the relationship between language and gender. Her current research includes the examination of the connections between the politics of language and the language of politics, e.g. in the media treatment of the Hill/Thomas hearings, Hillary Rodham Clinton, the O. J. Simpson trial, and the impeachment (cf. the last publication listed below). One of her latest publications is The Language War.

Introductory Remarks

American society, like many others, makes a sharp distinction between language and action, word and deed. Our proverbs and folktales reflect our contempt for the first as ineffectual, our respect for the latter as potent. Yet — especially in a representative democracy — if we insist on the absoluteness of the difference, we come up against a paradox: how do leaders convince themselves and their voters to adopt a particular course of action? And especially when that course of action produces or threatens to produce dubious results, how are both leaders and led convinced of its rightness and inevitability? Language is the major means of persuasion.

At the present writing, the United States is committed to a war in Iraq both the rationale for which and the ultimate benefits of which seem increasingly foggy. Daily the questions multiply: to what degree did the President and those around him misrepresent both motives and likely success to the people? Were the misrepresentations knowing lies, or wild exaggerations? In any case, why did the words — most notably in the President's State of the Union address in January, 2003, but on many other occasions, and by many other representatives and supporters of the present administration — get swallowed, and followed, with blind enthusiasm by the supposedly sophisticated media and their supposedly canny viewers, hearers, and readers? Through what linguistic means did they achieve control: words, sentence structure, narrative structures, discourse strategies? And if language changes the world, why are we so slow to see when it is manipulating us? Does our contempt for language as "just words", or "mere semantics", enable its skillful users to draw us into their web?

Edward S. Herman and Noam Chomsky have coined the phrase, "the manufacture of consent".[1] It is this manufacturing activity — the use of language to manipulate us into belief and action — that I want to examine: in particular, the knowing and sophisticated use of language by members of the Bush administration to induce complicity in beliefs and actions that otherwise citizens of the United States might subject to critical scrutiny.

While this book specifically addresses the war in Iraq, with the linguistic contribution examining how language has been used to justify and rationalize it, a complete answer to the question, "Why are we at war?" presuppose another: "how has this administration used language from the start in questionable ways to rationalize its complete agenda?" Just as the Iraq war is only one part of a larger agenda, so the language with which it has made this step plausible is merely the continuation of a linguistic policy previously put in place; U.S. involvement in Iraq is just one result of the linguistic activity that has enabled the Bush administration to accomplish a much larger and even more disturbing agenda. So my examination, while focusing on war rhetoric, will include consideration of the language of the administration as a whole.

My analysis will examine the discourse of several members of the Bush administration The president of the United States, and

---

[1] Edward S. Herman and Noam Chomsky, *Manufacturing Consent: The Political Economy of the Mass Media*. New York: Pantheon (1988).

this President in particular, hardly ever creates his own formal or ceremonial discourse. In the case of George W. Bush, there is a reasonable presumption that even apparently spontaneous throw-away lines have been sculpted by others in advance, ready to be slipped into an appropriate context. I will look at both the President's and others' formal orations and casual remarks; both oral and written utterances. The question I address is not, "What did he *mean* or intend by uttering that line?" Since language is ambiguous out of context, and since we can never put ourselves in the same context as another human being, we cannot reliably determine what a speaker meant or wanted to accomplish. But we can reliably determine what that utterance meant to representative hearers, and therefore how that utterance probably functioned in creating consensus.

For the sake of simplicity, I will attribute speech uttered by the President to him: "Bush said", "the President believes", and so forth. These expressions should not be taken to imply a belief that the words attributed to the President are in any real sense his own. "Bush" (etc.) should be taken as metonyms of "the people around Bush, those who control him".

Paths to Persuasion

Some uses of language by the Bush administration are, or appear to be, spontaneous, accidental, or unintentional, while others are polished and carefully orchestrated. The President's State of the Union addresses, for instance, are known to be carefully crafted by a stable of writers; his performances at occasional press conferences, on the other hand, have the appearance of off-the-cuff remarks. That apparent difference is deceptive: it is wise to assume that *everything* said by the President has been created beforehand. I suspect that the President's handlers want even his malapropisms (to be discussed below) to be part of his speech: had they wanted to exorcise a malapropism, they could easily have done so.

Political rhetoric has been the subject of analysis for over two millennia, with Aristotle's *Rhetoric* perhaps the earliest, and certainly the most influential, source. Aristotle saw persuasion as the aim of political speeches: inducing hearers to change their beliefs and perhaps their future course of action. He presented persuasion as a process involving three facets:

(1) *ethos*, or "character". The speaker must provide evidence of being a person worthy of the hearers' trust, whose arguments therefore they can rationally believe.

While the establishment of a speaker's *ethos* appears to be a universal prerequisite to rhetorical success, how that is achieved — what kinds of behavior and representations of self create trust — differ over time and space. For the Romans, a public speaker above all had to portray himself as possessing *gravitas*, "seriousness". A candidate for office wore a specially whitened toga; he spoke with the utmost formality, eschewing jokes and colloquialism, avoiding any appearance of spontaneity or folksiness. He was trusted by his audience because he was loftier, and therefore better, than they were, a man they could look up to.

For modern Americans, on the other hand, *gravitas* is a negative (recall the deconstruction of Al Gore in 2000 as "stiff"). On high occasions *gravitas* may be appropriate, but usually, to seem trustworthy a speaker must project "niceness": be friendly, a regular guy, informal and spontaneous. He must appear to be genuine. Above all he must be comforting: represent normal, conventional behavior, nothing that would put anyone off.

(2) *pathos*, or "feeling". The speaker and hearers share important emotions, are the same kinds of people with common interests. Those on the other side, however, do not share these interests and may not be fully human at all.

(3) *logos*, or "logical argument". The speaker speaks from authority. The speaker's claims are true and follow in a logical sequence from one point to the next. So if hearers accept the first point, acceptance of the remainder follows naturally.

From Aristotle's time to ours, audiences have flattered them-selves that they have been persuaded by *logos* alone (an instance of the overvaluation of reason above emotion, the stereotypically male over the stereotypically female). But *ethos* and *pathos* are the necessary precursors of and creators of any impression of *logos*: if a speaker can create trust and a sense of shared interests, the audience is much more likely to find the *logos* compelling — flawed though it might be. So it is essential to examine the Bush administration's mobilization of all three Aristotelian principles and to consider them all of equal importance. "Serious" contemporary analyses of American political have tended to focus on "logical" arguments, leaving the rest to "frivolous" pop analysts like the late-night comedians Jay Leno, David Letterman, and Bill Maher. But frivolous or not, these critics know something too many intellectuals don't. A complete analysis of how a democratic government seeks to persuade its citizens, and what those citizens are most apt to find persuasive, must consider all three arms of a persuasive discourse.

The Bush Administration Meets Aristotle

Administration ethos

Representations of *ethos* currently seem to involve explicit references to gender and gender differentiation: to be trustworthy, a male politician (women have other problems to consider) must come across as a *real man*. There are reasons why this representation has become so important. During the 1990s, gender roles underwent a profound change in America: the sharp line between *man* and *woman*, *masculine* and *feminine* was blurred or even erased. For many people, this abandonment of ancient stereotypes was liberating; for others, profoundly threatening. In many ways the electoral victory (if such it was) of George W. Bush and his conservative allies can be read as a (razor thin, but real) referendum against gender indeterminacy.

On the heels of this referendum came 9/11. Anxious times create nostalgia for the traditional and familiar. War has always been seen as men's work; during wartime (conventional or otherwise) gender roles and expectations are polarized.[2] Men make war. Men know how to make war. Men are the ones we trust to run the war. Only someone perceived as a macho male can be trusted to lead in wartime.

In many ways, George W. Bush is an odd choice as a talismanic or symbolic war-man. Although he is actually tall, he appears small, even childlike; his voice is a high-pitched petulant whine. Yet he has learned to project himself in many ways as a stereotypical male, and therefore a trustworthy leader: trustworthy both because he acts like a man, and because he has thereby redrawn the gender line in the sand erased by his predecessor.

For instance, he uses language in traditionally, and stereotypically, masculine ways. Men are often the ones who venture out into uncharted turf, linguistically as well as otherwise. They create and use the latest slang; they are not overly concerned with the niceties of grammar; they use words that are not heard in polite society.

With this in mind, a puzzling fact about the President's linguistic behavior, and Americans' response to it, makes sense. It has often been pointed out derisively that Bush's command of English is none too firm. He mispronounces words and uses the wrong words. His syntax degenerates into anacoluthon. His tone is often off in a vague but noticeable sort of way.

One is tempted to cite as an example of his mispronunciations his invariable pronunciation of "nuclear" as "nucular", except that this is so frequent everywhere as to be classifiable as a permissible variant pronunciation.

---

[2] Rosie the Riveter, the emblem of American women who went into the factories to work during World War II, is an obvious counterexample to this statement. But Rosie was created out of necessity: the factories needed to be productive, but the men who had worked in them were off to war. After the war, women were herded back to their homes and encouraged to return to conventional femininity.

The tone problem was noted soon after 9/11, when he used the term "crusade" to describe America's response to the act of terrorism, even as he and his administration were seeking to conciliate all the "good Arabs" in the world. Some felt his vow to "hunt 'em down and smoke 'em out", referring to the perpetrators, was lacking in *gravitas* especially considering the seriousness of events. More recently, questioned about his use of questionable intelligence in his 2003 State of the Union address, the President countered that "the intelligence I get is darn good intelligence". Again recently, in response to questions about counterinsurgency in Iraq, he bragged, "Bring 'em on."

To some commentators these seem inappropriate in affect and questionable as self-presentation, especially by the President of the last remaining superpower in times demanding high seriousness. But the interpretation is not quite so clear. Once upon a time, to be sure, the president of the United States was expected to speak, in his official capacity, with *gravitas*: to eschew colloquialism, pronounce words precisely and correctly, and draw from the formal literary vocabulary of English. His sentence structure was expected to pass muster, both in terms of grammaticality and complexity. (One need only think of FDR's "date that will live in infamy" as an exemplar of what used to be the rule.) But for the last twenty-odd years, *gravitas* has been seeping out of Presidential discourse, as the unmarked American style of speech and writing has become more and more colloquial. Ronald Reagan was applauded for his easy use of one-line colloquialisms from the movies: "Go ahead — make my day"; "Honey, I forgot to duck." Of course, Reagan was a former movie actor, so movie-talk was his native tongue. Likewise, Bush is a Texan, and Texans are supposed to be casual in speech and manner, macho men who venerate deeds, not words — unlike their counterparts in the sissified east. Real men drop their *g*'s; real men say "*ain't*".

Real men in contemporary culture don't worry about the niceties of correct expression: they're doers, not talkers. So although Bush's solecisms have provoked criticism among the intellectual elite, that is in all probability an asset in the eyes of the public at large. I am not suggesting that his cowboyisms, gangsterisms, and tough-guyisms are scripted for the President's use (although that is not out of the question). But I do think that they are kept in Bush's rhetorical bag for a reason. The people who are disturbed by the decline in presidential gravitas are not those whose opinion matters to this administration. In talking that way, the President implicitly reminds his hearers that he is a *real man*, someone you can trust in times that call for real men.

In the same informal category is the president's incessant use of nicknames, both for his inner circle ("Rummy", and "Condi"), for other Beltway types ("The Big O", reportedly, for Senator Olympia Snowe, R-Me.), and even for foreign leaders (Putin is "Pooty", for instance). To the more conventional, these nicknames seem crassly childish. But they are almost parodically masculine, going along with a slap on the shoulder and a genial insult ("you old S.O.B." is almost automatically expected to follow).

A related function of colloquialism and slang (because they are antithetical to the *gravitas* expected in serious times) is to suggest nonseriousness, nothing to worry about. The use of colloquialism suggests: "things are really OK, don't worry" — and if you do, you're a worry-wart, an unmanly Chicken Little who can't be taken seriously. Donald Rumsfeld's patented breeziness even when discussing matters of life and death, war and peace, has the same effect. Both Bush and Rumsfeld (W and Rummy) often adopt hyper-casual posture at press conferences and other somewhat formal speech events: the President bounces on the balls of his feet, and the Secretary of Defense leans an arm casually against the podium. Their breeziness makes a serious questioner look geeky and insecure by contrast, discouraging others.

Inarticulateness, real or feigned, serves other persuasive functions in current American rhetorical practice. Over the past half century or so, we have become a society in which the informal is the unmarked. Where previously we used title-last name address with people unless and until we got to know them well, by the 1970s it had become customary in many parts of the U.S. to move immediately to first naming. During the same period the normal style of public address grew much more informal, incorporating colloquialisms and jokes. As a result we increasingly see Bush style not as childish or inappropriate, but as "normal" — what we expect of our leaders.

The spontaneous feel of colloquial talk has one final advantage for the illegitimate persuader. Perhaps because of the inescapability of the smooth and sculpted message of the advertiser, we have become suspicious of language that seems prefabricated, glib, or even reasonably articulate, preferring the appearance of spontaneity, which we equate with straight from the shoulder honesty and truthfulness: if you're making it up as you go along, you can't be lying...right? If your utterance looks like the way you talk all the time, it can't be carefully constructed for a devious purpose...can it?

Verbal language is not the only, or indeed the most effective, channel of communication. Clothing, gesture, and physical appearance often create *ethos* more credibly than language, because they appear not to be deliberate or under conscious control. So the President's May, 2003 landing a plane on the deck of an aircraft carrier, and appearing for the photo op shortly thereafter in full military uniform (the first U.S. president ever to wear it) functioned as a powerful, and multiple, signifier of masculinity. Everything about it said: this is a manly man! He is the macho male that he appears to be.

Pathos: We are all good Americans (and they are not)

Once hearers are induced to like and trust a speaker, the next level of persuasion comes into play. The hearers' emotions are mobilized more readily because they are associated with someone who has already been proven trustworthy: your emotions are safe with him. Those emotions are of two types: individual (fears about one's own acceptability to the larger group, for example); or shared by the audience as a whole. The Bush administration's rhetoric often addresses both at once by implicit and explicit suggestions that disagreement equals disloyalty, and in some forms is tantamount to treason.

It is true that in wartime a higher degree of societal cohesiveness than usual is demanded. The enemy is necessarily demonized. They become *them*, the antithesis of *us*: the embodiment of evil, the not-quite-human (and therefore, whose annihilation is more readily countenanced). In wartime, solidarity is of the essence: any indication that *we* are not entirely cohesive is assumed to give aid and comfort to *them*. These are not unreasonable assumptions and rhetorical postures in dangerous times, and we all recognize that, in such times, it makes sense for everyone to guard against excessive compassion. But these reasonable stances can be used to justify illegitimate arguments and the quashing of rational dissent. Arguably the refusal to question government actions and decisions should be classified as disloyal, since it can lead us into errors that — all the more in dangerous times — can result in disaster that a thoughtful weighing of all existing options might have precluded.

American politicians have sometimes demanded loyalty tests to separate the "good" *us* from the "bad" *them*; but just as often American rhetoric is inclusive: Americans are all products of the melting pot. The fact that America is a country fused from many disparate elements has, most of the time, made it essential for public speakers to emphasize our similarities and common interests and goals. This administration is extraordinary for expending so much effort on divisiveness.

From right after 9/11, the President and his allies drew lines in the sand: the world had become an Armageddonlike battlefield between good and evil, right and wrong; every country must be either with us or against us. There was no possibility of nuance, no middle ground. The "enemy" was made into "varmints" that we would "hunt down and smoke out".

In November, 2001, the American Council of Trustees and Alumni (a group closely linked to Lynne Cheney, the Vice President's wife) put out a pamphlet entitled "Defending Civilization: How Our Universities Are Failing America and What Can Be Done About It". The title itself is apocalyptic, but the scariest thing about the nearly 40 page diatribe is in its assumptions. It examines many public utterances, oral and written, spontaneous and planned, by academics at many of the nation's most prestigious universities, about the events of 9/11, their interpretation, and the appropriate response to them. Those quoted are cited anonymously or semi-anonymously (e.g., "Professor of Hawaiian Studies, University of Hawaii"), with the anonymity being used purportedly to save them from embarrassment or retaliation, but at the same time suggesting that they *deserve* retribution: anonymous sources are often the authors of poison-pen writings and other scurrilous and irresponsible communications. (The authors of the pamphlet might, of course, have spared its subjects even more embarrassment and retaliation by not writing it at all.)

The ACTA response may appear to be harmless overenthusiasm in a moment of angst. But as a statement by a group with close ties to the administration in power, the pamphlet may inspire reasonable dismay. Problematic in a piece of writing allegedly intended to preserve our freedoms is the threat (all but explicit) of retaliation for verbal, constitutionally protected dissent. Even worse is the attempt to discourage the exploration of alternative perspectives and with them alternative solutions or mitigations. And then there is the overkill factor: politicians and their cronies are reading academic discourse as if it were electoral rhetoric. Academics use language in special ways and need to be understood as doing so.

Academics are by proclivity and training nuance-hounds. We nose out ambiguity like a pig hunting truffles. In this we differ from politicians, who tend to see the world as a place with simple answers to obvious problems. When academics worry over nuance and ambiguity we are only doing our jobs, trying to understand things in their full complexity, aiming at a complete answer but knowing it is seldom there for the taking: there are of necessity many truths, many answers.

Academics tend to like irony and other ways of achieving distance and expressing interpretive complexity. Irony is a protection from the emotions aroused by reality: we smile sardonically as we note the insolubility of a problem, rather than confronting it directly and giving in to despair.

So it is not surprising that, faced with an event that — to us as to everyone else — was as inexplicable as it was horrific, many academics saw it not as simple and explicable in terms of us/them or good/evil dichotomies, but as requiring for true understanding both ironic distance and nuanced explication. Some scholars noted correctly that U.S. interests were not identical to the interests of every other nation or culture in the world, and that, as the world's only superpower, we were treading on toes with scant appreciation of the rage we were creating. The U.S. was neither wholly good nor wholly blameless. Some, ironically or otherwise, saw the events of 9/11 from a Freudian perspective: those tall towers sheared off by those huge planes: who was emasculating whom? Perhaps Freudian perspectives on events like 9/11 are out of place, even a bit silly. But treasonous? You have to have remarkably thin skin to see it that way. Likewise, virtuously unambiguous responses ("We're right and they're wrong. It's as simple as that," Rudolph Giuliani, cited on p. 11) are juxtaposed against evil academic "moral equivocation" (p. 1): "What happened on September 11 was terrorism, but what happened during the Gulf War was also terrorism (p. 3)."

The problems created by demanding dichotomous good-versus-evil explanations for complex events are many. To cite a few:

- the interpretation is a poor fit with reality, and encourages misperceptions.
- it is an oversimplification, leading to simplistic and unsuccessful "solutions".
- exported to the rest of the world, these statements encourage a view of Americans as simple-minded and childlike, making others less likely to trust the one remaining superpower in the future.
- domestically these statements polarize at a time when cohesion and cooperation are essential, and make necessary compromise impossible.
- these statements alienate the many elsewhere in the world who take a more nuanced position (e.g. the "good Arabs" often cited in administration rhetoric).

Terrorism and war have not been the only excuses for us-versus-them argumentation. They have encouraged it and made it difficult to oppose, but the Bush administration was using it well before 9/11 for a different purpose: re-establishing the old stereotypical boundaries between the unmarked *us*, who need not explain ourselves and who "normally" receive rights and privileges) and the marked *them*, who must account for themselves but are not allowed the language to do so.

The Clinton administration, with the First Couple as exemplars, did a great deal to erase gender stereotypes. By mixing and crossing gender boundaries, the Clintons exposed themselves to a remarkable amount of personal hatred and vituperation (culminating in the impeachment).[3] The Bushes have gone to great lengths to undo the damage, with the President acting the part of the macho man and Laura, his wife, cast as the demure, self-abnegating, lady. One might even argue that the need to re-draw the gender lines was one (unacknowledged) reason for the war: since war more than any other human activity, separates the boys from the girls and enhances male prestige and authority, a war was needed to restore sexual order and hegemony.

Right after 9/11, three women in the Bush administration made a joint statement (as women) deploring the Taliban's oppression of women and explaining the purpose of our engagement in the war in Afghanistan as the liberation of Afghan women. That might seem a counterexample to my claims above: the Bush administration speaking with a feminine, and even feminist, voice. But there have been numerous reports since then that Afghan women are again being subjected to oppression: denied education, forced to resign from government jobs, made to wear the burkha — as well as reports that, in the increasingly fundamentalist atmosphere in Iraq, women are more and more subject to oppression. Yet I have not heard a single voice from the administration deploring these tendencies, much less seen any action designed to prevent them.

The administration's hypermasculine swagger might be viewed as harmless play-acting, but it is closely linked to decisions that

---

[3] See for discussion of these points my book *The Language War*. University of California Press (2000).

reinforce strict gender lines and male power over women. Think for example of the effective prohibition on stem cell research (on the grounds that aborted fetuses might be used in the research and thus it might provide encouragement of abortion). Or think of Republican attempts in Congress to pass laws giving fetuses the status of full-fledged victims when pregnant women are murdered, offering a sympathetic opening wedge to beliefs equating fetuses with "human beings" and, therefore, abortion with murder.

Consider the hysterical conservative response to the Supreme Court decision overturning sodomy laws. Senator Rick Santorum (R-PA) exclaimed that now there could no longer be laws to punish incest, bestiality, and other forms of sexual deviation. In response to the controversy thus engendered, the President referred to Santorum as "an inclusive man". Either the adjective was totally meaningless and its use totally cynical, or the message meant to be conveyed was that Santorum was in fact "inclusive", as long as those who were included were exclusively heterosexuals.

Just as after 9/11 every country had to declare itself "with us or against us" (good or evil), in the period surrounding the Iraq war, the same demand was made. A nation that refused to be part of the "coalition of the willing" (a remarkably tin-eared phrase) was vilified. That was the fate of France: France and the French were subjected to the kinds of rhetoric usually reserved for enemy nations with whom we are at war. Nasty old stereotypes about the French (involving cowardice and uncleanliness) resurfaced; just as we made euphemistic substitutions for German words in World War I ("liberty cabbage" for "sauerkraut", "Salisbury steak" for hamburger, and "hot dog" for frankfurter), we substituted "freedom" for "French": "freedom fries" were served in the Congressional restaurant.

So the message was sent out in many ways: dissent is disloyalty. But how should we define "patriotism" and "treason"? Who has the right to make the definitions, and on what basis can they properly be made? If someone (say, Lynne Cheney) can decide unilaterally that a particular form of expression is treasonable, and can therefore attack someone who has made such a statement as a traitor, that is a dangerously circular form of reasoning. It almost feels as if, while we were preoccupied by 9/11 and its aftermath, the loyal opposition lost an undeclared civil war without anyone noticing, thereby losing as well its right to make interpretations and determine the meanings of words and events.

In a simple definition, *patriotism* is supporting your country; *treason* is undermining it. But who decides what "support" and "undermining" mean? In this war-saturated society, these words have lost any reliable semantic reference, and now have only a pragmatic function as weapons to bludgeon the other side into silence and acquiescence.

The President has an unusual verbal habit which at first glance would seem to be a counterexample to the hypermacho image I attributed to him above. Stereotypically, adjectives are the province of the woman, as verbs are male. Writers are advised to eschew adjectives as weak, subjective, and emotional — stereotypically feminine. Yet the President rather often resorts to strings of adjectives to make his points. Even more striking, these tend to be the very adjectives that are thought the most "womanly" because the most empty: adjectives without clear referential meaning, used only to signal a speaker's positive or negative feelings toward her (or his) subject.[4]

Yet the President not infrequently — particularly in off-the-cuff performances — resorts to just such quintessentially "feminine" expressions. There are two examples in his news conference of May 30, 2003. The first occurs just after he has "take[n] responsibility" for his State of the Union assertion that Iraq was seeking to buy plutonium from Africa [see below for more discussion]. He says, "And I analyzed a thorough body of intelligence, *good, solid, sound* intelligence, that led me to the conclusion that it was necessary to remove Saddam Hussein from power." [Italics mine.]

---

[4] See for discussion Otto Jespersen, *Language: Its Nature, Development and Origin,* especially Chapter XIII: "The Woman," (pp. 237–254). London: Allen & Unwin (1922); and Robin Lakoff, *Language and Woman's Place.* New York: Harper & Row (1975).

Later, in response to suggestions that his national security adviser, Condoleezza Rice, bore some responsibility for the fiasco, he said, "Dr. Rice is an *honest, fabulous* person." [Italics mine.]

In neither case do the adjectives add anything to the meaning of the utterance, or increase the hearer's knowledge. Rather, in both cases, they seem merely to be used to underscore the speaker's certainty and authority — a ploy most commonly used by those whose authority is in question (like women, but unlike the president of the United States) — and to convey warmth and personal involvement. "Fabulous", in the second quotation, is even more remarkable in a serious, non-conversational context. It is the sort of word affected by teenagers or stereotypical women, meaning little more than a squeak of delight. But there may be a reason for these apparent weaknesses: macho swagger can be off-putting because of its denial of warm emotion. By the insertion of these words from a very different vocabulary, the President can induce warm, fuzzy feelings of identification in his hearers — the instantiation of Aristotelian *pathos*.

Logos: The appeal to logic: The appearance of intellectual persuasion

The third component of successful persuasion is intellectual: the speaker should be believed because his arguments make logical sense. The road to persuasion is paved with personal and emotional exhortations, but a skillful speaker still needs to arouse intellectual support for his arguments, so that — thinking it over later — hearers won't feel that they've been spoken down to or manipulated, but rather that they have been guided to an inevitable conclusion. If hearers have been emotionally won over by the first two tactics, they are apt to be more than willing to give the speaker the benefit of the doubt about questions of logic.

Logos in turn reinforces *ethos* and *pathos* because intellect is widely (if stereotypically) considered to be a male capacity, while feelings are female. So if *we* can reason together intellectually, that proves all the more that *we* are men, worthy and able to make war together.

Intellectual suasion also reinforces *pathos,* the appearance of consensus: we are reasoning *together,* by giving you my reasons I am making you privy to my thoughts. We must work together, in order to showcase *our* rationality against the irrational *them* (either the actual enemy, or those — womanly types — against the war).

Intellectual arguments for war often rely on misleading under-pinnings — arguments that look rigorous but are based on or contain hidden untruths or questionable beliefs. Phrases with apparent meaning, reiterated as catchwords, under examination may prove irrelevant, meaningless, or misleading. An argument may obscure the existence of a respectable and responsible middle ground.

There has been much discussion of the President's sixteen word comment in his 2003 State of the Union message that "the British government has learned that Saddam Hussein recently sought significant quantities of uranium from Africa". (One recent commentator noted a short pause before "from Africa", as if to suggest that there was something dark or strange about "Africa".) This statement has been cited as getting our government, and our President, off the hook: "the British" are responsible for the claim; the President is merely reporting it. But the wording does not permit this benign interpretation. "Learn" is what linguists call a "factive" verb: it presupposes the truth of its complement (the clause that follows it).[5] Compare a non-factive use: "The British government has said that ...." In selecting the verb "learn", the speechwriter meant for hearers to draw the inference that what followed was, in fact, true: Saddam Hussein did in truth seek uranium from Africa. The fact that the claim was cloaked in the presupposition of factivity, rather than being expressed as an assertion, does not weaken the persuasive power of the statement, but rather strengthens it. Presuppositions (like factivity), being embedded, are hard to question or controvert.

---

[5] The concept of factivity was introduced into linguistics in a paper by Paul and Carol Kiparsky, "Fact," which appeared in D. Steinberg and L. Jakobovits (eds.), *Semantics: an Interdisciplinary Reader in Philosophy, Linguistics, and Psychology.* Cambridge: Cambridge University Press (1971), 345–69.

The problem of the attribution of responsibility for the "sixteen words" is deeper than the simple overuse of adjectives or misuse of factive verbs. War is serious business: people get killed, infrastructure is destroyed, anger and resentment are created that may persist for generations to come. So it behooves a national leader who is urging war to be very sure his arguments rest on a basis of correct and reliable information. Moreover, he must take full responsibility for what he says and the reasoning behind it. The President of the United States, even more than most leaders, functions as a role model for his people and perhaps even the rest of the world. If he is seen as dishonest or evasive under the most serious circumstances, what lessons are the rest of us to derive? Even if we believe (as some members of his administration may) that even if the arguments are dubious, the end justifies the means, moral dishonesty vitiates any virtue that might arise out of the decision.

So the President's "sixteen words" deserve scrutiny. From one perspective, his language was merely ludicrous. From another, it is deeply disturbing.

Once it becomes clear that the claim in the State of the Union address was unfounded, the President had only one honorable option: to say immediately that making the statement was his deliberate choice, and he took full responsibility for it. Instead, for several weeks that responsibility floated in limbo, with one member of the administration after another taking the fall: first CIA head George Tenet, then deputy national security adviser and speechwriter Stephen J. Hadley, and finally Condoleezza Rice. But this serial blame-taking, aside from its farcical aspects, served only to absolve everyone from blame. Finally, in his press conference, the President said, "I take personal responsibility for everything I say, of course." That statement is a marvel of duplicity: seeming to do the manly thing, but finally achieving nothing because of its vagueness and generality, made even emptier by what came next: "I also take responsibility for making decisions on war and peace". The whole sounds like hyperbolic self-inflation: "See how important I am", rather than sober reflection on what the President had meant by the sixteen words, and to what extent he still stood by them. Taking responsibility for everything is taking responsibility for nothing.

The President's word-games do not stop here. Words and phrases that have been given specific meanings in earlier contexts have been taken from those contexts, recontextualized and given new meanings, without explicit warnings of the change. So the words have a comfortable, familiar ring, but they turn out to mean something else entirely. But the hearer identifies the words with their former connotations and comes away with emotions that may not be justified.

Two such phrases, used with specific reference in the course of the twentieth century, "the free world", and "revisionist history", have turned up in recent Presidential rhetoric. The first, from the end of World War II to the fall of the Soviet Union, was always used to contrast the non-Communist nations of the world to those behind the Iron Curtain. The second, which came into use more recently, was generally used of putative historians who denied the reality of the Holocaust. The first had strongly positive connotations, the second strongly negative.

In two speeches delivered in mid-June 2003, the President made use of both of these phrases. In Elizabeth, New Jersey, the President first brought the two phrases together: "There are some who would like to rewrite history — revisionist historians is what I like to call them. Saddam Hussein was a threat to America and the Free World in 1991, in 1998, [and] in 2003. He continually ignored the demands of the Free World, so the United States and friends and allies acted." The next day at Northern Virginia Community College, he said, "I know there's a lot of revisionist history now going on, but one thing is certain. He [Saddam Hussein] is no longer a threat to the Free World, and the people of Iraq are free."

Remarkable here are both the use of these phrases individually and their juxtaposition twice in two days. More remarkable still is that there is no mention that they are being used in new meanings. What is now the "Free World"? The old anti-communist bloc? Not likely. The U.S. and the Coalition of the Willing? Every nation but the Axis of Evil? Every nation but Iraq under Saddam? Such elastic words are dangerous: they seem to make sense and generate appropriate feelings, but torn from their original context, they may not mean what we think.

And who are these "revisionist historians"? There is a progression of the term from one day to the next. In his first (Elizabeth, New Jersey) speech, the President seems to be suggesting that he is using the words in a novel way: "…is what I like to call them". But he never provides an explicit new definition, nor any justification for attaching to generally benign and constitutionally permissible speech a term heretofore associated only with the most odious and unjustifiable kind of speech. By the next day, "revisionist history" is no longer introduced as a new term, but treated as familiar (presupposed) usage, beyond question or reproach. Who are these "revisionist historians? The President's "revisionist historians" are those who questioned America's going to war. These critics are now equated with the dubious scholars who deny that the Nazi Holocaust took place, making it difficult to see them in a respectable light.

The President and his men play other semantic games, often in ways that are not apparent to hearers or readers. In an extraordinary interview published in *Vanity Fair* (June 2003), Deputy Secretary of State Paul Wolfowitz offers a reason why the administration made a strong assertion that Iraq possessed weapons of mass destruction when in fact none were known to exist. The reason, he said, was that that was the only argument for war that everyone in the group could agree on. The implication, I think, is that the administration *could* have offered any of several other reasons (and therefore, that any reasons proffered to the public at large were simply cosmetic and were thrown out only to camouflage the real intentions of the administration, whatever those may have been). The reason selected, then, was selected only for reasons of expediency, not because it was true or even believed to be true. This is not precisely a lie, but it is not exactly truthful either.

J. L. Austin, the philosopher of language, considered words to be "speech acts": since their use altered reality, words were actions on a par with physical conduct.[6] But Austin only meant this equation of word and action to apply to performative expressions — verbs of linguistic communication used in the first person singular present indicative active: "I nominate", "I promise", and "I ask" — actions that can be performed purely by words and unilaterally by the speaker alone. Austin a bit sneakily extended the concept of performativity to all utterances, but only *qua* utterances: he never claimed that, by making an assertion that *p* is true, *p* is thereby made true. But Bush and his cohorts seem eager to extend the Austinian notion of performativity, at least for themselves, so that any claim they choose to make is *ipso facto* a reality, unquestionable and unchangeable.

A striking instance occurred in April, 2003, when the President declared the hostilities in Iraq to be at an end: that is, he declared the surrender of Iraq. Now, "surrender" is a possible performative verb, but only when its speaker is the one who is surrendering. The surrenderee cannot "surrender" the other side. Yet this is precisely what the President's statement was intended to do. Of course the chief executive of the world's only remaining superpower is a powerful man, but even a very powerful man cannot surrender someone else, or use a speech act to create another's surrender. But because he is powerful, and because we do have forms of language that can be used performatively in this way, many hearers undoubtedly heard Bush's declaration as literally ending the war, even though our original objective, the capture of Saddam Hussein, had not taken place.

Similarly the President declared the war in Afghanistan won although its original objective, the capture of Osama bin Laden "dead or alive" had not occurred. It is disturbing that the President of the United States, or the people who provide him with words, are unable to differentiate between reality and fantasy — or think that hearers cannot do so. Words are powerful, but they do not automatically convert wishes to actuality.

---

[6] J. L. Austin, *How to Do Things with Words.* Oxford: Clarendon Press (1962).

These examples of performative overuse are not precisely lies. Lies are assertive statements made infelicitously: when a speaker utters something he or she believes not to be true, with the intention of getting an addressee to believe it to the latter's disadvantage (or the speaker's advantage). But rather than false assertions, the President's utterances of this type are examples of other speech acts infelicitously used, for which we have no single-word description parallel to "lie". Normally infelicitous pragmatics marks a speaker as communicatively maladroit and therefore undeserving of credence. But when someone with preexisting power and authority misuses language in this way, the effect is often to confuse and demoralize hearers: it makes no sense for an authoritative person to make no sense. So they give up and go along, because it's the easiest thing to do.

Conclusions

In powerful circles, the close analysis of language is viewed as an empty academic exercise. Language, our proverbs and legends tell us, is "mere words." In this discussion I have tried to show that this is not the case. Words can be used to create, alter, and distort reality, and thereby to make us complicit in decisions we might otherwise reject.

In a democracy in which our vote depends, or should depend, on our grasp of the persuasive strategies of each side, it is the job of all citizens to become sophisticated linguistic analysts — savvy shoppers in the marketplace of ideas. We must develop protections against the blandishments of nice-guyism, appeals to shared identity, and seeming logic: we must be able to tell legitimate persuasion from what is questionable. Government agencies bring legal actions against corporations that engage in blatantly false rhetoric, or advertising, and misrepresent their wares; but there is no such protection for us consumers of political rhetoric.

Much of the time even the most arrant deceptiveness is essentially harmless: our political parties are no more different than

Tweedledum and Tweedledee, so being manipulated into voting for the wrong Tweedle is, in some eyes, of no matter. But in times of crisis, when human life and civil liberties are endangered and voters' decisions make a real difference, that comfortable cynicism fails. If we are being persuaded to make decisions this momentous on the basis of questionable language, we are abdicating our responsibilities if we let ourselves be persuaded by these illegitimate means. If we listen and analyze carefully, and are certain that we are being persuaded to a proper course of action, then we have done our job — but we have to do the hard work first. It is incumbent on all of us to look closely at the language in which our choices are wrapped; and the more attractive and seductive the arguments sound, the more on guard we should be.

Multilateralism and American Power

Roland Paris

Assistant Professor of Political Science and International Affairs at the University of Colorado at Boulder, he has won several awards for his teaching and writing, and is author of At War's End: Building Peace After Civil Conflict (New York: Cambridge University Press, forthcoming). This chapter was written in March 2003, just before the U.S. launched Operation Iraqi Freedom.

Since coming into office, the Bush Administration has undone international treaties, bypassed and disparaged multilateral institutions such as the UN and NATO, and insulted America's closest allies. The president and his senior advisors seem to view international organizations and multilateralism as impediments to the pursuit of American interests. That attitude, and the feelings of alienation and resentment it has elicited abroad, will make the reconstruction of postwar Iraq much more difficult.

President Bush has indicated that he intends Iraq to become a stable democracy after the war, initially under the tutelage of foreign occupiers. He argues that the creation of a democratic Iraqi government would foster the spread of democracy in the Middle East, and that the United States will remain in Iraq "as long as necessary" to ensure that Iraqis secure their right to "freedom and democracy".

Turning Iraq into a functioning democracy will be hard enough, even with the full support of the international community.

Most of the 150 tribes and 2,000 clans that comprise the society have been violently repressed for decades, and would happily exact revenge if given the opportunity. The country has no tradition of pluralist politics and peaceful compromise that is essential for democracy to function. Democratic nation-building will almost certainly require a lengthy transitional period of semi-authoritarian government to keep the country from collapsing into anarchy.

The U.S. government hasn't undertaken such a project since it occupied and remade Germany and Japan after World War II. Most of the expertise in this field now resides in international organizations, including the UN and the European Union, which have conducted "post-conflict peacebuilding" projects in roughly a dozen states over the past decade.

Yet these are precisely the institutions that the United States has estranged in recent months. The Administration's artless and heavy-handed diplomacy left Germany and France seething, Russia and China anxious about American unilateralism, and the United Nations in demoralized disarray. Now, the U.S. is about to turn to these same countries and institutions to seek their assistance in reconstructing Iraq. The president will probably gain some support from the UN, but convincing the European Union and other major states to participate in the American occupation of Iraq will be an uphill diplomatic battle.

It is not just the international community's expertise and money that the U.S. needs. More importantly, American occupiers will require the aura of international legitimacy that international institutions and multilateral efforts provide. The new American viceroy of Iraq may enjoy an initial period of popularity in the country as Iraqis celebrate the end of Saddam's regime, but he will soon begin to make decisions that are perceived to favor certain domestic factions, tribes or clans at the expense of others. He will in effect become the meanest, baddest clan leader of them all, no matter how much he claims to stand above the fray of Iraq's internal politics.

Nor will anyone be fooled by the creation of an indigenous Advisory Council to govern Iraq. Americans will remain the king-makers behind any new regime. In a society that is used to clientalistic forms of power, the façade of "self-government" will be obvious to most.

But are there any better options for rebuilding Iraq? The strategy touted by some Iraqi exiles — that of turning the country into a full-fledged democracy right away — is not a realistic alternative. If the peacebuilding missions of the 1990s taught anything, it was that overly rapid democratization can lead to chaos, as it most obviously did in Angola and Rwanda. In societies prone to conflict and lacking in experience with democracy, reliable institutional structures need to be built *before* the unleashing of electoral competition.

That means Iraq will need to be ruled by a semi-authoritarian government, at least for the first few years of its post-Saddam existence. The problem is that ordinary Iraqis may reject such arrangements as a form of foreign occupation. Once the fighting is over, the United States must therefore work immediately to counter perceptions that it is an imperialist power seeking to impose its rule on the Iraqi people, and the best way to do that is to reassure Iraqis that the "international community", rather than American occupiers, will oversee their transition to democracy.

First, however, the United States must win international support. And it can only do so if it treats multilateral institutions and its allies as partners in the management of global problems, not as underlings to be browbeaten and brought into line.

The Bush Administration seems increasingly aware of this problem. The president's recent speeches have been peppered with expressions of support for the United Nations as an institution. All signs point to his becoming a born-again multilateralist in the aftermath of the war.

But whether or not Bush succeeds in enlisting international help for reconstructing Iraq, there is a more fundamental problem to be fixed: The Administration talks about promoting U.S. national interests, yet it has failed to recognize that perceptions of legitimacy are themselves a form of real power in international politics — and that, in today's world, international institutions and the practices of multilateralism are the principal repositories of legitimacy.

Leadership based in legitimacy is ultimately more effective and less costly than leadership based on coercion. Powerful states that ignore this fact tend to provoke resistance and resentment. That is the paradox, and the danger, of Bush's fair-weather multilateralism.

The Burden of Nation-Building in Postwar Iraq[1]

Roland Paris

Building a stable democracy in postwar Iraq will require greater sacrifices than most Americans realize. President Bush says that the U.S. will remain in Iraq "as long as necessary" to ensure that Iraqis secure their right to "freedom and democracy." He invokes the rebuilding of Germany and Japan after World War II, noting that America "has made and kept this kind of commitment before."

What he does not say is that the Allies maintained military governments in Germany and Japan for ten and seven years respectively, and that thousands of American lawyers, engineers and economists devoted years to the reconstruction of these countries. Nor does he point out that Germany and Japan were largely homogeneous nation-states, whereas Iraq is deeply divided along ethnic and religious lines.

Does America have the determination and stamina to oversee such a transition in Iraq? The recent record of nation building in Afghanistan raises doubt.

When the U.S. launched its campaign against the Taliban and Al-Qaeda, senior American officials talked about "liberating" Afghanistan and creating a "representative government" that would ensure the country's "peace and stability." But there has been little

---

[1] This chapter was written in April 2003 as American forces were fighting their way toward Baghdad.

progress towards these goals. The writ of the new Hamid Karzai government does not extend much beyond the suburbs of Kabul; despotic warlords remain in control of nearly the entire country, including local police and security forces; and some observers report that local conditions are reverting to what they were during the period of Taliban rule. Even the American military commander in the country, Lt. Gen. Dan McNeill, says he is "frustrated" that the U.S. and its allies have "not made a more bold step" to rebuild Afghanistan.

In fact, the Bush administration seems to have lost interest in rebuilding Afghanistan. The draft foreign aid budget submitted to Congress [in February 2003] contained not one penny for reconstruction efforts in the country, leaving it to Congress to introduce a $300 million aid package. The administration has consistently rejected proposals to deploy the multi-national security force beyond the city limits of Kabul, which is the only part of the country it currently patrols, and Secretary of Defense Donald Rumsfeld insists that the roughly 8,500 American forces in Afghanistan will not perform peacekeeping functions or shift their attention away from hunting down pockets of terrorists. Meanwhile, U.S.-supported efforts to train a new national army have been painfully slow: only 1,700 troops had graduated from the program as of March [2003].

Rather than providing a model for postwar Iraq, developments in Afghanistan suggest how quickly the U.S. government can lose interest in a nation building project. Appearing before a Senate committee in February, Hamid Karzai made a poignant plea: "Don't forget us if Iraq happens." But lofty pledges to democratize and reconstruct Afghanistan are not being fulfilled.

If a similarly half-baked approach to nation building is pursued in postwar Iraq, the result could be disastrous. Security must be established and preserved throughout the country, including in the Kurdish northern areas and Shiite southern region. The emergence of a self-declared Kurdish political entity would pose an immediate threat to Turkey and Iran — and the latter can be expected to defend Shiite interests in the south, filling any power vacuum that might emerge. All of the surrounding countries, including Saudi Arabia, Jordan and Syria, fear the potentially destabilizing effects of chaos for their own security. Given the importance of the region to the global economy and the nervousness of Iraq's neighbors, any new government in Baghdad must have control over the entire country, not just the area around the capital.

Beyond the immediate need for security, what would it take for the United States to rebuild Iraq as a stable democracy? Administration officials have already hinted at their plan to organize a constituent assembly of Iraqis, which would draft a new democratic constitution and then hold elections. This may be complex and difficult, not least because the country's numerous factions will have to agree on the contents of a constitution. But similar processes have worked successfully in a number of war-torn states, most recently in East Timor.

Yet these measures are only a beginning. Without institutional structures to uphold the new democratic system, Iraq could quickly slip into civil conflict, or revert to authoritarian rule. Most importantly, the country needs an effective and politically neutral security apparatus. That means purging elements of the army and police that are closely associated with the existing regime, and training an entirely new cadre of officers to be loyal to the constitution, not to a particular faction or clan. Foreign forces cannot leave Iraq until this retraining has been largely accomplished.

Second, the survival of democracy in Iraq requires an independent and professional judiciary to defend the constitution against potential abuses by the regime itself. In Cambodia and Liberia, two countries that rewrote constitutions and held UN-supervised elections in the 1990s, democratically elected leaders immediately began to subvert their constitutions in order to retain power. Similarly, elected officials in Iraq, a country with no tradition of pluralistic politics, might decide that they really don't want to be voted out of office after all. If the U.S. wants democracy in Iraq to endure, it cannot afford to abandon the country before progress toward an independent judiciary is well underway, just as the court systems of Germany and Japan were remade after World War II.

A constitution can be drafted and elections held within two to three years, but reforming security and judicial institutions could take close to a decade. Assuming little armed resistance to U.S. forces after the war (and this may be an optimistic assumption) at least 75,000 troops will be needed to maintain order in the country. The Congressional Budget Office estimates that sustaining a force of this size would cost $16.8 billion per year. That does not include the costs of reconstruction, payment of Iraqi bureaucrats, or humanitarian aid.

Only a fraction of these expenses could be defrayed by drawing on frozen Iraqi assets or oil revenues. The frozen assets amount to little more than $2 billion, and oil revenues are already dedicated to humanitarian measures. In any case, the big ticket expense is the maintenance of the U.S. military in Iraq, and it would be politically awkward to use Iraqi oil income to subsidize foreign forces.

Having the United Nations administer the democratic transition in Iraq — something the administration now opposes — would be cheaper for U.S. taxpayers and probably more effective in the long run. The European Union and the governments of Germany and France have already indicated that they would contribute financially to nation building only if the UN is given a "central role". Working through the UN would also confer international legitimacy on the transitional process and defuse domestic Iraqi opposition to foreign occupation.

Even with extensive UN involvement, however, most of the duties and costs of nation building will be borne by the United States. And if armed resistance continues in the postwar period, more troops will be needed, costs will rise, and Americans will die.

Is America ready for this commitment? At this point, it has little choice. The war must be finished and a new Iraqi regime built. Replacing Saddam Hussein with a pro-Western dictator would avoid the travails of democracy building, but it would almost certainly radicalize the Iraqi populace, given that the hope of freedom has already been dangled before them. Recall what happened in neighboring Iran: the Shah's regime, installed in a U.S.-backed coup in 1953, provoked a fanatical backlash which brought anti-American Islamists to power.

Even more dangerous than replacing Saddam Hussein with a new dictator is the prospect that the United States will cut and run as soon as the first elections are held but before the country's democratic transition is secured. Iraq would be left in an unstable limbo, lacking the institutions required for durable democracy, but also lacking the coercive powers by which dictatorships maintain order.

The prognosis is not encouraging. Unless the American public is prepared for what lies ahead, support for the continued deployment of U.S. personnel and resources in postwar Iraq will quickly wane, and the nation building project will likely fail.

Moral Courage and Civil Society: Lessons from Yugoslavia[1]

Svetlana Broz

A cardiologist by profession, Dr. Broz is the granddaughter of the well-known communist former Yugoslavia head of state Marshal Tito. In the 1990s, she volunteered her services as a physician in war-torn Bosnia and discovered that her patients were not only in need of medical care, but that they urgently had a story to tell, a story suppressed by nationalist politicians and the mainstream media. What Dr. Broz heard drove her to devote herself over the next several years to the collection of first hand testimonies from the war, which she compiled into a compelling book Good People in an Evil Time: Complicity and Resistance in the Bosnian War. *Her book is extremely popular in the Balkans and a third edition has recently been published (Other Press, U.S., forthcoming, 2003).*

The wars in what used to be Yugoslavia, between 1991 and 1999, opened a new chapter in the history of handling conflict situations with international intervention. The United States and NATO employed military force to stop the war in Bosnia and Herzegovina in the fall of 1995 and with the signing of the peace accords in Dayton, Ohio. The persecution and violence against Kosovar Albanians was stopped with the NATO intervention of 1999.

Once peace had been introduced to Bosnia and Herzegovina and Kosovo, the international community appointed high representatives to govern, and in so doing realized a form of international

---

[1] The English translator for this article is Ellen Elias Bursac.

protectorate. Since these are among the first experiences of this kind, it is important to take a look at the countries where all this happened. From today's perspective (eight years later) it is clear that many grave mistakes were made, which should not be repeated in Afghanistan and Iraq.

The richness of the former Yugoslavia lay precisely in the shared diversity of the more than forty ethnic groups that lived there. They made it an interesting place for us to live and for foreigners to visit. The differences in mentality of the different peoples in that Yugoslavia gave rise to witty jokes that everyone was able to laugh at. Its culture was a value shared by all who lived there, and the existing ethnic subcultures were perceived as a part of the popular landscape.

After World War II the people of Yugoslavia raised the country from the ashes with their joint enthusiasm and this was something they were proud of for a full 45 years. The period immediately after the war was a time when people lived together, not merely next door to one another. There was a mutual respect for national and religious customs and holidays that people often celebrated together. There were strong friendships across ethnic lines. Children were raised in the spirit of tolerance; often enough they had no notion of which ethnic group a friend belonged to.

Mixed marriages, which in many regions comprised more than one third of the total, confirm the extent to which the lives of people were intermingled. The genetic strains of the six different ethnic groups joined in me are hardly an isolated example in the lands of my ancestors.

It is difficult to understand how such a country could disintegrate, erupt in so much bloodshed, with 250,000 victims, and more than 250,000 people held in concentration camps and more than 3,000,000 people displaced.

The trial of Slobodan Milosevic before the International War Crimes Tribunal in The Hague will give us a precise picture of the causes of the war in the former Yugoslavia.

When the Dayton Peace Accords were signed, most of the population of Bosnia and Herzegovina had hopes that they would be able to return to their pre-war lives with the support of the international community.

The Dayton Accords did, indeed, bring a halt to the bloody war in Bosnia and Herzegovina. But those same people who started the war and conducted it were also the Dayton signatories. Nothing happens by chance: when we see today who is fighting to hold to the letter of the Dayton Accords it becomes clear that Dayton was cobbled together along lines dictated by the nationalist leaders; the Accords were confirmation of their conquests.

The state of Bosnia and Herzegovina was created but it has not been able to function properly for a full eight years for the simple reason that the Agreement left all the nationalist parties in power. Only a handful of politicians, whose names appeared in the public indictments of the Hague Tribunal, have been forced out of public life.

One cannot help but wonder what would have happened in Europe after World War II if the Allies had left Germany to be run by Hitler's cronies? What would the elections have been like during the first ten years after the war? In such a political and psychological climate one can hardly expect the process of de-Nazification to begin, a process essential in Serbia, Montenegro, Croatia, Kosovo, Macedonia and some parts of Bosnia and Herzegovina.

Such a process first requires facing the truth, with a full awareness of what it was that happened during those horrible wars. The millions of people living in Serbia, Montenegro and Croatia are not prepared, even today, to face what was done in the name of their nation. So many people in those communities turn their heads from the truth out of fear of the question they must ask themselves, "What did I do to stop this from happening?" and the question, even more wrenching, "Am I at least in part morally responsible by the fact that I voted these politicians into office?"

I spent ten years in the field recording hundreds of testimonies of people whose lives had been touched, even saved, during the war by someone of another ethnicity, by someone risking his or her life to cross ethnic lines and extend a hand to a person in danger, in the hope that a book with its emphasis on wartime goodness rather than evil would help people face the truth of what had happened, and give them the courage to build a civil society in the postwar years. As I proceeded with the project I realized how invested the warmongers were in promoting evil. My work on human goodness was profoundly threatening to their war project. Indeed, the first tapes I brought home from my first round of interviews were stolen before I had the chance to transcribe them, so I had to go back a second time to collect another ninety testimonies. Since the book *Good People in an Evil Time* appeared in print in 1999 I have presented it at hundreds of readings in Bosnia and Herzegovina, Serbia and Croatia, and I have often found myself faced, even recently, with a press blockade, when regime journalists refuse to report on the excitement of the crowds of people who attend the readings and their relief at hearing stories that give them hope for the future of these societies.

There is a cloud of collective guilt hanging over entire ethnic communities, because the people responsible for the atrocities have still not been arrested, eight years after the end of the war. There is irony in the fact that Karadžić and Mladić are still at large today, though they were indicted years ago by the Hague Tribunal for genocide and other crimes against humanity.

Imagine the frustration and rage of the hundreds of thousands of survivors of war crimes, and more than a million family members of those murdered in Bosnia and Herzegovina when they watch SFOR (Security Forces) soldiers — numbering 80,000 immediately postwar and 16,000 eight years later — stand by and do nothing to arrest the men responsible for the deaths of more than 250,000 innocent people!

Only when these criminals have been brought to justice will victims be able to breathe freely. This will also disperse that cloud of collective guilt hovering over whole communities, and only then will others be able to turn to victims of the war and say the long awaited words, "I know that what happened was terrible. And I know that it must never happen again."

Today maniacal notions of the viability of ethnically pure regions in the minds of criminals steeped in gore continue to provoke murders. When members of a minority ethnic group make the courageous decision to return to the home they were forced out of during the war, they face the threat that even their children may be murdered as members of the majority group do whatever they can to intimidate them into giving up on their plan to return.

The wartime political elites created a country rife with crime and corruption from top to bottom in the economy, judiciary, school system, health care and the highest political echelons.

Bosnia and Herzegovina has been attempting three transitions: the first, the building of institutions and a stable peace; the second, the transition of property ownership from socialist to private; and finally, the transition from dependence on the international community to self-reliance.

The transition in property ownership, known as privatization, has sadly meant such asset-stripping that it has resulted in the destruction of the entire economy, already hit hard by the war. While companies were still owned by the state, their managers first ran them down as much as they could so as to diminish their net worth. Then when the company came up for sale, its management could purchase it for less. This resulted in staggering unemployment figures and a new source of postwar poverty. Unemployment in Bosnia is at 40%, with 60% of the population living on US$0.25 a day, while the UN standards set US$4.00 as the poverty line. I often wonder what one should call a life that goes on at an income that is at one sixteenth of the poverty level? Such extreme forms of impoverishment give rise to all manner of crimes, from drug sales, over trafficking in human beings, to prostitution. The judiciary, which should be sanctioning such activities, is inefficient, unprofessional, politically dependent and corrupt. The sad consequence of this condition is an upsurge in illiteracy among children, who spend their time on the streets, begging or in prostitution in order to feed their unemployed, ailing or invalid parents, instead of attending school.

War profiteers who first became wealthy by wartime looting have now become prominent citizens and businessmen, while their victims, witness to the source of the wealth these men enjoy, are, more likely, beggars.

Retired people who (many of them) owned not only their own apartments but also vacation homes on the seaside or in the mountains while they were still working before the war, have been left today with nothing but a meager pension of scarcely US$2.00 per day, half of the amount considered poverty-level subsistence.

Insistence on the differences among the various ethnic groups in Bosnia and Herzegovina has now been emphasized to the point of absurdity. This has gone so far that it has intruded on the education system. Children are often divided in the elementary and secondary schools by the ethnic membership of their parents into separate classrooms, and there are schools where teachers, swayed by fascist ideas, have raised wire fences 5–6 feet high across the middle of the playground to prevent physical contact between the various groups of school children during recess. No one asks the thousands of parents, and pupils who are the children of mixed marriages, how they feel about this madness. One cannot help but ask why it has taken the international community eight years to address this fundamental problem, as they finally have by imposing a law on elementary and secondary education that bans all forms of segregation. This catastrophic situation speaks volumes about how all the structural elements of society have been undermined, with the erosion of moral and ethical norms. Hague indictees are frequently painted as heroes by their own ethnic communities. Some in the press even call them "living saints".

In Bosnia and Herzegovina alone, the sum of direct and indirect losses to society comes to nearly US$100 billion. A total of between 71 and 81 billion US dollars has come from the international community during the war and in the post-Dayton period. According to information from the American Governmental Accounting Office, the total American military and civilian expenditures for the period of 1992–2000 comes to US$12.5 billion. If we compare the expenditures that the international community has spent in Bosnia and Herzegovina on normalizing the life of the country, with the "results" as described above, it is clear that this policy has been horrifyingly inefficient.

The wars in the former Yugoslavia, particularly in Bosnia and Herzegovina, were the first serious crisis of the post-cold-war period.

The lack of adequate and timely policies throughout this period has shed light on a far more serious problem: the inability of international participants to recognize the nature of this new kind of crisis, its causes and consequences. This confirms that the existing system of international security and the key international organizations that have developed in the post-colonial, bipolar world, do not fit conceptually within the process of globalization and a multipolar world. The international players have not been learning on the job.

The essential message was that when a war breaks out in a country, that country cannot resolve the war by itself, because the causes and consequences of the war are of a larger, regional character. The mistakes we have seen in Bosnia and Herzegovina need not be repeated elsewhere. The lessons learnt there can be applied not only in southeastern Europe, but in the necessary transformations of international organizations as well.

The fact of the matter is that without international support there would be no Bosnia and Herzegovina, politically, economically or socially. But the objective we should all be working toward is an economically and socially sustainable Bosnia and Herzegovina, a state with a stable civil existence, a democracy — in other words a politically stable community and an open society. This objective requires changes in the approach and concepts of international policies that have been designed to support the countries of southeastern Europe.

The interest the international community has shown for the four completely dysfunctional states that emerged from the collapse of Yugoslavia, based on crime and corruption, has carried over to the re-building of Afghanistan and now Iraq. If the lessons from Yugoslavia are not learned, and the same or similar mistakes are repeated in Afghanistan and Iraq, this will be a clear signal that the international community learns slowly, or, that a state of permanent instability in these countries is in reality its express goal.

The simplified way that conflicts between ethnic groups are portrayed comes down to a black-and-white stereotype. Black and white are not, in fact, colors, and the lives of the inhabitants of countries at war, during the mandates of leaders who foster evil ideas, are expressed in a palette of nuanced hues. Perception of these shades hinges on individual motivation, our unwillingness to tolerate evil, or stereotype offered by theoreticians who invariably miss the truth in their attempt to formulate generalizations.

Those inclined to explain inter-ethnic conflict as a clash of civilizations are not taking into account the centuries that these same groups have lived in mutual understanding with respect for one another's differences. As a rule, mini-nationalisms become an instrument in the hands of the ruling elite, who are followed by a minority of the larger population, albeit a minority armed with powerful weapons.

Knowing that they would be swiftly replaced or even jailed were they to allow the development of civil society and open elections, these rulers use all available means, the most powerful being the media, to frighten the members of their own ethnic groups. The scenario is always the same: they claim that members of one or all of the other ethnic groups threaten their vital interests by their very existence.

All they need is a critical mass of fear, rather than hatred, for them to be able to continue manipulating the passions of war, to justify the necessity of prolonging the mindset of war and the war itself.

Even then the average citizen is not prepared to murder his or her neighbor just because that person belongs to some other ethnic or religious group. Their reluctance to go along with the war program forced the authorities to engage criminals — many of whom were already serving time in prison — as well as mercenaries from other countries, drug addicts who were given their drugs free if they would engage in combat, and people from the militant émigré communities who came back to their homeland to promote the glorified goals of war.

In Bosnia and Herzegovina, for instance, it is impossible to find even the smallest village with an ethnically mixed community where its inhabitants are prepared to say that the war began with neighbors attacking neighbors. The story is always the same: someone from the side, from one of the neighboring countries came and committed the first atrocities, killing the first victim. At that moment the communities were polarized into two groups: those who felt they were potential victims, and those who were potentially guilty of aggression. This is the threshold moment that those who were intimidated for years through the media and other forms of psychological pressure, secretly furnished with arms in advance by the nationalist leaders who prepared the war, commenced to fight. Even after all that preparation it was often necessary to force them to fight, and there were soldiers who refused to take part in besieging their own cities, explaining that they could not bear to kill their fellow townspeople.

A fighter for the Bosnia and Herzegovina Army who defended Sarajevo during its three-year siege of the city by the Republika Srpska Army described the reluctance of many soldiers to fight:

"The first years of the war I spent several months during the first years of the war defending Sarajevo in a trench that was only 50 meters from the Serbian army trenches. Between us was an unmined, level meadow. If someone poked his head out on either side of the trench he could be killed. After several nights of us listening to and watching the enemy trench, one morning a man's voice called out from the other side, and astonished us, 'Hey, you guys. Let's play a round of soccer on the meadow!' We figured this had to be some kind of trick, but they said otherwise, 'We don't want to shoot you. This is a pointless war and we have decided we refuse to participate. If you are afraid, just say you won't shoot at us and we'll come up out of our trench first.' And so they did. We played soccer with them every day. If someone had seen us at that time they would have probably said we were insane. But looking back at that time from the vantage point of today it seems to me we were saner than most people. After two weeks of soccer, instead of fighting, the soldiers from the enemy side let us know that they would be going home for a two-week furlough, and that a new group of soldiers would be taking their place from some other part of Bosnia. The soldiers warned us to be careful. The new round of soldiers might not prefer soccer to fighting. 'Take care, because if you don't, who will we play soccer with two weeks from now when we get back!' they said. Off they went, and just as they had predicted, our boys could not even peek out of the trenches for the next two weeks because the new soldiers kept us constantly under fire.

I was frequently wounded by shrapnel during the war, but I will never forget the group of enemy soldiers we played soccer with, two weeks at a time, for almost a year."

The director of a factory testified to his experience in a small town in Central Bosnia:

"Armed soldiers who were part of the Croatian Defense Council and men from paramilitary units took people, including me and my family, Muslim by nationality, from their apartments and houses and brought them to the elementary school which they had made over into a prison camp. After several days they took forty of the prisoners, including my wife, our two five-year-old twin boys, and myself and lined us up in a row. Then they brought over a civilian, a man who was Croatian like they were, but who was also my closest friend. They ordered him to choose a dozen of us from the lines and to decide how we would be killed. I was horrified — he knew all of us so well. Without a second thought he turned to the armed murderers and said, 'You should be ashamed of yourselves! These people are innocent. Release them. Let them go home.' Then he turned to us and looking right into our eyes, said, 'I'm so sorry. This is all I can do. I know they will kill me tonight. I wish all of you the best.' His soldiers dragged him off somewhere and took us back to the prison camp.

My best friend was right. The criminal soldiers, his own kind, killed him that night. We were luckier. After several months we were saved through an exchange of prisoners. What I keep thinking about is: who has the right to speak of the collective guilt of any ethnic group?"

A young man who was held in a prison camp in eastern Bosnia, spoke of a local man, a house painter who helped the Muslims who were being persecuted at the hands of the Serbian paramilitary and military units — to survive the terror, killing and abuse. The criminals who set the camp up at the elementary school brought in the housepainter, and stood him up before the 450 internees held in the gym, saying, "This is what happens to Serbs who help Muslims," and right there in front of everyone shot the man in the head. He was killed by his own kind because he refused to accept what they were doing.

For the first time in history, rape has been declared a war crime by the International Criminal Tribunal for the former Yugoslavia.

A woman from northern Bosnia testified, "I was brought, alone, to a cellar. Six soldiers came in that day, one by one. Each one locked the door from inside and raped me. I did whatever I could to defend myself and screamed as loudly as I could. After the sixth man left, I sat there, miserable, in shock, when the seventh soldier came in. He locked the door, came halfway across the room, and said something softly. I couldn't hear him. He came over toward me slowly and whispered, "Scream. Please scream. I can't do what they did, but if you don't scream like you did before, the men out there will kill me."

Following the Soviet intervention in Afghanistan the country was devastated by war, and the various ethnic and national groups who lived there continued to follow leaders representing a wide range of interests. Now that the Taliban have been ousted from the government, Afghanistan has been undergoing an extremely complex process of forming a new government within which the conflicts of interest of the old and new leaders in various groups have persisted. Careful observers have observed that the number of victims was disproportionately low in comparison to the length of the conflict and the possibilities that their weaponry allowed. Fighters from the different groups most often had no idea what they were fighting for. Many of them were born in war, and war, for them, has been the only life they know. They have no sense of what peace is. Yet despite this, one can often hear them saying that they prefer not to kill their opponents unless they have no choice.

A Palestinian psychologist explained why he chose to dedicate his life to work for a shared life for Palestinians and Jews.

As a young man he was held in an Israeli military prison. He suffered for three days with several other prisoners in a cell with no water, because the commanding officer had ordered the soldiers guarding them not to give them water. On the fourth day a soldier came into the cell, and after checking that none of his superiors were watching, he pulled out a canteen and gave it, without a word, to the prisoners.

Several days later, the commanding officer beat the psychologist for refusing to sign a document written in a language he did not understand. After several blows he could hear the voice of the soldier guarding the office, "Aren't you ashamed of yourself for hitting this man just because he wouldn't sign something he couldn't read? I would never sign if I were in his place."

Two years ago, an Israeli paraglider, borne by strong gusts, was blown over onto Palestinian territory. The Palestinians who found him treated his wounds, packed up his equipment, fed him and gave him water, put him into a car and took him to the line of separation. They explained that the man had been in trouble and needed their help. They said they had nothing against the people of Israel and would always extend a helping hand to any person in need.

There are probably many people the world over who remember the news from Kashmir of the monster who cut a baby out of its living mother and then killed the child in front of her. Far less attention was accorded an article about a man who belonged to a religious group that had set fire to a train full of members of a different religious group. The man, horrified, ran into the blazing train and pulled out the first burning passenger he found, put out the fire and tried to save him. He explained that he was against what his own religious group had done, against the killing of innocent people for the purposes of religion or politics.

A man who lost most of his family during the Rwandan genocide, who survived only because he was studying abroad at the time, testified about the mother of one of the murderers. Every morning for four months, while her son went off to kill members of the other tribe, she brought into her home the entire family of the witness' aunt. The murderer's mother fed them, looked after their needs and hid them, knowing no one would look for members of the enemy tribe at her house. Every evening, when her son came back from his bloody work, she hid the family in the bush near her home, where they slept. That family is the only remnant of the man's large clan that managed to survive the genocide, thanks to this woman who found a way to oppose the ideas of her own son.

The judges, investigators and prosecutors at the International Criminal Tribunal for the former Yugoslavia in The Hague who came to my talk on good people in an evil time were surprised to hear that there were people in Bosnia and Herzegovina during the war who had the courage to stand up to crimes being committed against the innocent, even when they had no weapons to help them. Indeed the Tribunal archives contain countless testimonies given by surviving victims, which end with the explanation that they were saved, thanks to efforts by individuals from those same ethnic groups perpetrating the atrocities.

The media, political military analysts, sociologists, psychologists and even philosophers study the political, military and religious leaders who created or participated in what, *post festum*, international law qualifies as war crimes. There are dozens of institutes for peace the world over, but most of them work on war rather than on peace. Indeed, many universities have departments for Peace and War Studies, yet they work far more on war than they do on peace.

In all wars we find that one category of people is totally neglected and marginalized: people deserving of our greatest attention and respect. These are brave souls, fortunately to be found everywhere, who have said "NO" in the face of a totalitarian regime, of nationalist doctrine, ethnic cleansing and persecution. Each of these examples is a stone in a vast mosaic which will, one day, when it is put together, confirm that humanity in these wars did not depend on one's ethnic or religious background.

Ten years of experience in the field have shown me that the affirmation of examples of goodness coming from people who cross ethnic lines to help one another represents a useful way by which each of us can acknowledge the value of the act of goodness. At the same time this acknowledgement frees us from collective guilt.

Examples of goodness that knows no ethnic, religious, racial or political bounds are important documentary material from the wars, and they also represent an axis around which it is possible to build a healthy future. As such they are of enormous social, cultural and religious value. It is possible to find examples of goodness everywhere in the world where there have been conflicts. Their importance is universal.

Countries stricken by war and conflict should take advantage of the healing that such stories facilitate. One way to pull together the stories of how people used good to counter evil is to form an archive. The formation of an archive of testimonies of goodness and the building of a memorial can pave the way to reconciliation. Building democratic societies based on trust, understanding and a peaceful solution is a high-priority task for these governments and their population. Reconciliation is the key issue in postwar societies. An archive of stories of people who defied the evil imposed on them by warmongers can provide a model for future acts of kindness, resistance and civic courage. The stories of goodness in the face of evil encourage the fostering of tolerance. The archived stories offer ethical possibilities for teachers in classrooms and elsewhere to give both children and adults the chance to reflect on individual and group responsibility in the face of repressive regimes and their imposed brutalities. The archive and place it is housed can serve as a significant model for the implementation of restorative justice and prevention of future conflicts.

The difficult, psychological challenge of self-reflection, a stock-taking of individual and collective responsibility, cannot happen in the presence of extreme distrust and suspicion. Nor can it happen in the face of shame, self-recrimination, and the entrenched defenses and denial that these feelings produce. Stories of civic courage and kindness restore faith in humanity, remind citizens that in each of us lie seeds of goodness, and that even if we have been unkind or unethical at one point, the next moment we may find the strength to turn this around. Goodness allows for the redemption of the individual and the collective self. It creates a sense of dignity and allows us to act from a more mature perspective rather than from a stance of unmitigated blame.

By collecting examples of goodness and humanity, societies that have been torn apart by war, places like Bosnia and Herzegovina, Iraq and Afghanistan, have the opportunity to build forward-looking communities with a chance for hope.

The Iraq War and the Dialogue Among Civilizations

Akira Iriye

Charles Warren Professor of American History at Harvard University, Prof. Iriye is a specialist in the history of international relations and of U.S. foreign affairs. His recent books include Cultural Internationalism and World Order *(Baltimore, 1997) and* Global Community: The Role of International Organizations in the Making of the Contemporary World *(Berkeley, 2002). He is a contributor to the book* War & Peace in the 20th Century and Beyond *(World Scientific, 2002) and is currently at work on "A Global History of the Twentieth Century".*

Most wars are fought between states, each mobilizing its military and economic resources to protect what it considers to be its interests, whether security, commerce, prestige, or domestic order. The Iraq war, too, was such a conflict at one level, pitting the United States against the Iraqi state ruled by the Saddam Hussein regime. But it was also a confrontation involving the world's greatest military power and one of the world's great religions, Islam. To be sure, Islam was fractured within (and without) Iraq, but many Moslems, of various persuasions, viewed the war as a struggle for the future of Islam. Even those who had bitterly resented, or been brutally persecuted by, the Saddam regime did not necessarily welcome United States forces as occupiers of their land and administrators of their lives. So the struggle continued, and continues, months after the president of the United States declared an end to the military phase of the war.

The clash is not so much between civilizations as between power and civilization, or between power and culture. If it had been a clash of civilizations, Islamic nations would have sought to combine their forces against those representing Western civilization, and, equally important, European countries would have supported the United States rather than expressed their skepticism of the war. It would have been an occasion in which the West battled against a non-Western civilization. In fact, to the extent that the Iraq war was a clash of civilizations, it can be argued that the main protagonists in the drama were American and European civilizations. Precisely because the United States chose to use military force to effect "regime change" in Iraq, not to subvert or transform that country's culture, there was a great deal of confusion as to what should come after the initial military victory. European critics of the war, on their part, wondered to what ends American power would be used in a world that was becoming divided less by separate nations than by divergent religions and cultures. European nations such as France and Germany seemed to sense the ultimate futility of seeking to resolve inter-civilizational issues by force, that power could not be the answer to questions that were fundamentally cultural.

In a sense, the critics of the war were being heirs to the century-old movement that had sought to promote dialogue among civilizations.

At the Oslo conference of December 2001 in which I was privileged to participate, I argued that while the history of the twentieth century had been marked by unspeakable tragedies, above all by mutual misperception, mistrust, and fear among cultures and civilizations, strenuous efforts had been made to steer the world in a more constructive direction.[1] The world of 2000 would not have been what it was if those efforts had not borne fruit, albeit only partially, so that there was now a greater awareness of the need to promote dialogue among nations and cultures than a hundred years

---

[1] See Akira Iriye, "Misperception, Mistrust, Fear," in Geir Lundestad and Olav Njølstad (eds.), *War and Peace in the 20th Century and Beyond.* Singapore: World Scientific (2002), pp. 99–219.

earlier. The Nobel Peace Prize embodied such values, as did the numerous international organizations, both governmental and non-governmental, that had mushroomed throughout the course of the century in order to promote cultural exchange and intellectual cooperation with a view to promoting dialogue among cultures and civilizations.

At the beginning of the twentieth century, it was widely assumed that such dialogue was impossible, either because there was one civilization, that of the modern West, which towered over the rest, all considered to be pre-modern if not primitive, or because civilizations were viewed as expressions of people's foreordained identities so that they were inherently incompatible with one another. It took patient and sustained efforts by the League of Nations, UNESCO, and other organizations as well individuals who shared their vision to overcome this sort of fatalism and to argue that it was both desirable and possible to promote mutual understanding across civilizational boundaries. As a fitting climax to these efforts, the United Nations General Assembly in 1998 unanimously adopted a resolution to call 2001 "the year of dialogue among civilizations". It was as if the world organization was envisioning the new century as one in which dialogue among civilizations would be promoted even more seriously than ever before.

It is an irony of history that the very same year that was dedicated to this cause should also have witnessed one of the most barbaric assaults upon civilization in recent memory, the September 11 terrorist attacks in the United States. It was as if earnest attempts at promoting dialogue among civilizations were being brutally mocked by those who did not believe in such dialogue. The picture since then has often seemed to confirm such cynicism. With each day's news carrying stories about yet another bombing raid in the Middle East, South Asia, Southeast Asia, and elsewhere, it is difficult not to succumb to pessimism.

The Iraq war has done little to mitigate the sense of mistrust among civilizations. The war was ostensibly aimed at bringing democracy, a Western conception, to the Islamic people of Iraq. By giving the impression that Western ideas were being forced upon

Iraq, the war turned many Iraqis not only against the United States but also against the United Nations, viewing both as invaders. The image of the United States as a latter-day Roman empire, seeking to impose its will upon people of other civilizations, fit in with the history of often violent encounters among civilizations. Just as Rome brought its laws, its administration, and eventually its Christian religion, upon people of divergent cultures and religions, the United States gave the impression of seeking to envelope other countries under its influence.

That, however, would be a mis-reading of the circumstances surrounding the Iraq war. The European and American differences over the war tell a great deal about the nature of the conflict. Their disagreement concerns far more than geopolitics and national interests. At bottom is the fact that Europe and America have developed as distinct, if closely related, civilizations. Europeans have, particularly since the end of the Second World War, become conscious of their collective civilizational identity that transcends, but does not replace, separate national identities. European civilization, it may be said, is both multi-cultural and multi-national, whereas American civilization is multi-cultural and uni-national. That may be why Europeans feel uncomfortable with a conflict like the Iraq war that they view as another indication of the growing power of the United States in the globe. They, on their part, seem to feel that European civilizational identity is a product of history and geography through which Europe has been linked to the Middle East in a way the United States has never been (save perhaps to Israel).

The encounter among civilizations in Europe has involved wars of conquest going back several thousand years, but no one civilization has prevailed over the others, and in time European countries and people have evolved under the influence of multiple cultural traditions, all of which are considered integral parts of their collective civilization. In contrast, the United States has grown as a unitary nation assimilating different cultural traditions. One consequence of this contrast is that in external relations the United States has tended to behave as a great power, emphasizing military and economic means, whereas Europe, at least in the last several decades, has seemed to act as a culture, eschewing the use of military force as much as possible. There is irony in the fact that in the current world Europe seems to stand for culture, and the United States for power, whereas in earlier centuries the great powers of Europe vied with one another for extending their influence all over the world while the United States preferred to send out its missionaries and merchants to Americanize the globe through peaceful means.

The disagreement between the United States and Europe is as fundamental as the gap between power and culture. To the extent that human affairs are determined by cultural factors, the only plausible way to peace must be through dialogue among civilizations, not by force. Fortunately, efforts to promote such dialogue have been continuously carried forward despite the conflict in the Middle East. In 2001, several symposia were held on the theme, attended by delegates from all over the world. The one held in Vilnius, Lithuania, in April of that year adopted a resolution declaring, "No civilization can solely assume the responsibility for all humanity; neither can a single civilization claim exclusive rights to provide an ultimate and universally valid vision of how to be a human being in the complex and multifaceted world of today and tomorrow."[2] In response to the resolution's call to "all governments and civil societies...to take the initiative to further a dialogue among civilizations in such a way that it can become an instrument of transformation, a yardstick for peace and tolerance and a vehicle for diversity and pluralism", a major international conference on dialogue among civilizations was convened in New Delhi in July 2003, sponsored by UNESCO and the government of India. Over one hundred participants, representing a large number of countries, attended the gathering and spoke ardently of the need to continue to promote inter-civilizational dialogue through massive educational

---

[2] *Dialogue Among Civilizations*, International Conference in Vilnius, Lithuania, April 2001, pp. 17–19.

efforts by governments as well as by non-governmental organizations. As a working paper prepared by UNESCO for the conference pointed out, "the recent initiatives which have been taken to develop the theme of dialogue among civilizations constitute a major inspiring force for the development of new education for the new age....[We] have to construct the universally accepted human values into the philosophies of education without undermining the validity and dignity of diverse cultures."[3] It deserves attention that these expressions of faith in education as an instrument for promoting dialogue among civilizations were being aired at the very moment that United States administrators in occupied Iraq were experiencing difficulty in reforming the educational system in that country. If peace and stability were to come to Iraq, it would only be possible through international efforts to educate all people, not just in that country but all over the world, in fostering dialogue among civilizations.

Future historians may well look back upon these international gatherings and conclude that they were of even greater historical significance than the U.S.-led wars in Afghanistan and Iraq — of greater significance in that they exemplified the ongoing movement to develop a world of interdependence in which divergent civilizations existed in peaceful relationship to one another, in which wars among nations were becoming less frequent, in which military force was losing its legitimacy as an instrument for solving international or inter-civilizational affairs, and in which culture was finally triumphing over power.

---

[3] "Education: As An Instrument of Dialogue," New Delhi Conference, July 2003, pp. 9–10.

PART III

SERMONS IN CLOSING ...

A Sermon of Sorrow

Bishop Gunnar Stålsett

Dr. Stålsett has for fourteen years served as Member of the Nobel Peace Prize Committee. Former general secretary of the Lutheran World Federation (LWF), he was appointed as Bishop of Oslo in the (Lutheran) Church of Norway by the Norwegian Government in 1998. He is presently the chairman of the Niwano Peace Prize Committee (Tokyo) and an international president of the World Conference on Religion for Peace (New York). On March 22, 2003, he delivered the following sermon in the Oslo Cathedral.

> Blessed are those who grieve, for they shall be comforted!
> Blessed are you who create peace, for you shall be called God's Children.
> You are the salt of the earth. You are the light of the earth.
>
> (The Gospel according to St. Matthew.)

Let these words shape us in a time of war.

Today we seek comfort in a time without comfort. We turn to God, our creator. Everything that has been created carries the imprint of God. God has shown himself to us as a vulnerable human being. Jesus knew the force of violence on his body.

Christians around the world gather in church in order to be in a holy room which in the midst of the world allows us to be in the world. We are gathered in God's name, who is on the side of those who are assailed by violence and death — both in peace and in war. God is on the side of the wounded, because God himself is wounded. When we gather our thoughts in prayer for those who are suffering, then we know that God listens. For there is recognition by God in the cry: Oh, Lord, Oh, Lord why have you forsaken me.

433

A war rages. We see the pictures and hear the terse commentaries. We are gathered to take in the fact that war is not a picture or a commentary — not another form of Reality TV — but a bloody and painful reality. We are here in the church today to give room for the unease, anger, fear and the sorrow we are feeling, to express sadness that the will to wage war has triumphed over the will for peace.

The power of weapons during these early morning hours is poised not only against weapons of others, but also against tired and fearful human beings. In Iraq mothers and fathers are praying for their children, just like the mothers and fathers in the U.S. and England are praying for their sons and daughters who were sent to fight the war.

In the land of the Euphrates and the Tigris — a place of origin for civilization and culture — it is a long time since people have been able to feel happiness. Have they ever enjoyed human rights and freedom? Today they are assaulted even deeper than they ever have been in history. Exhausted after years of mismanagement, boycotts and deep human needs. Exhausted by the lack of freedom and food. Now they are trembling under the greatest war machine in the world.

We are gathered in the church to compose and order our thoughts, as well as to feel and show human fellowship. This is because war has to do with human beings. War is not about machines. It concerns body and soul, not only political systems. War has to do with vulnerable, God — created bodies, on both sides of the front lines. Behind armor and down in the bomb shelters, fear is the common denominator. We do not want to let the media seduce us with fancy video graphics — illustrations, the terse commentaries, analysis, the well-formulated reasons. We will not be caught in an illusion that war is a game. This is about human beings. This is about a message that becomes a prayer: You shall not kill me! This is about a child's face and a child's prayer. Let me live!

We are gathered in grief and prayer. War has broken out — a war that is supposed to portray for the entire world what a modern war power means. This is a war that intends to "shock and awe" the entire world. This is not a war to end all wars. This is a war to open the possibility for other wars. It is the warlords who postulate for the world and all the world's nations: if you are not with us, you are against us! If you don't want to join us, we will go to war alone. This is how powerful they have become. War creates the great uncertainty. Therefore, the world trembles.

The war is a fact. All the avenues to find a solution have been abandoned. Plentiful were the numbers of those who fell, even before the first victims fell under the shower of bombs. No one can doubt that there will be a victor on the battlefield. But it will be a victory without honor, even as the congratulations pour in. For the war is about more than breaking a tyrant and his ill equipped troops.

Today, among the first victims, we count human rights. The rule of law, to which nations together have committed themselves after two World Wars, is threatened. Two of the world's foremost nations in the fight for democracy and human rights, have set themselves outside the world order they themselves have been promoting. Therefore we grieve today.

Osama bin Laden and his terrorist network have succeeded in attacking the international community in a way that goes beyond all imagination. It can only bring joy to the political and religious fundamentalists among the Muslims that the foundation of democracy is shaken. They have not only attacked two physical towers and taken the lives of thousands of people. When terror causes war and more confusion, their dreams have come true. Together with the Christian fundamentalists of the same ilk, they can take pleasure in the fact that they have gotten a new war in their God's name.

We grieve that Saddam Hussein's grip of terror on his people has created such suffering. We grieve that a tyrant tries to take his people with him to his death, as he already so cruelly has murdered and tortured untold numbers of people in his own country and beyond its borders.

But there is no reason to grieve for the United Nations. The Security Council, which is the supreme body in our civilized world charged with securing humanity against the damnation of war, has stood its test. Those who regret that the Security Council did not buckle under the pressure and gather the world to war, exist in a different world. We grieve over leaders of states who let themselves be forced or bought to join a war against an independent nation and an already suffering population.

But most of all we grieve for the victims. We grieve for our sisters and brothers on God's earth — on the plot of land called Iraq — we grieve for those who will not experience freedom. And we grieve for those who may be living under the power of an alien occupation.

Today a prayer is lifted from the world's holy places, from homes and hearts, that the suffering must be short, and that lives will be spared. Prayer is not an extension of an intellectual exercise. Prayer is an extension of people's will to live. It is the power that lifts us out of a prison that limits our life and freedom. It is the human being's unconquerable will to a better future. Prayer is the human being's deepest life breath. When prayer dies, the human in us dies. Therefore, prayer is humanity's common language — believers or not. Dag Hammarskjøld once said: I pray to the God I don't believe in.

How can people believe in God after Auschwitz? So asked many while the battlefields of the Second World War were still warm with blood, while Europe was laying in ruins and the world shivered after the war's gloom. Should we not rather ask; how can we move on without believing in God? How can we regain the belief in people, without believing in a righteous and loving God? The alternative would be to hail the power of evil in all of us.

This is why we pray for those who hear sirens day and night, for those who feel the earth tremble and who cling to each other for protection and in prayer. We pray that the almighty and loving God will hold them close — hold watch over those who hold vigil, be close to those who hold watch, stroke the cheeks of those who are crying, let the angels watch over those who sleep.

Peace shall be won with prayer and work. Peace shall be won with willingness to sacrifice and cooperation. A country has to be raised out of ruins and a people have to learn what freedom and peace mean. That cannot be done by the might of arms. Therefore our responsibility is greater, if we want to be the salt of the earth and the light of the earth. Therefore our call to duty is greater if we want to resurrect the belief in God and the belief in the human being. It concerns Iraq and the Middle East, Israel and Palestine, Christians, Muslims and Jews, in a fellowship of future peace. But it also concerns our World.

How can we accomplish this? Only by coming together and seeing the seriousness, seeing the people, looking God in the eye. Only then, I believe, can we find new peacefulness, resolve and strength. That is why we are here. That is why we mourn and pray.

During the visit of Pope John Paul II to Hiroshima he gave a prayer which I will make ours today:

> "To you, Creator of nature and of human beings; of truth and beauty, I pray.
>
> Hear my voice, for it is the voice of the victims of all wars and crimes between individuals and nations.
>
> Hear my voice, for it is the voice of all children who suffer and will come to suffer when people put their trust in weapons and wars.
>
> Hear my voice when I ask you to awaken the wisdom of peace, the strength of justice and the joy of fellowship in all human hearts.
>
> Hear my voice, for I pray for the multitudes in each country, in each epoch in history who do not want war and who are afraid to walk the road of peace.
>
> Hear my voice and give us insight and strength so that we can always answer hatred with peace, injustice with by aligning ourselves with justice, poverty by giving of ourselves, war with peace.
>
> Oh Lord hear my voice and give to the world your everlasting peace."
>
> Amen.

A Memorial Service on the UN Tragedy

Bishop Gunnar Stålsett

The following sermon was delivered by Bishop Stålsett at The Cathedral of Oslo, August 29th 2003, for the victims of the bomb attack on the United Nations Headquarters in Baghdad.

Dear mourners, dear friends and servants of the United Nations,

Peace be with you!

We have heard the names of the victims. We have heard the names of the brave. To some of us they were friends and colleagues. To all of us they were champions in the cause of peace and justice. Peacemakers of extraordinary dedication. Carriers of hope to a people caught in the maelstrom of history, caught between error and terror. We are here to honour their memory and their mission.

At this moment of destiny for peace and world order, I share with you the words of the prophet as quoted by Jesus:

The people who live in darkness
will see a great light.
On those who live in the dark land of death
the light will shine. (Matthew 4:16)

In every place where humans dwell there is a house for worship.

In every heart there is a room for God. In very mind there is a need for meaning. In times of darkness we seek light in words of eternal truth and in the laws of nature. Many would join Dag

Hamarskjöld's words: "I pray to the One I do not know but to Whom I belong."

So we have come here to remember, to pray and to dedicate ourselves to the greater cause. We have gathered here with a deep sense of mourning, joining our hearts to mothers and fathers, children and loved ones whose loss is unbearable in these hours. We hear the words of Kofi Annan: "The ache in our souls is almost too much to bear." Therefore, no one should bear it alone.

There is a rhythm to life we all have come to expect and depend upon; Inhaling and exhaling, sunrise and sunset, waking and sleeping, life and death. It is these rhythms that help us maintain our equilibrium and give us a sense of security.

Into these rhythms there come events that awaken our souls to the complexity of living and the uncertainty of life. Hurricanes, earthquakes, heat waves and epidemics are part of the disorder of our global village. They cause us to wonder about the future of our planet, as we pause to remember and honour people who were caught in the web of the destruction caused by such phenomena.

But also, there are events and moments that, with cruelty and disregard for the very village we call home, would seek to destroy the fabric that makes us all one under the heavens. Events like those that occurred on September 11, the war on Iraq, the ongoing destruction of Israel and Palestine, such events shake the foundations on which people have built their houses of hope. As the wave of violent death continues, a sense of despair sets its cold grip on the heart of humanity.

We are here to say to each other and to the world that this barbaric act in Baghdad is an act of violence against the divine and the human. The attack on the UN headquarters in Iraq is seared into our consciousness as an attack against the only institution that is capable of bringing peace to a troubled world — if only it is allowed to do so.

In reflecting on the tragedy on August 19, I think again and again of the indelible image of Sergio Vieria de Mello, still alive, trapped by tons of concrete, finding it within himself to ask after the fate of his staff and others caught in the carnage of the Canal Hotel.

Even at this terrible moment, he thought of those in his charge — his co-workers and friends and those he had come to serve, the Iraqi people.

Such shining moments in the lives of those who perished in Baghdad, may be of small consolation to the loved ones of the victims as they struggle to come to terms with their loss. But the contributions to humanity by these servants of *our* United Nations in the end will far outweigh the evil that was visited upon them. They will not be forgotten, as the world has not forgotten another great leader of the United Nations, Dag Hamarskjöld. The decency and love that their work exemplified will outlast the brutality of the truck bomber.

We honour the victims today because no matter how difficult the situation was, these people — our representatives — were attempting to engage in constructive action, striving to enhance the participation and the dignity of the Iraqi people as they struggled to rebuild their shattered nation. Therefore Sergio's last words are a call to us all: "Don't let them pull the mission out!" Surely the United Nations' role in Iraq must not be abandoned. How shall the world honour the martyrs of peace if not by resolving to stay with the vision of a more peaceful and just world?

Today we grieve over the loss of life, the attack on hope, because of the planned and premeditated acts of a few on the representatives of our global village, the United Nations. In the context of Iraq this is a reminder that the principles enshrined in the United Nations Charter should not be treated as a matter of convenience, to be exalted or abandoned according to prevailing political moods. Just as the moral and ethical principles of religion should not be bent to the expediency of the moment, or invoked when all else has failed, so it is the case with the principles of the United Nations.

In this city of Oslo, The Secretary General of the United Nations, Kofi Annan said in his acceptance speech for the Nobel Peace Prize: "We have entered the third millennium through a gate of fire... New threats make no distinction between races, nations or regions. A new insecurity has entered every mind, regardless of wealth or status. A deeper awareness of the bonds that bind us all — in pain as in prosperity — has gripped young and old."

And he added: "In the 21st Century I believe the mission of the United Nations will be defined by a new, more profound, awareness of the sanctity and dignity of every human life regardless of race or religion.... The idea that there is one people in possession of the truth, one answer to the world's ills, or one solution to humanity's needs, has done untold harm throughout history — especially in the last century."

Indeed we have again been reminded that the dream of the Empire and the hallucination of eternal dominance is the same womb out of which fundamentalism of every breed is born.

The principles of universality, inclusiveness and multilateralism, must prevail, not the dictates of the strong. We the people must insist on wise policies based on truth. We must insist that in a world built on the moral standards of the United Nations, military force should only be a last resort. Force must never be a by-product of impatience or a substitute for the kind of dialogue and justice that is the underpinning of lasting peace.

Another Nobel laureate, Yitzhak Rabin, a general and statesman turned a champion of reconciliation, spoke of the "hundreds of cemeteries in our part of the Middle East — in our home in Israel — but also in Egypt, in Syria, Jordan, Lebanon, and Iraq — (and today we would add in Palestine). From the plane's window, from thousands of feet above them, the countless tombstones are silent. But the sound of their outcry has carried from the Middle East throughout the world for decades". This is the darkness that makes a land and a region a dark land of death longing for light.

It is high time that all parties to the Middle East conflict recognize that human dignity will not yield to force. Once again we must lift our voice in an absolute rejection of terrorism, wherever it may occur, whether in Baghdad, Jerusalem, Gaza, Jakarta or New York. Terrorist acts can not be legitimised as a way to address the issues of our time. War begets violence. Deceit begets mistrust. The law of nature is that we harvest what we sow. This is our tragedy today as turbulence continues where peace was promised.

Each and every one in the UN family mourns even as families and loved ones grieve all the more. They will carry the enduring burden of bereavement. They should find solace in the fact that the legacy their beloved ones left behind will continue as a light in the land of death.

The great man of peace Mahatma Gandhi once said: "We must be the change we wish to see." We must continue to use our reason and insights from history, our creativeness and courage. We must abide by the moral principles enshrined in humanity by its Creator, and in the dedication to love and mercy embodied in Christ. Thus shall their vision survive. Then can we dare to say that hope is possible beyond despair. The man-made inferno is not the last station, man-made suffering is not the final destiny. Darkness shall not prevail. The people who live in darkness will see a great light.

We must never let despair become the final response to the ambiguities of history.

Judaism, Christianity and Islam are founded on the promise of peace. This is a promise greatly betrayed today by us the followers. It is for us to make it become true: On those who live in the dark land of death, the light will shine. Their death shall not have been in vain. The great cause of their mission shall not fail. We make this our sacred covenant: The light of peace and justice will shine.

Therefore:

It is now for us, the living, peacemakers one and all, to both rally the forlorn while we endeavour to comfort the wounded.

It is now for us, the living, peacemakers one and all, to resolve again to announce that the hope of peace is more durable than the promise of violence.

It is now for us, the living, peacemakers, one and all, to replace the diabolical rhythm of hatred and murder, with the god-given rhythm of love and justice that provides villagers respite and security.

It is now for us, the living, peacemakers one and all, out of our various faith communities, to resolve again to proclaim that there is no God who desires death and there is no God who blesses destruction. There only is a God who desires for us "to do justice, seek mercy, and walk humbly" with our God.